THE PLAYS AND
POEMS OF
Philip Massinger

THE PLAYS AND POEMS OF

Philip Massinger

EDITED BY
PHILIP EDWARDS
AND
COLIN GIBSON

VOLUME III

OXFORD
AT THE CLARENDON PRESS
1976

Oxford University Press, Ely House, London W. 1

GLASGOW NEW YORK TORONTO MELBOURNE WELLINGTON
CAPE TOWN IBADAN NAIROBI DAR ES SALAAM LUSAKA ADDIS ABABA
DELHI BOMBAY CALCUTTA MADRAS KARACHI DACCA
KUALA LUMPUR SINGAPORE HONG KONG TOKYO

ISBN 0 19 811894 5

© *Oxford University Press 1976*

*Printed in Great Britain
at the University Press, Oxford
by Vivian Ridler
Printer to the University*

CONTENTS

THE ROMAN ACTOR

INTRODUCTION

(a) *Date*

The latest date for the composition of *The Roman Actor* is established
by Malone's record of Sir Henry Herbert's licence for performance,
dated 11 October 1626: '*The Roman Actor*, by Philip Massinger,
licensed for the King's Company.'[1]

Of the few passages which may contain topical allusions—
mainly to conditions in the theatre—none helps to fix the date of
composition very precisely, though there is some suggestion of early
rather than late 1626.[2] Boyle thought that he had found in the
description of the storm accompanying Ascletario's death (V. i.
227 ff.) an allusion to a severe storm which swept London on
12 June, and which excited contemporary comment, recorded in
Rushworth's *Historical Collections of Private Passages of State* (*1618–
1629*), 1659, p. 391, and in *The Court and Times of Charles I*, ed.
R. F. Williams, 1848, i. 113–14.[3] However, heavy rain and electrical
storms were frequent in England from June until August, and there
is insufficient specific detail in Massinger's lines to relate them to
any particular occasion.

Herbert's licence is the only reliable means of dating the writing
of the tragedy, and there can be little doubt that it was completed
shortly before October 1626.

(b) *Sources*

The sources of *The Roman Actor* have been discussed by the editor
in *AUMLA: Journal of the Australasian Universities Language and
Literature Association*, xv (1961), 60–72.

It is clear that as usual with him Massinger read widely in search
of material for his Roman play. Suetonius's life of Domitian in the

---

[1] Adams, *Herbert*, p. 31.
[2] See the notes to I. i. 3–4, 16–17, and 62–5.
[3] Article on Philip Massinger, in *DNB*, xxxvii (1884), 13.

B

De Vita Caesarum, viii, was his main source for the plot,[1] but he also
drew on Dio Cassius's *Roman History*, Tacitus, Juvenal, Horace,
Ovid, Seneca the Elder, and the anonymous *Epitome de Caesaribus*.
It is further obvious that the dramatist carefully studied Jonson's
treatment of Roman history in *Sejanus* (1603).[2]

Almost all the major events in *The Roman Actor* are founded on
Suetonius, though the historian is followed closely only in the last
Act, which covers the events leading up to the assassination. Elsewhere Massinger freely compresses, elaborates, and reinterprets
what he borrows, fashioning a story of imperial tyranny and bloody
revenge, moralized as an indictment of unreasoning passion and
unchecked will.

Additional sources were needed to supplement the story of
Domitian's relationship with his wife. Tacitus's account of Nero's
infatuation with Poppaea (*Annals*, iii. 46), and of an unsuccessful plot
against Agrippina, his mother, by a group which included Domitia,
his aunt, and an actor named Paris (*Annals*, iii. 19–21), became
Parthenius's description of the emperor's love for Domitia (I. ii.
17–43), and the accusation made against Domitia by Aretinus,
Parthenius, and the princesses (IV. i and ii). Dio Cassius's *Roman
History*, lxvii. 15 was used for the scene dramatizing Domitia's
final break with her husband,[3] and in the *Epitome de Caesaribus*
Massinger found an explicit link between Domitia's part in the
conspiracy against Domitian and her illicit love for Paris.

The portrait of the 'prodegie of mankind, bloudie *Domitian*' is
clearly influenced by the hostile accounts of Tacitus in the *Agricola*
and Juvenal in his *Satires*; specific borrowings are noted in the
Commentary. Juvenal's Paris, idolized actor and powerful court
favourite,[4] provided the groundwork for Massinger's Roman Actor,
though, in keeping with the defence of the acting profession offered

---

[1] Massinger knew enough Latin and Greek to read the original, but there is evidence
that he at least consulted Philemon Holland's translation, *The Historie of Twelve
Cæsars*, published in 1606. Further, in his footnotes Holland cites the authors of almost
all of Massinger's supplementary sources as authorities on the life of Domitian.

[2] The parallels between *Sejanus* and *The Roman Actor* listed by W. D. Briggs, 'The
Influence of Jonson's Tragedy in the Seventeenth Century', *Anglia*, xxxv (1912),
316–18, are supplemented in C. A. Gibson's edition of *The Roman Actor*, unpublished
doctoral thesis, University of Otago, 1962.

[3] Massinger also took from Dio some of the details of Domitian's vision (V. i. 181–
212), and gave thematic elaboration to Dio's statement that Minerva was Domitian's
patron goddess (*Roman History*, lxvii. 1).

[4] *Satires*, vi. 82–7; vii. 86–92.

in the play, Massinger's Paris is idealized as being virtuous, wise, and generous.

The first play within the play, *The Cure of Avarice*, together with the exchange between Philargus and Parthenius which opens the second Act, is based on material in Horace's *Satires*, II. iii. 108–26, 142–57. For the second play, *Iphis and Anaxarete*, Massinger used Ovid's version of the fable in the *Metamorphoses*, xiv. 698 ff. This is prefaced by Paris's address to the hard-hearted porter, modelled on Ovid's *Amores*, I. vi. There are analogues to the third play, *The False Servant*, in the story of Joseph and Potiphar's wife, and in the Hippolytus–Phaedra myth. O. M. Villarejo has argued that Massinger is indebted to Lope de Vega's *Lo fingido verdadero*, published at Madrid in 1621,[1] but a stronger case has been made by Dr. Bertha Hensman that the inset play was constructed from material drawn from three of Seneca the Elder's *Controversiae*, each of which presents charge and counter-charge rising out of a situation involving the discovery of adultery.[2]

Some 90 lines of *The Roman Actor* come directly from Jonson's *Sejanus*, but there are more than verbal correspondences between the two plays.

Massinger's exposition, a discussion of the degeneracy of Rome and its ruler by a group of disgruntled nobles, is also Jonson's. Rusticus and Sura watch and comment on the arrest of Paris just as Lepidus and Arruntius comment on the removal of Nero (*Sejanus*, iv. 323 ff.) The second scene, in which Parthenius tells Domitia that the emperor loves her, has its parallel in the opening scene of Act II of *Sejanus*, in which Livia is courted by Sejanus and congratulated for it by the physician Eudemus. The whole of Massinger's third scene, the arraignment of Paris (for which there was no classical model), closely imitates the trial of Cordus in Act III of Jonson's play. Aretinus's report to Domitian, which leads to the emperor's action against Lamia (II. i. 112 ff.), recalls Sejanus's provocative account of the activities of Agrippina, Nero and Drusus. Act III, scene i, in which Domitilla and Julia resolve to suffer rather than to act against Domitian, elaborates on *Sejanus*, iv. 1 ff., where Agrippina and her sons take a similar resolve, and in

---

[1] 'Lope de Vega and the Elizabethan and Jacobean Drama', unpublished doctoral thesis, Columbia University, 1953. Villarejo takes the view that Lope's play as a whole is a main source for *The Roman Actor*.

[2] *Controversiae*, II. vii, 'Peregrinus Negotiator'; IV. vii, 'Tyrannicida Adulter Tyranni'; IX. i, 'Cimon Ingratus Calliae'.

Domitian's dismissal of his guard shortly before his assassination can be seen a repetition of Sejanus's behaviour prior to his fall (*Sejanus*, v. 424 ff.)

Massinger also follows Jonson's prescription for the style proper to tragedy.[1] His language is frequently sententious or proverbial; much material is drawn from Greek and Latin writers such as Livy, Ovid, Pliny, Plutarch, and Seneca, and there is a wealth of reference to classical myth, legend, and history. Wherever possible, Massinger's classical sources are noted in the Commentary.

(c) *Text*

The only seventeenth-century edition of *The Roman Actor* was published in 1629, in quarto, for Robert Allot; the printers were Bernard Alsop and Thomas Fawcett.[2] The edition was not entered in the Stationers' Register, but is mentioned there once in connection with a transfer, on Allot's death, of his rights over sixty-one titles to John Legatt and Andrew Crooke.[3]

M[r]. Legatt & Andrew Crooke.   Entred for their Copies by Consent of M[rs]. Allott & by order of a full Co[rt]. holden the Seauenth day of Nouember last All the Estate Right Title & Interest w[ch]. the said M[rs]. Allott hath in these Copies and parts of Copies hereafter following w[ch]. were M[r]. Robte Allotts dec[d]. saluo Iure cuiuscunꝗ   xxx[s]. vj[d].

Number 52 in the list of titles is 'Romane Actor. by M[r] Massinger.' The entry is dated 1 July 1637. The play is also named in booksellers' catalogues in 1656, 1661, 1663 and 1671.[4]

The 1629 edition will be referred to from now on as *29*; the title-page is reproduced on p. 13. *29* is in quarto, A–K[4] (40 leaves); see Greg, *Bibliography*, no. 424 (ii. 574). The contents are: A1[r], *title*; A1[v], 'The persons presented. The principall Actors.'; A2[r], *dedication begins*, 'To my much Honoured, and most *true Friends, Sir* PHILIP KNYVET, Knight and Baronet. And to Sir THOMAS IEAY, Knight. And THOMAS BELLINGHAM of *Newtimber* in *Sussex* Esquire.'; A2[v], *dedication ends, signed 'Philip Massinger.'*; A3[r],

---

[1] See *Roman Actor*, Dedication 24–31 and note.

[2] There can be no doubt of the interpretation of the initials *B. A.* and *T. F.* on the title-page. Alsop, in association with Fawcett from 1625, had already printed Dekker and Massinger's *The Virgin Martyr* in 1622, and *The Duke of Milan* in 1623.

[3] Register D 361–2; Greg, *Bibliography*, i. 46; Arber, iv. 387–8. See also 'Philip Chetwind and the Allott Copyrights', H. Farr, *The Library*, 4th Series xv (1935), 129–60.

[4] Greg, *Bibliography*, iii. 1326, 1336, 1350, and iv. 1660.

poem, '*To his deare Friend the Author.*', *signed* '*T. I.*'; A3ᵛ, *poem*, '*In* Philippi Massingeri, *Poetæ elegantiss: Actorem Romanum, typis excusum.* δεκαϛικον.', *signed* 'THO: G.', *poem*, '*To his deseruing Friend Mr.* Philip Massinger, *vpon his Tragædie, the Roman Actor.*', *signed* '*Tho: May.*'; A4ʳ, *poem*, '*Vpon Mr.* MASSINGER *His Roman Actor.*', *signed* '*Iohn Foorde.*', *untitled poem, signed* '*Robert Harvey.*'; A4ᵛ, *poem*, '*To His long knowne and lou'd Friend, Mr.* PHILIP MASSINGER, *vpon His Roman Actor.*', *signed* '*Ioseph Taylor.*'; B1ʳ, 'THE ROMAN ACTOR, A Tragedie.', *text begins*; K4ᵛ, *text ends*, '*FINIS.*'. The text is in roman, 20 lines measuring approximately 80 mm. There are usually 38 lines to the page (34 on C3ʳ; 37 on C3ᵛ and H4ʳ).

Two skeletons were used in the printing, but for sheet C the outer forme set of titles was used for both outer and inner formes. In sheet D the set for the outer forme changes place with the set for the inner forme, and the new positions are retained in later sheets. The general style of composition remains the same throughout, and a spelling analysis indicates that a single compositor set up the text of the whole play.[1] The number of misprints, turned and wrong fount letters, and errors in spelling and punctuation left standing in the text suggest that the setting up was done hastily or casually. Sheet H was composed with particular carelessness. It contains 78 of the total of 155 press corrections, and in the first state of the inner forme the type-pages on H3ᵛ and H4ʳ are transposed.

It might be expected that Massinger would take special care over the printing of the play which he considered to be his finest work, and the press corrections of 29 suggest that he did assist in proof reading at the press. Thirteen of the twenty formes are variant; B (i), H (o), and K (i) exist in three states. Among the corrections are many minor changes in spelling and punctuation which are probably due to the author himself (e.g. I. i. 99, 108, I. ii. 83, III. i. 99, III. ii. 64, 273). A number of errors escaped his notice and that of the printing house corrector; some of these were finally recognised and corrected by hand in the Harbord copy (e.g. I. ii. 33, 85, III. i. 30, 58, IV. ii. 70, 229).

The copy for the printer was probably the author's manuscript.

---

[1] Of four invariable spellings in *Believe As You List* (*wee, mee, doe, noe*), the first two are usually altered in *The Roman Actor* to *we* and *me*; the spelling *doe* is consistently preserved, and the spelling *noe* equally consistently altered to *no*. The exceptional spellings *wee, mee, do*, and *noe* are distributed throughout the play, and occur on inner and outer formes.

Instances of mislineation are few and insignificant, and there is little sign of serious confusion or alteration; this indicates the use of a fair copy rather than Massinger's foul papers. The compositor has imposed his own spelling on words like *would, giue, guard*, and *these*, but even within this group there are traces of authorial spelling. The mistaken *grieue* for *giue* (I. i. 115) for instance, suggests an original *gieue*, the dramatist's preferred spelling. Massinger's preference for *w* rather than *u* appears in *sawcie, plowd, powre; rancke, sincke, truncke* show another of the author's spelling habits. A selection of well-attested authorial spellings in the quarto would include *cyndars, guift, falne, prodegie, tyranne, fabrique* and *affoord; gamsome*, by an easy minim error, appears as *gainsome*. The combination of light and spasmodically heavy pointing, the separation by a comma of two limbs of a phrase ('good, and glorious actions'), the tendency for lines to remain unstopped at their end, all recall the punctuation of *Believe As You List*. Stage directions are often elaborate and literary: '*Enter Domitia, vsherd in by Aretinus, her traine with all state borne vp by Julia, Cænis, and Domitilla*'; '*The Hangmen torment 'em, they still smiling.*' References to music are descriptive of an effect sought ('*A sad musicke*'; '*A dreadfull Musicke sounding*'), rather than practical instructions. There is good evidence that the quarto was not printed from a manuscript prepared as theatrical prompt-copy. Exits and entrances are not always marked; on B4^v occurs the direction '*Exeunt omnes preter Longinum.*' The prompter could hardly have known that this name, which does not appear elsewhere in the text, indicates that Lamia, as he is called everywhere in the play, should remain on stage, since Longina was the cognomen of Lamia's wife, Domitia. Few properties are mentioned, and when Massinger corrects the printed text he gives the matter only intermittent attention.

There are copies of 29 in the following libraries and institutions: Bamburgh Castle Library; the Bodleian Library (2 copies); the Boston Public Library; the British Museum (4 copies); the Chapin Library; the University of Chicago; the Library of Congress; Eton College; the Folger Shakespeare Library (5 copies); Harvard University; the Henry E. Huntington Library; the University of Illinois; King's College, Cambridge; King's College, Newcastle (2 copies); the Brotherton Library, University of Leeds; the University of Liverpool; the University of London; the Pierpont Morgan Library; the Newberry Library; the University of Pennsylvania;

the Carl H. Pforzheimer Collection; Princeton University; the National Library of Scotland; the University of Texas (3 copies); the Victoria and Albert Museum (3 copies); Worcester College, Oxford; and Yale University.

The present text has been prepared from the Bodleian Library copy, Malone 236 (4).

The Harbord copy, now in the Folger Shakespeare Library (Gosse 5299), contains manuscript corrections which, since Greg's examination of them in 1924, have been accepted as Massinger's.[1] At times the work of correction has been done carefully, at others superficially; there are occasional miscorrections and frequent oversights. On H4^r, for instance, Massinger makes one substantive correction, one spelling correction, and amends a turned letter, but passes over four misprints, two wrong fount letters and one turned ligature. However, the strong probability that the edition of 1629 was set up from the author's manuscript, together with the fact of Massinger's examination of the printed text,[2] provides the modern editor with a comparatively reliable original text of the play.

There are other seventeenth-century manuscript corrections in a British Museum copy of *29* (162. d. 8) which occasionally anticipate the emendations of later editors, and have been admitted into the present text (siglum *B.M. MS*). One emendation proposed by H. D. Sykes, in 'Elizabethan and Jacobean Plays: Suggested Textual Emendations', *NQ*, iii (1917), is recorded in the apparatus (siglum *Sykes*).

Besides the collected editions, *The Roman Actor* appeared in *The Best Plays of the Old Dramatists: Philip Massinger*, edited by Arthur Symons, vol. ii, 1889, and in *Philip Massinger*, edited by L. A. Sherman, New York, 1912.[3]

W. L. Sandidge's *A Critical edition of Massinger's The Roman Actor* (Princeton Studies in English, 4) Princeton, 1924, was the first critical old-spelling edition of the play. A. K. McIlwraith edited

---

[1] W. W. Greg, 'More Massinger Corrections', *The Library*, 4th Series, v (1925), 59–91. See also A. H. Cruickshank, *Philip Massinger*, 1920, pp. 215–23; J. E. Gray, 'Still more Massinger Corrections', *The Library*, 5th Series v (1951), 132–9; A. K. McIlwraith, 'The Manuscript Corrections in Massinger's Plays,' *The Library*, 5th Series vi (1952), 213–16. See further the General Introduction, vol. i, pp. xxxii–xxxiii.

[2] The Harbord copy contains only four formes in an uncorrected or early state: B (i), G (i), H (i), K (i).

[3] According to Sandidge (p. 1) the quarto was 'reproduced' in octavo, London, 1729, but no trace has been found of such an edition.

The Roman Actor in his unpublished doctoral thesis 'The Life and Works of Philip Massinger', Oxford, 1931, and printed a modernized text in *Five Stuart Tragedies*, 1953. The tragedy was also edited by C. A. Gibson, an unpublished doctoral thesis, University of Otago, 1962.

A few alterations and shortened versions of the play have been printed. For the versions of 1722 and 1854 see pp. 9–12. *Beauties of Massinger*, printed for John Porter in 1817, contained twelve passages from *The Roman Actor*, selected to illustrate 'the striking eloquence' of the play. In 1830 Murray published the bowdlerized *The Plays of Philip Massinger, adapted for family reading*, edited by W. Harness, and containing I. i and iii, and part of II. Harper published an American edition under the same title in 1831. Extensive selections from the whole play were printed by Henry Morley in *English Plays*, pp. 271–87 (vol. iii of *Cassell's Library of English Literature*, 5 vols., 1876–81). M. Horn-Monval, *Répertoire bibliographique des traductions et adaptations françaises du théâtre étranger*, Paris, 1963, v, no. 282, records an undated manuscript translation by Joseph de Smet, *L'Acteur de Rome*. Extracts from this translation were published in *Les Cahiers du Sud*, June–July 1933, 128–9, and in *Le Théâtre Élisabéthain* (*Cahiers du Sud*, Paris, 1940), 165–7. A translation into Hungarian by Miklós Szenczi was published in *Angol Reneszánsz Drámák: Shakespeare Kortarsai*, Budapest, 1961, vol. ii.

(d) *Stage History*

As seen already, *The Roman Actor* was licensed for performance by the King's men by Sir Henry Herbert on 11 October 1626. Apart from this fact and the statement on the title-page of the 1629 quarto that the play is published 'As it hath diuers times beene, with good allowance Acted, at the private Play-house in the *Black-Friers*, by the Kings Majesties Servants' little is known of the stage history of the tragedy down to the closing of the theatres in 1642. For the cast list printed with the text of the play see p. 14.

In his Dedication, Massinger presumes that his play will be condemned by '*such as are onely affected with Iigges and ribaldrie*' (line 16), and some scholars have taken this to mean that *The Roman Actor* did not succeed on stage. However, the tragedy was intended for the more sophisticated audiences at Blackfriars; the Dedication is best read as a self-assured defiance of popular taste, and flattery of the private-theatre type of playgoer and reader.[1] In his verse tribute, Thomas Goffe speaks plainly enough of several performances of the play, and of a favourable reception; *The Roman Actor* is 'a work, which, it is clear, has so often pleased the gay theatre when acted' (Verse II, l. 9).

It is possible that the scene (II. i) in which Parthenius attempts to cure Philargus of his avarice by means of a play attracted the attention of other dramatists. Ford's *The Lover's Melancholy* (1628), contains an episode (III. iii) in which the physician Corax presents a masque illustrating the kinds of melancholia, in order to cure Prince Palador of his love melancholy; and in Brome's *The Antipodes* (1638), a doctor presents a whole series of playlets to cure the demented Peregrine of his love for travel.[2]

After the Restoration, to limit the keen competition for plays which had been in the repertoires of the pre-war companies, Killigrew, the manager of the King's Majesty's Servants at the New Theatre, was given rights over 108 plays, including *The Roman Actor*, on 12 January 1669.[3] J. G. McManaway points out that a manager's interest in the acquisition of plays is seldom anything but practical, and suggests that performances may have been given,[4] but if so, no records of them are known.

When Killigrew's company combined with the rival Duke's Company in 1682, *The Roman Actor* became available to Betterton who, according to Davies in the 1789 edition of Downes's *Roscius Anglicanus*, 'took a fancy to the Part of *Paris*' (p. 26). This revival may have taken place about 1682 or as late as 1692, for a playbill of 1722 refers to the piece as 'acted but once these 30 years.'[5] Baker mentions that Betterton 'gained great applause and reputation in the part of the Roman Actor, which he himself performed.'[6]

In 1722 a revision of the play (probably the work of Betterton) was performed at Lincoln's Inn Fields Theatre. *The History and Fall of*

---

[1] *The Fair Maid of the Inn*, written by Fletcher and Massinger for the same Black-friars audience, and licensed early in 1626, has a prologue expressing similar sentiments: ''Tis scurvy, when for approbation / A Jigg shall be clapt at, and every rhime / Prais'd and applauded by a clamorous chime ... Hither / Come nobler Judgements, and to those the strain, / Of our invention is not bent in vain.'

[2] Noted by C. E. Andrews, *Richard Brome: A Study of his Life and Works* (Yale Studies in English, 4), New York, 1913, pp. 123–4.

[3] Nicoll, *History of English Drama*, i (1955), 353–4.   [4] *Studies*, p. 17.

[5] *The London Stage (1660–1800)*, Part 2, ed. E. L. Avery, Carbondale, Illinois, 1960, ii. 681.

[6] *Biographica Dramatica*, 1812, iii. 217.

Domitian; or, *The Roman Actor* was given on 13, 15, 20 and 25 June. The cast included Walker (Paris), Boheme (Domitian), Ogden (Parthenius), Leigh (Lamia), Diggs (Rusticus), Hulett (1st Tribune), Mrs. Seymour (Domitia), Mrs. Spiller (Domitilla), and Mrs. Parlour (Julia). On 22 November of the same year a benefit performance 'for a gentleman under Misfortune' netted £66. There was some rearrangement of the cast, and Quin, Ryan, and Egleton are named in the parts of Aretinus, Parthenius, and Stephanus.[1] *The Roman Actor. A Tragedy. Written Originally by Philip Massinger: And since Reviv'd with Alterations* was printed for Mears, Chetwood, Woodman, and Chapman in 1722, and may represent the text used for the revival. The alterations consist of the replacement of words and allusions thought archaic, and cuts or changes on stylistic, moral, and religious grounds. Nicoll identifies the anonymous reviser as Betterton himself.

In 1781, Tate Wilkinson introduced *The Roman Actor* to Kemble at York, and 'afforded our *English* actor an opportunity to deliver the splendid declamation of Paris, one of the most spirited pieces of that peculiar master of oratory, Massinger.'[2] Under the title of a 'Theatrical Fête', Kemble gave 'The Defence of the Stage' (*The Roman Actor*, I. iii), together with *Julius Caesar*, III, 1 *Henry IV*, IV, and a three-act tragedy, Young's *The Brothers*. Performances were also given at Hull, Leeds, and Edinburgh. In 1781–2 Kemble performed his own two-act version of the play in Ireland. Genest comments that 'Kemble was particularly impressive in Paris, and acted the part . . . at Dublin with great applause.'[3] On 23 May 1796, the programme for Mrs. Kemble's retiring performance at Drury Lane included the same version of *The Roman Actor*. The cast consisted of Palmer (Domitian), Aickin (Lamia), Caulfield (Aretinus), Maddocks (Rusticus), Webb (Sura), ?C. Kemble (Parthenius), Trueman (Cornelius), Kemble (Paris), Whitfield (Aesopus), Packer (Latinus), Mrs Powell (Domitia), Miss De Camp (Julia), Miss Heard (Domitilla), and Miss Miller (Galeria).[4] There is a manuscript of the text in the Larpent collection, Larpent 1040. A reviewer in *The Monthly*

---

[1] Genest, iii. 82; Avery, *The London Stage (1660–1800)*, Part 2, ii. 681, 696.

[2] J. Boaden, *Memoirs of the Life of John Philip Kemble*, 1825, i. 35. In *The Wandering Patentee*, York, 1795, ii. 105–12, Wilkinson printed a playbill for 18 May, and the text of the scene from *The Roman Actor* (I. iii. 31 ff.)

[3] vii. 244.

[4] *The London Stage (1660–1800)*, Part 5, ed. C. B. Hogan, Carbondale, Illinois, 1968, iii. 1861.

Mirror, ii (May 1796), 52, commented, 'Massinger's play, compressed into two acts, is yet deficient of the interest which can alone make it popular. Mr Kemble, the most gracious and majestic actor we ever saw, or expect to see, in that noble defence and eulogium of the stage, which Paris makes before the consuls, gave an additional proof of the soundness of his judgement, and the unequalled force of his declamation.' Kemble's text consists of the Paris–Domitia thread of the plot, culled from the published play with very little alteration to Massinger's verse.

On 2 and 7 September 1812, at the Theatre Royal, Birmingham, William Macready the elder introduced *The Roman Actor*, as an after-piece to *The Virgin of the Sun*. The playbills describe it as 'a petit Piece . . . written by Philip Massinger, and since corrected, revised, and adapted to the present Time . . . Tending to elucidate the real Purposes for which the Stage was first erected'.[1] The cast consisted of the younger Macready (Paris), Thompson (Latinus), Gomersal (Oesopus), Evatt (Aretinus), Bishop (Lamia), Butler (Rusticus), Wood and Cuffley (Lictors). These character names and the playbill description of the piece suggest that Macready only performed *The Roman Actor*, I. i. and iii, thus anticipating Kean's selection from Massinger's tragedy.

Edmund Kean presented *The Curia* at Drury Lane on 3 June 1822, with himself in the rôle of Paris. He then took part in *The Mountaineers* and *The Watermen*. There was a small house, and the proceeds were only £5. 17s. 7d. At the Theatre Royal, Dublin, on 12 August of the same year (his benefit night) Kean repeated the performance.[2] The dramatic critic of *The London Magazine* for July, 1822, thought that Kean's Paris was exceedingly bad, 'overbearing, familiar, sarcastic, pompous without dignity, and violent without energy.'[3] Sandidge conjectures that *The Drama's Vindication: or the Roman Actor. Compressed from Massinger's celebrated play*, published in 1854, represents the text used by Kean. He is probably right, since a contemporary journal reported that 'The scene from MASSINGER's play of *The Roman Actor* was produced as a sort of appeal to the public on the merits of the stage; and seemed

---

[1] Playbills for both performances are in the 1810–12 volume of Theatre Royal playbills in the Birmingham Reference Library. See also A. S. Downer, *The Eminent Tragedian: William Charles Macready*, 1966, p. 34.

[2] Genest, ix. 152–3; Levey and O'Rorke, *Annals of the Theatre Royal, Dublin*, 1880, p. 11.

[3] Quoted by H. N. Hillebrand, *Edmund Kean*, 1933, p. 227.

to have a particular reference to that neglect which Drury Lane Theatre has so long laboured under.'[1] The published text consists of part of Act I. i and the whole of I. iii. French published an acting edition under the same title in 1888.

As usual, provincial companies imitated Kean's London programme. On 12 May, 1830, at the Theatre Royal, Bath, a performance of *Riches* (see vol. iv, p. 14) was preceded by *The Roman Actor: or, The Drama's Vindication*, 'an entertainment in one act . . . for the benefit of Mr. Stuart.' The playbill, at the Reference Library, Bath, gives the cast as Stuart (Paris), Griffith (Aesopus), Field (Latinus), Mathews and Lodge (two Lictors), Trevena (Aretinus), Lansdowne (Rusticus), Cooke (Falcinius), and Connor (Domitian's messenger).

The one great speech which had prolonged the life of *The Roman Actor* continued to be used. It was given by Chalmers at Philadelphia on 18 May 1795, and at Boston on 20 May, and by Hackett at the Park Theatre, New York, on 19 September 1827.[2] John Coleman, in his *Fifty Years of an Actor's Life*, 1904, ii. 488, recalled that 'we did *Othello*, and I delivered Paris's defence of the stage from Massinger's now obsolete play *The Roman Actor*. There was a very good house.' This was at the Gravesend Theatre in 1850.

---

[1] *The Drama; or, Theatrical Pocket Magazine*, 1822, iii. 36.
[2] Sandidge, p. 5.

THE
ROMAN
ACTOR.

A
TRAGÆDIE.

As it hath diuers times beene, with
good allowance Acted, at the priuate
Play-house in the *Black-Friers*,
by the Kings Majesties
Servants.

WRITTEN
By PHILIP MASSINGER.

LONDON.
Printed by *B.A.* and *T.F.* for ROBERT ALLOT, and
are to be sold at his Shop at the signe of the *Beare*
in *Pauls* Church-yard. 1629.

The persons presented. The principall Actors.

Domitianus Cæsar.	IOHN LOWIN.
Paris the Tragædian.	IOSEPH TAYLOR.
Parthenius a free-man of *Cæsars.*	RICHARD SHARPE.
Ælius Lamia, and *Stephanos.*	THOMAS POLLARD. 5
Iunius Rusticus.	ROBERT BENFIELD.
Aretinus Clemens, Cæsars spie.	EYLLARDT SWANSTONE.
Æsopus a Player.	RICHARD ROBINSON.
Philargus a rich Miser.	ANTHONY SMITH.
Palphurius Sura, a Senator.	WILLIAM PATTRICKE. 10
[*Fulcinius* a Senator.]	
[*Ascletario* an Astrologer.]	
[*Sijeius* and *Entellus,* Conspirators.]	
Latinus a Player.	CVRTISE GREVILL.
3. Tribunes.	15
2. Lictors.	GEORGE VERNON.
	IAMES HORNE.
Domitia the wife of *Ælius Lamia.*	IOHN TOMPSON.
Domitilla cousin germane to *Cæsar.*	IOHN HVNNIEMAN.
Iulia, Titus Daughter.	WILLIAM TRIGGE. 20
Cænis, Vespatians Concubine.	ALEXANDER GOVGH.
[A Ladie.]	
[A Centurion.]	
[Souldiers.]	
[Captaines.]	25
[Prisoners.]	
[Hangmen.]	
[Seruants.]	
[Guard.]	

5. *Ælius*] *Massinger MS*; ∼, 29   11. *Fulcinius* . . . Senator.] *Coxeter*; *not in 29*
12–13. *Ascletario* . . . Conspirators.] *Gifford*; *not in 29*   13. *Sijeius*] *Gifford*;
Sigerus Sandidge   22–28. A Ladie . . . Seruants.] *Gifford*; *not in 29*
29. Guard.] *editor*; *not in 29*

To my much Honoured, and most *true Friends*,
Sir PHILIP KNYVET, Knight and Baronet.
And to Sir THOMAS IEAY, Knight. And
THOMAS BELLINGHAM of *Newtimber* in
Sussex Esquire.

5

*How much I acknowledge my selfe bound for your so many, and
extraordinary fauors confer'd vpon me (as farre as it is in my power)
posterity shall take notice, I were most vnworthy of such noble friends,
if I should not with all Thankefulnesse, professe, and owne em. In the
composition of this Tragædie you were my only Supporters, and it* 10
*being now by your principall encouragement to be turn'd into the world,
it cannot walke safer, then vnder your protection. It hath beene happie*
*in the suffrage of some learned, and iudicious Gentlemen when it was
presented, nor shall they find cause I hope in the pervsall, to repent
them of their good opinion of it. If the grauity and height of the subject* 15
*distaste such as are onely affected with Iigges, and ribaldrie (as I pre-
sume it will,) their condemnation of me, and my Poem, can no way
offend me: my reason teaching me such malicious, and ignorant detractors deserue rather contempt, then satisfaction. I euer held it the
most perfit birth of my* Minerua; *and therefore, in iustice offer it to* 20
*those that haue best deseru'd of me, who I hope in their courteous
acceptance will render it worth their receiuing, and euer, in their gentle
construction of my imperfections, beleeue they may at their pleasure
dispose of him, that is wholly, and sincerelie*

Devoted   25

to their seruice.

Philip Massinger.

---

7. *me (as]* Massinger MS; ~, ~ 29   *power)]* Massinger MS; ~ ^ 29

To his deare Friend the Author.

I AM no great admirer of the Playes,
  Poets, or Actors, that are now adayes:
Yet in this Worke of thine me thinkes I see
  Sufficient reason for Idolatrie.
Each line thou hast taught CEASAR is, as high   5
  As Hee could speake, when groueling Flatterie,
And His owne pride (forgetting Heavens rod)
  By His Edicts stil'd himselfe great Lord and God.
By thee againe the Lawrell crownes His Head;
  And thus reviu'd, who can affirme him dead?   10
Such power lyes in this loftie straine as can
  Giue Swords, and legions to DOMITIAN.
And when thy PARIS pleades in the defence
  Of Actors, every grace, and excellence
Of Argument for that subject, are by Thee   15
  Contracted in a sweete Epitome.
Nor doe thy Women the tyr'd Hearers vexe,
  With language no way proper to their sexe.
Iust like a cunning Painter thou lets fall
  Copies more faire then the Originall.   20
I'll adde but this. From all the moderne Playes
  The Stage hath lately borne, this winnes the Bayes.
And if it come to tryall boldly looke
  To carrie it cleere, Thy witnesse being thy Booke.

T. I.

In Philippi Massingeri, *Poetæ elegantiss:*
Actorem Romanum, typis excusum.
δεκαςικον.

Ecce *Philippinæ, celebrata Tragœdia Musæ*
   Quam Roseus Britonum Roscius egit, adest.
Semper, fronde ambo vireant Parnasside, semper
   Liber ab invidiæ dentibus esto, Liber.
Crebra papyriuori spernas incendia pæti   5
   Thus, Vænum expositi tegmina suta libri:
Nec metuas raucos, Momorum Sybila, rhoncos
   Tam bardus nebulo si tamen vllus, erit.
Nam toties festis, actum, placuisse Theatris
   Quod liquet, hoc, Cusum, crede, placebit, opus.   10

THO: G.

2. *Roseus*] *Massinger MS*; *Roseus* 29 (*defective* e)   *egit*] *Massinger MS*; *egit* 29
(*defective* e)

To his *deseruing Friend Mr.* Philip Massinger, *vpon his Tragædie, the Roman Actor.*

PARIS, the best of Actors in his age
  Acts yet, and speakes vpon our Roman Stage
Such lines by thee, as doe not derogate
  From *Romes* proud heights, and Her then learned State.
Nor great *Domitians* fauour; not th'embraces   5
  Of a faire Empresse, nor those often graces
Which from th'applauding Theaters were pay'd
  To His braue Action, nor His ashes layd
In the *Flaminian* way, where people strow'd
  His Graue with flowers, and *Martialls* wit bestow'd   10
A lasting Epitaph, not all these same
  Doe adde so much renowne to *Paris* name,
As this that thou present'st his Historie
  So well to vs. For which in thankes would Hee
(If that His soule, as thought *Pithagoras*   15
  Could into any of our Actors passe)
Life to these Lines by action gladly giue
  Whose Pen so well has made His storie liue.

                                    Tho: May.

Vpon Mr. MASSINGER *His Roman Actor.*

To write, is growne so common in our Time
  That euery one, who can but frame a Rime
Howeuer monstrous, giues Himselfe that praise
  Which onely Hee should claime, that may weare Bayes
By their Applause whose judgements apprehend   5
  The weight, and truth, of what they dare commend.
In this besotted Age (friend) 'tis thy glory
  That Heere thou hast out-done the Roman story.
Domitians pride; His wiue's lust vnabated
  In death; with *Paris*, meerly were related   10
Without a Soule, Vntill thy abler Pen
  Spoke them, and made them speake, nay Act agen
In such a height, that Heere to know their Deeds
  Hee may become an Actor that but Reades.

Iohn Foorde.

9. wiue's] *Massinger MS*; wiues 29

Long'st thou to see proud *Cæsar* set in State,
His Morning greatnesse, or his Euening fate?
With admiration heere behold him fall
And yet out-liue his tragique Funerall:
For 'tis a question whether *Cæsars* Glorie   5
Rose to its heighth before, or in this Storie.
Or whether *Paris* in *Domitians* fauour
Were more exalted, then in this thy labour.
Each line speakes him an Emperour, eu'ry phrase
Crownes thy deseruing temples with the Bayes;   10
  So that reciprocally both agree
  Thou liu'st in him and Hee suruiues in Thee.

Robert Harvey.

To His long knowne and lou'd Friend,
Mr. PHILIP MASSINGER,
vpon His Roman Actor.

IF that my Lines being plac'd before thy Booke
  Could make it sell, or alter but a looke
Of some sowre Censurer, who's apt to say
  No one in these Times can produce a Play
Worthy his reading since of late, 'tis true   5
  The old accepted are more then the new.
Or could I on some Spot o'the Court worke so
  To make him speake no more then He doth know;
Not borrowing from His flattering flatter'd friend
  What to dispraise, or wherefore to commend.   10
Then (gentle Friend) I should not blush to bee
  Rank'd 'mongst those worthy ones, which heere I see
Vshering this Worke, but why I write to Thee
  Is to professe our loues Antiquitie,
Which to this *Tragœdie* must giue my test,   15
  Thou hast made many good, but this thy best.

                     Ioseph Taylor.

The Roman Actor

A Tragedie

Actus I. Scæna 1.

Enter PARIS, LATINUS, ÆSOPUS.

Æsopus. WHAT doe wee acte to day?
Latinus.   *Agaves* phrensie
With *Pentheus* bloudie end.
 Paris.   It skils not what;
The times are dull, and all that wee receiue
Will hardly satisfie the dayes Expence.
The *Greekes* (to whom we owe the first inuention   5
Both of the buskind scæne and humble socke)
That raigne in euery noble familie
Declaime against vs: and our *Amphitheater*,
Great *Pompies* worke, that hath giu'n full delight
Both to the eye, and eare of fifty thousand   10
Spectators in one day, as if it were
Some vnknowne desert, or great *Rome* vnpeopl'd,
Is quite forsaken.
 Latinus. Pleasures of worse natures
Are gladly entertayn'd, and they that shun vs,
Practise in priuate sports the *Stewes* would blush at. 15
A Litter borne by eight Liburnian slaues,
To buy Diseases from a glorious strumpet,
The most censorious of our Roman gentrie,
Nay of the guarded robe the Senators,
Esteeme an easie purchase,
 Paris.   Yet grudge vs   20
(That with delight joyne profit, and endeauour
To build their mindes vp faire, and on the Stage

I. i. 6. socke] *Coxeter, Massinger MS* (socc.); stocke *29* 8. *Amphitheater*] *29*;
theatre *Gifford* 12. *Rome*] *Coxeter*; Roome *29*

B1^v Decipher to the life what honours waite
On good, and glorious actions, and the shame
That treads vpon the heeles of vice) the salarie   25
Of six Sestertij.
    Æsopus.   For the profit *Paris*,
And mercinarie gaine they are things beneath vs
Since while you hold your grace, and power with *Cæsar*,
We from your bounty finde a large supply,
Nor can one thought of want euer approach vs,   30
    Paris. Our aime is glorie, and to leaue our names
To after times.
    Latinus.   And would they giue vs leaue
There ends all our ambition.
    Æsopus.   Wee haue enemies,
And great ones too, I feare. 'Tis giuen out lately
The Consull *Aretinus* (*Cæsars* spie)   35
Sayd at his Table ere a moneth expir'd
(For being galld in our last Comedie)
He would silence vs for euer.
    Paris.   I expect
No fauour from him, my strong Auentine is
That great *Domitian*, whom we oft haue cheer'd   40
In his most sullen moodes will once returne,
Who can repayre with ease, the Consuls ruines.
    Latinus. 'Tis frequent in the Citie, he hath subdued
The Catti, and the Daci, and ere long,
The second time will enter *Rome* in triumph.   45

Enter two LICTORS.

    Paris. Ioue hasten it, with vs? I now beleeue
The Consuls threates *Æsopus.*
    1. *Lictor.*   You are summon'd
T'appeare to day in Senate.
    2. *Lictor.*   And there to answer
What shall be vrg'd against you.
    Paris.   We obey you.

25. vice) the] *Massinger MS* (vice) The); vice. The *29*   32. times] *29*^{2, 3}; time
*29*¹   37. galld] *Massinger MS*; gald *29*   44. Catti . . . Daci] *Massinger MS*,
29^{2, 3}; Catta . . . Dacie *29*¹   46. vs?] *Massinger MS*, *29*^{2, 3}; ~. *29*¹   49. obey
you.] *Massinger MS*, *29*^{2, 3}; ~ ~_∧ *29*¹

Nay droope not fellowes, innocence should be bould. 50
B2^r We that haue personated in the Scæne
The ancient Heroes, and the falles of Princes
With loude applause, being to act our selues,
Must doe it with vndaunted confidence.
What ere our sentence be thinke 'tis in sport. 55
And though condemn'd lets heare it without sorrow,
As if we were to liue againe to morrow.
  1. *Lictor*. 'Tis spoken like your selfe.

Enter ÆLIUS LAMIA, IUNIUS RUSTICUS, PALPHURIUS SURA.

  Lamia.   Whether goes *Paris*?
  1. *Lictor*. He's cited to the Senate.
  Latinus.   I am glad the State is
So free from matters of more waight and trouble 60
That it has vacant time to looke on vs.
  Paris. That reuerend place, in which the affaires of Kings,
And prouinces were determin'd, to descend
To the censure of a bitter word, or iest,
Drop'd from a Poets pen! peace to your Lordships, 65
We are glad that you are safe.
               Exeunt LICTORS, PARIS, LATINUS, ÆSOPUS.
  Lamia.   What times are these?
To what is *Rome* falne? may we being alone
Speake our thoughts freely of the Prince, and State,
And not feare the informer?
  Rusticus.   Noble *Lamia*,
So dangerous the age is, and such bad acts 70
Are practis'd euery where, we hardly sleepe
Nay cannot dreame with safetie. All our actions
Are cal'd in question, to be nobly borne
Is now a crime; and to deserue too well
Held Capitall treason. Sonnes accuse their Fathers, 75
Fathers their sonnes; and but to winne a smile
From one in grace in Court, our chastest Matrons
Make shipwracke of their honours. To be vertuous

---

50. bould.] *Massinger MS*; ~ ∧ *29*   51. Scæne] *Massinger MS*; Sceane *29*
56. sorrow,] *Massinger MS*; ~ ∧ *29*   58 SD. ÆLIUS ... SURA] *Gifford, Massinger
MS* (Ælius Lamia, Junius, Rusticus, Palphuris, Sura); Ælius, Lamia, Junius, Rusticus
Palphuris, Sura *29*   77. in Court] *29*; at Court *Coxeter*

Is to bee guilty. They are onely safe
That know to sooth the Princes appetite,   80
And serue his lusts.
B2ᵛ   *Sura.*   Tis true; and tis my wonder
That two sonnes of so different a nature,
Should spring from good *Vespatian*. We had a *Titus*,
Stilde iustly the delight of all mankinde,
Who did esteeme that day lost in his life   85
In which some one or other tasted not
Of his magnificent bounties. One that had
A readie teare when he was forc'd to signe
The death of an offender. And so farre
From pride, that he disdain'd not the conuerse   90
Euen of the poorest Roman.
     Lamia.   Yet his brother
Domitian, that now swayes the power of things,
Is so inclin'd to bloud, that noe day passes
In which some are not fastend to the hooke,
Or throwne downe from the Gemonies. His freemen   95
Scorne the Nobilitie, and he himselfe
As if he were not made of flesh and bloud,
Forgets he is a man.
     Rusticus.   In his young yeeres
He shew'd what he would be when growne to ripenes:
His greatest pleasure was, being a childe,   100
With a sharp pointed bodkin to kill flies,
Whose roomes now men supply. For his escape
In the *Vitellian* warre he rais'd a Temple
To *Iupiter*, and proudly plac'd his figure
In the bosome of the God. And in his edicts   105
He does not blush, or start to stile himselfe
(As if the name of Emperour were base)
Great Lord, and God *Domitian*.
     Sura.   I haue letters
He's on his way to *Rome*, and purposes
To enter with all glorie. The flattering Senate   110
Decrees him divine Honours, and to crosse it
Were death with studied torments; for my part
I will obey the time, it is in vaine

79. bee] *Massinger MS, 29²˒³; eb 29¹*

To striue against the torrent.
 Rusticus.   Lets to the Curia
B3ʳ And though vnwillingly, gieue our suffrages　　115
Before we are compeld.
 Lamia.   And since we cannot
With safetie vse the actiue, lets make vse of
The passiue fortitude, with this assurance
That the state sicke in him, the gods to friend,　　119
Though at the worst will now begin to mend.　　*Exeunt.*

Actus I. Scæna 2.

Enter DOMITIA, *and* PARTHENIUS *with a letter.*

 Domitia. To me this reuerence?
 Parthenius.   I pay it Ladie
As a debt due to her thats *Cæsars* mistris.
For vnderstand with ioy he that commands
All that the Sunne giues warmth to, is your seruant.
Be not amaz'd, but fit you to your fortunes.　　5
Thinke vpon state, and greatnesse, and the Honours
That waite vpon *Augusta*, for that name
Ere long comes to you: still you doubt your vassall:
But when you haue read this letter, writ, and sign'd
With his imperiall hand, you will be freed　　10
From feare, and jealousie; and I beseech you,
When all the beauties of the earth bowe to you,
And Senators shall take it for an honour,
As I doe now to kisse these happie feete;
When euery smile you giue is a preferment,　　15
And you dispose of Prouinces to your creatures,
Thinke on *Parthenius.*
 Domitia.   Rise. I am transported,
And hardly dare beleeue what is assur'd here.
The meanes, my good *Parthenius*, that wrought *Cæsar*
(Our God on earth) to cast an eye of fauour　　20
Vpon his humble handmaide!

---

 115. gieue] *Massinger MS*; grieue *29*   I. ii. 1 SD. PARTHENIUS . . . *letter.*]
Massinger MS (*Parthenius.* with a letter); *Parthenius. 29* 8. vassall:] *Massinger
MS*; ∼, *29*

Parthenius.   What but your beautie?
When nature fram'd you for her master peece,
As the pure abstract of all rare in woman,
B3ᵛ She had no other ends but to designe you
To the most eminent place. I will not say   25
(For it would smell of arrogance to insinuate
The seruice I haue done you) with what zeale
I oft haue made relation of your Vertues,
Or how I haue sung your goodnesse; or how *Cæsar*
Was fir'd with the relation of your storie;   30
I am rewarded in the acte, and happie
In that my proiect prosper'd.
Domitia.   You are modest,
And were it in my power I woulde be thankefull.
If that when I was mistris of my selfe,
And in my way of youth, pure, and vntainted,   35
The Emperour had vouchsaf'd to seeke my fauours,
I had with ioy giuen vp my virgin fort
At the first summons to his soft embraces:
But I am now anothers, not mine owne.
You know I haue a husband, for my honour   40
I would not be his strumpet, and how lawe
Can bee dispenc'd with to become his wife.
To mee's a riddle.
Parthenius.   I can soone resolue it.
When power puts in its Plea the lawes are silenc'd.
The world confesses one *Rome*, and one *Cæsar*,   45
And as his rule is infinite, his pleasures
Are vnconfin'd; this sillable, his will,
Stands for a thousand reasons.
Domitia.   But with safetie,
Suppose I should consent, how can I doe it?
My husband is a Senator of a temper,   50
Not to be iested with.

                    Enter LAMIA.

Parthenius.   As if hee durst
Be *Cæsars* riuall. Heere he comes, with ease

29. goodnesse;] *Massinger MS*; ∼ₐ *29*   30. storie;] *Massinger MS*; ∼, *29*
33. I woulde] *Massinger MS*; for to *29¹*; I would to *29²,³*   35. way] *29*; May
Sykes   44. its] *Massinger MS*; his *29*   46. rule] *B.M. MS*; rules *29*

I will remoue this scruple.

   Lamia.   How! so priuate!
Mine owne house made a brothell! Sir how durst you,
Though guarded with your power in Court, and greatnesse,   55
Hould conference with my wife? as for you Minion
B4r I shall hereafter treate—

   Parthenius.   You are rude, and sawcie,
Nor know to whom you speake.

   Lamia.   This is fine ifaith!

   Parthenius. Your wife? but touch her, that respect forgotten
That's due to her, whom mightiest *Cæsar* fauours,   60
And thinke what 'tis to die. Not to loose time,
She's *Cæsars* choice. It is sufficient honor
You were his taster in this heauenly nectar,
But now must quit the office.

   Lamia.   This is rare.
Cannot a man be master of his wife   65
Because she's young, and faire, without a pattent?
I in mine owne house am an Emperour,
And will defend whats mine, where are my knaues?
If such an insolence escape vnpunish'd—

   Parthenius. In your selfe *Lamia*, *Cæsar* hath forgot   70
To vse his power, and I his instrument,
In whom though absent, his authoritie speakes,
Haue lost my faculties.   *Stampes.*

      Enter a Centurion with Souldiers.

   Lamia.   The Guard! why am I
Design'd for death?

   Domitia.   As you desire my fauour
Take not so rough a course.

   Parthenius.   All your desires   75
Are absolute commaunds. Yet giue me leaue
To put the will of *Cæsar* into acte.
Heer's a bill of Diuorce betweene your Lordship,
And this great Lady. If you refuse to signe it,
And so as if you did it vncompell'd,   80

---

56. you] *Coxeter*; your *29*   58. ifaith!] *29*; ifaith! / Is she not my wife? *Coxeter*
60. fauours,] *Massinger MS*; ~ˌ *29*   66. pattent?] *Massinger MS*; ~. *29*
70. *Lamia*,] *B.M. MS*; ~. *29*

Wonne to it by reasons that concerne your selfe,
Her honour to vntainted, here are Clearkes
Shall in your best bloud write it newe, till torture
Compell you to performe it.
    Lamia.   Is this legall?
    Parthenius. Monarkes that dare not doe vnlawfull things,   85
Yet bare them out, are Constables, not Kings.
Will you dispute?
B4ᵛ   *Lamia.*   I know not what to vrge
Against my selfe, but too much dotage on her,
Loue and obseruance.
    Parthenius.   Set it vnder your hand
That you are impotent, and cannot pay   90
The duties of a husband, or that you are mad,
(Rather then want iust cause wee'l make you so)
Dispatch, you know the danger els, deliuer it.
Nay on your knee. Madam you now are free
And Mistris of your selfe.
    Lamia.   Can you *Domitia*   95
Consent to this?
    Domitia.   'Twould argue a base minde
To liue a seruant, when I may commaund.
I now am *Cæsars*, and yet in respect
I once was yours, when you come to the Pallace,
(Prouided you deserue it in your seruice)   100
You shall find me your good Mistris. Waite me *Parthenius.*
And now farewell poore *Lamia.*
                    Exeunt omnes preter LONGINUM.
    Lamia.   To the Gods
I bend my knees, (for tyrannie hath banish'd
Iustice from men) and as they would deserue
Their Altars, and our vowes, humbly inuoke 'em   105
That this my rauish'd wife may proue as fatall
To proud *Domitian*, and her embraces
Affoord him in the end as little ioy,
As wanton *Helen* brought to him of *Troy.*   *Exit.*

85. *Parthenius.* Monarkes] *Massinger MS* (pa: monarkes); New workes *29¹*; *Par.*
Monarchs *29²·³*   87. Will . . . dispute?] *Massinger MS*; *Parth.* Will . . . dispute.
29¹; *Parth.* Will . . . dispute? *29²·³*   88. her,] *Gifford*; ~ₐ *29*   93. it.] *Massinger MS*; ~ₐ *29*

Actus I. Scæna 3.

Enter LICTORS, ARETINUS, FULCINIUS, RUSTICUS, SURA, PARIS,
LATINUS, ÆSOPUS.

Aretinus. Fathers conscript may this our meeting be
Happie to *Cæsar* and the common wealth.
Lictor. Silence.
Aretinus.   The purpose of this frequent Senate
Is first to giue thankes to the Gods of *Rome*,
That for the propagation of the Empire,   5
C1ʳ Vouchsafe vs one to gouerne it like themselues.
In height of courage, depth of vnderstanding,
And all those vertues, and remarkeable graces,
Which make a Prince most eminent, our *Domitian*
Transcend's the ancient Romans. I can neuer   10
Bring his praise to a period. What good man
That is a friend to truth, dares make it doubtfull,
That he hath *Fabius* stay'dnesse, and the courage
Of bould *Marcellus* (to whom *Hanibal* gaue
The stile of Target, and the Sword of *Rome*.)   15
But he has more, and euery touch more Roman,
As *Pompey's* dignitie, *Augustus* state,
Antonies bountie, and great *Iulius* fortune,
With *Catoes* resolution. I am lost
In th'Ocean of his vertues. In a word   20
All excellencies of good men in him meet,
But no part of their vices.
Rusticus.   This is no flatterie!
Sura. Take heed, you'l be obseru'd.
Aretinus.   'Tis then most fit
That we (as to the Father of our Countrie,
Like thankefull sonnes, stand bound to pay true seruice   25
For all those blessings that he showres vpon vs)
Should not conniue, and see his gouernment
Deprau'd, and scandaliz'd by meaner men
That to his fauour, and indulgence owe
Themselues and being.

I. iii. 14. *Marcellus* (to] *Massinger MS*; *Marcellus, to* 29   15. *Rome.*)] *Massinger
MS*; ∼.ᴧ 29   24. as] 29; who *conj. Mason*   28. Deprau'd,] *Massinger MS*; ∼ᴧ 29

Paris.	Now he points at vs.	30

Aretinus. Cite *Paris* the Tragedian.

Paris.   Here.

Aretinus.   Stand forth.

In thee, as being the chiefe of thy profession,
I doe accuse the qualitie of treason,
As libellers against the state and *Cæsar.*

    Paris. Meere accusations are not proofes my Lord,   35
In what are we delinquents?

    Aretinus.   You are they
That search into the secrets of the time,
And vnder fain'd names on the Stage present
Actions not to be toucht at; and traduce
Persons of rancke, and qualitie of both Sexes,   40
And with satiricall, and bitter iests
Make euen the Senators ridiculous
To the Plebeans.

    Paris.   If I free not my selfe,
(And in my selfe the rest of my profession)
From these false imputations, and proue   45
That they make that a libell, which the Poet
Writ for a Comedie, so acted too,
It is but Iustice that we vndergoe
The heauiest censure.

    Aretinus.   Are you on the Stage
You talke so boldly?

    Paris.   The whole world being one   50
This place is not exempted, and I am
So confident in the iustice of our cause,
That I could wish *Cæsar* (in whose great name
All Kings are comprehended) sate as iudge,
To heare our Plea, and then determine of vs.   55
If to expresse a man sould to his lusts,
Wasting the treasure of his time and Fortunes,
In wanton dalliance, and to what sad end
A wretch thats so giuen ouer does arriue at;
Deterring carelesse youth, by his example,   60

CI^v appears at left margin beside line 39.

31. *rearranged by Coxeter*; *one line in* 29   46. libell,] *Massinger MS*; ∼ ⌃ 29
50. world] *Coxeter*; word 29   53. *Cæsar* (in] *Massinger MS*; *Cæsar*, in 29
54. comprehended)] *Massinger MS*; ∼ ⌃ 29   59. at;] *Massinger MS*; ∼, 29

From such licentious courses; laying open
The snares of baudes, and the consuming arts
Of prodigall strumpets, can deserue reproofe,
Why are not all your golden principles
Writ downe by graue Philosophers to instruct vs   65
To chuse faire Vertue for our guide, not pleasure,
Condemnd vnto the fire?
   Sura.   There's spirit in this.
   Paris. Or if desire of honour was the base
On which the building of the Roman Empire
Was rais'd vp to this height; if to inflame   70
The noble youth with an ambitious heate
T'indure the frosts of danger, nay of Death
C2ʳ To be thought worthy the triumphall wreath
By glorious vndertakings, may deserue
Reward, or fauour, from the common wealth,   75
Actors may put in for as large a share
As all the sects of the Philosophers.
They with could precepts (perhaps seldome reade)
Deliver what an honourable thing
The actiue vertue is. But does that fire   80
The bloud, or swell the veines with emulation
To be both good, and great, equall to that
Which is presented on our Theaters?
Let a good Actor in a loftie Sceane
Show great *Alcides* honour'd in the sweate   85
Of his twelue labours; or a bould *Camillus*
Forbidding *Rome* to be redeem'd with gold,
From the insulting *Gauls*; or *Scipio*
After his victories imposing Tribute
On conquer'd *Carthage*. If done to the life,   90
As if they saw their dangers, and their glories,
And did partake with them in their rewardes,
All that haue any sparke of *Roman* in them,
The slothfull artes layd by, contend to bee
Like those they see presented.
   Rusticus.   He has put   95

---

67. Condemnd] *Massinger MS*; Condemne *29*   78. with] *Massinger MS*;
which *29*   86. *Camillus*] *Massinger MS* (Camillus); *Cancillus 29*   87. gold,]
Massinger MS; ∼ₐ *29*

The Consuls to their whisper.
   Paris.   But 'tis vrg'd
That we corrupt youth, and traduce superiours:
When doe we bring a vice vpon the Stage,
That does goe off vnpunish'd? doe we teach
By the successe of wicked vndertakings,   100
Others to tread, in their forbidden steps?
We show no arts of *Lidian* Pandarisme,
Corinthian poysons, *Persian* flatteries,
But mulcted so in the conclusion that
Even those spectators that were so inclin'd,   105
Go home chang'd men. And for traducing such
That are aboue vs, publishing to the world
Their secret crimes, we are as innocent
C2ᵛ As such as are borne dumbe. When we present
An heyre, that does conspire against the life   110
Of his deare parent, numbring euery houre
He liues as tedious to him, if there be
Among the auditors one whose conscience tells him,
He is of the same mould, we cannot helpe it.
Or bringing on the stage a loose adultresse,   115
That does maintaine the ryotous expence
Of him that feedes her greedie lust, yet suffers
The lawfull pledges of a former bed
To starue the while for hunger, if a Matron
Howeuer great in fortune, birth, or titles,   120
Guilty of such a foule vnnaturall sinne,
Crie out tis writ by me, we cannot helpe it:
Or when a couetous man's express'd, whose wealth
Arithmetique cannot number, and whose Lordships
A Falcon in one day cannot flie ouer,   125
Yet he so sordid in his mind, so griping
As not to affoord himselfe the necessaries
To maintaine life, if a Patrician,
(Though honourd with a Consulship) finde himselfe
Touch'd to the quicke in this, we cannot helpe it.   130
Or when we show a Iudge that is corrupt,
And will giue vp his sentence as he fauours
The person, not the cause, sauing the guiltie

    122. by] *29*; for *Coxeter*   124. Arithmetique] *Massinger MS*; Arithmatique *29*

If of his faction, and as oft condemning
The innocent out of particular spleene,   135
If any in this reuerend assemblie,
Nay e'ne your selfe my Lord, that are the image
Of absent *Cæsar*, feele something in your bosome
That puts you in remembrance of things past,
Or things intended tis not in vs to helpe it.   140
I haue said, my Lord, and now as you finde cause
Or censure vs, or free vs with applause.
   Latinus. Well pleaded on my life! I neuer saw him
Act an Orators part before.
   Æsopus.   We might haue giuen
Ten double fees to *Regulus*, and yet   145
C3ʳ Our cause deliuered worse.   *A shoute within.*

Enter PARTHENIUS.

   Aretinus.   What shoute is that?
   Parthenius. Cæsar our Lord married to conquest, is
Returnd in triumph.
   Fulcinius.   Lets all hast to meete him.
   Aretinus. Breake vp the Court, we will reserue to him   149
The Censure of this cause.
   All.   Long life to *Cæsar.*   *Exeunt omnes.*

Actus I. Scæna 4.

Enter IULIA, CÆNIS, DOMITILLA, DOMITIA.

   Cænis. Stand backe, the place is mine.
   Iulia.   Your's? am I not
Great *Titus* daughter, and *Domitians* neece?
Dares any claime precedence?
   Cænis.   I was more;
The mistris of your father, and in his right
Claime dutie from you.
   Iulia.   I confesse you were vsefull   5
To please his appetite.
   Domitia.   To end the controuersie,
For Ile haue no contending, Ile be bold
To leade the way my selfe.

Domitilla. You, Minion!
Domitia. Yes
And all ere long shall kneele to catch my fauours.
Iulia. Whence springs this floud of greatnesse?
Domitia. You shall know
To soone for your vexation, and perhaps 11
Repent too late, and pine with enuie when
You see whom *Cæsar* fauours.
Iulia. Obserue the sequel.

C3ᵛ *Enter at one doore Captaines with Lawrels,* DOMITIAN,
in his Triumphant Chariot, PARTHENIUS, PARIS, LATINUS,
ÆSOPUS, *met by* ARETINUS, SURA, LAMIA, RUSTICUS,
FULCINIUS, *Prisoners led by him.*

Cæsar. As we now touch the height of humane glorie,
Riding in triumph to the Capitoll, 15
Let these whom this victorious arme hath made
The scorne of Fortune, and the flaues of *Rome,*
Tast the extreames of miserie. Beare them off
To the common prisons, and there let them proue
How sharpe our axes are. [*Exeunt Captaines with Prisoners.*]
Rusticus. A bloudie entrance! 20
Cæsar. To tell you, you are happie in your Prince
Were to distrust your loue, or my desert
And either were distastefull. Or to boast
How much, not by my Deputies, but my selfe,
I haue enlargd the Empire; or what horrors 25
The Souldier in our conduct hath broke through,
Would better suite the mouth of *Plautus* bragart,
Then the adored Monarch of the world.
Sura. This is no boast.
Cæsar. When I but name the Daci,
And gray ey'd *Germans* whom I haue subdu'd, 30
The Ghost of *Iulius* will looke pale with envie,
And great *Vespatians,* and *Titus* triumph,
(Truth must take place of Father and of Brother)
Will be no more remembred. I am aboue

I. iv. 8. You,] *Coxeter;* ~ ₍ 29   13 SD. FULCINIUS,] *Massinger MS* (*Fulcinius,*);
Fulcinius, and 29   20 SD. *Exeunt . . . Prisoners.*] *after Gifford; not in* 29   21. you
are] *Coxeter;* your are 29

All honours you can giue me. And the stile   35
Of Lord, and God, which thankefull subiects giue me
(Not my ambition) is deseru'd.
    Aretinus.   At all parts
Cœlestiall Sacrifice is fit for *Cæsar*
In our acknowledgement.
    Cæsar.   Thankes *Aretinus*,
Still hold our fauour. Now; the God of warre,   40
And famine, bloud, and death, *Bellonas* Pages,
Banish'd from *Rome* to *Thrace* in our good fortune,
With iustice he may taste the fruits of peace,
Whose sword hath plowd the ground, and reap'd the harvest
Of your prosperitie. Nor can I thinke   45
That there is one among you so vngratefull,
Or such an enemie, to thriuing vertue,
That can esteeme the iewell he holds deerest
Too good for *Cæsars* vse.
    Sura.   All we possesse.
    Lamia. Our liberties.
    Fulcinius.   Our children.
    Parthenius.   Wealth.
    Aretinus.   And throates   50
Fall willingly beneath his feete.
    Rusticus.   Base flattery.
What Roman could indure this?
    Cæsar.   This cals on
My loue to all, which spreads it selfe among you.
The beauties of the time! receiue the honour
To kisse the hand, which rear'd vp thus, holds thunder;   55
To you 'tis an assurance of a calme.
Iulia my neece and *Cænis* the delight
Of old *Vespatian*, *Domitilla* to,
A princesse of our bloud.
    Rusticus.   Tis strange his pride
Affords no greater courtesie to Ladies   60
Of such high birth and rancke.
    Sura.   Your wifes forgotten.
    Lamia. No, shee will bee remembred feare it not;
She will bee grac'd and greas'd.

Cæsar.   But when I looke on
Diuine *Domitia*, mee thinkes we should meete
(The lesser gods applauding the encounter)   65
As *Iupiter*, the Giants lying dead
On the *Phlegræan* plaine, imbrac't his *Iuno*.
Lamia 'tis your honour that she's mine.
    Lamia. You are too great to be gainesaid.
    Cæsar.   Let all
C4ᵛ That feare our frowne, or doe affect our fauour,   70
Without examining the reason why,
Salute her (by this kisse I make it good)
With the title of *Augusta*.
    Domitia.   Still your seruant.
    All. Long liue *Augusta*, great *Domitians* Empresse.
    Cæsar. Paris my hand.
    Paris.   The Gods still honour *Cæsar*.   75
    Cæsar. The wars are ended, and our armes layd by
We are for soft delights. Command the Poets
To vse their choisest, and most rare inuention
To entertaine the time, and be you carefull
To giue it action. Wee'l prouide the people   80
Pleasures of all kindes. My *Domitia* thinke not
I flatter, though thus fond. On to the Capitoll!
Tis death to him that weares a sullen browe:
This tis to be a Monarch when alone   84
He can command all, but is aw'd by none.   *Exeunt.*

The end of the first Acte.

[II. i]   *Actus II. Scæna 1.*

Enter PHILARGUS, PARTHENIUS.

    Philargus. Mʏ sonne to tutor me! Know your obedience
And question not my will.
    Parthenius.   Sir were I one
Whom want compeld to wish a full possession
Of what is yours; or had I euer numbred

64. *Domitia*] *B.M. MS*; *Domitian* 29   II. i. 4. yours; or] *Massinger MS* (yours;
Or); yours. Or *29*

Your yeeres; or thought you liu'd to long, with reason   5
You then might nourish ill opinions of me.
Or did the suite that I prefer to you
Concerne my selfe, and aim'd not at your good
You might denie, and I sit downe with patience,
And after neuer presse you,
   Philargus.   I' the name of *Pluto*   10
What wouldst thou haue me doe?
D1ʳ *Parthenius.*   Right to your selfe,
Or suffer me to doe it. Can you imagine
This nastie hat, this tatterd cloke, rent shooe,
This sordid linnen can become the master
Of your faire fortunes? whose superfluous meanes   15
(Though I were burthensome) could cloth you in
The costliest Persian silkes, studded with iewels
The spoyles of Prouinces, and euery day
Fresh change of Tirian purple.
   Philargus.   Out vpon thee,
My monyes in my coffers melt to heare thee.   20
Purple! hence Prodigall. Shall I make my Mercer
Or Taylor my heyre? or see my Ieweller purchase?
No, I hate pride.
   Parthenius.   Yet decencie would doe well.
Though for your outside you will not be alterd,
Let me preuaile so farre yet, as to winne you   25
Not to denie your bellie nourishment;
Neither to thinke you haue feasted when 'tis cramm'd
With mouldie barley bread, onions, and leekes,
And the drinke of bondmen, water.
   Philargus.   Wouldst thou haue me
Bee an *Apicius*, or a *Lucullus*,   30
And ryot out my state in curious sawces?
Wise nature with a little is contented,
And following her, my guide, I cannot erre.
   Parthenius. But you destroy her in your want of care
(I blush to see, and speake it) to maintaine her   35
In perfect health and vigor, when you suffer
(Frighted with the charge of Phisicke) Rheumes, Catars,

The Scurfe, Ach in your bones to grow vpon you,
And hasten on your fate with too much sparing,
When a cheape Purge, a Vomit and good dyet   40
May lengthen it. Giue me but leaue to send
The Emperors Doctor to you.
    Philargus.   Ile be borne first
Halfe rotten to the fire, that must consume me!
His Pills, his Cordials, his Electuaries,
D1ᵛ His Sirrups, Iulips, Bezerstone nor his   45
Imagin'd Vnicornes horne comes in my bellie,
My mouth shall be a draught first. 'Tis resolu'd.
No; I'le not lessen my deare golden heape,
Which euerie houre increasing does renew
My youth, and vigor, but if lessen'd, then,   50
Then my poore hartstrings cracke. Let me enioy it,
And brood ore't while I liue, it being my life,
My soule, my all. But when I turne to dust,
And part from what is more esteem'd by me
Then all the Gods, *Romes* thousand Altars smoke to,   55
Inherit thou my adoration of it,
And like me serue my Idoll.   *Exit* PHILARGUS.
    Parthenius.   What a strange torture
Is Auarice to it selfe! what man that lookes on
Such a penurious spectacle but must
Know what the fable meant of *Tantalus*,   60
Or the Asse whose backe is crack'd with curious viands
Yet feedes on thistles. Some course I must take,
To make my Father know what crueltie
He vses on himselfe.

Enter PARIS.

    Paris.   Sir, with your pardon,
I make bould to enquire the Emperours pleasure,   65
For, being by him commanded to attend,
Your fauour may instruct vs what's his will
Shall be this night presented?
    Parthenius.   My lou'd *Paris*,
Without my intercession you well know
You may make your owne approaches, since his eare   70

To you is euer open.
    Paris.   I acknowledge
His clemencie to my weakenesse, and if euer
I doe abuse it, lightning strike me dead.
The grace he pleases to conferre vpon me
(Without boast I may say so much) was neuer   75
Imploy'd to wrong the innocent, or to incense
His furie.
    Parthenius. 'Tis confess'd many men owe you
D2ʳ For Prouinces they nere hop'd for; and their liues,
Forfeited to his anger. You being absent,
I could say more.
    Paris.   You still are my good Patron.   80
And lay it in my fortune to deserue it,
You should perceiue the poorest of your clients
To his best abilities thankefull.
    Parthenius.   I belieue so.
Met you my Father?
    Paris.   Yes Sir, with much griefe
To see him as he is. Can nothing worke him   85
To be himselfe?
    Parthenius.   O *Paris* 'tis a waight
Sits heauie here, and could this right hands losse
Remoue it, it should off, but he is deafe
To all perswasion.
    Paris.   Sir, with your pardon,
I'll offer my aduice! I once obseru'd   90
In a Tragedie of ours, in which a murther
Was acted to the life, a guiltie hearer
Forc'd by the terror of a wounded conscience,
To make discouerie of that, which torture
Could not wring from him. Nor can it appeare   95
Like an impossibilitie, but that
Your Father looking on a couetous man
Presented on the Stage as in a mirror
May see his owne deformity, and loath it.
Now could you but perswade the Emperour   100
To see a Comedie we haue that's stilde

---

79. anger. You] *Massinger MS* (anger. you); anger, you *29*   88. off,] *Massinger MS*; ~ ∧ *29*

The Cure of Avarice, and to command
Your Father to be a spectator of it,
He shall be so Anotamiz'd in the Scæne,
And see himselfe so personated; the basenes   105
Of a selfe torturing miserable wretch
Truely describ'd, that I much hope the obiect
Will worke compunction in him.
  Parthenius.   There's your fee;
I ne're bought better counsaile. Be you in readines;
D2ᵛ I will effect the rest.
  Paris.   Sir when you please   110
Wee'l be prepar'd to enter. Sir the Emperour. *Exit* PARIS.

    Enter CÆSAR, ARETINUS, *Guard.*

  Cæsar. Repine at vs?
  Aretinus.   Tis more, or my informers
That keepe strict watch vpon him are deceiu'd
In their intelligence: there is a list
Of malecontents, as *Iunius Rusticus,*   115
Palphurius Sura, and this *Ælius Lamia,*
That murmure at your triumphs as meere Pageants;
And at their midnight meetings tax your iustice
(For so I stile what they call tyrannie)
For *Pætus Thrasea's* death, as if in him,   120
Vertue her selfe were murther'd; nor forget they
Agricola who (for his seruice done
In the reducing *Britaine* to obedience)
They dare affirme to be remou'd with poyson,
And he compeld to write you a cohæyre   125
With his daughter, that his testament might stand,
Which else you had made void. Then your much loue
To *Iulia* your neece, censur'd as incest,
And done in scorne of *Titus* your dead brother;
But the divorce *Lamia* was forc'd to signe   130
To her, you honour with *Augusta's* title,
Being onely nam'd, they doe conclude there was
A *Lucrece* once, a *Collatine,* and a *Brutus,*
But nothing Roman left now, but in you

114. intelligence:] *Massinger MS*; ∼ₐ 29 116. *Palphurius*] *Coxeter*; *Palphu-*
rius, 29 *Ælius*] *Massinger MS*; ∼, 29 123. *Britaine*] *Gifford*; *Britanie* 29

The lust of *Tarquin*.

    Cæsar.   Yes. His fire, and scorne   135
Of such as thinke that our vnlimited power
Can be confin'd. Dares *Lamia* pretend
An interest to that which I call mine?
Or but remember, she was euer his
That's now in our possession? fetch him hither. *The Gard goe of.*
I'll giue him cause to wish he rather had   141
D3ʳ Forgot his owne name then e're mention'd hers.
Shall we be circumscrib'd? let such as cannot
By force make good their actions, though wicked,
Conceale, excuse or qualifie their crimes: 145
What our desires grant leaue, and priuiledge to
Though contradicting all divine decrees,
Or lawes confirm'd by *Romulus*, and *Numa*,
Shall be held sacred.

    Aretinus.   You should else take from
The dignitie of *Cæsar*.

    Cæsar.   Am I master   150
Of two and thirtie Legions, that awe
All Nations, of the triumphed world,
Yet tremble at our frowne? yeeld an accompt
Of whats our pleasure to a priuate man?
Rome perish first, and *Atlas* shoulders shrinke,   155
Heav'ns fabrique fall; the Sunne, the Moone, the Stars
Loosing their light, and comfortable heate,
Ere I confesse, that any fault of mine
May be disputed.

    Aretinus.   So you preserue your power
As you should; equall, and omnipotent heere,   160
With *Iupiters* aboue.   PARTHENIUS *kneeling whispers to* CÆSAR.

    Cæsar.   Thy suite is granted
What ere it be *Parthenius* for thy seruice
Done to *Augusta*. Onely so? a trifle.
Command him hither. If the Comedie faile
To cure him, I will minister something to him   165
That shall instruct him to forget his gold,
And thinke vpon himselfe.

137. confin'd. Dares] *Massinger MS* (confin'd. dares); confin'd, dares 29
153. frowne?] *editor*; ~,29;~! *Symons*   yeeld an]29; to yield an *Mason*; to yield *Gifford*

Parthenius.   May it succeed well
Since my intents are pious.   *Exit* PARTHENIUS.
     Cæsar.   We are resolu'd
What course to take, and therefore *Aretinus*
Inquire no farther. Goe you to my Empresse,   170
And say I doe entreate (for she rules him
Whom all men else obey) she would vouchsafe
The musicke of her voice, at yonder window,
D3ᵛ When I aduance my hand thus. I will blend   *Exit* ARETINUS.
My crueltie with some scorne, or else tis lost.   175
Reuenge, when it is vnexpected, falling
With greater violence; and hate clothed in smiles,
Strikes, and with horror, dead the wretch that comes not
Prepar'd to meete it.

                    Enter LAMIA *with the Guard.*

                    Our good *Lamia* welcome.
So much we owe you for a benefit   180
With willingnes on your part conferd vpon vs,
That 'tis our studie (we that would not liue
Ingag'd to any for a courtesie)
How to returne it.
     Lamia.   'Tis beneath your fate
To be oblig'd that in your owne hand graspe   185
The meanes to be magnificent.
     Cæsar.   Well put off
But yet it must not doe. The Empire, *Lamia*,
Diuided equally can hold no waight,
If ballanc'd with your guift in faire *Domitia*.
You that could part with all delights at once,   190
The magazine of rich pleasures being contain'd
In her perfections, vncompell'd deliuer'd
As a Present fit for *Cæsar*. In your eyes
With teares of ioy, not sorrow, 'tis confirm'd
You glory in your act.
     Lamia.   Derided too!   195
Sir this is more—
     Cæsar.   More then I can requite,

182. (we] *Massinger MS*; we 29   183. courtesie)] *Massinger MS*; ~, 29
187. doe. The] *Massinger MS* (doe. the); doe, the 29

It is acknowledg'd *Lamia*. There's no drop
Of melting nectar I tast from her lippe,
But yeeldes a touch of immortalitie
To the blest receiuer; euery grace and feature,   200
Priz'd to the worth, bought at an easie rate,
If purchas'd for a Consulship. Her discourse
So rauishing, and her action so attractiue,
That I would part with all my other senses
Prouided I might euer see, and heare her.   205
The pleasures of her bed I dare not trust
The windes or ayre with, for that would draw downe
D4ʳ In enuie of my happinesse, a warre
From all the Gods vpon mee.
    Lamia.   Your compassion
To me in your forbearing to insult   210
On my calamitie which you make your sport,
Would more appease those Gods you haue prouok'd,
Then all the blasphemous comparisons,
You sing vnto her praise.
    Cæsar.   I sing her praise?
'Tis farre from my ambition to hope it. *Musicke aboue and a song.*
It being a debt she onely can lay downe,   216
And no tongue else discharge. Harke. I thinke prompted
With my consent that you once more should heare her,
She does begin. An vniuersall silence
Dwell on this place. 'Tis death with lingring torments   220
To all that dare disturbe her.
                 The song ended CÆSAR *goe on.*
             Who can heare this
And falls not downe and worships? in my fancie,
Apollo being iudge on *Latmos* hill,
Faire hayr'd *Calliope* on her iuorie Lute
(But something short of this) sung *Ceres* prayses   225
And grieslie *Pluto's* rape on *Proserpine*.
The motion of the Spheares are out of time
Her musicall notes but heard. Say *Lamia*, say,
Is not her voice Angelicall?
    Lamia.   To your eare.

212. prouok'd,] *Massinger MS*; ~ˌ *29*   217. prompted] *Massinger MS*;
promped *29*   223. *Latmos*] *Mason*; *Latinos 29*   227. time] *29*; tune *Mason*

But I alas am silent.
    Cæsar.   Bee so euer,   230
That without admiration canst heare her.
Malice to my felicitie strikes thee dumbe,
And in thy hope, or wish to repossesse
What I loue more then Empire, I pronounce thee
Guiltie of treason. Off with his head. Doe you stare ?   235
By her, that is my Patronesse, *Minerua*,
(Whose Statue I adore of all the Gods)
If he but liue to make reply thy life
Shal answer it.
                    The Guard lead off LAMIA *stopping his mouth.*
             My feares of him are freed now
And he that liu'd to vpbraid me with my wrong,   240
For an offence he neuer could imagine,
In wantonnes remou'd. Descend my dearest.
Plurality of husbands shall no more
Breede doubts or iealousies in you. 'Tis dispatch'd
And with as little trouble heere, as if   245
I had kild a flye.

Enter DOMITIA, *vsherd in by* ARETINUS, *her traine with all state
borne vp by* IULIA, CÆNIS, *and* DOMITILLA.

             Now you appeare and in
That glorie you deserue, and these that stoope
To doe you seruice in the acte much honourd.
Iulia forget that *Titus* was thy Father,
Cænis and *Domitilla* ne're remember   250
Sabinus, or *Vespatian*. To be slaues
To her, is more true liberty then to liue
Parthian or *Asian* Queenes. As lesser stars
That waite on *Phœbe* in her full of brightnes
Compar'd to her you are. Thus I seate you   255
By *Cæsars* side, commanding these that once
Were the adored glories of the time
To witnes to the world they are your vassals
At your feete to attend you.
    Domitia.   Tis your pleasure

D4ᵛ

---

   239 SD. *The . . . mouth.*] *Coxeter*; *follows* life (l. 238) 29   *lead*] 29²; *had* 29¹
255. are. Thus] *Coxeter*; are (thus 29; are; & thus *conj. McIlwraith*

And not my pride. And yet when I consider 260
That I am yours, all duties they can pay
I doe receiue as circumstances due
To her you please to honour.

Enter PARTHENIUS *with* PHILARGUS.

Parthenius.   *Cæsars* will
Commaunds you hither, nor must you gaine-say it.
Philargus. Loose time to see an Enterlude? must I pay to 265
For my vexation?
Parthenius.   Not in the Court,
It is the Emperours charge.
Philargus.   I shall endure
My torment then the better.
Cæsar.   Can it bee
This sordid thing *Parthenius* is thy Father?
No actor can expresse him. I had held 270
The fiction for impossible in the Scæne,
E1ʳ Had I not seene the substance. Sirrha sit still,
And giue attention; if you but nod
You sleepe for euer. Let them spare the Prologue,
And all the Ceremonies proper to our selfe 275
And come to the last act, there where the cure
By the Doctor is made perfect. The swift minutes
Seeme yeeres to me *Domitia* that diuorce thee
From my embraces. My desires encreasing
As they are satisfied, all pleasures else 280
Are tedious as dull sorrowes. Kisse me, againe:
If I now wanted heate of youth, these fires
In *Priams* veines would thaw his frozen bloud,
Enabling him to get a second *Hector*
For the defence of *Troy.*
Domitia.   You are wanton! 285
Pray you forbeare. Let me see the Play.
Cæsar. Begin there.

Enter PARIS *like a Doctor of Physicke,* ÆSOPUS. LATINUS *brought
forth a sleepe in a chayre, a key in his mouth.*

Æsopus.   O master Doctor he is past recouerie;

285. wanton!] *29* (wanton?); wanton Sir. *McIlwraith*

A lethargie hath ceas'd him. And howeuer
His sleepe resemble death his watchfull care
To guard that treasure he dares make no vse of,   290
Workes strongly in his soule.
    Paris.   What's that he holdes
So fast betweene his teeth?
    Æsopus.   The key that opens
His iron chests cramn'd with accursed gold,
Rustie with long imprisonment. There's no dutie
In me his sonne, nor confidence in friends,   295
That can perswade him to deliuer vp
That to the trust of any.
    Philargus.   He is the wiser;
We were fashion'd in one mould.
    Æsopus.   He eates with it,
And when deuotion calles him to the Temple
E1ᵛ Of *Mammon*, whom of all the Gods he kneeles to,   300
That held thus still, his orisons are payde;
Nor will he, though the wealth of *Rome* were pawn'd
For the restoring of it, for one short houre
Be wonne to part with it.
    Philargus.   Still, still my selfe.
And if like me he loue his gold, no pawne   305
Is good securitie.
    Paris.   I'll trie if I can force it.
It will not be. His auaritious mind
(Like men in riuers drown'd) makes him gripe fast
To his last gaspe what he in life held dearest.
And if that it were possible in nature   310
Would carry it with him to the other world.
    Philargus. As I would doe to hell rather then leaue it.
    Æsopus. Is he not dead?
    Paris.   Long since to all good actions
Or to himselfe, or others, for which wise men
Desire to liue. You may with safetie pinch him,   315
Or vnder his nayles sticke needles, yet he stirs not;
Anxious feare to loose what his soule dotes on
Renders his flesh insensible. We must vse
Some meanes to rouse the sleeping faculties

Of his mind, there lies the Lethargie. Take a Trumpet   320
And blowe it into his eares, tis to noe purpose.
The roring noyse of thunder cannot wake him.
And yet despaire not; I haue one tricke yet left.
Æsopus. What is it?
Paris.   I will cause a fearefull Dreame
To steale into his fancie, and disturbe it   325
With the horror it brings with it, and so free
His bodyes Organs.
Domitia.   'Tis a cunning fellow,
If he were indeed a Doctor as the play sayes,
He should be sworne my seruant, gouerne my slumbers
And minister to me waking.
Paris.   If this faile   *A chest brought in.*
I'll giue him ore. So with all violence   331
E2ʳ Rend ope this iron chest. For here his life lyes
Bound vp in fetters, and in the defence
Of what he values higher, 'twill returne
And fill each veine and arterie. Lowder yet.   335
'Tis open, and alreadie he begins
To stirre, marke with what trouble.   LATINUS *stretches himselfe.*
Philargus.   As you are *Cæsar*
Defend this honest thriftie man, they are theeues,
And come to rob him.
Parthenius.   Peace, the Emperour frownes.
Paris. So now powre out the bags vpon the Table,   340
Remoue his iewels, and his bonds. Againe,
Ring a second golden peale, his eyes are open.
He stares as he had seene *Medusas* head,
And were turn'd marble. Once more.
Latinus.   Murther, murther,
They come to murther me. My sonne in the plot?   345
Thou worse then paricide if it bee death
To strike thy Fathers body, can all tortures,
The furies in hell practise, be sufficient
For thee that doest assassinate my soule?
My gold! my bonds! my iewels! dost thou envie   350

323. yet left] *29*; left *Coxeter*   332. his] *Coxeter*; is *29*   341. bonds.
Againe,] *Massinger MS* (bonds. againe,); bonds, againe. *29*   345. come to murther
me] *29²*; will vs murther, murther *29¹*

My glad possession of them for a day?
Extinguishing the Taper of my life
Consum'd vnto the snuffe?
    Paris.   Seem not to mind him.
    Latinus. Haue I to leaue thee rich denied my selfe
The ioyes of humaine being? Scrap'd and horded   355
A masse of treasure, which had *Solon* seene
The *Lidian Crœsus* had appear'd to him
Poore as the begger *Irus*? And yet I
Sollicitous to encrease it, when my intrayles
Were clem'd with keeping a perpetuall fast,   360
Was deafe to their loud windie cries, as fearing
Should I disburse one peny to their vse,
My heyre might curse me. And to saue expence
In outward ornaments, I did expose
My naked body to the Winters cold,   365
And Summers scorching heate. Nay when diseases
E2ᵛ Grew thicke vpon mee, and a little cost
Had purchas'd my recouerie, I chose rather
To haue my ashes clos'd vp in my vrne,
By hasting on my fate, then to diminish   370
The gold my prodigall sonne (while I am liuing)
Carelessely scatters.
    Æsopus.   Would you would dispatch and die once.
Your Ghost should feele in hell, that is my slaue
Which was your master.
    Philargus.   Out vpon thee varlet.
    Paris. And what then followes al your carke, and caring,   375
And selfe affliction when your staru'd truncke is
Turn'd to forgotten dust? This hopefull youth
Vrines vpon your monument. Ne're remembring
How much for him you suffer'd. And then tells
To the companions of his lusts, and ryots,   380
The hell you did indure on earth to leaue him
Large meanes to be an Epicure, and to feast
His senses all at once, a happines
You neuer granted to your selfe. Your gold then

---

   353. *rearranged by Coxeter; one line in 29*   367. mee] *Massinger MS*; me 29
(*defective* e)   371. sonne (while . . . liuing)] *Massinger MS*; sonne, while . . .
liuing, 29

(Got with vexation, and preseru'd with trouble)   385
Maintaines the publicke stewes, pandars, and ruffians
That quaffe damnations to your memorie,
For liuing so long here.
    Latinus.   'Twill be so, I see it.
O that I could redeeme the time that's past!
I would liue, and die like my selfe; and make true vse   390
Of what my industrie purchas'd.
    Paris.   Couetous men
Hauing one foote in the graue lament so euer.
But grant that I by Art could yet recouer
Your desperate sicknes, lengthen out your life
A dozen of yeeres, as I restore your body   395
To perfect health, will you with care endeuour
To rectifie your mind?
    Latinus.   I should so liue then
As neither my heyre should haue iust cause to thinke
I liu'd too long for being close handed to him,
E3ʳ Or cruell to my selfe.
    Paris.   Haue your desires.   400
Phœbus assisting mee, I will repayre
The ruin'd building of your health, and thinke not
You haue a sonne that hates you; the truth is
This meanes with his consent I practis'd on you,
To this good end, it being a deuice   405
In you to shew the *Cure of Avarice.*

             Exeunt PARIS, LATINUS, ÆSOPUS.
    Philargus. An old foole to be guld thus! had he died
As I resolue to doe, not to be alter'd,
It had gone off twanging.
    Cæsar.   How approue you sweetest,
Of the matter, and the Actors?
    Domitia.   For the subiect   410
I like it not, it was filch'd out of *Horace,*
Nay I haue read the Poets, but the fellow
That play'd the Doctor did it well by *Venus*;
He had a tunable tongue and neate deliuery,
And yet in my opinion he would performe   415

389. redeeme] *Massinger MS*; redeeme 29 (*second* e *defective*)   412. haue]
Massinger MS; hauə 29

A louers part much better. Prethee *Cæsar*,
For I grow wearie, let vs see to morrow
Iphis and *Anaxerete*.
    Cæsar.   Any thing
For thy delight *Domitia*. To your rest
Till I come to disquiet you. Wayte vpon her.   420
There is a busines that I must dispatch
And I will straight be with you.
       Exeunt ARETINUS, DOMITIA, IULIA, CÆNIS, DOMITILLA.
    Parthenius.   Now my dread Sir
Endeuour to preuayle.
    Cæsar.   One way or other.
Wee'l cure him neuer doubt it. Now *Philargus*
Thou wretched thing, hast thou seene thy sordid basenesse?   425
And but obseru'd what a contemptible creature
A couetous miser is? dost thou in thy selfe
Feele true compunction? with a resolution
To be a new man?
    Philargus.   This craz'd bodies *Cæsars*,
But for my minde—
E3ᵛ   *Cæsar*.   Trifle not with my anger.   430
Canst thou make good vse of what was now presented?
And imitate in thy suddaine change of life,
The miserable rich man, that expres'd
What thou art to the life?
    Philargus.   Pray you giue me leaue
To dye as I haue liu'd. I must not part with   435
My gold, it is my life. I am past cure.
    Cæsar. No; by *Minerua* thou shalt neuer more
Feele the least touch of auarice. Take him hence
And hang him instantly. If there be gold in hell
Inioy it, thine here and thy life together   440
Is forfeited.
    Philargus. Was I sent for to this purpose?
    Parthenius. Mercie for all my seruice, *Cæsar* mercie!
    Cæsar. Should *Ioue* plead for him, 'tis resolu'd he dyes,
And he that speakes one sillable to disswade me.
And therefore tempt me not. It is but iustice.   445

418. *Iphis*] *Coxeter*; *Iplus 29*   443. him, 'tis] *Massinger MS* (him, 'Tis); him.
'Tis *29*   444. me.] *Massinger MS*; me, *29*

Since such as wilfully, will hourely dye,
Must tax themselues, and not my crueltie.   *Exeunt omnes.*

The end of the second Act.

Actus III. Scæna 1.

Enter IULIA, DOMITILLA, STEPHANOS.

Iulia. No *Domitilla*, if you but compare
What I haue suffer'd with your iniuries,
(Though great ones I confesse) they will appeare
Like molehils to *Olimpus.*
Domitilla.   You are tender
Of your owne wounds, which makes you loose the feeling   5
And sense of mine. The incest he committed
With you, and publikely profes'd, in scorne
Of what the world durst censure may admit
Some weake defence, as being borne headlong to it,
But in a manly way to enioy your beauties.   10
Besides, wonne by his periuries that he would
Salute you with the title of *Augusta*,
Your faint deniall show'd a full consent,
And grant to his temptations. But poore I
That would not yeeld, but was with violence forc'd   15
To serue his lusts, and in a kinde *Tiberius*
At *Capræ* neuer practis'd, haue not heere
One conscious touch to rise vp my accuser,
I in my will being innocent.
Stephanos.   Pardon mee
Great Princesses, though I presume to tell you,   20
Wasting your time in childish lamentations,
You doe degenerate from the bloud, you spring from:
For there is something more in *Rome* expected
From *Titus* daughter, and his vncles heyre,
Then womanish complaints after such wrongs   25
Which mercie cannot pardon. But you'l say
Your hands are weake, and should you but attempt
A iust reuenge on this inhumaine monster,
This prodegie of mankind, bloudie *Domitian*,

E4ʳ

Hath readie swords at his command, aswell 30
As Islands to confine you, to remoue
His doubts, and feares, did he but entertaine
The least suspition you contriu'd or plotted
Against his person.
    Iulia.   'Tis true *Stephanos.*
The legions that sack'd *Hierusalem* 35
Vnder my Father *Titus* are sworne his,
And I no more remembred.
    Domitilla.   And to loose
Our selues by building on impossible hopes,
Were desperate madnes.
    Stephanos.   You conclude too fast.
One single arme whose master does contemne 40
His owne life holds a full command ore his,
Spite of his guards. I was your bondman Ladie,
And you my gracious patronesse; my wealth,
And libertie your guift; and though no souldier,
To whom or custome, or example makes 45
Grimme death appeare lesse terrible, I dare dye
To doe you seruice in a faire reuenge,
And it will better sute your births and honours
To fall at once, then to liue euer slaues
To his proud Empresse that insults vpon 50
Your patient sufferings. Say but you goe on,
And I will reach his heart, or perish in
The noble vndertaking.
    Domitilla.   Your free offer
Confirmes your thankefulnesse, which I acknowledge
A satisfaction for a greater debt 55
Then what you stand ingag'd for: but I must not
Vpon vncertaine grounds hazard so gratefull,
And good a seruant. The immortall powers
Protect a Prince though sould to impious acts,
And seeme to slumber till his roaring crimes 60
Awake their iustice: but then looking downe

E4ᵛ

III. i. 30. swords] *Massinger MS*; words *29*   command,] *Massinger MS*; ~ₐ*29*
31. you, to remoue] *Massinger MS*; you to remoue. *29*   35. sack'd] *29²*; sacred
29¹   37. *Domitilla.*] *Coxeter*; *Domit. 29*   48. sute] *Massinger MS*; suite *29*
52. reach] *Massinger MS*; retch *29*   53. *Domitilla.*] *Coxeter*; *Domit. 29*   58. im-
mortall] *Massinger MS* (imortall); mortall *29*

And with impartiall eyes, on his contempt
Of all religion, and morrall goodnesse,
They in their secret iudgements doe determine
To leaue him to his wickednesse, which sinckes him   65
When he is most secure.
   Iulia.   His crueltie
Increasing dayly of necessitie
Must render him as odious to his souldiers,
Familiar friends, and freemen, as it hath done
Alreadie to the Senate; then forsaken   70
Of his supporters, and growne terrible
Eu'n to himselfe, and her, he now so dotes on,
We may put into act, what now with safetie
We cannot whisper.
   Stephanos.   I am still prepar'd
To execute when you please to command mee: 75
Since I am confident he deserues much more
That vindicates his countrie from a tyranne,
Then he that saues a citizen.

Enter CÆNIS.

   Iulia.   O heere's *Cænis.*
F1^r   *Domitilla.* Whence come you?
   Cænis.   From the Empresse who seeme; mou'd
In that you waite no better. Her prides growne   80
To such a height that shee disdaines the service
Of her owne women; and esteemes her selfe
Neglected! when the Princesses of the bloud
On everie course imployment, are not readie
To stoope to her commands.
   Domitilla.   Where is her greatnes?   85
   Cænis. Where you would little thinke she could descend
To grace the roome or persons.
   Iulia.   Speake; where is she?
   Cænis. Among the Players, where all state layd by,
She does enquire who acts this part, who that,
And in what habits? blames the tire-women   90
For want of curious dressings; and so taken

---

64. secret] *Coxeter*; secrets *29*   77. tyranne] *Massinger MS*; tyrannie *29*
84. On] *29²*; One *29¹*

She is with *Paris* the Tragedians shape
That is to act a Louer, I thought once
She would haue courted him.
    Domitilla.   In the meane time
How spends the Emperour his houres?
    Cænis.   As euer   95
He hath done heretofore; in being cruell
To innocent men, whose vertues he calles crimes.
And but this morning if't be possible
He hath out-gone himselfe, hauing condemn'd
At *Aretinus* his informers suite,   100
Palphurius Sura, and good *Iunius Rusticus*,
Men of the best repute in *Rome* for their
Integritie of life; no fault obiected
But that they did lament his cruell sentence
On *Pætus Thraseas* the Philosopher,   105
Their Patron and instructer.
    Stephanos.   Can *Ioue* see this
And hold his thunder!
    Domitilla.   *Nero* and *Caligula*
Commanded onely mischiefes, but our *Cæsar*
Delights to see 'em.
  F1ᵛ   *Iulia.*   What we cannot helpe,
We may deplore with silence.
    Cænis.   We are call'd for   110
By our proud mistresse.
    Domitilla.   We a while must suffer.
    Stephanos. It is true fortitude to stand firme against
All shocks of fate, when cowards faint and dye
In feare to suffer more calamitie.   *Exeunt.*

Actus III. Scæna 2.

[III. ii]

Enter CÆSAR, PARTHENIUS.

Cæsar. They are then in fetters?
Parthenius.   Yes Sir. But
Cæsar.   But? What?
I'll haue thy thoughts. Deliuer them.

105. *Thraseas*] 29²; *Thracea* 29¹   111. *Domitilla.*] *Coxeter*; *Domit.* 29

Parthenius.   I shall Sir.
But still submitting to your God-like pleasure,
Which cannot be instructed—
    Cæsar.   To the point.
    Parthenius. Nor let your sacred Maiestie belieue   5
Your vassall, that with drie eyes look'd vpon
His Father drag'd to death by your command,
Can pitty these, that durst presume to censure
What you decreed.
    Cæsar.   Well. Forward.
    Parthenius.   'Tis my zeale
Still to preserue your clemencie admi'rd   10
Temper'd with iustice, that emboldens me
To offer my aduice. Alas I know Sir
These Bookemen, *Rusticus*, and *Palphurius Sura*,
Deserue all tortures. Yet in my opinion,
They being popular Senators, and cried vp   15
With loud applauses of the multitude,
For foolish honestie, and beggerly vertue,
T'would rellish more of pollicie to haue them
Made away in priuate, with what exquisite torments
You please, it skils not, then to haue them drawne   20
To the degrees in publike; for 'tis doubted
That the sad obiect may beget compassion
In the giddie rout, and cause some sudaine vprore
That may disturbe you.
    Cæsar.   Hence pale spirited coward!
Can we descend so farre beneath our selfe   25
As, or to court, the peoples loue, or feare
Their worst of hate? Can they that are as dust
Before the whirlewinde of our will and power,
Adde any moment to vs? Or thou thinke
If there are Gods aboue, or Goddesses,   30
(But wise *Minerua* that's mine owne and sure)
That they haue vacant houres to take into
Their serious protection, or care,
This many headed monster? mankind liues
In few, as potent Monarchs, and their Peeres;   35
And all those glorious constellations

F2ʳ

III. ii. 26. court] *29²*; count *29¹*   35. potent] *29*; ~, *McIlwraith*

That doe adorne the firmament, appointed
Like groomes with their bright influence to attend
The actions of Kings, and Emperours,
They being the greater wheeles that moue the lesse.   40
Bring forth those condemn'd wretches; let me see
One man so lost, as but to pittie 'em
And though there lay a million of soules
Imprison'd in his flesh, my Hangmens hookes
Should rend it off and giue 'em libertie.   45
Cæsar hath said it.   *Exit* PARTHENIUS.

Enter PARTHENIUS, ARETINUS, *and the Guard, Hangmen dragging*
in IUNIUS RUSTICUS, *and* PALPHURIUS SURA, *bound backe to*
backe.

    Aretinus.   'Tis great *Cæsars* pleasure
That with fix'd eyes you carefully obserue
The peoples lookes. Charge vpon any man
That with a sigh, or murmure does expresse
A seeming sorrow for these traytors deaths.   50
You know his will, performe it.
    Cæsar.   A good bloud-hound,
And fit for my imployments.
    Sura.   Giue vs leaue
To dye fell tyrant.
    Rusticus.   For beyond our bodies
Thou hast no power.
    Cæsar.   Yes, I'll afflict your soules.
And force them groaning to the *Stigian* lake   55
Prepar'd for such to howle in, that blaspheame
The power of Princes, that are Gods on earth;
Tremble to thinke how terrible the dreame is
After this sleepe of death.
    Rusticus.   To guiltie men
It may bring terror, not to vs, that know   60
What 'tis to dye, well taught by his example
For whom we suffer. In my thought I see
The substance of that pure vntainted soule,
Of *Thraseas* our master made a starre,

F2ᵛ (margin left of "You know his will, performe it.")

43. there] *29²*; their *29¹*   46 SD. IUNIUS] *Coxeter*; *Iunius, 29*   53. tyrant]
29²; tyrannie *29¹*

That with melodious harmonie invites vs   65
(Leauing this dunghill *Rome*, made hell by thee,)
To trace his heauenly steps, and fill a Spheare
Aboue yon Chrystall Canopie.
    Cæsar.   Doe inuoke him
With all the aydes his sanctitie of life
Haue wonne on the rewarders of his vertue,   70
They shall not saue you. Dogs doe you grinne? torment 'em.
So take a leafe of *Seneca* now and proue
If it can render you insensible
Of that which but begins here. Now an oyle
                The Hangmen torment 'em, they still smiling.
Drawne from the Stoicks frozen principles,   75
Predominant ouer fire, were vsefull for you.
Againe, againe. You trifle. Not a groane,
Is my rage lost? What cursed charmes defend 'em!
Search deeper, villaines. Who lookes pale? or thinkes
That I am cruell?
    Aretinus.   Ouer mercifull.   80
'Tis all your weakenesse Sir.
    Parthenius.   I dare not show
A signe of sorrow, yet my synnewes shrinke
The spectacle is so horrid.   *Aside.*
    Cæsar.   I was neuer
O'recome till now. For my sake rore a little,
And show you are corporeall, and not turn'd   85
Aeriall spirits. Will it not do? By *Pallas*
It is vnkindly done to mocke his furie
Whom the world stiles omnipotent. I am tortur'd
In their want of feeling torments. *Marius* storie
That does report him to haue sate vnmou'd   90
When cunning Chirurgions rip'd his arteries,
And veines, to cure his goute, compar'd to this
Deserues not to bee nam'd. Are they not dead?
If so, wee wash an *Æthiope.*
    Sura.   No, wee liue.
    Rusticus. Liue to deride thee, our calme patience treading   95
Vpon the necke of tyrannie. That securely,
(As t'were a gentle slumber,) we indure

    71. you.] *Massinger MS*; ∼ₐ *29*

F3ʳ

Thy hangmens studied tortures, is a debt
Wee owe to graue Philosophie, that instruct's vs
The flesh is but the clothing of the soule,   100
Which growing out of fashion though it bee
Cast of, or rent, or torne, like ours, 'tis then
Being it selfe diuine, in her best luster.
But vnto such as thou, that haue no hopes
Beyond the present, euerie little scar;   105
The want of rest; excesse of heate or cold,
That does informe them, onely they are mortall,
Pierce through, and through them.
    Cæsar.   We will heare no more.
    Rusticus. This onely, and I giue thee warning of it.
Though it is in thy will to grinde this earth,   110
As small as *Atomes*, they throwne in the Sea to,
They shall seeme recollected to thy sense,
And when the sandie building of thy greatnes,
Shall with its owne weight totter; looke to see me
As I was yesterday, in my perfect shape,   115
F3ᵛ   For I'll appeare in horror.
    Cæsar.   By my shaking
I am the guiltie man, and not the Iudge.
Drag from my sight, these cursed ominous wizards,
That as they are now, like to double fac'd *Ianus*,
Which way soe're I looke, are furies to me.   120
Away with 'em. First show them death, then leaue
No memory of their ashes. I'll mocke fate.
               Exeunt Hangmen with RUSTICUS *and*
               SURA, STEPHANOS *following.*
Shall words fright him, victorious armies circle?
No, no, the feuer does begin to leaue me.

        Enter DOMITIA, IULIA, CÆNIS.

Or were it deadly, from this liuing fountaine   125
I could renue the vigor of my youth,
And be a second *Virbius.* O my glory!

---

105. scar] *29²*; starre *29¹*   107. them, onely] *29*; them onely, *McIlwraith*
108. Pierce] *29²*; *Cæs.* Pierce *29¹*   *Cæsar.* We] *29²*; We *29¹*   112. thy] *29²*;
the *29¹*   122 SD. *Exeunt . . . following.*] *Coxeter*; *follows* leaue (l. 121) *29*
127. *Virbius*] *Massinger MS*; *Verbius 29*

My life! command! my all!   *Embracing and kissing mutually.*
  Domitia.   As you to me are.
I heard you were sad; I haue prepar'd you sport
Will banish melancholie. Sirrha, *Cæsar*,   130
(I hugge my selfe for't) I haue beene instructing
The Players how to act, and to cut off
All tedious impertinencie, haue contracted
The Tragedie, into one continued Sceane.
I haue the art of 't, and am taken more   135
With my abilitie that way, then all knowledge
I haue but of thy loue.
  Cæsar.   Thou art still thy selfe,
The sweetest, wittiest—
  Domitia.   When wee are a bed
I'll thanke your good opinion. Thou shalt see
Such an *Iphis* of thy *Paris*, and to humble   140
The pride of *Domitilla* that neglects mee
(How e're she is your cousin) I haue forc'd her
To play the part of *Anaxerete*.
You are not offended with it?
  Cæsar.   Any thing
That does content thee yeilds delight to mee.   145
My faculties, and powers are thine.
  Domitia.   I thanke you.
Prethee lets take our places. Bid 'em enter
Without more circumstance.

    After a short flourish, enter PARIS *as Iphis.*
        How doe you like
That shape? me thinkes it is most sutable
To the aspect of a despairing louer.   150
The seeming late falne, counterfeited teares
That hang vpon his cheekes, was my deuice.
  Cæsar. And all was excellent.
  Domitia.   Now heare him speake.
  Paris. That she is faire (and that an Epethite
To foule to expresse her) or descended nobly,   155
Or rich, or fortunate, are certaine truthes

F4ʳ (margin at "Prethee lets take our places")

128. command!] 29; ~ₐ *Coxeter*   148. circumstance. How] *Massinger MS*
(circumstance. how); circumstance, how 29   148 SD. *After . . . Iphis.*] *Coxeter*;
follows enter (l. 147) 29   156. are] *Coxeter*; and 29

In which poore *Iphis* glories. But that these
Perfections, in no other Virgin found,
Abus'd, should nourish crueltie, and pride,
In the diuinest *Anaxarete*,   160
Is, to my loue-sicke languishing soule, a riddle,
And with more difficultie to be dissolu'd,
Then that, the monster *Sphinx* from the steep rocke
Offer'd to *Oedipus*. Imperious loue,
As at thy euer flaming Altars *Iphis*   165
Thy neuer tyred votarie hath presented
With scalding teares whole Hecatombes of sighes,
Preferring thy power, and thy *Paphian* mothers,
Before the thunderers, *Neptunes*, or *Pluto's*
(That after *Saturne* did diuide the world   170
And had the sway of things, yet were compell'd
By thy vneuitable shafts to yeeld
And fight vnder thy ensignes) be auspicious
To this last tryall of my sacrifice
Of loue, and seruice.
    Domitia.   Do's he not act it rarely?   175
Obserue with what a feeling he deliuers
His orisons to *Cupid*; I am rap'd with't.
    Paris. And from thy neuer emptied quiuer take
A golden arrow, to transfix her heart
And force her loue like me, or cure my wound   180
With a leaden one, that may beget in me
Hate and forgetfulnesse, of what's now my Idoll.
F4ᵛ But I call backe my prayer, I haue blaspheam'd
In my rash wish. 'Tis I that am vnworthy,
But she all merit, and may in iustice challenge   185
From the assurance of her excellencies
Not loue, but adoration. Yet beare witnesse
All knowing powers, I bring along with me
As faithfull aduocates to make intercession
A loyall heart, with pure, and holy flames   190
With the foule fires of lust neuer polluted.
And as I touch her threshold (which with teares,
My limbes benumb'd with cold, I oft haue wash'd)

   163. steep] *Massinger MS*; steepie *29*   167. whole] *Coxeter*; whose *29*
191. With] *29*; Which *B.M. MS*

With my glad lips I kisse this earth growne proud
With frequent fauours from her delicate feete.   195
   Domitia. By *Cæsars* life he weepes. And I forbeare
Hardly to keepe him companie.
   Paris.   Blest ground thy pardon
If I prophane it with forbidden steps.
I must presume to knocke, and yet attempt it
With such a trembling reuerence as if   200
My hands held vp for expiation
To the incensed Gods to spare a kingdome.
Within there, hoe! something divine come forth
To a distressed mortall.

Enter LATINUS *as a Porter.*

   Latinus.   Ha! Who knockes there?
   Domitia. What a churlish looke this knaue has!
   Latinus.   Is't you Sirrha?
Are you come to pule and whine? avaunt, and quickly.   206
Dogwhips shall driue you hence else.
   Domitia.   Churlish deuill!
But that I should disturbe the Sceane, as I liue
I would teare his eyes out.
   Cæsar.   'Tis in iest *Domitia.*
   Domitia. I doe not like such iesting; if he were not   210
A flintie hearted slaue, he could not vse
One of his forme so harshly. How the toade swells
At the others sweete humilitie!
   Cæsar.   'Tis his part,
Let 'em proceed.
Gı *Domitia.*   A Rogues part, will ne're leaue him.
   Paris. As you haue gentle Sir, the happinesse   215
(When you please) to behold the figure of
The master peice of nature, limn'd to the life,
In more then humane *Anaxerete*,
Scorne not your seruant, that with suppliant hands
Takes hold vpon your knees, coniuring you   220
As you are a man, and did not sucke the milke

---

   201. for] *29²*; or *29¹*   204 SD. *Enter . . . Porter.*] *29²*; *follows* there? *29¹*
   205. has!] *Massinger MS*; ~ₐ *29*   214. part, will] *29*; part will *Coxeter*; part,
t'will *conj. McIlwraith*   216. you] *Coxeter*; yon *29*

Of Wolues, and Tigres, or a mother of
A tougher temper, vse some meanes these eyes
Before they are wept out, may see your Ladie.
Will you be gracious Sir?

 Latinus.   Though I loose my place for't 225
I can hold out no longer.
 Domitia.   Now hee melts
There is some little hope hee may die honest.
 Latinus. Madam.

Enter DOMITILLA *for Anaxerete.*

 Domitilla. Who calls? what obiect haue we heere?
 Domitia. Your cousin keepes her proud state still; I thinke
I haue fitted her for a part.
 Domitilla.   Did I not charge thee 230
I ne're might see this thing more?
 Paris.   I am indeed
What thing you please, a Worme that you may tread on.
Lower I cannot fall to shew my duty,
Till your disdaine hath dig'd a graue to couer
This bodie with forgotten dust, and when 235
I know your sentence, (cruellest of women)
I'll by a willing death remoue the obiect
That is an eyesore to you.
 Domitilla.   Wretch thou darst not.
That were the last, and greatest seruice to mee
Thy doting loue could boast of. What dull foole 240
But thou could nourish any flattering hope
One of my height, in youth, in birth and fortune
Could e're desend to looke vpon thy lownesse?
Much lesse consent to make my Lord of one
I would not accept, though offer'd for my slaue. 245
G1ᵛ My thoughts stoope not so lowe.
 Domitia.   There's her true nature,
No personated scorne.
 Domitilla.   I wrong my worth
Or to exchange a syllable, or looke,
With one so farre beneath me.
 Paris.   Yet take heed,

228/230/238/247/265/299. *Domitilla.*] *B.M. MS*; *Domit.* 29

Take heed of pride, and curiouslie consider   250
How brittle the foundation is, on which
You labour to aduance it. *Niobe*,
Proud of her numerous issue, durst contemne
Latonas double burthen but what follow'd?
She was left a childlesse mother, and mourn'd to marble.   255
The beautie you o're-prize so, time, or sicknes
Can change to loth'd deformitie; your wealth
The prey of theeues; Queene *Heccuba*, *Troy* fir'd,
Vlisses bond woman. But the loue I bring you
Nor time, nor sicknesse, violent theeues, nor fate   260
Can rauish from you.
    Domitia.   Could the Oracle
Giue better counsaile?
    Paris.   Say will you relent yet?
Reuoking your decree that I should dye?
Or shall I doe what you command? resolue;
I am impatient of delay.
    Domitilla.   Dispatch then.   265
I shall looke on your Tragedie vnmou'd,
Peraduenture laugh at it, for it will proue
A Comedie to me.
    Domitia.   O diuell! diuell!
    Paris. Then thus I take my last leaue. All the curses
Of louers fall vpon you; and hereafter   270
When any man like me contemn'd, shall studie
In the anguish of his soule to giue a name
To a scornfull cruell mistresse, let him onely
Say this most bloudie woman is to me,
As *Anaxarete* was to wretched *Iphis*.   275
Now feast your tyrannous mind, and glorie in
G2ʳ The ruines you haue made: for *Hymens* bands
That should haue made vs one, this fatall halter
For euer shall diuorce vs; at your gate
As a trophee of your pride, and my affliction,   280
I'll presently hang my selfe.
    Domitia.   Not for the world.
Restraine him as you loue your liues.
    Cæsar.   Why are you
Transported thus *Domitia*? 'tis a play,

Or grant it serious, it at no part merits
This passion in you.

    Paris.　　　　　I nere purpos'd Madam　　　285
To do the deed in earnest, though I bowe
To your care, and tendernesse of me.

    Domitia.　　　　　Let me Sir,
Intreate your pardon, what I saw presented
Carried me beyond my selfe.

    Cæsar.　　　　　To your place againe
And see what followes.

    Domitia.　　　　　No, I am familiar　　　290
With the conclusion, besides vpon the sudaine
I feele my selfe much indispos'd.

    Cæsar.　　　　　To bed then.
I'll be thy Doctor.

    Aretinus.　　　There is something more　　　*[Aside.]*
In this then passion, which I must find out,
Or my intelligence freezes.

    Domitia.　　　　　Come to me *Paris*　　　295
To morrow for your reward.

        [Exeunt all but DOMITILLA *and* STEPHANOS.]
    Stephanos.　　　　　Patronesse heare mee!
Will you not call for your share? sit downe with this,
And the next action like a *Gaditane* strumpet
I shall looke to see you tumble.

    Domitilla.　　　　　Prethee be patient.
I that haue sufferd greater wrongs beare this;　　　300
And that till my reuenge my comfort is.　　　　　*Exeunt.*

      The end of the third Act.

G2ᵛ
[IV. i]

Actus IIII. Scæna 1.

Enter PARTHENIUS, IULIA, DOMITILLA, CÆNIS.

Parthenius. WHY 'tis impossible! *Paris*?

    Iulia.　　　　　You obseru'd not
(As it appeares) the violence of her passion,

---

293 SD. *Aside.*] *Coxeter; not in* 29　　296 SD. *Exeunt . . .* STEPHANOS.] *Symons;*
not in 29

When personating *Iphis*, he pretended
(For your contempt faire *Anaxerete*)
To hang himselfe.
 Parthenius. Yes, yes, I noted that;   5
But neuer could imagine it could worke her
To such a strange intemperance of affection,
As to dote on him.
 Domitilla. By my hopes I thinke
That she respects not though all heere saw, and mark'd it;
Presuming she can mould the Emperours will   10
Into what forme she likes, though we, and all
Th'informers of the world conspir'd to crosse it.
 Cænis. Then with what eagernesse this morning vrging
The want of health, and rest, she did intreate
Cæsar to leaue her.
 Domitilla. Who no sooner absent   15
But she calls *Dwarfe* (so in her scorne she stiles me)
Put on my pantofles, fetch pen, and paper,
I am to write, and with distracted lookes,
In her smocke, impatient of so short delay
As but to haue a mantle throwne vpon her,   20
She seal'd I know not what, but 'twas indors'd
To my lou'd *Paris.*
 Iulia. Adde to this I heard her
Say, when a page receiu'd it; let him waite me
And carefully in the walke, cal'd our retreate,
Where *Cæsar* in his feare to giue offence,   25
Vnsent for neuer enters.
 Parthenius. This being certaine
(For these are more then iealous suppositions)
Why doe not you that are so neere in bloud
Discouer it?
 Domitilla. Alas you know wee dare not.
'Twill be receaued for a malicious practise   30
To free vs from that slauerie, which her pride
Imposes on vs. But if you would please
To breake the ice on paine to be suncke euer

IV. i. 8/15/29/56/66/81/92/99/112/115/119/154 *Domitilla.*] *Coxeter*; *Domit.* 29
8. thinke] *Massinger MS*; thinke not 29   9. respects not] *Massinger MS*; respects 29 28. you] *Coxeter*; yon 29
8118945.3   D

G3ʳ (marginal)

We would auerre it.
  Parthenius.   I would second you,
But that I am commanded with all speede   35
To fetch in *Ascletario* the *Chaldæan*,
Who in his absence is condemn'd of treason
For calculating the natiuitie
Of *Cæsar*, with all confidence fore-telling
In euerie circumstance when he shall die   40
A violent death. Yet if you could approue
Of my directions I would haue you speake
As much to *Aretinus*, as you haue
To me deliuer'd. He in his owne nature
Being a spie, on weaker grounds no doubt   45
Will vndertake it, not for goodnesse sake
(With which he neuer yet held correspondence)
But to endeare his vigilant obseruings
Of what concernes the Emperour, and a little
To triumph in the ruines of this *Paris*   50
      Enter ARETINUS.
That cros'd him in the Senate house. Here he comes
His nose held vp; he hath something in the winde,
Or I much erre, alreadie. My designes
Command me hence great Ladies, but I leaue
My wishes with you.   *Exit* PARTHENIUS.
  Aretinus.   Haue I caught your greatnes 55
In the trap my proud *Augusta*?
  Domitilla.   What is't raps him?
  Aretinus. And my fine Roman Actor? is't euen so?
No courser dish to take your wanton palate
Saue that which but the Emperour none durst tast off?
T'is very well. I needs must glory in   60
This rare discouerie, but the rewards
G3ᵛ Of my intelligence, bid me thinke even now,
By an edict from *Cæsar* I haue power,
To tread vpon the necke of slauish *Rome*,
Disposing offices, and Prouinces,   65
To my kinsmen, friends and clients.
  Domitilla.   This is more
Then vsuall with him.
  Iulia.   *Aretinus?*

 Aretinus.   How?
No more respect and reuerence tender'd to mee
But *Aretinus*! 'tis confess'd that title
When you were Princesses, and commanded all   70
Had beene a fauour; but being as you are
Vassals to a proud woman, the worst bondage,
You stand oblig'd with as much adoration
To entertaine him, that comes arm'd with strength,
To breake your fetters, as tand gallie-slaues   75
Pay such as doe redeeme them from the oare.
I come not to intrap you, but aloud
Pronounce that you are manumiz'd, and to make
Your libertie sweeter, you shall see her fall,
(This Empresse, this *Domitia*, what you will)   80
That triumph'd in your miseries.
 Domitilla.   Were you serious
To proue your accusation, I could lend
Some helpe.
 Cænis. And I.
 Iulia.   And I.
 Aretinus.   No atome to mee.
My eyes, and eares are euery where, I know all,
To the line and action in the play that tooke her;   85
Her quicke dissimulation to excuse
Her being transported, with her morning passion;
I brib'd the boy that did conuey the letter,
And hauing perus'd it, made it vp againe:
Your griefes, and angers, are to me familiar;   90
That *Paris* is brought to her, and how farre
He shall be tempted.
 Domitilla.   This is aboue wonder.
 Aretinus. My gold can worke much stranger miracles
Then to corrupt poore waiters. Heere ioyne with me,
'Tis a complaint to *Cæsar*. This is that   95
Shall ruine her, and raise you. Haue you set your hands
To the accusation?
 Iulia.   And will iustifie
What we haue subscrib'd to.
 Cænis.   And with vehemencie.

34ʳ

95. complaint] *Massinger MS, 29²*; compliant *29¹*

Domitilla. I will deliuer it.
Aretinus.   Leaue the rest to me then.

Enter CÆSAR *with his Guard.*

Cæsar. Let our Lieutenants bring vs victory,   100
While we enioy the fruites of peace at home,
And being secur'd from our intestine foes,
(Far worse then forreine enemies) doubts, and feares,
Though all the skie were hung with blazing meteors,
Which fond Astrologers giue out to be   105
Assur'd presages of the change of Empires,
And deaths of Monarchs, wee vndaunted yet,
Guarded with our owne thunder, bid defiance,
To them, and fate, we being too strongly arm'd
For them to wound vs.
Aretinus.   *Cæsar.*
Iulia.   As thou art   110
More then a man.
Cænis.   Let not thy passions bee
Rebellious to thy reason.   *The Petition deliuer'd.*
Domitilla.   But receiue
This tryall of your constancie, as vnmou'd
As you goe to, or from the Capitoll,
Thankes giuen to *Ioue* for triumphs!
Cæsar.   Ha!
Domitilla.   Vouchsafe   115
A while to stay the lightning of your eyes.
Poore mortalls dare not looke on.
Aretinus.   There's no veine
Of yours, that rises high with rage, but is
An earthquake to vs.
Domitilla.   And if not kept clos'd
With more then humaine patience, in a moment   120
Will swallow vs to the center.
Cænis.   Not that we
Repine to serue her, are we her accusers.
Iulia. But that she's falne so low.
Aretinus.   Which on sure proofes
We can make good.

102. intestine] *Coxeter*; intestiue 29

Domitilla.　　　　　And show she is vnworthie
Of the least sparke of that diuiner fire　　　　　125
You haue confer'd vpon her.
　　Cæsar.　　　　　I stand doubtfull,
And vnresolu'd what to determine of you.
In this malicious violence you haue offer'd
To the Altar of her truth, and purenesse to me,
You haue but fruitlesly labour'd to sullye　　　　　130
A white robe of perfection, blackmouth'd enuie
Could belch no spot on. But I will put off
The deitie, you labour to take from me,
And argue out of probabilities with you
As if I weare a man. Can I beleeue　　　　　135
That she, that borrowes all her light from me,
And knowes to vse it, would betray her darknesse
To your intelligence, and make that apparent,
Which by her perturbations in a play
Was yesterday but doubted, and find none,　　　　　140
But you that are her slaues, and therefore hate her,
Whose aydes she might imploy to make way for her?
Or *Aretinus* whom long since she knew
To be the Cabinet counsailor, nay the key
Of *Cæsars* secrets? could her beauty raise her　　　　　145
To this vnequald height to make her fall
The more remarkable? or must my desires
To her, and wrongs to *Lamia* be reuengd
By her, and on her selfe that drewe on both?
Or she leaue our imperiall bed to court　　　　　150
A publicke actor?
　　Aretinus.　　　　　Who dares contradict
These more then humain reasons, that haue power
To cloth base guilt, in the most glorious shape
Of innocence?
　　Domitilla.　　　To wel she knew the strength,
And eloquence of her patron to defend her,　　　　　155
And thereupon presuming fell securely;
Not fearing an accuser, nor the truth,
Produc'd against her, which your loue and fauour
Will ne're discerne from falshood.

149. both?] *Massinger MS, 29*²; ∼ₐ *29*¹'²

Cæsar.   I'll not heere
A syllable more that may inuite a change   160
In my opinion of her. You haue rais'd
A fiercer war within me by this fable,
(Though with your liues you vowe to make it storie)
Then if, and at one instant, all my legions
Reuolted from me, and came arm'd against me.   165
Heere in this paper are the swords predestin'd
For my destruction; heere the fatall stars
That threaten more then ruine; this the deaths head
That does assure me, if she can proue false
That I am mortall, which a sudaine feauer   170
Would prompt me to beleeue, and fayntly yeeld to.
But now in my full confidence what she suffers,
In that, from any witnesse but my selfe,
I nourish a suspition she's vntrue,
My toughnes returnes to me. Lead on Monsters,   175
And by the forfeit of your liues confirme
She is all excellence, as you all basenesse,
Or let mankinde for her fall, boldly sweare
Hı^v There are no chast wiues now, nor euer were.   *Exeunt omnes.*

[IV. ii]   *Actus IIII. Scæna 2.*

Enter DOMITIA, PARIS, *Seruants.*

Domitia. Say we command, that none presume to dare
On forfeit of our fauour, that is life,
Out of a sawcie curiousnesse to stand
Within the distance of their eyes, or eares,
Till we please to be waited on. And sirrha   *Exeunt Seruants.*
Howe're you are excepted, let it not   6
Beget in you an arrogant opinion
'Tis done to grace you.
    Paris.   With my humblest seruice
I but obey your summons, and should blush else
To be so neare you.
    Domitia.   'Twould become you rather   10
To feare, the greatnesse of the grace vouchsaf'd you

163. liues] *Coxeter*; lines 29   170. which] 29²; with 29¹,²

May ouerwhelme you, and 'twill doe no lesse,
If when you are rewarded, in your cups
You boast this priuacie.
    Paris.   That were, mightiest Empresse,
To play with lightning.
    Domitia.   You conceiue it right.   15
The meanes to kill, or saue, is not alone
In *Cæsar* circumscrib'd, for if incens'd
We haue our thunder to, that strikes as deadly.
    Paris. 'Twould ill become the lownesse of my fortune
To question what you can doe, but with all   20
Humilitie to attend what is your will,
And then to serue it.
    Domitia.   And would not a secret
(Suppose we should commit it to your trust)
Scald you to keepe it?
    Paris.   Though it rag'd within me
Till I turn'd cyndars, it should ne're haue vent.   25
To be an age a dying, and with torture,
Onely to bee thought worthy of your counsaile,
Or actuate what ever you command mee
A wretched obscure thing, not worth your knowledge,
Were a perpetuall happinesse.
    Domitia.   We could wish   30
That we could credit thee, and cannot find
In reason but that thou whom oft I haue seene
To personate a Gentleman, noble, wise,
Faithfull, and gamsome, and what vertues else
The Poet pleases to adorne you with,   35
But that (as vessels still pertake the odour
Of the sweete pretious liquors they contain'd)
Thou must be reallie in some degree
The thing thou dost present. Nay doe not tremble.
We seriouslie beleeue it, and presume   40
Our *Paris* is the volume in which all
Those excellent guifts the Stage hath seene him grac'd with

IV. ii. 20. with all] *Coxeter*; withall *29*   27. bee] *Massinger MS*; pe *29¹*; be
29²   28. ever you command mee] *Massinger MS* (ever you comand mee); yuu
command to me *29¹*; you command to me *29²*   34. gamsome] *McIlwraith*; gainsome *29*   39. tremble.] *Massinger MS*; tremele, *29¹*; tremble, *29²*

Are curiouslie bound vp.

 Paris.   The argument
Is the same great *Augusta*, that I acting,
A foole, a coward, a traytor or cold cinique   45
Or any other weake, and vitious person,
Of force I must be such. O gracious Madam,
How glorious soeuer, or deform'd,
I doe appeare in the Sceane, my part being ended,
And all my borrowed ornaments put off,   50
I am no more, nor lesse then what I was
Before I enter'd.

 Domitia. Come, you would put on
A wilfull ignorance, and not vnderstand,
What 'tis we point at. Must we in plaine language,
Against the decent modestie of our sex,   55
Say that we loue thee, loue thee to enioy thee,
Or that in our desires thou art preferr'd,
And *Cæsar* but thy second? thou in iustice
(If from the height of Maiestie we can
Looke downe vpon thy lownesse and embrace it,) 60
Art bound with feruor to looke vp to me.

H2ᵛ *Paris.* O Madam heare me with a patient eare
And be but pleas'd to vnderstand the reasons
That doe deterre me from a happinesse
Kings would be riuals for. Can I that owe   65
My life, and all that's mine to *Cæsars* bounties
Beyond my hopes, or merits showr'd vpon me,
Make payment for them with ingratitude,
Falshood, and treason? Though you haue a shape
Might tempt *Hypolitus*, and larger power   70
To helpe, or hurt, then wanton *Phædra* had,
Let loyaltie, and dutie plead my pardon
Though I refuse to satisfie.

 Domitia.   You are coy,
Expecting I should court you. Let meane Ladies
Vse prayers, and intreaties to their creatures   75
To rise vp instruments to serue their pleasures;
But for *Augusta* so to loose her selfe

---

 44. great] *Massinger MS, 29²*; geeat *29¹* 70. Hypolitus] *Massinger MS*; *Hypo-*
llitus 29¹, ²; *Hyppollitus 29²*

That holds command o're *Cæsar*, and the world,
Were pouertie of spirit. Thou must, thou shalt,
The violence of my passions knowes no meane,   80
And in my punishments, and my rewards
I'll vse no moderation, take this onely
As a caution from me. Thread-bare Chastitie,
Is poore in the aduancement of her seruants,
But wantonnesse magnificent; and 'tis frequent   85
To haue the Salarie of vice waigh downe
The pay of vertue. So without more trifling
Thy sudaine answer.
    Paris.   In what a straight am I brought in!
Alas I know that the denial's death
Nor can my grant discouer'd threaten more.   90
Yet to dye innocent, and haue the glorie
For all posteritie to report that I
Refus'd an Empresse to preserue my faith
To my great master, in true iudgement must
Show fairer then to buy a guilty life,   95
With wealth, and honours. 'Tis the base I build on,
I dare not, must not, will not.
    Domitia.   How, contemn'd?
Since hopes, nor feares in the extreames preuaile not
I must vse a meane. Thinke who 'tis sues to thee.
Denie not that yet which a brother may   100
Grant to his sister: as a testimonie

      CÆSAR, ARETINUS, IULIA, DOMITILLA, CÆNIS *aboue.*

I am not scorn'd. Kisse me. Kisse me againe.
Kisse closer. Thou art now my *Troyan Paris*
And I thy *Helen.*
    Paris.   Since it is your will.
    Cæsar. And I am *Menelaus.* But I shall be   105
Something I know not yet.   *CÆSAR descends.*
    Domitia.   Why lose we time
And opportunitie? These are but sallads
To sharpen appetite. Let vs to the feast.   *Courting* PARIS *wantonly.*

---

82. moderation, take] *Massinger MS*; moderation take *29¹˒ ²*; moderation. Take *29³*
88. In] *29*; Oh! *Coxeter*   97. dare not] *29²˒ ³*; dare not not *29¹*   99. I must]
29²˒ ³; must *29¹*   102. I am] *29²˒ ³*; am *29¹*

Where I shall wish that thou wert *Iupiter*
And I *Alcmena*, and that I had power   110
To lengthen out one short night into three,
And so beget a *Hercules*.

> [*Enter* CÆSAR *and Guard.*]

    Cæsar.   While *Amphitrio*
Stands by, and drawes the curtaines.
    Paris.   Oh?—   *Falls on his face.*
    Domitia.   Betrai'd?
    Cæsar. No, taken in a net of *Vulcans* filing,
Where in my selfe the *Theater* of the Gods   115
Are sad spectators, not one of em daring
To witnesse with a smile he does desire
To be so sham'd for all the pleasure that
You haue sold your being for. What shall I name thee?
Ingratefull, trecherous, insatiate, all   120
Inuectiues, which in bitternes of spirit
Wrong'd men haue breath'd out against wicked women,
Cannot expresse thee. Haue I rays'd thee from
Thy lowe condition to the height of greatnesse,
Command, and Maiestie, in one base act   125
To render me that was (before I hugg'd thee
An adder in my bosome) more then man
A thing beneath a beast? did I force these
Of mine owne bloud as handmaids to kneele to
H3ᵛ Thy pompe, and pride, hauing my selfe no thought   130
But how with benefits to binde thee mine;
And am I thus rewarded? not a knee?
Nor teare? nor signe of sorrow for thy fault?
Breake stubborne silence. What canst thou alleage
To stay my vengeance?
    Domitia.   This. Thy lust compell'd me   135
To be a strumpet, and mine hath return'd it

---

112. a] *29³*; an *29¹, ²*   SD. *Enter...Guard.*] *editor; not in 29*   115. Where
in] *conj. Mason;* Wherein *29*   119. for. What] *29³, Massinger MS* (for. what); for,
what *29¹, ²*   123. thee. Haue] *29³, Massinger MS* (thee. haue); thee, haue *29¹, ²*
126. that was (before ... thee] *Massinger MS*; (that was before ... thee *29¹*; (that was
before ... thee) *29², ³*   127. bosome)] *Massinger MS;* ~, *29*   130-97. *H3ᵛ*
and H4ʳ are transposed in 29¹, ². On H3ᵛ of the Harbord copy Massinger writes this page
followes the later; *on H4ʳ,* this page misplaced.

In my intent, and will, though not in act,
To cuckold thee.
    Cæsar.   O impudence! take her hence,
And let her make her entrance into hell,
By leauing life with all the tortures that   140
Flesh can be sensible of. Yet stay. What power
Her beautie still holds o're my soule! that wrongs
Of this vnpardonable nature cannot teach me
To right my selfe and hate her!—Kill her.—Hold.
O that my dotage should increase from that   145
Which should breed detestation. By *Minerua*
If I looke on her longer I shall melt
And sue to her, my iniuries forgot,
Againe to be receiu'd into her fauour
Could honour yeild to it! Carrie her to her Chamber,   150
Be that her prison till in cooler bloud
I shall determine of her.   *Exit [Guard] with* DOMITIA.
    Aretinus.   Now step I in   *[Aside.]*
While he's in this calme mood for my reward—
Sir, if my seruice hath deseru'd—
    Cæsar.   Yes. Yes,
And I'll reward thee, thou hast rob'd me of   155
All rest, and peace, and bin the principall meanes
To make me know that, of which if againe   *Enter Guard.*
I could be ignorant of, I would purchase it
With the losse of Empire; strangle him, take these hence to
And lodge them in the dungeon! Could your reason   160
Dull wretches flatter you with hope to thinke
That this discouerie that hath showr'd vpon me
Perpetuall vexation should not fall
H4ʳ Heauie on you? away with 'em, stop their mouthes,
I will heare no reply.
        Exeunt Guard, ARETINUS, IULIA, CÆNIS, DOMITILLA.
        O *Paris, Paris*   165
How shall I argue with thee? how begin,
To make thee vnderstand before I kill thee,
With what griefe and vnwillingnes 'tis forc'd from me?
Yet in respect I haue fauourd thee, I will heere

---

142. soule!] *Massinger MS*; ~ₐ 29   152 SD. *Exit Guard*] *Coxeter*; *Exit* 29
Aside.] *editor*; *not in* 29

What thou canst speake to qualefie, or excuse 170
Thy readinesse to serue this womans lust,
And wish thou couldst giue me such satisfaction
As I might burie the remembrance of it.
Looke vp. We stand attentiue.

    Paris.   O dread *Cæsar*,
To hope for life, or pleade in the defence 175
Of my ingratitude were againe to wrong you.
I know I haue deseru'd death. And my suit is
That you would hasten it: yet that your highnes
When I am dead (as sure I will not liue)
May pardon me I'll onely vrge my frailtie, 180
Her will, and the temptation of that beautie
Which you could not resist. How coulde poore I then
Fly that which followd me, and *Cæsar* su'd for?
This is all. And now your sentence.

    Cæsar.   Which I know not
How to pronounce. O that thy fault had bin 185
But such as I might pardon; if thou hadst
In wantonnesse (like *Nero*) fir'd proud *Rome*,
Betraide an armie, butcherd the whole Senate,
Committed Sacriledge, or any crime
The iustice of our *Roman* lawes cals death, 190
I had preuented any intercession
And freely sign'd thy pardon.

    Paris.   But for this
Alas you cannot, nay you must not Sir;
Nor let it to posteritie be recorded
That *Cæsar* vnreueng'd, sufferd a wrong, 195
Which yf a priuate man should sit downe with it
Cowards would baffell him.

H4ᵛ   *Cæsar.*   With such true feeling
Thou arguest against thy selfe, that it
Workes more vpon me, then if my *Minerua*
(The grand protectresse of my life, and Empire,) 200
On forfeite of her fauour, cry'd aloud
Cæsar show mercie. And I know not how,
I am inclinde to it. Rise. I'll promise nothing,

182. coulde] *Massinger MS*; would *29*   191. had] *Massinger MS, 29²*; ꝗad *29¹*
196. yf a] *Massinger MS*; ifa *29¹*; if a *29²*

Yet cleare thy cloudie feares and cherish hopes,
What we must doe, we shall doe; we remember   205
A Tragedie, we oft haue seen with pleasure,
Call'd, the *False Seruant*.
    Paris.   Such a one we haue Sir.
    Cæsar. In which a great Lord takes to his protection
A man forlorne, giuing him ample power
To order, and dispose of his estate   210
In his absence, he pretending then a iourney.
But yet with this restraint that on no tearmes
(This Lord suspecting his wiues constancie,
She hauing playd false to a former husband)
The seruant though sollicited should consent,   215
Though she commanded him to quench her flames.
    Paris. That was indeed the argument.
    Cæsar.   And what
Didst thou play in it?
    Paris.   The false seruant Sir.
    Cæsar. Thou didst indeed. Do the Players waite without?
    Paris. They doe Sir and prepar'd to act the storie   220
Your Maiestie mention'd.
    Cæsar.   Call 'em in. Who presents
The iniur'd Lord?

       Enter ÆSOPUS, LATINUS, *a* BOY *drest for a Ladie.*

    Æsopus.   T'is my part Sir.
    Cæsar.   Thou didst not
Doe it to the life. We can performe it better.
Off with my Robe, and wreath; since *Nero* scorn'd not
The publike *Theater*, we in priuate may   225
11ʳ Disport our selues. This cloake, and hat without
Wearing a beard, or other propertie
Will fit the person.
    Æsopus.   Onely Sir a foyle,
The point, and edge rebutted, when you are
To doe the murther. If you please to vse this   230

208. *Cæsar*. In] *29³* (*Cæs.* In); In *29¹˒²*   213. (This] *Massinger MS*; This *29*
214. She] *Massinger MS, 29¹*; (She *29²˒³*   216. commanded] *29²˒³*; command *29¹*
217. *Paris*. That] *29³* (*Par.* That); That *29¹˒²*   229. rebutted] *29*; rebated *Gifford*
are] *Massinger MS*; act *29*

And lay aside your owne sword.

  Cæsar.   By no meanes.
In iest or earnest this parts neuer from me.
We'l haue but one short Sceane. That where the Ladie
In an imperious way commands the seruant
To be vnthankefull to his patron. When   235
My cue's to enter prompt me, nay begin
And doe it spritely. Though but a new Actor,
When I come to execution you shall find
No cause to laugh at me.

  Latinus.   In the name of wonder
What's *Cæsars* purpose?

  Æsopus.   There is no contending.   240

  Cæsar. Why when?

  Paris.   I am arm'd.
And stood death now within my view and his
Vneuitable dart aim'd at my breast
His cold embraces should not bring an ague
To any of my faculties, till his pleasures   245
Were seru'd, and satisfied, which done *Nestors* yeeres,
To me would be vnwelcome.

  Boy.   Must we intreate,
That were borne to command, or court a seruant
(That owes his foode and cloathing to our bountie)
For that, which thou ambitiouslie shouldst kneele for? 250
Vrge not in thy excuse the fauours of
Thy absent Lord, or that thou standst ingag'd
For thy life to his Charitie; nor thy feares
Of what may follow, it being in my power
To mould him any way.

  Paris.   As you may me   255
In what his reputation is not wounded

I1ᵛ Nor I his creature in my thankefulnesse suffer.
I know you are young, and faire; be vertuous too
And loyall to his bed, that hath aduanc'd you
To th'height of happinesse.

  Boy.   Can my louesicke heart 260
Be cur'd with counsell? or durst reason euer
Offer to put in an exploded plea

232. or] *Massinger MS*; nor *29*   242. stood] *Massinger MS*; stood grim *29*

In the Court of *Venus*? My desires admit not
The least delay. And therefore instantly
Giue me to vnderstand what I shall trust to.   265
For if I am refus'd, and not enioy
Those rauishing pleasures from thee, I run mad for;
I'll sweare vnto my Lord at his returne
(Making what I deliuer good with teares)
That brutishly thou wouldst haue forc'd from me   270
What I make suit for. And then but imagine
What 'tis to dye with these words slaue, and traytor,
With burning corrasiues writ vpon thy forehead,
And liue prepar'd for't.
   Paris.   This he will beleeue   *[Aside.]*
Vpon her information. 'Tis apparent.   275
And then I am nothing. And of two extreames
Wisedome sayes chose the lesse.—Rather then fall
Vnder your indignation, I will yeeld.
This kisse, and this confirmes it.
   Æsopus.   Now Sir, now.
   Cæsar. I must take them at it.
   Æsopus.   Yes Sir, be but perfect.   280
   Cæsar. O villaine! thankelesse villaine! I should talke now;
But I haue forgot my part. But I can doe,
Thus, thus, and thus.   *Kils* PARIS.
   Paris.   Oh, I am slaine in earnest.
   Cæsar. 'Tis true, and 'twas my purpose my good *Paris.*
And yet before life leaue thee, let the honour   285
I haue done thee in thy death bring comfort to thee.
If it had beene within the power of *Cæsar,*
His dignitie preseru'd, he had pardon'd thee.
But crueltie of honour did deny it.
I2ʳ Yet to confirme I lou'd thee, 'twas my study   290
To make thy end more glorious to distinguish
My *Paris* from all others, and in that
Haue showne my pittie. Nor would I let thee fall
By a Centurions sword, or haue thy limbes
Rent peece meale by the hangmans hooke (howeuer   295

---

274 SD. *Aside.*] *Coxeter*; *not in 29*   278. yeeld.] *Coxeter*; ~ₐ 29   286. thee.]
Massinger MS; ~ₐ 29   290. thee,] *Massinger MS*; ~? 29   295. (howeuer]
Massinger MS) ((~:); ~: 29

Thy crime deseru'd it) but as thou didst liue
Romes brauest Actor, 'twas my plot that thou
Shouldst dye in action, and to crowne it dye
With an applause induring to all times,
By our imperiall hand. His soule is freed   300
From the prison of his flesh, let it mount vpward.
And for this truncke, when that the funerall pile
Hath made it ashes, we'l see it inclos'd
In a golden vrne. Poets adorne his hearse
With their most rauishing sorrowes, and the stage   305
For euer mourne him, and all such as were
His glad spectators weepe his suddaine death,
The cause forgotten in his Epitaph.

> *Exeunt. A sad musicke, the Players bearing off*
> PARIS *body,* CÆSAR *and the rest following.*

The end of the fourth Act.

[V. i]

Actus V. Scæna 1.

Enter PARTHENIUS, STEPHANOS, *Guard.*

Parthenius. KEEPE a strong guard vpon him, and admit not
Accesse to any, to exchange a word,
Or syllable with him, till the Emperour pleases
To call him to his presence. The relation   [*Exit Guard.*]
That you haue made me *Stephanos* of these late   5
Strange passions in *Cæsar*, much amaze me.
The informer *Aretinus* put to death
For yeelding him a true discouerie
Of th'Empresse wantonnesse; poore *Paris* kild first
And now lamented; and the Princesses   10
I2ᵛ Confin'd to seuerall Islands, yet *Augusta*,
The machine on which all this mischiefe mou'd,
Receiu'd againe to grace?
    Stephanos.   Nay courted to it,
(Such is the impotence of his affection.)
Yet, to conceale his weaknesse he giues out   15
The people made suit for her, whom they hate more

Then ciuill warre, or famine. But take heed
My Lord, that nor in your consent nor wishes
You lent or furtherance, or fauour to
The plot contriu'd against her; should she proue it,   20
Nay doubt it onely you are a lost man,
Her power o're doting *Cæsar* being now
Greater then euer.
    Parthenius.   'Tis a truth I shake at.
And when there's opportunitie—
    Stephanos.   Say but doe,
I am yours, and sure.
    Parthenius.   I will stand one tryall more   25
And then you shall heare from me.
    Stephanos.   Now obserue
The fondnesse of this tyranne, and her pride.

Enter CÆSAR *and* DOMITIA.

    Cæsar. Nay all's forgotten.
    Domitia.   It may be on your part.
    Cæsar. Forgiuen to, *Domitia*: 'tis a fauour
That you should welcome with more cheerefull lookes.   30
Can *Cæsar* pardon what you durst not hope for
That did the iniurie, and yet must sue
To her whose guilt is wash'd off by his mercy
Onely to entertaine it?
    Domitia.   I ask'd none,
And I should be more wretched to receiue   35
Remission (for what I hold no crime)
But by a bare acknowledgement then if
By sleighting, and contemning it, as now,
I dar'd thy vtmost furie. Though thy flatterers
Perswade thee, that thy murthers, lusts, and rapes   40
Are vertues in thee, and what pleases *Cæsar*
Though neuer so vniust is right, and lawfull;
Or worke in thee a false beliefe that thou
Art more then mortall; yet I to thy teeth
(When circl'd with thy Guards, thy rods, thy axes,   45
And all the ensignes of thy boasted power)
Will say *Domitian*, nay adde to it *Cæsar*,

13ʳ

                19. lent] *29*; lend *Gifford*

Is a weake feeble man, a bondman to
His violent passions, and in that my slaue,
Nay more my slaue, then my affections made me   50
To my lou'd *Paris*.
    Cæsar.   Can I liue, and heare this?
Or heare and not reuenge it? come, you know
The strength that you hold on me, doe not vse it
With too much crueltie, for though 'tis granted
That *Lidian Omphale* had lesse command   55
O're *Hercules*, then you vsurpe ore me,
Reason may teach me to shake off the yoke
Of my fond dotage.
    Domitia.   Neuer, doe not hope it,
It cannot be. Thou being my beauties captiue
And not to be redeem'd, my Empire's larger   60
Then thine *Domitian*, which I'll exercise
With rigor on thee, for my *Paris* death.
And when I haue forc'd those eyes now red with fury
To drop downe teares, in vaine spent to appease me,
I know thy feruor such to my embraces   65
(Which shall be, though still kneel'd for, stil deni'd thee)
That thou with languishment shalt wish my Actor
Did liue againe, so thou might'st be his second
To feede vpon those delicates, when he's sated.
    Cæsar. O my *Minerua*!
    Domitia.   There she is, inuoke her: 70
Shee cannot arme thee with abilitie
To draw thy sword on me, my power being greater.
Or onely say to thy Centurions
I3ᵛ Dare none of you doe what I shake to thinke on?
And in this womans death remoue the furies   75
That euery houre afflict mee? *Lamias* wrongs
When thy lust forc'd mee from him, are in mee
At the height reveng'd, nor would I out-liue *Paris*
But that thy loue increasing with my hate
May adde vnto thy torments, so with all   80
Contempt I can I leaue thee.   *Exit* DOMITIA.
    Cæsar.   I am lost

80. with all] *Coxeter*; withall 29

Nor am I *Cæsar*. When I first betray'd
The freedome of my faculties, and will
To this imperious Siren, I layd downe
The Empire of the world, and of my selfe   85
At her proud feete. Sleepe all my irefull powers?
Or is the magique of my dotage such
That I must still make suite to heare those charmes
That doe increase my thraldome? wake my anger,
For shame breake through this Lethargie, and appeare   90
With vsuall terror, and enable mee
(Since I weare not a sword to pierce her heart,
Nor haue a tongue to say this, let her dye)
Though 'tis done with a feauer-shaken hand *Pulls out a Table booke.*
To signe her death; assist mee great *Minerua*   95
And vindicate thy votarie. So shee's now   *Writes.*
Among the list of those I haue proscrib'd,
And are, to free mee of my doubts, and feares,
To dye to morrow.
    Stephanos.   That same fatall booke
Was neuer drawne yet, but some men of rancke   100
Were mark'd out for destruction.
    Parthenius.   I begin
To doubt my selfe.   [*Exit* STEPHANOS.]
    Cæsar.   Who waites there?
    Parthenius.   *Cæsar.*
    Cæsar.   So.
These that command arm'd troupes quake, at my frownes,
And yet a woman sleights 'em. Where's the Wizard
Wee charg'd you to fetch in?
14ʳ   *Parthenius.*   Readie to suffer   105
What death you please t'appoint him.
    Cæsar.   Bring him in.
                [*Exit* PARTHENIUS.]

       Enter ASCLETARIO, *Tribunes, Guard.*
We'll question him our selfe. Now you that hold
Intelligence with the starres, and dare prefixe

82. *Cæsar.* When] *Massinger MS* (*Cæsar.* when); *Cæsar*, when 29   96 SD. *Writes.*]
Gifford²; (*Writes.*) 29 (*at l.* 99)   97. proscrib'd] *Massinger MS*; prescrib'd 29
102 SD. *Exit* STEPHANOS.] *Gifford*; *not in* 29   106 SD. *Exit* PARTHENIUS.]
editor; *not in* 29

The day and houre in which we are to part
With life and Empire, punctually fore-telling   110
The meanes, and manner of our violent end,
As you would purchase credit to your art
Resolue me, since you are assur'd of vs,
What fate attends your selfe?
   Ascletario.   I haue had long since
A certaine knowledge, and as sure as thou   115
Shalt dye to morrow, being the fourteenth of
The Kalends of *October*, the houre fiue,
Spite of preuention, this carkasse shall be
Torne and deuourd by dogs, and let that stand
For a firme prediction.
   Cæsar.   May our body, wretch,   120
Find neuer nobler Sepulcher if this
Fall euer on thee. Are we the great disposer
Of life, and death yet cannot mocke the starres
In such a trifle? Hence with the impostor,
And hauing cut his throat, erect a pile   125
Guarded with souldiers, till his cursed truncke
Be turn'd to ashes: vpon forfeite of
Your life, and theirs, performe it.
   Ascletario.   'Tis in vaine.
When what I haue foretold is made apparent
Tremble to thinke what followes.
   Cæsar.   Drag him hence   130
And doe as I command you.   *The* [*Tribunes and*] *Guard beare*
      I was neuer   *off* ASCLETARIO.
Fuller of confidence, for hauing got
The victorie of my passions, in my freedome
From proud *Domitia* (who shall cease to liue
Since she disdaines to loue) I rest vnmou'd,   135
And in defiance of prodigious meteors,
Chaldeans vaine predictions, iealous feares
Of my neere friends, and freemen, certaine hate
14ᵛ Of kindred, and alliance, or all terrors
The souldiers doubted faith, or peoples rage   140
Can bring to shake my constancie I am arm'd.

115. as sure] *Massinger MS*; assure *29*   119–20. stand / For] *Coxeter*; *undivided*
29   130 SD. *Tribunes and Guard*] *Gifford*; *Guard 29*

That scrupulous thing stil'd Conscience is sear'd vp
And I insensible of all my actions
For which by morrall and religious fooles
I stand condemn'd, as they had neuer beene.   145
And since I haue subdu'd triumphant loue
I will not deifie pale captiue feare
Nor in a thought receiue it. For till thou
Wisest *Minerua*, that from my first youth,
Hast beene my sole protectresse, dost forsake me,   150
Not *Iunius Rusticus* threatned apparition,
Nor what this Southsayer but eu'n now foretold
(Being things impossible to humane reason)
Shall in a dreame disturbe me. Bring my couch there.

                Enter with couch.

A sudaine but a secure drousinesse   155
Inuites me to repose my selfe. Let Musicke
With some choyse dittie second it. I' the meane time
Rest there deare booke, which open'd when I wake
Shall make some sleepe for euer.
            Layes the booke vnder his Pillow. The Musicke and song.
                                        CÆSAR *sleepes.*

        Enter PARTHENIUS *and* DOMITIA.

Domitia.   Write my name
In his bloudie scrole *Parthenius*? the feare's idle;   160
He durst not, could not.
    Parthenius.   I can assure nothing
But I obseru'd when you departed from him
After some little passion, but much furie,
He drew it out: whose death he sign'd I know not
But in his lookes appear'd a resolution   165
Of what before he staggerd at. What he hath
Determin'd of is vncertaine, but too soone
Will fall on you, or me, or both, or any,
His pleasure knowne to the Tribunes, and Centurions,
Who neuer vse to enquire his will but serue it.   170
Now if out of the confidence of your power,

  142. stil'd] *Massinger MS*; still'd 29   150. me,] *Massinger MS*; ~ˏ 29
  157. I' the] *Symons*; I the *29*; In the *Coxeter*; The *Gifford*

The bloudie Catalogue being still about him,
Kᵢʳ As he sleepes you dare peruse it, or remoue it
You may instruct your selfe or what to suffer,
Or how to crosse it.
    Domitia.   I would not be caught   175
With too much confidence. By your leaue Sir. Ha!
No motion! you lye vneasie Sir,
Let me mend your Pillow.
    Parthenius.   Haue you it?
    Domitia.   'Tis heere.
    Cæsar. Oh.
    Parthenius. You haue wak'd him; softly gracious Madam
While we are vnknowne, and then consult at leisure.   180
                Exeunt PARTHENIUS, *and* DOMITIA.

A dreadfull Musicke sounding, Enter IUNIUS RUSTICUS, *and*
PALPHURIUS SURA, *with bloudie swords, they waue them ouer his*
head. CÆSAR, *in his sleepe troubled, seemes to pray to the Image,*
they scornefully take it away.

    Cæsar. Defend me goddesse, or this horrid dreame
Will force me to destraction. Whether haue
These furies borne thee? Let me rise! and follow!
I am bath'd o're with the cold sweat of death,
And am depriu'd of organs to pursue   185
These sacriligious spirits. Am I at once
Robd of my hopes, and being? No, I liue   *Rises destractedly.*
Yes liue, and haue discourse to know my selfe
Of Gods, and men forsaken. What accuser
Within me cries aloud, I haue deseru'd it,   190
In being iust to neither? Who dares speake this?
Am I not *Cæsar*? how! againe repeate it?
Presumptuous traytor thou shalt dye. What traytor?
He that hath beene a traytor to himselfe
And stands conuicted heere. Yet who can sit   195
A competent Iudge ore *Cæsar*? *Cæsar.* Yes
Cæsar by *Cæsar's*, sentenc'd, and must suffer.
Minerua cannot saue him. Ha! where is she?
Where is my goddesse? vanish'd! I am lost then.

181. *Cæsar.* Defend] *Coxeter*; Defend 29   191. In] *Coxeter*; It 29   193. dye.
What] *Massinger MS* (dye. what); dye, what 29

No, 'twas no dreame, but a most reall truth   200
K1ᵛ That *Iunius Rusticus*, and *Palphurius Sura*,
Although their ashes were cast in the sea
Were by their innocence made vp againe
And in corporeall formes but now appear'd,
Wauing their bloudie swordes aboue my head,   205
As at their deathes they threatned. And me thought
Minerua rauish'd hence whisper'd that she
Was for my blasphemies disarm'd by *Ioue*
And could no more protect me. Yes 'twas so,
                                    Thunder and lightning.
His thunder does confirme it, against which   210
Howe're it spare the lawrell, this proud wreath
Is no assurance.

                    Enter 3. TRIBUNES.

                    Ha! come you resolu'd
To be my executioners?
     1. *Tribune.*   Allegeance
And faith forbid that we should lift an arme
Against your sacred head.
     2. *Tribune.*   We rather sue   215
For mercie.
     3. *Tribune.* And acknowledge that in iustice
Our liues are forfeited for not performing
What *Cæsar* charg'd vs.
     1. *Tribune.*   Nor did we transgresse it
In our want of will, or care, for being but men
It could not be in vs to make resistance,   220
The Gods fighting against vs.
     Cæsar.   Speake, in what
Did they expresse their anger? wee will heere it
But dare not say vndaunted.
     1. *Tribune.*   In briefe thus Sir.
The Sentence giuen by your imperiall tongue
For the Astrologer *Ascletario's* death   225
With speede was put in execution.
     Cæsar.   Well.
     1. *Tribune.* For his throate cut, his legs bound, and his armes

209 SD. *Thunder ... lightning.*] *Gifford; follows* which (l. 210) 29

Pinion'd behinde his backe, the breathlesse truncke
Was with all scorne dragg'd to the field of *Mars*
And there a pile being rais'd of old dry wood,   230
Smeer'd o're with oyle, and brimstone, or what else
K2r Could helpe to feede, or to increase the fire
The Carkasse was throwne on it. But no sooner
The stuffe, that was most apt, began to flame;
But sudainely to the amazement of   235
The fearelesse souldier, a sudaine flash
Of lightning breaking through the scatter'd cloudes
With such a horrid violence forc'd its passage,
And as disdaining all heate but it selfe
In a moment quench'd the artificiall fire.   240
And before we could kindle it againe
A clap of thunder follow'd, with such noyse,
As if then *Ioue* incens'd against mankind,
Had in his secret purposes determin'd
An vniuersall ruine to the world.   245
This horror past, not at *Deucalions* floud
Such a stormie shower of raine (and yet that word is
To narrow to expresse it) was e're seene.
Imagine rather Sir, that with lesse furie
The Waues rush downe the Cataracts of *Nile*;   250
Or that the Sea spouted into the ayre
By the angry *Orke*, endaungering tall ships
But sayling neere it, so falls downe againe.
Yet heere the wonder ends not, but begins,
For as in vaine we labour'd to consume   255
The witches bodye, all the Dogs of *Rome*
Howling, and yelling like to famish'd wolues
Brake in vpon vs, and though thousands were
Kild in th'attempt some did ascend the pile
And with their eager fangs ceas'd on the carkasse.   260
    Cæsar. But haue they torne it?
    1. *Tribune.*   Torne it, and deuour'd it.
    Cæsar. I then am a dead man, since all predictions
Assure me I am lost. O my lou'd souldiers

---

228. Pinion'd] 29³, *Massinger MS* (pinion'd); Pinn'd 29¹, ²   238. passage,]
Massinger MS; ~ₐ 29   242. follow'd,] *Massinger MS*; ~ₐ 29   262. man,]
Massinger MS; ~ₐ 29

Your Emperour must leaue you: yet howeuer
I cannot grant my selfe a short reprieue   265
I freely pardon you. The fatall houre
Steales fast vpon me. I must dye this morning
By fiue my souldiers, that's the latest houre
2ᵛ You e're must see me liuing.
    1. *Tribune*.   *Ioue* auert it!
In our swords lies your fate, and we will guard it.   270
    Cæsar. O no, it cannot be, it is decreed
Aboue, and by no strengths heere to be alterd.
Let proud mortalitie but looke on *Cæsar*
Compass'd of late with armies, in his eyes
Carrying both life, and death, and in his armes   275
Fadoming the earth; that would be stilde a God,
And is for that presumption cast beneath
The low condition of a common man,
Sincking with mine owne waight.
    1. *Tribune*.   Doe not forsake
Your selfe, wee'll neuer leaue you.
    2. *Tribune*.   We'll draw vp   280
More cohorts of your Guard, if you doubt treason.
    Cæsar. They cannot saue me. The offended Gods
That now sit iudges on me, from their enuie
Of my power and greatnesse heere, conspire against me.
    1. *Tribune*. Endeauour to appease them.
    Cæsar.   'Twill be fruitlesse, 285
I am past hope of remission. Yet could I
Decline this dreadfull houre of fiue, these terrors
That driue me to despaire would soone flye from me
And could you but till then assure me,
    1. *Tribune*.   Yes Sir,
Or wee'll fall with you, and make *Rome* the vrne   290
In which wee'll mix our ashes.
    Cæsar.   Tis said noblie,
I am something comforted. Howere to dye
Is the full period of calamitie.   *Exeunt*.

Actus V. Scæna 2.

Enter PARTHENIUS, DOMITIA, IULIA, CÆNIS, DOMITILLA,
STEPHANOS, SIJEIUS, ENTELLUS.

Parthenius. You see we are all condemnd, there's no euasion,
K3ʳ We must doe or suffer.
Stephanos.   But it must be sudaine,
The least delay is mortall.
Domitia.   Would I were
A man to giue it action.
Domitilla. Could I make my approaches, though my stature   5
Does promise little, I haue a spirit as daring
As hers, that can reach higher.
Stephanos.   I will take
That burthen from you Madam. All the art is
To draw him from the Tribunes that attend him,
For could you bring him but within my swords reach   10
The world should owe her freedome from a tyranne,
To *Stephanos.*
Sijeius.   You shall not share alone
The glorie of a deed that will endure
To all posteritie.
Entellus.   I will put in
For a part my selfe.
Parthenius.   Be resolute, and stand close.   15
I haue conceiu'd a way, and with the hazard
Of my life I'll practise it to fetch him hither.
But then no trifling.
Stephanos.   We'l despatch him feare not;
A dead dog neuer bites.
Parthenius.   Thus then at all.

          PARTHENIUS *goes off, the rest stand aside.*

Enter CÆSAR *and the* TRIBUNES.

Cæsar. How slowe pac'd are these minutes! in extreames   20
How miserable is the least delay!
Could I impe feathers to the wings of time

V. ii. 5. *Domitilla.] Coxeter; Domit. 29   9. him,] Massinger MS; ~ₐ 29
12. Sijeius.] Coxeter; Sige. 29   18. not;] Coxeter; ~ₐ 29   22. impe] Massinger
MS; iumpe 29*

Or with as little ease command the Sunne
To scourge his coursers vp heauens easterne hill
Making the houre I tremble at past recalling   25
As I can moue this dyals tongue to six,
My veines, and arteries emptied with feare
Would fill and swell againe. How doe I looke?
Doe you yet see death about me?

K3ᵛ   1. *Tribune*.   Thinke not of him.
There is no danger, all these prodegies   30
That doe affright you rise from naturall causes,
And though you doe ascribe them to your selfe,
Had you ne're beene, had happen'd.
   Cæsar.   'Tis well said,
Exceeding well braue souldier. Can it be
That I that feele my selfe in health, and strength   35
Should still beleeue I am so neare my end,
And haue my guards about me? perish all
Predictions, I grow constant they are false
And built vpon vncertainties.
   1. *Tribune*.   This is right.
Now *Cæsar's* heard like *Cæsar*.
   Cæsar.   We will to   40
The Campe, and hauing there confirmd the souldier
With a large *Donatiue*, and increase of pay
Some shall—I say no more.

Enter PARTHENIUS.

   Parthenius.   All happinesse,
Securitie, long life attend vpon
The Monarch of the World.
   Cæsar.   Thy lookes are cheerefull.   45
   Parthenius. And my relation full of ioy and wonder.
Why is the care of your imperiall body
My Lord, neglected? the fear'd houre being past
In which your life was threatned.
   Cæsar.   Is't past fiue?

23. ease] *29*; care *conj. McIlwraith*   26. six] *Coxeter*; fix *29*   28. I] *Massinger MS*; I *29* (*defective*)   30. danger,] *Massinger MS*; ~ₐ *29*   35. health,] *Massinger MS*; ~ₐ *29*   40. heard] *Massinger MS*; hard *29*   48. neglected?] *Massinger MS*; ~ₐ *29*

Parthenius. Past six vpon my knowledge, and in iustice   50
Your Clocke master should dye that hath deferd
Your peace so long. There is a post new lighted
That brings assur'd intelligence, that your legions
In *Siria* haue wonne a glorious day,
And much enlarg'd your Empire. I haue kept him   55
Conceal'd that you might first pertake the pleasure
In priuate, and the Senate from your selfe
Be taught to vnderstand how much they owe
To you and to your fortune.
    Cæsar.   Hence pale feare then.
K4ʳ Lead me *Parthenius.*
    1. *Tribune.*   Shall we waite you?
    Cæsar.   No.   60
After losses Guards are vsefull, know your distance.
                Exeunt CÆSAR *and* PARTHENIUS.
    2. *Tribune.* How strangely hopes delude men, as I liue
The houre is not yet come.
    1. *Tribune.*   Howere we are
To pay our duties, and obserue the sequele.   *Exeunt* TRIBUNES

    Enter CÆSAR, *and* PARTHENIUS.

Domitia. I heare him comming, be constant.
    Cæsar.   Where *Parthenius*
Is this glad messenger?
    Stephanos.   Make the doore fast. Heere,   66
A messenger of horror.
    Cæsar.   How! betraid?
    Domitia. No, taken tyranne.
    Cæsar.   My *Domitia,*
In the conspiracie!
    Parthenius.   Behold this booke.
    Cæsar. Nay then I am lost. Yet though I am vnarm'd   70
I'll not fall poorely.   *Orethrowes* STEPHANOS.
    Stephanos.   Helpe me.
    Entellus.   Thus, and thus.
    Sijeius. Are you so long a falling?

50. in iustice] *29*¹˒²; iniustice *29*³   65–9. *rearranged by Gifford; 29 reads* I . . .
constant. / Where . . . messenger. / Make . . . horror. / How! betraid? / No . . . tyranne. /
My . . . conspiracie. / Behold . . . booke.   68. *Domitia*,] *Massinger MS*; ∼ˌ *29*

Cæsar.   'Tis done, 'tis done basely.
                                         Falls, and dyes.
Parthenius. This for my Fathers death.
Domitia.   This for my *Paris*.
Iulia. This for thy Incest.   *These seuerally stab him.*
Domitilla.   This for thy abuse
Of *Domitilla*.

                  Enter TRIBUNES.

  I. *Tribune*. Force the doores. O *Mars*!   75
What haue you done?
   Parthenius.   What *Rome* shall giue vs thanks for.
   Stephanos. Despatch'd a Monster.
   I. *Tribune*.   Yet he was our Prince
How euer wicked, and in you 'tis murther
Which whosoe're succeeds him will reuenge.
Nor will we that seru'd vnder his command   80
Consent that such a monster as thy selfe
(For in thy wickednesse, *Augusta's* title
Hath quite forsooke thee) thou that wert the ground
Of all these mischiefes, shall goe hence vnpunish'd.
Lay hands on her. And drag her to her sentence;   85
We will referre the hearing to the Senate
Who may at their best leisure censure you.
Take vp his body. He in death hath payd
For all his cruelties. Heere's the difference:
Good Kings are mourn'd for after life, but ill   90
And such as gouern'd onely by their will
And not their reason, vnlamented fall;
No Goodmans teare shed at their Funerall.   *Exeunt omnes. Florish.*

                  FINIS.

  74 *Domitilla*.] *Coxeter*; *Domit*. 29   74–5 abuse / Of] *Gifford*; *undivided* 29
78. 'tis] *Massinger MS*; this 29   85. to her] *Massinger MS* (to Her); to 29
92. reason, vnlamented fall;] *Gifford*; reason. Vnlamented fall 29

THE GREAT DUKE OF FLORENCE

INTRODUCTION

(a) *Date*

Malone noted that '*The Great Duke* was licensed for the Queen's Servants, July 5, 1627';[1] there can be little doubt that by this title *The Great Duke of Florence* was meant: the title-page of the first edition in 1636 confirms the theatrical company—'her Maties Servants at the Phœnix'—and it is unlikely that one company would have two plays of such similar names. But if we are to date *The Great Duke of Florence* in 1627 it becomes the only play written by Massinger for a company other than the King's men after the death of Fletcher in 1625; this has perturbed Johanne Stochholm, who edited the play in 1933, and also Bentley. Miss Stochholm suggested that the play was written in 1624 and that the licensing was delayed. Bentley accepts the licence as indicating the approximate date of composition 'with serious misgivings' (iv. 788). Although the long list of plays written exclusively for the King's men after 1625 suggests that there must have been an agreement of some kind between Massinger and the company, there is no certainty that he was under contract to them. If a contract did exist, it might not have been arranged immediately after Fletcher's death. *The Great Duke of Florence* may have been the last play written by Massinger as a freelance. If Massinger *was* under contract to the King's men in 1627, then we must assume (*a*) that the submission of *The Great Duke of Florence* was illegitimate, or (*b*) that Massinger had in earlier times undertaken to produce the play for Beeston, had been paid for it, but was very slow in delivering the copy, or (*c*) that Beeston had kept the play from before 1625 and took his time to have it licensed and performed, or (*d*) that the King's men were offered the play and refused it, or (*e*) that Herbert's licence refers to another play. Of these possibilities (*b*) seems by far the most likely. There is no strong reason for questioning 1627 as the date of the play.

---

[1] Variorum Shakespeare, 1821, iii. 230; Adams, *Herbert*, p. 31.

(b) *Source*

No immediate source for *The Great Duke of Florence* is known. The basic plot, concerning a ruler who, intending to marry, sends one of his nobles to report on the beauty of a certain young woman, and then is deceived by the nobleman who has fallen in love with the girl himself and tells a false tale of her ugliness, derives from the legend of the English king Edgar's wooing of Alfrida, first told by William of Malmesbury in the twelfth century. The various versions of this story are described at length by Johanne Stochholm in her edition. Holinshed wrote it up in 1578, and then came the anonymous play, *A Knack to Know a Knave*, acted in 1592 and published in 1594; this tedious work weaves its moral way round a simple retelling of the Edgar–Alfrida story and then changes the usual savage conclusion into a happy ending.[1] It seems that Massinger must have known this play, because it contains the device by which the nobleman attempts to justify his untrue report of the young lady's plainness: the substitution of a kitchen wench for the real person. Massinger not only takes over this incident but also echoes the language of the earlier play in the kitchen-maid's words to the scandalized ruler:

> Come I pray, sit down, you are welcome by my troth,
> As God saue me heres neuer a napkin, fie, fie.
> Come on, I pray eat some plums, they be sugar,
> Heres good drinke by Ladie, why do you not eate?[2]

In the parallel scene in Massinger, we have the following:

> Will your Dukeship
> Sit down and eat some Sugar-plums? . . .
>
> . . . .
>
> . . . and here is wine too
> As good as e're was tap'd.
>
> (IV. ii. 163–8)

There is no real contact between the plays except in this incident.

Johanne Stochholm gave a detailed account of Lope de Vega's play based on the Edgar–Alfrida legend, *Comedia famosa de la hermosa Alfreda* (supposed to have been written by 1601). It seems

---

[1] For a full comparison of the old play with Massinger's, see Stochholm, and also H. A. Shands, 'Massinger's "The Great Duke of Florence" und seine Quellen', Halle, 1902 (dissertation).

[2] Malone Society Reprint, lines 1508–11.

to have no relation with Massinger's play. Indeed there is no known source for Massinger's introduction of Giovanni and the love between him and Lidia, nor for making a mystery of the Duke's intentions towards Lidia. The performance of a play called 'cosmo' or 'cossmo' was recorded by Henslowe in 1593, and if this means Cosimo Duke of Florence it may be connected with a play called *Der Herzog von Florenz* which was acted by an English touring company in Austria and Saxony in 1608 and 1626.[1] We know that in this latter play the Duke falls in love with a nobleman's daughter, and we should keep open the possibility that Massinger was in some way indebted to it. But it is more than likely that translating the Edgar–Alfrida story to Florence was his own idea, and that, following his usual custom, he boldly treated a traditional fiction as though it were comparatively recent European history (Cosimo I was Duke of Florence from 1537 to 1574; Cosimo II from 1609 to 1621).

(c) *Text*

The Great Duke of Florence was entered in the Stationers' Register on 7 December, 1635:

M^r. Marriott.   Entred for his Copie vnder the hands of S^r. Henry Herbert & M^r. Smethwicke warden The great Duke of fflorence a Comicall history by Phil: Massinger   vj^d.

(Register D 325; Greg, *Bibliography*, i. 44; Arber, iv. 351)

The play was regularly published by John Marriot in 1636. This edition, the only early one, will be referred to as *36*; the title-page is reproduced on p. 101. The printer's name is not mentioned. Sayle (*Early English Printed Books*, no. 4137) thought the printer was probably Miles Flesher, and McIlwraith confirmed this (Thesis, i. 461) by noting that Thomas Goodwin's *A Childe of Light* . . . printed in 1636 by 'M. F.' contains what seems to be identical type, similar watermarks, and uses three times the ornament which heads A3^r in *36*. (Christopher Dow's *A Discourse of the Sabbath* printed by 'M. Flesher' in 1636 also uses this ornament.)

36 is in quarto, A^4 (–A1), B–K^4, L1 (40 leaves); see Greg, *Bibliography*, no. 505; ii. 650. The last page of the text, L1, is really the first leaf of A, on the remaining leaves of which the preliminaries were printed. In the Huntington copy, the commendatory verses

---

[1] Stochholm's edition, pp. xv–xxii.

by George Donne and Ford, on an unsigned leaf usually found as A4 in the preliminaries, follow L1 and the two leaves are conjugate. A4 has been noted as following A2 in two copies, and as missing in another. When properly bound up, the contents are: A2^r, *title*; A2^v, 'The Actors names.'; A3^r, *dedication begins*, 'TO THE TRULY HONORED, AND MY NOBLE Favourer, Sir ROBERT WISEMAN Knight, of *Thorrells* Hall in ESSEX.'; A3^v, '*The Epistle Dedicatorie.*', *dedication ends*, *signed* 'PHILIP MASSINGER.'; A4^r, *verse epistle*, 'On his great Duke of Florence; To M^r. PHILIP MASSINGER, my much esteemed friend.', *signed* 'GEORGE DONNE.'; A4^v, *verse epistle*, 'To the deserving memory, of this worthy Worke, and the Author, M^r. PHILIP MASSINGER.', *signed* 'IOHN FORD.'; B1^r, 'A COMICAL HISTORY OF THE GREAT DVKE OF FLORENCE.', *text begins*; L1^v, *text ends*, '*The end.*'. The text is in roman, 20 lines measuring approximately 80 mm.

Slight irregularities in this well-printed play do not present a serious problem. There are normally 38 lines to a page, but F2^v, H1^v, I1^v have 39 lines each, and K4^r, K4^v, and L1^r have 37 lines each. The variation in the number of lines, coupled with occasional crowding of the verse, suggests that the copy had been inaccurately cast off. The evidence of the type used in the headlines makes it clear that two skeleton formes were used in the printing; the skeletons were changed about (inner for outer and *vice versa*) in imposing sheet C, and returned to their original placings again at sheet E. A curious inconsistency in the text is that proper names, regularly italicized in sheets B and C, begin to appear in roman in sheet C, and are printed almost entirely in roman in the remaining sheets. Unfortunately, there is insufficient evidence for differentiating the work of compositors, so that it is impossible to say whether the roman names are the result of an individual quirk or a printing-house decision. The letters v and j are printed in the modern way throughout the play, though occasional lapses show that this procedure was still novel (see the introduction to *The Maid of Honour*); in successive lines we have 'Juno' and 'Iupiter' (IV. ii. 179–80); V sometimes appears for U.

In fourteen copies collated, McIlwraith found variant readings in four formes out of the twenty; Miss Stochholm's collations of eleven copies add two further press-corrections; a total of eight corrections are entered in the present edition.

The neat printing suggests a tidy manuscript. The full stage-directions are interesting examples of Massinger's concern to indicate action and gesture; the best is, '*This spoke as if shee studied an evasion.*' (IV. i. 106). We have also '*Claps him on the shoulder.*' (IV. i. 43); '*Rises and resignes his chair.*' (IV. ii. 207); '*The Duke admiring Lidia.*' (V. ii. 79); '*Calandrino still looking on his instructions.*' (II. i. 38); '*Makes Antique curtesies.*' (II. i. 53). There are many other detailed directions. Although Massinger's spellings are not preserved, it is more than likely that the capitalised 'Hee' in the first few pages of the text is preserved from his autograph (it is frequent in *Believe As You List*). The frequency of permissive entries ('*and others*', for example) makes it unlikely that the manuscript had been worked over for the theatre. The most cogent evidence that the printer's copy was Massinger's own autograph manuscript lies in the misnaming of minor characters: Massinger was forgetfully generous with the name Lodovico and at different times gave it to three different characters (see note to V. i. 30); the error would not have remained in a revised manuscript, certainly not in one intended for use in the theatre.

There are copies of *36* in the following libraries and institutions: University of Arizona; Bodleian Library (2 copies); Boston Public Library; British Museum (4 copies); Cambridge University Library; Chapin Library, Williamstown; Chetham's Library, Manchester; University of Chicago; Clark Library, University of California; Library of Congress; Folger Shakespeare Library; University of Glasgow, Hunterian Collection; Harvard College Library; Huntington Library; University of Illinois; King's College, Cambridge; University of Leeds, Brotherton Library; University of Liverpool (2 copies); University of London; Merton College, Oxford; University of Michigan; Pierpont Morgan Library; National Library of Scotland; Newberry Library; University of Newcastle; New York Public Library; Ohio State University; University of Pennsylvania; Pforzheimer Collection; Princeton University; Royal Library, The Hague; Shakespeare Birthplace Trust, Stratford-upon-Avon; University of Texas (2 copies); Trinity College, Cambridge; Alexander Turnbull Library, Wellington, New Zealand; Victoria and Albert Museum (3 copies); Wadham College, Oxford; Worcester College, Oxford; Yale University (2 copies).

The text of the present edition has been prepared from the British Museum copy, 644. e. 80.

The Great Duke of Florence has been very rarely reprinted; apart from appearing in the standard collected editions, it was published in Harness's selection of expurgated texts in 1830, and Symons included it in volume i of his Mermaid selection, 1887. Johanne M. Stochholm published a full edition with introduction and notes in 1933 (Baltimore); it had been submitted for the degree of Ph.D. at Bryn Mawr College; it is referred to in the text-notes as *Stochholm*.

A German translation appeared in 1904 in vol. ii of Robert Prölss' *Alt englisches Theater* (see Chelli, *Étude sur la collaboration*, p. 287).

(d) *Stage History and Adaptation*

The Great Duke of Florence was first performed, as we have seen, by Christopher Beeston's company, Queen Henrietta Maria's men, at the Phœnix in 1627. It remained in repertory at the Phœnix (or Cockpit), for it is one of the plays protected for William Beeston by the Lord Chamberlain in 1639 (Bentley, i. 330–1). So far as is known, the play was not staged again until the present century. A. H. Cruickshank has a note in his book on Massinger published in 1920 that 'Mr. Ben Greet's Company has from time to time given a charming alfresco performance of *The Great Duke of Florence*' (p. 70). Sir Ben Greet, the actor-manager (1857–1936), was a pioneer of open-air performances of Shakespeare, and one of those responsible for founding the Shakespeare tradition at the Old Vic during the first world war. From 23 to 25 February 1922, an amateur group including 'Mr Ledward, Mr Colbourne and Mr Ramage, reinforced by Miss Cathleen Nesbitt and Miss Elizabeth Pollock' performed *The Great Duke of Florence* in the Middle Temple Hall in aid of the Inns of Court Mission.[1]

In 1927, William Archer published *Three Plays*, the third of which is *Lidia: Comedy in Four Acts, Suggested by Massinger's 'Great Duke of Florence'*. It is very bad, written in a ridiculous kind of antique blank verse and full of whimsy. The plot is a good deal altered.[2]

---

[1] See *The Spectator*, 18 Feb. 1922; a programme has been preserved at the Bodleian, in *The Poetical Register*, ii. 2 (Thorn-Drury. d. 6).

[2] *Lidia* is really better forgotten; it is difficult to see why Jonas M. Barish thinks it worth comparing it with the original and demolishing it. See 'The New Theatre and the Old: Reversions and Rejuvenations', in *Reinterpretations of Elizabethan Drama*, ed. N. Rabkin (English Institute Essays) 1969, pp. 8–9.

THE
GREAT DVKE
OF
FLORENCE.

A Comicall Historie.

As it hath beene often presented with good
allowance by her Maties Servants at the
Phœnix in Drurie Lane.

Written by PHILIP MASSINGER.

LONDON:
Printed for JOHN MARRIOT.   1636.

Cozimo, *Duke of* Florence.
Giovanni, *Nephew to the Duke.*
Lodovico Sanazarro, *the Dukes Favorite.*
Carolo Charomonte, *Giovanni his Tutor.*   5
Contarino, *Secretary to the Duke.*
Alphonso, ⎱
Hippolito, ⎰ *Counsailors of State.*
Hieronimo, ⎰
Calandrino, *A merrie fellow, servant to* Giovanni.   10
Bernardo, ⎱
Caponi, ⎰ *Servants to* Carolo Charomonte.
Petruchio, ⎰
[Gentleman.]
[Servant.]   15
Fiorinda, *Dutchesse of* Urbin.
Lidia, *daughter to* Carolo Charomonte.
Calaminta, *Servant to* Fiorinda.
Petronella, *Servant to* Lidia.

14. Gentleman.] *Gifford*; *not in 36*   15. Servant.] *editor*; *not in 36*

To the Truly Honored, and my Noble Favourer, Sir ROBERT WISEMAN Knight, of *Thorrells* Hall in ESSEX.

SIR:

As I dare not be ungratefull for the many benefits you have hereto- 5
fore conferr'd upon me, so I have just reason to feare that my
attempting this way to make satisfaction (in some measure) for so
due a debt, will further ingage me. However examples encourage me.
The most able in my poore Quality have made use of Dedications
in this Nature, to make the world take notice (as farre as in them 10
lay) who, and what they were that gave supportment, and protection
to their Studies, being more willing to publish the Dooer, then
receive a benefit in a corner. For my selfe, I wil freely, and with
A3ᵛ a zealous thankfulnesse acknowledge, that for many yeares I had
but faintly subsisted, if I had not often tasted of your Bounty. But 15
it is above my strength, and faculties, to celebrate to the desert,
your noble inclination, (and that made actuall) to raise up, or to
speak more properly, to rebuild the ruines of demolish'd Poesie.
But that is a worke reserved, and will be, no doubt, undertaken, and
finished, by one that can to the life expresse it. Accept I beseech you 20
the tender of my service, and in the list of those you have obliged
to you, contemne not the Name of

Your true and

faithfull Honorer

PHILIP MASSINGER. 25

On his great Duke of Florence;
To M^r. PHILIP MASSINGER, my
much esteemed friend.

Enjoy thy Lawrell! 'tis a noble choice,
　Not by the suffrages of voice
Procur'd; but by a conquest so atchiev'd
　As that thou hast at full reliev'd
Almost neglected Poetrie; whose Bayes　　　　　　5
　(Sullid by childish thirst of praise)
Wither'd into a dulnesse of Despaire,
　Had not thy later labour (heire
Vnto a former industrie) made knowne
　This Work, which thou may'st call thine owne,　　10
So rich in worth, that th'ignorant may grudge
To finde true vertue is become their Iudge.

GEORGE DONNE.

To the deserving memory, of this worthy Worke,
and the Author, Mʳ. PHILIP MASSINGER.

Action *gives many Poems right to live,*
This Piece *gave life to* Action*; and will give*
For state, and language, in each change of Age,
To Time, delight; and honour to the stage.
Should late prescription faile which fames that Seat,   5
This Pen, might style The Duke of Florence Great.
Let many Write; Let much be Printed; read,
And censur'd; Toyes; no sooner hatch't, then dead.
Here, without blush to Truth of commendation,
Is prov'd, how Art hath out-gone Imitation.   10

IOHN FORD.

A Comical History of
The Great Duke of Florence

Actus primi Scena prima.

CAROLO CHAROMONTE. CONTARINO.

Carolo. YOU bring your welcome with you.
Contarino. Sir, I finde it
In every circumstance.
Carolo. Againe most welcome.
Yet give me leave to wish (and pray you excuse mee,
For I must use the freedome I was borne with)
The great Dukes pleasure had commanded you   5
To my poore house upon some other service,
Not this you are designde to; but his will
Must be obeyde, how ere it ravish from me
The happy conversation of one
As deere to me as the old Romans held   10
Their houshold *Lars*, whom they beleev'd had power
To blesse and guard their Families.
Contarino. 'Tis receiv'd so
On my part Signior; nor can the Duke
But promise to himselfe as much as may
Be hop'd for from a Nephew. And t'were weaknesse   15
In any man to doubt, that *Giovanni*
Train'd up by your experience and care
In all those Arts peculiar, and proper
To future Greatnesse, of necessity
Must in his actions being growne a man   20
Make good the Princely education
Which Hee deriv'd from you.
Carolo. I have discharg'd,

To the utmost of my power, the trust the Duke
Committed to me, and with joy perceive
B1ᵛ The seed of my endeavours was not sowen   25
Upon the barren sands, but fruitfull glebe,
Which yeelds a large encrease; my noble Charge,
By his sharp wit, and pregnant apprehension
Instructing those that teach him; making use
Not in a vulgar and pedantique forme   30
Of what's read to him, but 'tis streight digested
And truly made his owne. His grave discourse,
In one no more indebted unto yeares,
Amazes such as heare him; horsmanship
And skill to use his weapon are by practise   35
Familiar to him; as for Knowledge in
Musique, He needs it not, it being borne with him,
All that He speaks being with such grace deliver'd
That it makes perfit harmony.
    Contarino.   You describe
A wonder to me.
    Carolo.   Sir, he is no lesse,   40
And that there may be nothing wanting that
May render him compleat, the sweetnesse of
His disposition so winnes on all
Appointed to attend him, that they are
Rivalls ev'n in the coursest office, who   45
Shall get præcedencie to doe him service:
Which they esteeme a greater happinesse
Then if they had beene fashion'd, and built up
To hold command o're others.
    Contarino.   And what place
Does he now blesse with his presence?
    Carolo.   He is now   50
Running at the ring, at which he's excellent.
He does alott for every exercise
A severall houre, for Sloath the Nurse of vices
And rust of action, is a stranger to him.
But I feare I am tedious, let us passe   55
If you please to some other subject, though I cannot
Deliver him as he deserves.
    Contarino.   You have giv'n him

B2ʳ A noble character.

    Carolo.   And how I pray you
(For we that never looke beyond our villa's
Must be inquisitive) are State affaires   60
Carried in Court?

    Contarino.   There's little alteration.
Some rise, and others fall; as it stands with
The pleasure of the Duke, their great disposer.

    Carolo. Does *Lodovico Sanazarro* hold
Waight, and grace with him?

    Contarino.   Every day new honours   65
Are showr'd upon him, and without the envie
Of such as are good men; since all confesse
The service done our Master in his warres
'Gainst *Pisa*, and *Sienna*, may with justice
Claime what's conferr'd upon him.

    Carolo.   'Tis said nobly.   70
For Princes never more make knowne their wisdome
Then when they cherish goodnesse, where they finde it;
They being men, and not Gods, *Contarino*,
They can give wealth and titles, but no vertues;
That is without their power. When they advance   75
(Not out of judgement, but deceiving fancie)
An undeserving man, how ere set of
With all the trim of greatnesse, state, and power,
And of a creature ev'n growne terrible
To him from whom he tooke his Gyant forme,   80
This thing is still a Comet, no true starre;
And when the bounties feeding his false fire
Begin to faile, will of it selfe goe out,
And what was dreadfull, prooves ridiculous.
But in our *Sanazarro* 'tis not so,   85
He being pure and tride gold, and any stamp
Of grace to make him currant to the world
The Duke is pleas'd to give him, will adde honor
To the great bestower, for he though allow'd
Companion to his Master, still preserves   90
His Majestie in full lustre.

B2ᵛ   *Contarino.*   Hee indeede

              67. men;] *Coxeter*; ~. *36*

At no part does take from it, but becomes
A partner of his cares, and eases him,
With willing shoulders, of a burthen, which
Hee should alone sustaine.
 Carolo.   Is Hee yet married?   95
 Contarino. No Signior, still a Batchelor, how e're
It is apparent, that the choycest Virgin
For beauty, bravery, and wealth in *Florence*,
Would with her Parents glad consent, be woon
(Were his affection, and intent but knowne)   100
To be at his devotion.
 Carolo.   So I think too.

    Enter GIOVANNI *and* CALANDRINO.

But break we off. Here comes my Princely charge.
Make your approaches boldly, you will finde
A courteous entertainment.
 Giovanni.   Pray you forbeare
My hand, good Signior. 'Tis a ceremony   105
Not due to me. 'Tis fit we should embrace
With mutuall armes.
 Contarino. It is a favour Sir
I grieve to be denide.
 Giovanni.   You shall o're-come.
But 'tis your pleasure, not my pride that grants it.
Nay pray you Guardian, and good Sir, put on: 110
How ill it shewes to have that reverend head
Be uncover'd to a Boy!
 Carolo.   Your Excellence
Must give me liberty to observe the distance
And duty that I owe you.
 Giovanni.   Owe me duty?
I doe professe, and when I doe denie it   115
Good fortune leave me, you have beene to me
A second Father, and may justly challenge
(For trayning up my youth in Arts, and Armes)
As much respect, and service, as was due
To him that gave me life. And did you know Sir   120
Or will beleeve from me, how many sleepes
B3ʳ Good *Charomonte* hath broken in his care

To build me up a man, you must confesse
Chiron the Tutor to the great *Achilles*
Compar'd with him, deserves not to be nam'd.   125
And if my gracious Uncle the great Duke
Still holds me worthy his consideration,
Or findes in me ought worthy to be lov'd,
That little rivolet flow'd from this spring,
And so from me report him.
    Contarino.   Fame already   130
Hath fill'd his Highnesse eares with the true story
Of what you are, and how much better'd by him.
And 'tis his purpose to reward the travaile
Of this grave Sir with a magnificent hand.
For though his tendernesse hardly could consent   135
To have you one houre absent from his sight,
For full three yeares he did denie himselfe
The pleasure Hee tooke in you, that you, here
From this great Master might arrive unto
The Theory of those high mysteries   140
Which you by action must make plaine in Court.
'Tis therefore his request (and that from him
Your Excellence must grant a strict command)
That instantly (it being not five houres riding)
You should take horse, and visit him. These his letters   145
Will yeeld you farther reasons.
    Calandrino.   To the Court!
Farewell the flower then of the Countries garland.
This is our Sunne, and when Hee's set, we must not
Expect or Spring, or Summer, but resolve
For a perpetuall Winter.
    Carolo.   Pray you observe   150
The frequent changes in his face.   GIOVANNI *reading the Letter.*
    Contarino.   As if
His much unwillingnesse to leave your house,
Contended with his duty.
    Carolo.   Now he appeares
Collected and resolv'd.
    Giovanni.   It is the Duke!
The Duke upon whose favour, all my hopes   155
And fortunes doe depend. Nor must I check

B3ᵛ

At his commands for any private motives
That doe invite my stay here, though they are
Almost not to be master'd. My obedience
In my departing suddenly shall confirme   160
I am his Highnesse creature. Yet I hope
A little stay to take a solemne farewell
For all those ravishing pleasures I have tasted
In this my sweet retirement, from my Guardian,
And his incomparable daughter, cannot meete   165
An ill construction.
    Contarino.   I will answer that,
Use your owne will.
    Giovanni.   I would speake to you Sir
In such a phrase as might expresse the thanks
My heart would gladly pay. But—
    Carolo.   I conceive you:
And something I would say, but I must doe it   170
In that dumb rhetorique, which you make use of;
For I doe wish you all—I know not how,
My toughnesse melts, and spite of my discretion
I must turne woman.
    Contarino.   What a sympathie
There is betweene em.
    Calandrino.   Were I on the Rack   175
I could not shed a teare. But I am mad,
And ten to one shall hang my selfe for sorrow
Before I shift my shirt. But heare you Sir,
(I'll separate you) when you are gone, what will
Become of me?
    Giovanni.   Why thou shalt to Court with me.   180
    Calandrino. To see you worried?
    Contarino.   Worried *Calandrino*?
    Calandrino. Yes Sir. For bring this sweet face to the Court
There will be such a longing 'mong the Madames,
Who shall ingrosse it first, nay fight and scratch for't,
That if they be not stop'd, for entertainment   185
They'll kisse his lips off. Nay, if you'll scape so
And not be tempted to a farther danger,
These *Succubæ* are so sharp set, that you must

163. For] *36*; Of *Gifford²*   179. (I'll . . . you)] *after Mason*; ⌃ I'll . . . you. *36*

Give out you are an Eunuch.
   Contarino.   Have a better
Opinion of Court-Ladies, and take care   190
Of your owne stake.
   Calandrino.   For my stake 'tis past caring,
I would not have a bird of uncleane feathers
Hansell his Limetwig, and so much for him.
There's something else that troubles me.
   Contarino.   What's that?
   Calandrino. Why how to behave my self in Court, and tytely. 195
I have beene told the very place transformes men,
And that not one of a thousand, that before
Liv'd honestly in the Country, on plaine Sallads,
But bring him thither, marke me that, and feed him
But a moneth or two with Custards and Court Cakebread,   200
And he turnes Knave immediatly. I would be honest;
But I must follow the fashion, or die a beggar.
   Giovanni. And if I ever reach my hopes, beleeve it
We will share fortunes.
   Carolo.   This acknowledgement
Bindes me your debtor ever.

Enter LIDIA.

                      Here comes one   205
In whose sad lookes you easily may reade
What her heart suffers, in that she is forc'd
To take her last leave of you.
   Contarino.   As I live
A beauty without parallel.
   Lidia.   Must you goe then
So suddenly?
   Giovanni.   There's no evasion, *Lydia*,   210
To gaine the least delay, though I would buy it
At any rate. Greatnesse with private men
Esteem'd a blessing, is to me a curse.
And we, whom for our high births, they conclude
The onely free men, are the onely slaves: 215
Happy the golden meane! had I beene borne
In a poore sordid Cottage; not nurs'd up
With expectation to command a Court:

I might, like such of your condition (Sweetest)
Have tooke a safe and middle course, and not   220
As I am now against my choyse compell'd
Or to lye groveling on the earth, or rais'd
So high upon the pinnacles of State,
That I must either keepe my height with danger,
Or fall with certaine ruine.
    Lidia.   Your owne goodnesse   225
Will be your faithfull guard.
    Giovanni.   O *Lidia.*
    Contarino. So passionate!
    Giovanni.   For had I beene your equall
I might have seene and lik'd with mine own eyes,
And not as now with others; I might still,
And without observation, or envie,   230
As I have done, continued my delights
With you, that are alone in my esteeme
The abstract of Society; we might walke
In solitary Groves, or in choyce Gardens;
From the variety of curious flowers   235
Contemplate natures workmanship, and wonders.
And then for change, neare to the murmur of
Some bubling fountaine, I might heare you sing,
And from the well-tun'd accents of your tongue
In my imagination conceive   240
With what mellodious harmony a Quire
Of Angells sing above, their Makers praises.
And then with chast discourse, as we return'd,
Impe feathers to the broken wings of Time,
And all this I must part from.
    Contarino.   You forget   245
The hast impos'd upon us.
    Giovanni.   One word more
And then I come. And after this, when with
Continued innocence, of love, and service,
Cı^r I had growne ripe for Hymenæall joyes,
Embracing you, but with a lawfull flame,   250
I might have beene your husband.
    Lidia.   Sir, I was
And ever am your servant, but it was,

And 'tis farre from me, in a thought to cherish
Such sawcie hopes: If I had beene the heire
Of all the Globes and Scepters mankind bowes to,   255
At my best you had deserv'd me; as I am
How e're unworthy, in my virgin zeale
I wish you as a partner of your bed,
A Princesse equall to you, such a one
That may make it the study of her life,   260
With all th'obedience of a wife to please you.
May you have happy issue, and I live
To be their humblest handmayde.
     Giovanni.   I am dumb,
And can make no reply.
     Contarino.   Your Excellence
Will be benighted.
     Giovanni.   This kisse bath'd in teares   265
May learne you what I should say.
     Lidia.   Give me leave
To wayt on you to your horse.
     Carolo.   And me to bring you
To the one halfe of your journey.
     Giovanni.   Your love puts
Your age to too much trouble.
     Carolo.   I grow young
When most I serve you.
     Contarino.   Sir, the Duke shal thank you.   270
                                        Exeunt omnes.

Actus primi Scæna secunda.

ALPHONSO, HIPPOLITO, HIERONIMO, *with a Petition.*

Alphonso. His Highnesse cannot take it ill.
     Hippolito.   However,
We with our duties shall expresse our care
For the safety of his Dukedome.
     Hieronimo.   And our loves

               Enter COZIMO *the Duke.*
To his person. Here he comes. Present it boldly.

Cozimo. What needs this form? we are not grown so proud   5
As to disdaine familiar conference
With such as are to counsaile, and direct us.
This kinde of adoration shew'd not well
In the old Roman Emperors, who forgetting
That they were flesh and blood, would be styl'd gods,   10
In us to suffer it were worse. Pray you rise.
Still the old suit; with too much curiousnesse   *Reades.*
You have too often search'd this wound, which yeelds
Security and rest, not trouble to me.
For here you grieve, that my firme resolution   15
Continues me a Widdower; and that
My want of issue to succeede me in
My government, when I am dead, may breed
Distraction in the State, and make the name
And family of the Medices, now admir'd,   20
Contemptible.
    Hippolito. And with strong reasons Sir.
    Alphonso. For were you old and past hope to beget
The modell of your selfe, we should be silent.
    Hieronimo. But being in your height and pride of yeeres
As you are now great Sir, and having too   25
In your possession the daughter of
The deceas'd Duke of *Vrbin*, and his heire,
Whose Guardian you are made, were you but pleas'd
To think her worthy of you, besides children
The Dukedome she brings with her for a dower,   30
Will yeeld a large encrease of strength and power
To those faire territories, which already
Acknowledge you their absolute Lord.
    Cozimo.   You presse us
With solid arguments we grant, and though
We stand not bound to yeeld account to any   35
Why we doe this or that (the full consent
Of our Subjects being included in our Will)
We out of our free bounties will deliver
The motives that divert us. You well know
That three yeeres since to our much griefe, we lost   40
Our Dutches, such a Dutches, that the world
In her whole course of life, yeelds not a Lady

C2r

That can with imitation deserve
To be her second: in her grave we buried
All thoughts of woman: let this satisfie   45
For any second marriage. Now whereas
You name the heire of *Vrbin*, as a Princesse
Of great revenues, 'tis confess'd she is so;
But for some causes private to our selfe,
We have dispos'd her otherwise. Yet despaire not,   50
For you ere long with joy shall understand,
That in our Princely care we have provided
One worthy to succeed us.

     Enter LODOVICO SANAZARRO.

Hippolito.   We submit,
And hold the counsailes of great *Cozimo*
Oraculous.
 Cozimo. My *Sanazaro*. Nay,   55
Forbeare all ceremony. You looke sprightly friend,
And promise in your cleare aspect some novell
That may delight us.
 Sanazarro.   O Sir, I would not be
The Harbinger of ought that might distast you.
And therefore know (for 'twere a sinne to torture   60
Your Highnesse expectation) your Vice-Admirall
By my directions hath surpriz'd the Gallies
Appointed to transport the Asian tribute
Of the great Turke, a richer Prize was never
Brought into *Florence*.
 Cozimo.   Still my Nightingale,   65
That with sweet accents doest assure me, that
My Spring of happinesse comes fast upon me.
Embrace me boldly. I pronounce that wretch
An enemy to brave and thriving action,
That dares beleeve, but in a thought, we are   70
Too prodigall in our favours to this man,
Whose merits, though with him we should devide
Our Dukedome, still continue us his debtor.
 Hippolito. 'Tis farre from me.
 Alphonso.   We all applaud it.
 Cozimo. Nay, blush not *Sanazarro*, we are proud   75

Of what we build up in thee, nor can our
Election be disparag'd; since we have not
Receiv'd into our bosome and our grace
A glorious lazie Droane, growne fat with feeding
On others toyle, but an industrious Bee   80
That crops the sweet flowers of our enemies,
And every happy evening returnes
Loaden with wax and hony to our Hive.
    Sanazarro. My best endevours never can discharge
The service I should pay.
    Cozimo.   Thou art too modest,   85
But we will study how to give, and when,
Before it be demanded.

Enter GIOVANNI *and* CONTARINO.

Giovanni!

My Nephew; let me eye thee better Boy.
In thee me thinks my Sister lives againe:
For her love I will be a Father to thee,   90
For thou art my adopted Sonne.
    Giovanni.   Your Servant
And humblest Subject.
    Cozimo.   Thy hard travaile Nephew
Requires soft rest, and therefore we forbeare
For the present an account, how thou hast spent
Thy absent houres. See Signiors, see, our care   95
Without a second bed provides you of
A hopefull Prince. Carrie him to his Lodgings,
And for his farther honour *Sanazarro*
With the rest doe you attend him.
    Giovanni.   All true pleasures
Circle your Highnesse.
    Sanazarro.   As the rising Sunne   100
We doe receive you.
    Giovanni.   May this never set,
But shine upon you ever.
Exeunt GIOVANNI, SANAZARRO, HIERONIMO,
ALPHONSO, HIPPOLITO.

C3ʳ   *Cozimo.*   Contarino!

I. ii. 102 SD. HIPPOLITO] *Gifford*; *Lodovico 36*

Contarino. My gracious Lord.

Cozimo.   What entertainment found you
From *Carolo de Charamonte*?

Contarino.   Free
And bountifull. He's ever like himselfe   105
Noble and hospitable.

Cozimo.   But did my Nephew
Depart thence willingly?

Contarino.   He obey'd your summons
As did become him. Yet it was apparent
But that he durst not crosse your will, he would
Have sojourn'd longer there, he ever finding   110
Variety of sweetest entertainment;
But there was something else, nor can I blame
His youth, though with some trouble he took leave
Of such a sweet companion.

Cozimo.   Who was it?

Contarino. The daughter sir of Signior *Carolo*,   115
Faire *Lidia*, a virgin at all parts,
But in her birth and fortunes, equall to him.
The rarest beauties *Italy* can make boast of,
Are but meere shadowes to her, she the substance
Of all perfection. And what encreases   120
The wonder Sir, her bodies matchlesse forme
Is better'd by the purenesse of her soule.
Such sweet discourse, such ravishing behaviour,
Such charming language, such inchanting manners,
With a simplicity that shames all Courtship,   125
Flow hourely from her, that I doe beleeve
Had *Circe*, or *Calipso* her sweet graces,
Wandring *Vlisses* never had remembred
Penelope, or *Ithaca*.

Cozimo.   Be not rap'd so.

Contarino. Your Excellence would be so had you seen her. 130

Cozimo. Take up. Take up. But did your observation
Note any passage of affection
Betweene her and my Nephew?

Contarino.   How it should
Be otherwise betweene 'em, is beyond
My best imagination. *Cupids* arrowes   135

Were uselesse there, for of necessity
Their yeeres and dispositions doe accord so
They must wound one another.
    Cozimo. Umh! Thou art
My Secretary *Contarino*, and more skill'd
In politique designes of State, then in   140
Thy judgement of a beauty; give me leave
In this to doubt it. Here. Goe to my Cabinet,
You shal find there Letters newly receiv'd
Touching the state of *Vrbin*.
Pray you with care peruse them, leave the search   145
Of this to us.
    Contarino. I doe obey in all things.   *Exit* CONTARINO.
    Cozimo. Lydia! A Diamond so long conceal'd,
And never worne in Court! of such sweet feature?
And he on whom I fixe my Dukedomes hopes,
Made Captive to it! Vmh! 'tis somewhat strange,   150
Our eyes are every where, and we will make
A strict enquiry. *Sanazarro*!

           Enter SANAZARRO.

    Sanazarro. Sir!
    Cozimo. Is my Nephew at his rest?
    Sanazarro. I saw him in bed Sir.
    Cozimo. 'Tis well, and does the Princes *Fiorinda*
(Nay, doe not blush, she is rich *Vrbins* heire)   155
Continue constant in her favours to you?
    Sanazarro. Dread sir, she may dispense them as she pleases,
But I looke up to her as on a Princesse
I dare not be ambitious of, and hope
Her prodigall graces shall not render me   160
Offended to your Highnesse.
    Cozimo. Not a scruple.
He whom I favour as I doe my friend,
May take all lawfull graces that become him.
But touching this hereafter; I have now
(And though perhaps it may appeare a trifle)   165
Serious imployment for thee.

143–4. receiv'd / Touching] *Gifford; undivided 36*   161. Offended] *36*; Offending
Mason; Offender *Gifford*

4ʳ   *Sanazarro.*   I stand ready
For any act you please.
    Cozimo.   I know it friend,
Have you ne're heard of *Lidia* the daughter
Of *Carolo Charamonte*?
    Sanazarro.   Him I know sir
For a noble Gentleman, and my worthy friend,   170
But never heard of her.
    Cozimo.   She is deliver'd
And feelingly to us by *Contarino*
For a master-peece in nature, I would have you
Ride suddenly thither to behold this wonder:
But not as sent by us, that's our first caution: 175
The second is, and carefully observe it,
That though you are a Batchelor, and endow'd with
All those perfections that may take a virgin,
On forfeit of our favour doe not tempt her.
It may be her faire graces doe concerne us.   180
Pretend what businesse you think fit, to gaine
Accesse into her Fathers house, and there
Make full discovery of her, and returne me
A true relation; I have some ends in it
With which we will acquaint you.
    Sanazarro.   This is Sir   185
An easie taske.
    Cozimo.   Yet one that must exact
Your secrecie, and diligence. Let not
Your stay be long.
    Sanazarro.   It shall not sir.
    Cozimo.   Farewell,
And be, as you would keepe our favour, carefull.

Finis Actus primi.

Actus secundi Scæna prima.

FIORINDA. CALAMINTA.

    Fiorinda. HOw does this dressing show?
    Calaminta.   'Tis of itselfe
4ᵛ   Curious and rare: but borrowing ornament

As it does from your Grace, that daines to weare it,
Incomparable.
Fiorinda.   Thou flatter'st me.
Calaminta.   I cannot,
Your Excellence is above it.
    Fiorinda.   Were we lesse perfect,   5
Yet being as we are an absolute Princesse,
We of necessity must be chast, wise, faire,
By our prerogative. Yet all these faile
To move where I would have them. How receiv'd
Count *Sanazarro* the rich Scarfe I sent him   10
For his last Visit?
    Calaminta.   With much reverence,
I dare not say affection. He express'd
More ceremonie in his humble thanks
Then feeling of the favour; and appear'd
Wilfully ignorant in my opinion   15
Of what it did invite him to.
    Fiorinda.   No matter,
He's blinde with too much light. Have you not heard
Of any private Mistresse he's ingag'd to?
    Calaminta. Not any, and this does amaze me Madame,
That he, a Souldier, one that drinks rich wines,   20
Feedes high, and promises as much as *Venus*
Could wish to finde from *Mars*, should in his manners
Be so averse to women.
    Fiorinda.   Troth I know not,
He's man enough, and if he has a haunt,
He preyes farre off like a subtill Fox.
    Calaminta.   And that way   25
I doe suspect him. For I learnt last night
(When the great Duke went to rest) attended by
One private follower, he tooke horse, but whither
He's rid, or to what end I cannot guesse at,
But I will finde it out.
    Fiorinda.   Doe faithfull servant,   30
We would not be abus'd.
               Enter CALANDRINO.
               Who have we here?
D1ʳ   *Calaminta.* How the foole stares!

Fiorinda.   And lookes as if he were
Conning his neck-verse.
    Calandrino.   If I now proove perfect
In my A. B. C. of Courtship, *Calandrino*
Is made for ever; I am sent, let me see,   35
On a how doe you, as they call't.
    Calaminta.   What would'st thou say?
    Calandrino. Let me see my notes. These are her lodgings. Well.
    Calaminta. Art thou an Asse?
    Calandrino.   Peace, thou art a Court wagtaile
To interrupt me.   CALANDRINO *still looking*
    Fiorinda.   He has giv'n it you.   *on his instructions.*
    Calandrino. And then say to th'illustrious *Fi. o. rin. da.*   40
I have it. Which is she?
    Calaminta.   Why this; Fopdoodle.
    Calandrino. Leave chattering Bulfinch: you would put me out,
But 'twill not doe. Then after you have made
Your three obeysances to her, kneele and kisse
The skirt of Gowne. I am glad it is no worse.   45
    Calaminta. And why so sir?
    Calandrino.   Because I was afraid
That after the Italian garbe I should
Have kiss'd her backward.
    Calaminta.   This is sport unlook'd for.
    Calandrino. Are you the Princesse?
    Fiorinda.   Yes sir.
    Calandrino.   Then stand faire
(For I am cholerick) and doe not nip   50
A hopefull blosome. Out againe. Three low   *Reades.*
Obeysances.
    Fiorinda. I am ready.
    Calandrino.   I come on then.
    Calaminta. With much formality.
    Calandrino.   Umph. One. two. three.
                      Makes Antique curtesies.
Thus farre I am right. Now for the last. O rare!
Shee is perfum'd all over! Sure great women   55
Instead of little dogges are priviledg'd
Dɪᵛ To carrie Musk Cats.

      II. i. 37. my] *Coxeter*; thy *36*   45. Gowne] *36*; her gown *Gifford*

Fiorinda. Now the ceremony
Is pass'd, what is the substance?
    Calandrino. I'll peruse
My instructions, and then tell you: Her skirt kiss'd,
Informe her Highnesse, that your Lord,
    Calaminta. Who's that? 60
    Calandrino. Prince Giovanni, who entreates your Grace,
That he with your good favour may have leave
To present his service to you. I think I have nick'd it
For a Courtier of the first forme.
    Fiorinda. To my wonder:

        Enter GIOVANNI *and a* GENTLEMAN.

Returne unto the Prince: but he prevents 65
My answer. Calaminta take him off,
And for the neate delivery of his message
Give him ten Duccats, such rare parts as yours
Are to be cherish'd.
    Calandrino. We will share. I know
It is the custome of the Court, when ten 70
Are promis'd, five is faire. Fie, fie, the Princesse
Shall never know it, so you dispatch me quickly,
And bid me not come to morrow.
    Calaminta. Very good sir.
        Exeunt CALANDRINO *and* CALAMINTA.
    Giovanni. Pray you friend
Informe the Duke I am putting into act 75
When he commanded.
    Gentleman. I am proud to be imploy'd sir.
        Exit GENTLEMAN.
    Giovanni. Madam, that without warrant I presume *They salute.*
To trench upon your Privacies, may argue
Rudenesse of manners. But the free accesse
Your Princely courtesie vouchsafes to all 80
That come to pay their services, gives me hope
To finde a gracious pardon.
    Fiorinda. If you please, not
To make that an offence in your construction,
Which I receive as a large favour from you,
There needes not this Apologie.

Giovanni.   You continue   85
·2ʳ As you were ever, the greatest Mistresse of
Faire entertainment.
      Fiorinda.   You are Sir the Master,
And in the Country have learnt to out-doe
All that in Court is practis'd. But why should we
Talke at such distance? You are welcome sir.   90
We have beene more familiar, and since
You wil impose the Province, you should governe,
Of boldnesse on me, give me leave to say
You are too punctuall. Sit sir, and discourse
As we were us'd.
      Giovanni.   Your Excellence knowes so well   95
How to command, that I can never erre
When I obey you.
      Fiorinda.   Nay, no more of this.
You shall o'recome; no more I pray you sir.
And what delights, pray you be liberall
In your relation, hath the Country life   100
Afforded you?
      Giovanni.   All pleasures gracious Madame,
But the happinesse to converse with your sweet vertues.
I had a grave Instructer, and my houres
Design'd to serious Studies yeelded me
Pleasure with profit in the knowledge of   105
What before I was ignorant in; the Signior
Carolo de Charomonte being skilfull
To guide me through the labyrinth of wilde passions,
That labour'd to imprison my free soule
A slave to vitious Sloath.
      Fiorinda.   You speake him well.   110
      Giovanni. But short of his deserts. Then for the time
Of recreation I was allow'd
(Against the forme follow'd by jealous Parents
In Italy) full liberty to pertake
His daughters sweet society. She's a virgin   115
Happy in all endowments, which a Poet
Could fancie in his Mistresse: being her selfe
A Schoole of goodnesse, where chast Mayds may learne
Ɔ2ᵛ (Without the aydes of forraigne Principles)

By the example of her life and purenesse   120
To be as she is, excellent. I but give you
A briefe Epitome of her vertues, which
Dilated on at large, and to their merit,
Would make an ample Story.
  Fiorinda.   Your whole age
So spent with such a Father, and a Daughter,   125
Could not be tedious to you.
  Giovanni.   True great Princesse:
And now since you have pleas'd to grant the hearing
Of my times expence in the Country, give me leave
To entreate the favour, to be made acquainted
What service, or what objects in the Court   130
Have in your Excellence acceptance, prov'd
Most gracious to you?
  Fiorinda.   I'll meete your demand,
And make a plaine discovery. The Dukes care
For my estate and person holds the first
And choycest place. Then the respect the Courtiers   135
Pay gladly to me, not to be contemn'd.
But that which rais'd in me the most delight
(For I am a friend to valour) was to heare
The noble actions truly reported
Of the brave Count *Sanazarro.* I professe   140
When it hath beene, and fervently deliver'd,
How boldly in the horror of a fight
Cover'd with fire and smoake, and as if nature
Had lent him wings, like lightning he hath falne
Upon the Turkish Gallies, I have heard it   145
With a kinde of pleasure, which hath whisper'd to me
This Worthy must be cherish'd.
  Giovanni.   'Twas a bounty
You never can repent.
  Fiorinda.   I glory in it.
And when he did returne (but still with conquest)
His Armour off, not young Antinous   150
Appear'd more Courtly; all the Graces that
D3^r Render a mans Society deere to Ladies,
Like Pages wayting on him, and it does
Worke strangely on me.

Giovanni.   To divert your thoughts
Though they are fixt upon a noble Subject,   155
I am a suitor to you.
    Fiorinda.   You will aske
I doe presume, what I may grant, and then
It must not be deni'd.
    Giovanni.   It is a favour
For which I hope your Excellence will thank me.
    Fiorinda. Nay, without circumstance.
    Giovanni.   That you would please 160
To take occasion to move the Duke,
That you with his allowance may command
This matchlesse virgin Lidia (of whom
I cannot speake too much) to waite upon you.
She's such a one, upon the forfeit of   165
Your good opinion of me, that will not
Be a blemish to your trayne.
    Fiorinda.   'Tis ranke! He loves her;   *Aside.*
But I will fit him with a suit. I pause not
As if it bred or doubt or scruple in me
To doe what you desire, for I'll effect it,   170
And make use of a faire and fit occasion.
Yet in returne I aske a boone of you,
And hope to finde you, in your grant to me
As I have beene to you.
    Giovanni.   Command me Madame.
    Fiorinda. 'Tis neere allyde to yours. That you would be 175
A Suitor to the Duke, not to expose
(After so many trialls of his faith)
The noble *Sanazarro* to all dangers,
As if he were a wall to stand the furie
Of a perpetuall batterie: but now   180
To grant him after his long labours, rest
And liberty to live in Court, his Armes
And his victorious sword and shield hung up
3ᵛ For monuments.
    Giovanni.   Umph. I'll embrace, faire Princesse,
The soonest oportunity.

<hr>

184. embrace, faire Princesse,] *Coxeter*; embrace ∧ faire Princes ∧ *36*

Enter COZIMO.

The Duke!   185

Cozimo. Nay, blush not; we smile on your privacie,
And come not to disturbe you. You are equalls,
And without prejudice to eithers Honors,
May make a mutuall change of love and Courtship,
Till you are made one, and with holy rites,   190
And we give suffrage to it.

    Giovanni.   You are gracious.

    Cozimo. To our selfe in this. But now break off. Too much
Taken at once of the most curious viands
Dulls the sharp edge of appetite. We are now
For other sports, in which our pleasure is   195
That you shall keepe us company.

    Fiorinda.   We attend you.   *Exeunt.*

[II. ii]   *Actus secundi Scæna secunda.*

BERNARDO. CAPONI. PETRUCHIO.

Bernardo. Is my Lord stirring?

Caponi.   No; He's fast.

Petruchio.   Let us take then
Our morning draught. Such as eate store of Beefe,
Mutton, and Capons, may preserve their healths
With that thin composition call'd small Beere,
As 'tis said they doe in England. But Italians   5
That think when they have sup'd upon an Olive,
A Root, or bunch of Raysins, 'tis a Feast,
Must kill those crudities, rising from cold hearbs,
With hot and lusty wines.

    Caponi.   A happinesse
Those Tramontaines ne're tasted.

    Bernardo.   Have they not   10
Store of wine there?

    Caponi.   Yes, and drink more in two houres
Then the Dutchmen, or the Dane in foure and twenty.

    Petruchio. But what is't? French trash, made of rotten grapes

II. ii. 10. Those] *36²*; These *36¹*

4ʳ And dregs, and lees of Spaine, with Welch Metheglyn,
A drench to kill a horse, but this pure Nectar   15
Being proper to our climate, is too fine
To brook the roughnesse of the Sea. The spirit
Of this begets in us quick apprehensions
And active executions, whereas their
Grosse feeding makes their understanding like it.   20
They can fight, and that's their all.   *They drink.*

> *Enter* SANAZARRO. *A* SERVANT.

Sanazarro.   Security
Dwells about this house I think; the gate's wide open,
And not a servant stirring. See the horses
Set up, and cloath'd.
Servant.   I shall Sir.   [*Exit.*]
Sanazarro.   I'll make bold
To presse a little further.
Bernardo.   Who is this,   25
Count *Sanazarro?*
Petruchio.   Yes, I know him. Quickly
Remove the Flaggon.
Sanazarro.   A good day to you friends.
Nay, doe not conceale your Physick, I approve it,
And if you please will be a Patient with you.
Petruchio. My noble Lord.   *Drinks.*
Sanazarro.   A health to yours. Well done,   30
I see you love your selves. And I commend you,
'Tis the best wisedome.
Petruchio.   May it please your Honour
To walk a turne in the Gallery, I'll acquaint
My Lord with your being here.   *Exit* PETRUCHIO.
Sanazarró.   Tell him I come
For a Visit onely. 'Tis a hansome pile this.   *Exit* SANAZARRO.
Caponi. Why here is a brave fellow, and a right one,   36
Nor wealth, nor greatnesse makes him proud.
Bernardo.   There are
Too few of them, for most of our new Courtiers
(Whose Fathers were familiar with the prices

---

24 SD. *Exit.*] *Gifford*; *not in 36*   37–8. are / Too] *Coxeter*; *undivided in 36*
8118945.3   F

Of oyle, and corne, with when, and where to vent 'em,   40
And left their heires rich from their knowledge that way)
Like gourds shot up in a night, disdaine to speake
D4ᵛ But to cloath of Tissue.

Enter CAROLO CHAROMONTE *in a night-Gown,*
PETRUCHIO *following.*

Carolo.   Stand you prating, knaves,
When such a guest is under my roofe? See all
The roomes perfum'd. This is the man that carries   45
The sway, and swinge of the Court; and I had rather
Preserve him mine with honest offices, then—
But I'll make no comparisons. Bid my daughter
Trim her selfe up to the height, I know this Courtier
Must have a smack at her, and perhaps by his place   50
Expects to wriggle further. If he does
I shall deceive his hopes, for I'll not taint
My Honour for the Dukedome. Which way went he?
Caponi. To the round Gallerie.
Carolo.   I will entertain him   54
As fits his worth, and quality, but no farther.   *Exeunt.*

[II. iii]   *Actus secundi Scæna tertia.*

SANAZARRO *solus.*

Sanazarro. I cannot apprehend, yet I have argu'd
All wayes I can imagine, for what reasons
The great Duke does imploy me hither, and
What does encrease the miracle, I must render
A strict and true account, at my returne   5
Of Lidia this Lords daughter, and describe
In what she's excellent, and where defective.
'Tis a hard task; he that will undergoe
To make a judgement of a womans beauty,
And see through all her plaistrings, and paintings,   10
Had neede of Linceus eyes, and with more ease
May looke like him through nine mud walls, then make
A true discovery of her. But th'intents
And secrets of my Princes heart must be
Serv'd and not search'd into.

40. and where] *Mason*; and to where 36

Enter CAROLO CHAROMONTE.

Carolo.   Most noble Sir   15
Excuse my age subject to ease, and Sloath,
That with no greater speed I have presented
My service with your welcome.
:ı⁻   *Sanazarro.*   'Tis more fit
That I should aske your pardon for disturbing
Your rest at this unseasonable houre.   20
But my occasions carrying me so neere
Your hospitable house, my stay being short to;
Your goodnesse, and the name of friend, which you
Are pleas'd to grace me with, gave me assurance
A Visit would not offend.
Carolo.   Offend, my Lord?   25
I feele my selfe much younger for the favour.
How is it with our gracious Master?
Sanazarro.   He Sir
Holds still his wonted Greatnesse, and confesses
Himselfe your debtor, for your love, and care
To the Prince Giovanni, and had sent   30
Particular thanks by me, had his Grace knowne
The quick dispatch of what I was design'd to
Would have licenc'd me to see you.
Carolo.   I am rich
In his acknowledgement.
Sanazarro.   Sir, I have heard
Your happinesse in a daughter.
Carolo.   Sits the winde there?   [*Aside.*]
Sanazarro. Fame gives her out for a rare master-peece.   36
Carolo. 'Tis a plaine Village Girle Sir, but obedient,
That's her best beauty Sir.
Sanazarro.   Let my desire
To see her, finde a faire construction from you,
I bring no loose thought with me.
Carolo.   You are that way   40
My Lord free from suspition. Her owne manners
(Without an imposition from me)

II. iii. 35 SD. *Aside.*] *Coxeter; not in 36*

Enter LIDIA *and* PETRONELLA.

I hope will prompt her to it. As she is
She's come to make a tender of that service
Which she stands bound to pay.

    Sanazarro.   With your faire leave   45
I make bold to salute you.

    Lidia.   Sir, I, you have it.

E1ᵛ   *Petronella.* I am her Gentlewoman, wil he not
Kisse me to? This is course ifaith.

    Carolo.   How he falls off!

    Lidia. My Lord, though silence best becomes a Mayde,
And to be curious to know but what   50
Concernes my selfe, and with becomming distance,
May argue me of boldnesse, I must borrow
So much of modesty as to enquire
Prince Giovannies health?

    Sanazarro.   Hee cannot want
What you are pleas'd to wish him.

    Lidia.   Would 'twere so,   55
And then there is no blessing that can make
A hopefull and a noble Prince compleat,
But should fall on him. O, he was our North star,
The light and pleasure of our eyes.

    Sanazarro.   Where am I?
I feele my selfe another thing! Can charmes   60
Be writ on such pure Rubies? Her lips melt
Assoone as touch'd! not those smooth gales that glide
O're happy Arabie, or rich Sabæa,
Creating in their passage gummes and spices,
Can serve for a weake simile to expresse   65
The sweetnesse of her breath. Such a brave stature
Homer bestow'd on Pallas, every limbe
Proportion'd to it.

    Carolo.   This is strange; my Lord.

    Sanazarro. I crave your pardon, and yours, matchlesse Mayd,
For such I must report you.

---

46. Sir, I, you] *36*; Sir, you *Coxeter*   47–8. *rearranged by McIlwraith*; I . . . not
kisse me to? / This *36*   50–1. what / Concernes] *Coxeter*; *undivided 36*
53–4. enquire / Prince] *Coxeter*; *undivided 36*   54–5. want / What] *Coxeter*; *undivided 36*

Petronella.   There's no notice   70
Taken all this while of me.
Sanazarro.   And I must adde
If your discourse and reason parallel
The rarenesse of your more then humane forme,
You are a wonder.
Carolo.   Pray you my Lord make triall:
She can speak I can assure you, and that my presence   75
May not take from her freedome, I will leave you.
For know my Lord, my confidence dares trust her
Where, and with whom she pleases.—If he be
2ʳ Taken the right way with her, I cannot fancie
A better match; and for false play I know   80
The tricks, and can discerne them.—Petronella!
Petronella. Yes my good Lord.
Carolo.   I have imployment for you.
          Exeunt CAROLO *and* PETRONELLA.
Lidia. What's your will Sir?
Sanazarro. Madame, you are so large a theame to treat of,
And every Grace about you offers to me   85
Such copiousnesse of language, that I stand
Doubtfull which first to touch at. If I erre,
As in my choyce I may, let me entreat you
Before I doe offend, to signe my pardon,
Let this the Emblem of your innocence   90
Give me assurance.
Lidia.   My hand joyn'd to yours
Without this superstition confirmes it.
Nor neede I feare you will dwell long upon me,
The barrennesse of the subject yeelding nothing
That Rhetorick with all her tropes and figures   95
Can amplifie. Yet since you are resolv'd
To prove your selfe a Courtier in my praise,
As I am a woman (and you men affirme
Our sex loves to be flatter'd) I'll endure it.   CAROLO *above.*
Now when you please begin.   [SANAZARRO] *turnes from her.*
Sanazarro.   Such Lædas paps were,   100
Down pillowes styl'd by Jove. And their pure whitenesse

82 SD. *Exeunt* ... PETRONELLA.] *Coxeter; after* Lord *in* 36   100 SD. SANAZARRO]
editor; not in 36

Shames the Swans Down, or snow. No heat of lust
Swells up her Azure veines. And yet I feele
That this chast Ice but touch'd fans fire in me.
 Lidia. You neede not noble Sir be thus transported,
Or trouble your invention to expresse
Your thought of me: the plainest phrase and language
That you can use, will be too high a straine
For such an humble Theme.
 Sanazarro.   If the great Duke
Made this his end to try my constant temper, 110
Though I am vanquish'd, 'tis his fault, not mine.
For I am flesh and blood, and have affections
E2ᵛ Like other men. Who can behold the Temples,
Or holy Altars, but the Objects worke
Devotion in him? And I may as well 115
Walke over burning iron with bare feet
And be unscorch'd, as looke upon this beauty
Without desire, and that desire pursu'd to,
Till it be quench'd with the enjoying those
Delights, which to atchieve danger is nothing, 120
And loyalty but a word.
 Lidia.   I ne're was proud,
Nor can finde I am guilty of a thought
Deserving this neglect, and strangenesse from you.
Nor am I amorous.
 Sanazarro. Suppose his Greatnesse
Loves her himselfe, why makes he choyce of me 125
To be his agent? it is tyrannie
To call one pinch'd with hunger to a feast,
And at that instant cruelly deny him
To taste of what he sees. Alleageance
Tempted too farre, is like the triall of 130
A good sword on an Anvill; as that often
Flies in peeces without service to the owner;
So trust enforc'd too farre prooves treachery,
And is too late repented.
 Lidia.   Pray you Sir,
Or licence me to leave you, or deliver 135
The reasons which invite you to command
My tedious wayting on you.

Carolo.   As I live
I know not what to think on't. Is't his pride,
Or his simplicity?
Sanazarro.   Whither have my thoughts
Carried me from my selfe? in this my dulnesse,   140
I have lost an oportunity.   *He turnes to her.*
    Lidia.   'Tis true,   *She falls off.*
I was not bred in Court, nor live a starre there,
Nor shine in rich embroideries, and pearle,
As they that are the Mistresses of great fortunes,
Are every day adorn'd with.
    Sanazarro.   Will you vouchsafe   145
Your eare sweet Lady?
    Lidia.   Yet I may be bold
For my integrity, and fame, to ranke
With such as are more glorious. Though I never
Did injurie, yet I am sensible
When I am contemn'd, and scorn'd.
    Sanazarro.   Will you please to heare me?
Lidia. O the difference of natures. Giovanni,   151
A Prince in expectation, when he liv'd here,
Stole courtesie from heaven, and would not to
The meanest servant in my Fathers house
Have kept such distance.
    Sanazarro.   Pray you doe not think me   155
Unworthy of your eare, it was your beauty
That turn'd me statue, I can speake, faire Lady.
    Lidia. And I can heare. The harshnesse of your Courtship
Cannot corrupt my curtesie.
    Sanazarro.   Will you heare me
If I speake of love?
    Lidia.   Provided you be modest,   160
I were uncivill else.
    Carolo.   They are come to parlee,
I must observe this neerer.   CAROLO *descends.*
    Sanazarro.   You are a rare one,
And such (but that my hast commands me hence)
I could converse with ever. Will you grace me
With leave to visit you againe?

162 SD. CAROLO *descends.*] *Coxeter; opposite* else (161) *in 36*

Lidia.   So you   165
At your returne to Court, doe me the favour
To make a tender of my humble service
To the Prince Giovanni.
   Sanazarro.   Ever touching   [*Aside.*]
Upon that string?—And will you give me hope
Of future happinesse?
   Lidia.   That, as I shall finde you.   170
The Fort that's yeelded at the first assault,
E3ᵛ Is hardly worth the taking.

                    Enter CAROLO.

   Carolo.   O, they are at it.
Sanazarro. She is a Magazine of all perfection,
And 'tis death to part from her, yet I must,—
A parting kisse faire Maid.
   Lidia.   That custome grants you.   175
   Carolo. A homely breakfast does attend your Lordship,
Such as the place affords.
   Sanazarro.   No, I have feasted
Already here, my thanks, and so I leave you.
I will see you againe. Till this unhappy houre
I was never lost, and what to doe or say   180
I have not yet determin'd.   *Exit* SANAZARRO.
   Carolo.   Gone so abruptly?
'Tis very strange.
   Lidia.   Under your favour Sir,
His comming hither was to little purpose
For any thing I heard from him.
   Carolo.   Take heede Lidia!
I doe advise you with a Fathers love,   185
And tendernesse of your honour: as I would not
Have you course and harsh in giving entertainment,
So by no meanes be credulous. For great men
Till they have gain'd their ends are Giants in
Their promises, but those obtain'd, weake Pigmies   190
In their performance. And it is a maxime
Alow'd among them, so they may deceive
They may sweare any thing; for the Queen of love

168 SD. *Aside.*] *Gifford*; *not in 36*

As they hold constantly, does never punish,
But smile at Lovers perjuries. Yet be wise too,   195
And when you are su'd to in a noble way,
Be neither nice, nor scrupulous.
    Lidia.   All you speake Sir
I heare as Oracles, nor will digresse
From your directions.
    Carolo.   So shall you keepe   199
Your fame untainted.
    Lidia.   As I would my life Sir.   *Exeunt.*

           Finis Actus secundi.

Actus tertij Scæna prima.

SANAZARRO. SERVANT.

  Sanazarro. LEAVE the horses with my Groomes; but be you
    carefull
With your best diligence, and speed to finde out
The Prince, and humbly in my name entreat him
I may exchange some private conference with him
Before the great Duke know of my arrivall.   5
  Servant. I hast my Lord.
  Sanazarro.   Here I'll attend his comming,
And see you keepe your selfe as much as may be
Conceal'd from all men else.
  Servant.   To serve your Lordship
I wish I were invisible.   *Exit* SERVANT.
  Sanazarro.   I am driven
Into a desperate streight, and cannot steere   10
A middle course; and of the two extreames
Which I must make election of, I know not
Which is more full of horror. Never servant
Stood more ingag'd to a magnificent Master
Then I to Cozimo. And all those honors   15
And glories by his Grace conferr'd upon me,
Or by my prosperous services deserv'd,
If now I should deceive his trust, and make
A shipwrack of my loyalty, are ruin'd.

And on the other side, if I discover   20
Lidias divine perfections, all my hopes
In her are sunke, never to be boy'd up:
For 'tis impossible, but assoone as seene
She must with adoration be su'd to.
A Hermit at his beades, but looking on her,   25
Or the cold Cinique, whom Corinthian Lais,
Not mov'd with her lusts blandishments, call'd a stone,
At this object would take fire. Nor is the Duke
Such an Hippolitus, but that this Phædra
But seene, must force him to forsake the Groves   30
And Dians Huntmanship, proud to serve under
E4ᵛ Venus soft Ensignes. No, there is no way
For me to hope fruition of my ends,
But to conceale her beauties; and how that
May be effected, is as hard a taske   35
As with a vayle to cover the Sunnes beames,
Or comfortable light. Three yeares the Prince
Liv'd in her company, and Contarino
The Secretary, hath possess'd the Duke
What a rare peece she is. But he's my creature,   40
And may with ease be frighted to denie
What he hath said. And if my long experience
With some strong reasons I have thought upon,
Cannot o're-reach a youth, my practise yeelds me
But little profit.

             Enter GIOVANNI *and the* SERVANT.

Giovanni.   You are well return'd Sir.   45
Sanazarro. Leave us.   *Exit* SERVANT.
             When that your Grace shall know the motives
That forc'd me to invite you to this trouble,
You will excuse my manners.
Giovanni.   Sir, there needs not
This circumstance betweene us. You are ever
My noble friend.
Sanazarro.   You shall have further cause   50
To assure you of my faith and zeale to serve you.
And when I have committed to your trust

         III. i. 46 SD. *Exit* SERVANT.] *Gifford*; *at line 48 in 36*

(Presuming still on your retentive silence)
A secret of no lesse importance, then
My honor, nay my head, it will confirme   55
What value you hold with me.
 Giovanni.   Pray you beleeve Sir
What you deliver to me, shall be lock'd up
In a strong Cabinet; of which you your selfe
Shall keepe the key. For here I pawne my Honor
(Which is the best security I can give yet)   60
It shall not be discover'd.
 Sanazarro.   This assurance
Is more then I with modesty could demand
From such a paymaster, but I must be suddaine,
And therefore to the purpose. Can your Excellence
In your imagination conceive   65
On what designe, or whither the Dukes will
Commanded me hence last night?
 Giovanni.   No I assure you,
And it had beene a rudenesse to enquire
Of that I was not call'd to.
 Sanazarro.   Grant me hearing,
And I will make you truly understand,   70
It onely did concerne you.
 Giovanni.   Me my Lord?
 Sanazarro. You in your present state, and future fortunes,
For both lye at the stake!
 Giovanni.   You much amaze me.
Pray you resolve this riddle.
 Sanazarro.   You know the Duke,
If he die issue-lesse (as yet he is)   75
Determines you his Heire.
 Giovanni.   It hath pleas'd his Highnesse
Oft to professe so much.
 Sanazarro.   But say, he should
Be woone to prove a second wife, on whom
He may beget a sonne, how in a moment
Will all those glorious expectations, which   80
Render you reverenc'd and remarkable,
Be in a moment blasted, how e're you are
His much lov'd sisters sonne!

Giovanni.   I must beare it
With patience, and in me it is a duty
That I was borne with: and 'twere much unfit   85
For the receiver of a benefit
To offer for his owne ends, to prescribe
Lawes to the givers pleasure.
      Sanazarro.   Sweetly answer'd,
And like your noble selfe. This your rare temper
So winnes upon me, that I would not live   90
(If that by honest Arts I can prevent it)
To see your hopes made frustrate. And but think
How you shall be transform'd from what you are,
Fɪᵛ Should this (as heaven avert it) ever happen;
It must disturbe your peace. For whereas now,   95
Being as you are receiv'd for the Heire apparant,
You are no sooner seene, but wondred at;
The Signiors making it a businesse to
Enquire how you have slep'd; and as you walke
The streetes of Florence, the glad multitude   100
In throngs presse but to see you, and with joy
The Father, pointing with his finger, tells
His sonne, This is the Prince, the hopefull Prince,
That must hereafter rule, and you obey him.
Great Ladies begge your picture, and make love   105
To that, despairing to enjoy the substance.
And but the last night, when 'twas onely rumor'd
That you were come to Court (as if you had
By Sea past hither from another world)
What generall showts, and acclamations follow'd,   110
The bells rung lowd, the boonfires blaz'd, and such
As lov'd not wine, carrowsing to your health,
Were drunk, and blush'd not at it. And is this
A happinesse to part with?
      Giovanni.   I allow these
As flourishes of Fortune, with which Princes   115
Are often sooth'd, but never yet esteem'd 'em
For reall blessings.
      Sanazarro.   Yet all these were pay'd
To what you may be, not to what you are,
For if the great Duke but shew to his servants

A sonne of his owne, you shall like one obscure   120
Passe unregarded.
    Giovanni.   I confesse, command
Is not to be contemn'd, and if my Fate
Appoint me to it, as I may I'll beare it
With willing shoulders. But my Lord as yet
You have tolde me of a danger comming towards me,   125
But have not nam'd it.
    Sanazarro.   That is soone deliver'd;
Great Cozimo your Uncle, as I more
Then guesse, for 'tis no frivolous circumstance
That does perswade my judgement to beleeve it,
Purposes to be married.
    Giovanni.   Married, Sir?   130
With whom, and on what termes, pray you instruct me?
    Sanazarro. With the faire Lidia.
    Giovanni.   Lidia?
    Sanazarro.   The daughter
Of Signior Charomonte.
    Giovanni.   Pardon me
Though I appeare incredulous, for on
My knowledge, he ne're saw her.
    Sanazarro.   That is granted;   135
But Contarino hath so sung her praises,
And giv'n her out for such a master-peece,
That he's transported with it Sir. And love
Steales sometimes through the eare into the heart
As well as by the eye. The Duke no sooner   140
Heard her describ'd, but I was sent in post
To see her, and returne my judgement of her.
    Giovanni. And what's your censure?
    Sanazarro.   'Tis a pretie creature.
    Giovanni. She's very faire.
    Sanazarro.   Yes, yes, I have seene worse faces.
    Giovanni. Her limbs are neatly form'd.
    Sanazarro.   She hath a waste   145
Indeede siz'd to loves wish.
    Giovanni.   A delicate hand too.
    Sanazarro. Then for a legge and foote.
    Giovanni.   And there I leave you,

For I presum'd no further.
    Sanazarro.   As she is Sir
I know she wants no gracious part that may
Allure the Duke, and if he onely see her   150
She is his owne. He will not be deni'd,
And then you are lost. Yet if you'll second me
(As you have reason, for it most concernes you)
I can prevent all yet.
F2ᵛ   *Giovanni.*   I would you could
A noble way.
    Sanazarro. I will cry downe her beauties;   155
Especially the beauties of her minde,
As much as Contarino hath advanc'd 'em,
And this I hope, will breed forgetfulnesse,
And kill affection in him: but you must
Joyne with me in my report, if you be question'd.   160
    Giovanni. I never told a lye yet, and I hold it
In some degree blasphemous to dispraise
What's worthy admiration. Yet for once
I will dispraise a little, and not varie
From your relation.
    Sanazarro.   Be constant in it.   165

Enter ALPHONSO.

Alphonso. My Lord, the Duke hath seen your man, and wonders
You come not to him. See if his desire
To have conference with you hath not brought him hither
In his owne person.

Enter COZIMO, CONTARINO, HIPPOLITO *and Attendants.*

    Cozimo.   They are comely coursers,
And promise swiftnesse.
    Contarino.   They are of my knowledge   170
Of the best race in Naples.
    Cozimo.   You are Nephew,
As I heare, an excellent horseman, and we like it.
'Tis a faire grace in a Prince. Pray you make triall
Of their strength and speed, and if you think them fit

168–9. *rearranged by Gifford*; To have . . . brought / Him *36*   169 SD. HIPPO-
LITO] *Gifford*; *not in 36*

For your imployment, with a liberall hand   175
Reward the Gentleman, that did present 'em
From the Viceroy of Naples.
   Giovanni.   I will use
My best endevour Sir.
   Cozimo.   Wayte on my Nephew.
              Exeunt GIOVANNI, ALPHONSO, HIPPOLITO.
Nay stay you Contarino, be within call,
It may be we shal us you. You have rode hard Sir,   180
And we thank you for it. Every minute seemes
Irksome, and tedious to us, till you have
Made your discovery. Say friend, have you seene
This Phænix of our age?
   Sanazarro.   I have seene a Mayde Sir,
3ʳ But if that I have judgement, no such wonder   185
As she was deliver'd to you.
   Cozimo.   This is strange.
   Sanazarro. But certaine truth, it may be she was look'd on
With admiration in the Country Sir,
But if compar'd with many in your Court,
She would appeare but ordinary.
   Cozimo.   Contarino   190
Reports her otherwise.
   Sanazarro.   Such as ne're saw Swannes,
May think Crowes beautifull.
   Cozimo.   How is her behaviour?
   Sanazarro. 'Tis like the place she lives in.
   Cozimo.   How her wit,
Discourse, and entertainment?
   Sanazarro.   Very course,
I would not willingly say poore, and rude,   195
But had she all the beauties of faire women,
The dulnesse of her soule would fright me from her.
   Cozimo. You are curious Sir, I know not what to think on't.
Contarino!
   Contarino. Sir.
   Cozimo.   Where was thy judgement man
To extoll a virgin, Sanazarro tells me   200
Is neerer to deformity?

      178 SD. *Exeunt* . . . HIPPOLITO.] *Coxeter*; *at line 177 in 36*

Sanazarro.   I saw her,
And curiously perus'd her, and I wonder
That she that did appeare to me, that know
What beauty is, not worthy the observing,
Should so transport you.
    Contarino.   Troth my Lord I thought then—   205
    Cozimo. Thought? Didst thou not affirme it?
    Contarino.   I confesse Sir
I did beleeve so then, but now I heare
My Lords opinion to the contrary,
I am of another faith: for 'tis not fit
That I should contradict him. I am dimme Sir,   210
But he's sharpe sighted.

F3ᵛ   *Sanazarro.*   This is to my wish.   [*Aside.*]
    Cozimo. We know not what to think of this, yet would not

Enter GIOVANNI, HIPPOLITO, ALPHONSO.

Determine rashly of it. How doe you like
My Nephewes horsemanship?
    Hippolito.   In my judgement Sir
It is exact and rare.
    Alphonso.   And to my fancie   215
He did present great Alexander mounted
On his Bucephalus.
    Cozimo.   You are right Courtiers,
And know it is your duty to cry up
All actions of a Prince.
    Sanazarro.   Doe not betray   *Aside to* GIOVANNI.
Your selfe, you are safe, I have done my part.
    Giovanni.   I thanke you,   220
Nor will I faile.
    Cozimo.   What's your opinion Nephew
Of the horses?
    Giovanni.   Two of them are in my judgement
The best I ever back'd. I meane the roane Sir,
And the browne bay: but for the chesnut colour'd,
Though he be full of mettall, hot, and fierie,   225
He treads weake in his pasternes.
    Cozimo.   So, come neerer;

211 SD. *Aside.*] *Coxeter; not in 36*   212 SD. ALPHONSO] *Gifford;* Lodovico 36

This exercise hath put you into a sweat,
Take this and dry it: and now I command you
To tell me truly what's your censure of
Charomontes daughter Lidia.
    Giovanni.   I am Sir   230
A novice in my judgement of a Lady,
But such as it is, your Grace shall heare it freely.
I would not speake ill of her, and am sorie
If I keepe my selfe a friend to truth, I cannot
Report her as I would, so much I owe   235
Her reverend Father. But I'll give you Sir
As neere as I can her character in little.
She's of a goodly stature, and her limbs
Not disproportion'd; for her face it is
Farre from deformity, yet they flatter her   240
That style it excellent: her manners are
Simple and innocent: but her discourse
And wit deserve my pittie, more then praise.
At her best my Lord, she is a hansome picture,
And that said, all is spoken.
    Cozimo.   I beleeve you,   245
I ne're yet found you false.
    Giovanni.   Nor ever shall Sir.
Forgive me matchlesse Lidia! too much love   *Aside.*
And jealous feare to lose thee, doe compell me
Against my will, my reason, and my knowledge
To be a poore ditracter of that beauty,   250
Which fluent Ovid, if he liv'd againe,
Would want words to expresse.
    Cozimo.   Pray you make choyce of
The richest of our furniture for these horses,   *To* SANAZARRO.
And take my Nephew with you, we in this
Will follow his directions.
    Giovanni.   Could I finde now   255
The Princesse Fiorinda, and perswade her
To be silent in the suit, that I mov'd to her,
All were secure.
    Sanazarro.   In that my Lord I'll ayde you.
    Cozimo. We wil be private, leave us.   *Exeunt omnes.*
                      All my studies

And serious meditations ayme no further   260
Then this young mans good. He was my sisters son,
And she was such a sister when she liv'd
I could not prize too much, nor can I better
Make knowne how deere I hold her memory,
Then in my cherishing the onely issue   265
Which she hath left behind her. Who's that?

                    Enter FIORINDA.

    Fiorinda.   Sir.
    Cozimo. My faire charge, you are welcome to us.
    Fiorinda. I have found it Sir.
    Cozimo.   All things goe well in Urbin.
    Fiorinda. Your gracious care to me an Orphan, frees me
From all suspition, that my jealous feares   270
Can drive into my fancie.
F4ᵛ   *Cozimo*.   The next Summer
In our owne person, we will bring you thither,
And seat you in your owne.
    Fiorinda.   When you think fit Sir.
But in the mean time, with your Highnesse pardon,
I am a suitor to you.
    Cozimo.   Name it Madame,   275
With confidence to obtaine it.
    Fiorinda.   That you would please
To lay a strict command on Charomonte,
To bring his daughter Lidia to the Court,
And pray you think Sir that 'tis not my purpose
To imploy her as a servant, but to use her   280
As a most wish'd companion.
    Cozimo.   Ha. Your reason?
    Fiorinda. The hopefull Prince your Nephew Sir hath given her
To me for such an abstract of perfection,
In all that can be wish'd for in a virgin,
As beauty, musique, ravishing discourse,   285
Quicknesse of apprehension, with choyce manners
And learning to, not usuall with women;
That I am much ambitious (though I shall
Appeare but as a foyle to set her off)

                    270–1. feares / Can] *Coxeter; undivided 36*

To be from her instructed, and suppli'd   290
In what I am defective.
 Cozimo.   Did my Nephew
Seriously deliver this?
 Fiorinda.   I assure your Grace
With zeale, and vehemencie, and even when
With his best words he striv'd to set her forth
(Though the rare subject made him eloquent)   295
He would complaine, all he could say came short
Of her deservings.
 Cozimo.   Pray you have patience.—
This was strangely caried. Ha! are we trifled with?   [*Aside.*]
Dare they doe this? is Cozimos furie, that
Of late was terrible, growne contemptible?   300
Well; we will cleare our browes, and undermine
Their secret works, (though they have dig'd like Moles,)
And crush 'em with the tempest of my wrath
When I appeare most calme. He is unfit
To command others, that knowes not to use it,   305
And with all rigour, yet my sterne lookes shall not
Discover my intents, for I will strike
When I begin to frowne.—You are the Mistresse
Of that you did demand.
 Fiorinda. I thank your Highnesse,
But speed in the performance of the grant   310
Doubles the favour Sir.
 Cozimo. You shall possesse it sooner then you expect,
Onely be pleas'd to be ready when my Secretary
Waites upon you, to take the fresh ayre.—My Nephew!   [*Aside.*]
And my bosome friend so to cheat me, 'tis not faire!   315

   Enter GIOVANNI, SANAZARRO.

 Sanazarro. Where should this Princesse be? nor in her lodgings,
Nor in the private walks, her owne retreat
Which she so much frequented?
 Giovanni.   By my life
She's with the Duke. And I much more then feare
Her forwardnesse to prefer my suit, hath ruin'd   320

298 SD. *Aside.*] Coxeter (*at 308*); *not in 36* 311. favour] *Coxeter*; favours *36*
314 SD. *Aside.*] *Coxeter*; *not in 36*

What with such care we built up.

Cozimo.		Have you furnish'd
Those Coursers, as we will'd you?

Sanazarro.		There's no signe
Of anger in his lookes.

Giovanni.		They are compleat Sir.

Cozimo. 'Tis well. To your rest. Soft sleepes wayt on you Madame.
To morrow with the rising of the Sunne			325
Be ready to ride with us.—They with more safety
Had trod on fork-tongu'd Adders, then provok'd me.

						Exit COZIMO.

Fiorinda. I come not to be thank'd Sir for the speedy
Performance of my promise touching Lidia,
It is effected.

Sanazarro. We are undone.

Fiorinda.		The Duke			330
No sooner heard me with my best of language
G1ᵛ Describe her excellencies, as you taught me,
But he confirm'd it. You looke sad, as if
You wish'd it were undone.

Giovanni.		No gracious Madame,
I am your servant for't.

Fiorinda.		Be you as carefull			335
For what I mov'd to you. Count *Sanazarro,*
Now I perceive you honour me, in vouchsafing
To weare so sleight a favour.

Sanazarro.		'Tis a grace
I am unworthy of.

Fiorinda.		You merit more
In prizing so a trifle. Take this Diamond,			340
I'll second what I have begun. For know
Your valour hath so woone upon me, that
'Tis not to be resisted. I have said Sir,
And leave you to interpret it.		*Exit* FIORINDA.

Sanazarro.		This to me
Is Wormewood. 'Tis apparant we are taken			345
In our owne nooze. What's to be done?

Giovanni.		I know not.
And 'tis a punishment justly falne upon me
For leaving truth, a constant Mistresse, that

Ever protects her servants, to become
A slave to lyes, and falshood. What excuse   350
Can we make to the Duke? what mercy hope for,
Our packing being laid open?
 Sanazarro.   'Tis not to
Be question'd, but his purpos'd journey is
To see faire Lidia.
 Giovanni. And to divert him
Impossible.
 Sanazarro. There's now no looking backward.   355
 Giovanni. And which way to goe on with safety not
To be imagin'd.
 Sanazarro. Give me leave. I have
An Embrion in my braine, which, I despaire not,
May be brought to forme and fashion, provided
You will be open breasted.
 Giovanni.   'Tis no time now,   360
Our dangers being equall, to conceale
A thought from you.
 Sanazarro.   What power hold you o're Lidia?
Doe you think that with some hazard of her life
She would prevent your ruine?
 Giovanni.   I presume so,
If in the undertaking it, she stray not   365
From what becomes her innocence, and to that
'Tis farre from me to presse her, I my selfe
Will rather suffer.
 Sanazarro. 'Tis enough, this night
Write to her by your servant Calandrino
As I shall give directions, my man   370

    Enter CALANDRINO.

Shall beare him company. See Sir to my wish
He does appeare, but much transform'd from what
He was when he came hither.
 Calandrino.   I confesse
I am not very wise, and yet I finde
A foole, so he be parcell knave, in Court   375
May flourish and grow rich.

   375. knave, in Court] *Coxeter*; knave in Court, *36*

Giovanni.   Calandrino.
Calandrino.   Peace.
I am in contemplation.
Giovanni.   Doe not you know me?
Calandrino. I tell thee, no, on forfeit of my place,
I must not know my selfe, much lesse my Father,
But by Petition. That Petition lin'd too   380
With golden birds, that sing to the tune of Profit,
Or I am deafe.
Giovanni.   But you have your sense of feeling.   *Offering to*
Sanazarro. Nay pray you forbeare.   *kick him.*
Calandrino.   I have all that's requisite
To the making up of a Signior. My spruce ruffe,
My hooded cloake, long stockin, and pain'd hose,   385
My Case of tooth-picks, and my silver forke,
To convey an Olive neatly to my mouth,
G2ᵛ And what is all in all, my pockets ring
A golden peale. O that the Pesants in the Country
(My quondam fellowes) but saw me as I am,   390
How they would admire and worship me!
Giovanni.   As they shall,
For instantly you must thither.
Calandrino.   My grand Signior
Vouchsafe a *bezolus manus*, and a cringe
Of the last edition.
Giovanni.   You must ride post with Letters
This night to Lidia.
Calandrino.   And it please your Grace   395
Shall I use my Coach, or foot-cloath Mule?
Sanazarro.   You Whidgin,
You are to make all speed, think not of pompe.
Giovanni. Follow for your instructions Sirra.
Calandrino.   I have one suit to you
My good Lord.
Sanazarro.   What is't?
Calandrino.   That you would give me
A subtill Court charme, to defend me from   400
Th'infectious ayre of the Country.
Giovanni.   What's the reason?

398–9. *Verse as 36*; have / One *Gifford*; suit / To *McIlwraith*

Calandrino. Why, as this Court ayre taught me knavish wit,
By which I am growne rich, if that againe
Should turne me foole and honest; Vaine hopes farewell,
For I must die a beggar.
    Sanazarro.   Goe too Sirrha,   405
You'll be whip'd for this.
    Giovanni.   Leave fooling, and attend us. *Exeunt.*

The end of the third Act.

Actus quarti Scæna prima.

CAROLO CHAROMONTE, LIDIA.

Carolo. DAUGHTER I have observ'd since the Prince left us
(Whose absence I mourn with you) and the visit
Count Sanazarro gave us, you have nourish'd
Sad and retired thoughts, and parted with
That freedome, and alacrity of spirit   5
With which you us'd to cheere me.
    Lidia.   For the Count, Sir,
All thought of him does with his person die;
But I confesse ingenuously I cannot
So soone forget the choyce, and chast delights
The curteous conversation of the Prince,   10
And without staine I hope, afforded me
When he made this house a Court.
    Carolo.   It is in us
To keepe it so without him. Want we know not,
And all we can complaine of (heaven be prais'd for't)
Is too much plenty, and we will make use of   15
All lawfull pleasures.

Enter Servants.

          How now fellowes, when
Shall we have this lusty dance?
    Caponi.   In the after-noone Sir,
'Tis a device I wis of my owne making,
And such a one, as shal make your Signiorship know
I have not beene your Butlar for nothing, but   20
I have crotchets in my head. We'll trip it titely,

IV. i. 14. for't] *Coxeter*; for 36

And make my sad young Mistresse merry againe,
Or I'll forsware the Cellar.
 Bernardo.   If we had
Our fellow Calandrino here to dance
His part, we were perfect.
 Petruchio.   O, he was a rare fellow;   25
But I feare the Court hath spoil'd him.
 Caponi.   When I was young
I could have cut a caper on a pinnacle,
But now I am old and wise; keepe your figure faire,
And follow but the sample I shall set you,
The Duke himselfe will send for us, and laugh at us, 30
And that were credit.

      Enter CALANDRINO.

 Lidia.   Who have we here?
 Calandrino.   I finde
What was brawne in the Country, in the Court growes tender.
The bots on these joulting Jades, I am bruis'd to jelly.
A Coach for my mony! and that the Curtezans know well,
Their riding so, makes them last three yeares longer 35
Then such as are hacknei'd.
 Carolo.   Calandrino, 'tis he.
 Calandrino. Now to my postures. Let my hand have the honor
To convey a kisse from my lips to the cover of
Your foote deere Signior.
 Carolo.   Fie, you stoope too low Sir.
 Calandrino. The hemme of your vestment Lady. Your Glove is
 for Princes,   40
Nay, I have con'd my distances.
 Lidia.   'Tis most Courtly.
 Caponi. Fellow Calandrino!
 Calandrino.   Signior de Caponi,
Grand Botelier of the Mansion.
 Bernardo.   How is't man?
         Claps him on the shoulder.
 Calandrino. Be not so rustique in your salutations,
Signior Bernardo, Master of the accounts.   45
Signior Petruchio, may you long continue
Your function in the chamber.

G3ᵛ

Caponi.   When shall we learne
Such gambolls in our villa?
Lidia.   Sure he's mad.
Carolo. 'Tis not unlike, for most of such mushroomes are so.
What newes at Court?
Calandrino.   Basto! they are mysteries,   50
And not to be reveal'd. With your favour Signior,
I am in private to conferre a while
With this Signiora. But I'll pawne my honour,
That neither my terse language, nor my habit
How e're it may convince, nor my new shrugs,   55
Shall render her enamour'd.
Carolo.   Take your pleasure.
A little of these apish tricks may passe,
Too much is tedious.   *Exit* CAROLO.
Calandrino.   The Prince in this paper
Presents his service. Nay, it is not Courtly
To see the seale broke open. So I leave you.   60
Signiors of the Villa, I'll descend to be
Familiar with you.
Caponi. Have you forgot to dance?
Calandrino.   No, I am better'd.
Petruchio. Will you joyne with us?
Calandrino.   As I like the project.
Let me warme my braines first with the richest Grape,   65
And then I am for you.
Caponi.   We will want no wine.
                         Exeunt. Manet LIDIA.
Lidia. That this comes onely from the best of Princes,
With a kinde of adoration does command me
To entertaine it, and the sweet contents   *Kissing the letter.*
That are inscrib'd here by his hand, must be   70
Much more then musicall to me. All the service
Of my life at no part can deserve this favour.
O what a virgin longing I feele on me
To unrip the seale, and reade it, yet to breake
What he hath fastned, rashly, may appeare   75
A sawcie rudenesse in me. I must doe it,
(Nor can I else learne his commands, or serve 'em)

But with such reverence, as I would open
Some holy Writ, whose grave instructions beat downe
Rebellious sinnes, and teach my better part   80
How to mount upward. So, 'tis done, and I   *Opens the Letter.*
With Eagles eyes wil curiously peruse it.   *Reads the Letter.*

 Chast Lidia: the favours are so great
  On me by you conferr'd, that to intreat
 The least addition to 'em, in true sense   85
  May argue me of blushlesse impudence.
 But such are my extreames, if you denie
  A farther grace, I must unpittied die.
 Hast cuts off circumstance; as you are admir'd
  For beauty, the report of it hath fir'd   90
 The Duke my Vncle, and I feare you'll prove,
  Not with a sacred, but unlawfull love.
 If he see you, as you are, my hop'd-for light
  Is chang'd into an everlasting night.
 How to prevent it, if your goodnesse finde,   95
  You save two lives, and me you ever binde,
  The honourer of your vertues, Giovanni.

G4ᵛ Were I more deafe then Adders, these sweet charmes
Would through my eares finde passage to my soule,
And soone inchant it. To save such a Prince   100
Who would not perish? Vertue in him must suffer,
And piety be forgotten. The Dukes lust
Though it rag'd more then Tarquins, shall not reach me.
All quaint inventions of chast virgins ayde me!
My prayers are heard, I have't. The Duke ne're saw me,   105
Or if that faile, I am againe provided.   *This spoke*
But for the servants! They wil take what forme   *as if shee*
I please to put upon them. Giovanni,   *studied an*
Be safe, thy servant Lidia assures it.   *evasion.*
Let mountaines of afflictions fall on me,   110
Their waight is easie, so I set thee free.   *Exit.*

[IV. ii]   *Actus quarti Scæna secunda.*

COZIMO, GIOVANNI, SANAZARRO, CAROLO, *Servants.*

Sanazarro. Are you not tyr'd with travaile Sir?

Cozimo.   No, no,
I am fresh and lustie.
   Carolo.   This day shall be ever
A holy day to me, that brings my Prince
Under my humble roofe.   *Weepes.*
   Giovanni.   See Sir, my good Tutor
Sheds teares for joy.
   Cozimo.   Dry them up Charomonte,   5
And all forbeare the roome, while we exchange
Some private words together.
   Giovanni.   O my Lord,
How grosly have we overshot our selves!
   Sanazarro. In what Sir?
   Giovanni.   In forgetting to acquaint
My Guardian with our purpose; all that Lidia   10
Can doe, availes us nothing, if the Duke
Finde out the truth from him.
   Sanazarro.   'Tis now pass'd helpe,
And we must stand the hazard, hope the best Sir!
            Exeunt GIOVANNI, SANAZARRO[, *Servants*].
H1r   *Carolo.* My loyalty doubted Sir?
   Cozimo.   'Tis more. Thou hast
Abus'd our trust, and in a high degree   15
Committed treason.
   Carolo.   Treason? 'tis a word
My innocence understands not. Were my breast
Transparent, and my thoughts to be discern'd,
Not one spot shall be found to taynt the candor
Of my alleageance. And I must be bold   20
To tell you Sir (for he that knowes no guilt
Can know no feare) 'tis tyrannie to o're-charge
An honest man, and such till now I have liv'd,
And such my Lord I'll die.
   Cozimo.   Sir, doe not flatter
Your selfe with hope, these great and glorious words   25
Which every guilty wretch, as well as you,
That's arm'd with impudence, can with ease deliver,
And with as full a mouth, can work on us!
Nor shall gay flourishes of language cleare

     IV. ii. 13 SD. *Servants*] *after Gifford*; *not in 36*

What is in fact apparent.

    Carolo.   Fact? What fact? 30
You that know onely, what it is, instruct me,
For I am ignorant.

    Cozimo.   This then Sir: we gave up
(On our assurance of your faith and care,)
Our Nephew Giovanni, nay, our heire
In expectation, to be train'd up by you 35
As did become a Prince.

    Carolo.   And I discharg'd it.
Is this the treason?

    Cozimo.   Take us with you Sir.
And in respect we knew his Youth was prone
To women, and that living in our Court
He might make some unworthy choyce, before 40
His weaker judgement was confirm'd, we did
Remove him from it; constantly presuming
You with your best endevours, rather would
Have quench'd those heates in him, then light a Torch,
As you have done to his loosenesse.

    Carolo.   I? my travaile 45
Is ill requited Sir, for by my soule
I was so curious that way, that I granted
Accesse to none could tempt him, nor did ever
One syllable, or obscæne accent touch
His eare that might corrupt him.

    Cozimo.   No? Why then 50
With your allowance did you give free way
To all familiar privacie, betweene
My Nephew and your daughter? Or why did you
(Had you no other ends in't but our service)
Reade to 'em, and together (as they had beene 55
Schollers of one forme) Grammar, Rhetorique,
Philosophie, Storie, and interpret to 'em
The close temptations of lascivious Poets?
Or wherefore (for we still had spies upon you)
Was she still present, when by your advice 60
He was taught the use of his weapon, horsmanship,
Wrastling, nay swimming, but to fan in her
A hot desire of him? and then forsooth

H1ᵛ

His exercises ended, cover'd with
A faire pretence of recreation for him,   65
When Lidia was instructed in those graces
That add to beauty, he brought to admire her,
Must heare her sing, while to her voyce, her hand
Made ravishing Musick; and this applauded, dance
A light Levalto with her.
    Carolo.   Have you ended   70
All you can charge me with?
    Cozimo.   Nor stop'd you there,
But they must unattended walke into
The silent Groves, and heare the amorous birds
Warbling their wanton notes, here a sure shade
Of barren Sicamours (which the all-seeing Sunne   75
Could not pierce through:) neere that an arbor hung
With spreading Eglantine, there a bubling spring
Watring a banke of Hyacinths, and Lillies,
With all allurements, that could move to lust.
  2ʳ And could this, Charomonte, (should I grant   80
They had beene equalls both in birth and fortune)
Become your gravity? Nay, 'tis cleare as ayre
That your ambitious hopes to match your daughter
Into our family, gave connivence to it;
And this, though not in act, in the intent   85
I call high treason.
    Carolo.   Heare my just defence Sir,
And though you are my Prince, it wil not take from
Your Greatnesse to acknowledge with a blush,
In this my accusation you have beene
More sway'd by spleene, and jealous suppositions,   90
Then certaine grounds of reason. You had a Father
(Blest be his memory) that made frequent proofes
Of my loyalty, and faith, and (would I boast
The dangers I have broke through in his service)
I could say more. Nay, you your selfe, dread Sir,   95
When ever I was put unto the test,
Found me true gold, and not adulterate metall,
And am I doubted now?
    Cozimo.   This is from the purpose.
    Carolo. I wil come to it Sir, your Grace wel knew

Before the Princes happy presence made   100
My poore house rich, the chiefest blessing which
I gloried in, (though now it prove a curse)
Was an onely daughter. Nor did you command me,
As a security to your future feares,
To cast her off: which had you done, how e're   105
She was the light of my eyes, and comfort of
My feeble age; so farre I priz'd my duty
Above affection, she now had beene
A stranger to my care. But she is faire.
Is that her fault, or mine? Did ever Father   110
Hold beauty in his issue for a blemish?
Her education and her manners tempt to.
If these offend, they are easily remov'd;
You may, if you think fit, before my face,
In recompence of all my watchings for you,   115
With burning corrasives transforme her to
An ugly Leper; and this done to taint
Her sweetnes, prostitute her to a loathsom brothel.
This I will rather suffer Sir, and more,
Then live suspected by you.
    Cozimo.   Let not passion   120
Carie you beyond your reason.
    Carolo.   I am calme Sir,
Yet you must give me leave to grieve, I finde
My actions misinterpreted. Alas Sir,
Was Lidias desire to serve the Prince
Call'd an offence? or did she practise to   125
Seduce his youth, because with her best zeale
And fervour she endevoured to attend him?
'Tis a hard construction: though she be my daughter
I may thus farre speake her. From her infancy
She was ever civill, her behaviour neerer   130
Simplicity then craft; and malice dares not
Affirme in one loose gesture, or light language,
She gave a signe she was in thought unchast:
I'll fetch her to you Sir, and but looke on her
With equall eyes, you must in justice grant   135
That your suspition wrongs her.

101. blessing] *Mason*; blessings 36

H2ᵛ

Cozimo.   It may be,
But I must have stronger assurance of it
Then passionate words. And not to trifle time,
As we came unexpected to your house,
We will prevent all meanes that may prepare her   140
How to answer that, with which we come to charge her.
And howsoever it may be receiv'd
As a foule breach to hospitable rites,
On thy alleageance, and boasted faith,
Nay forfeit of thy head, we doe confine thee   145
Close prisoner to thy Chamber, till all doubts
Are clear'd that doe concerne us.
    Carolo.   I obey Sir,
And wish your Grace had followed my hearse
To my Sepulchre, my loyalty unsuspected,
Rather then now—but I am silent Sir,   150
And let that speake my duty.   *Exit* CAROLO.
    Cozimo.   If this man
Be false, disguised treacherie ne're put on
A shape so neere to truth. Within there.

Enter GIOVANNI *and* SANAZARRO *ushering in* PETRONELLA.
    CALANDRINO *and others setting forth a banquet.*

Sanazarro.   Sir.
Cozimo. Bring Lidia forth.
Giovanni.   She comes Sir of her selfe
To present her service to you.
    Cozimo.   Ha. This personage   155
Cannot invite affection.
    Sanazarro.   See you keepe State.
Petronella. I warrant you.
    Cozimo.   The manners of her minde
Must be transcendent, if they can defend
Her rougher out-side; may we with your liking
Salute you Lady?
    Petronella.   Let me wipe my mouth Sir   160
With my Cambrick handkercher, and then have at you.
    Cozimo. Can this be possible?
    Sanazarro.   Yes sir, you will finde her
Such as I gave her to you.

Petronella.   Will your Dukeship
Sit down and eat some Sugar-plums? here's a Castle
Of March-Pane too, and this Quince Marmalade   165
Was of my owne making. All summ'd up together
Did cost the setting on, and here is wine too   *Drinks all off.*
As good as e're was tap'd. I'll be your taster,
For I know the fashion, now you must doe me right Sir,
You shall nor will, nor choose.
     Giovanni.   She's very simple.   170
     Cozimo. Simple, 'tis worse. Doe you drink thus often Lady?
     Petronella. Still when I am thirsty, and eate when I am hungry.
Such Junkets come not every day. Once more to you,
With a heart and a halfe ifaith.
     Cozimo.   Pray you pawse a little,
If I hold your Cards, I shall pull downe the side,   175
I am not good at the game.
H3ᵛ   *Petronella.*   Then I'll drink for you.
     Cozimo. Nay, pray you stay. I'll finde you out a pledge
That shall supply my place, what think you of
This compleat Signior? You are a Juno,
And in such state must feast this Jupiter,   180
What think you of him?
     Petronella.   I desire no better.
     Cozimo. And you will undertake this service for me?
You are good at the sport.
     Calandrino.   Who I? A pidler Sir.
     Cozimo. Nay, you shall sit inthron'd, and eate, and drink
As you were a Duke.
     Calandrino.   If your Grace will have me,   185
I'll eate and drink like an Emperour.
     Cozimo.   Take your place then,
We are amaz'd.
     Giovanni.   This is grosse. Nor can the imposture
But be discover'd.
     Sanazarro.   The Duke is too sharpe sighted
To be deluded thus.
     Calandrino.   Nay, pray you eate faire,
Or devide, and I will choose. Cannot you use   190

171. thus] *Gifford*; this *36*   179-81. *rearranged by Gifford*; This ... state /
Must ... him? *36*

Your fork as I doe? Gape and I will feed you.   *Feedes her.*
Gape wider yet, this is Court-like.
   Petronella.   To choke Dawes with,
I like it not.
   Calandrino. But you like this.   *They drink.*
   Petronella.   Let it come Boy.
   Cozimo. What a sight is this! we could be angry with you,
How much you did belye her when you told us   195
She was onely simple, this is barbarous rudenesse,
Beyond beliefe.
   Giovanni.   I would not speake her Sir
Worse then she was.
   Sanazarro.   And I my Lord chose rather
To deliver her better parted then she is,
Then to take from her.

               Enter CAPONI.

   Caponi.   Ere I'll loose my dance,   200
I'll speake to the purpose. I am Sir no Prologue,
But in plaine termes must tell you, we are provided
Of a lusty Hornepipe.
   Cozimo.   Prethee let us have it,
For we grow dull.
   Caponi.   But to make up the medley,
For it is of severall colours, we must borrow   205
Your Graces Ghost here.
   Calandrino.   Pray you Sir depose me,
It will not doe else. I am sir the engine
By which it moves.   *Rises and resignes his chaire.*
   Petronella.   I will dance with my Duke too,
I will not out.
   Cozimo. Begin then. There's more in this   *Dance.*
Then yet I have discover'd. Some Oedipus   210
Resolve this riddle.
   Petronella.   Did I not foot it roundly?   *Falls downe.*
   Cozimo. As I live stark drunk. Away with her. We'll reward you,
When you have cool'd your selves in the Cellar.
   Caponi.   Heaven preserve you.
                           Exeunt dancers.

205. we] *Coxeter*; for we 36

Cozimo. We pitty Charomonte's wretched fortune
In a daughter, nay, a monster. Good old man!   215
The place growes tedious. Our remove shall be
With speed. We'll onely in a word or two
Take leave and comfort him.
Sanazarro.   'Twill rather Sir
Encrease his sorrow, that you know his shame,
Your Grace may doe it by Letter.
Cozimo.   Who sign'd you   220
A Pattent to direct us? Waite our comming
In the Garden.
Giovanni.   All will out.
Sanazarro.   I more then feare it.
                    Exeunt GIOVANNI *and* SANAZARRO.
Cozimo. These are strange Chimeras to us! what to judge of't
Is past our apprehension! One command
Charomonte to attend us. Can it be   *Exit Servant.*
That Contarino could be so besotted   226
As to admire this prodigie! or her Father
To dote upon it! or does she personate
For some ends unknowne to us? this rude behaviour
Within the Scæne presented, would appeare   230
Ridiculous and impossible.

                    Enter CAROLO.

                    O you are welcome.
We now acknowledge the much wrong we did you
In our unjust suspition. We have seene
The wonder Sir, your daughter.
Carolo.   And have found her
Such as I did report her. What she wanted   235
In Courtship, was I hope suppli'd in civill
And modest entertainment.
Cozimo.   Pray you tell us,
And truly we command you, Did you never
Observe she was given to drink?
Carolo.   To drink Sir?
Cozimo.   Yes.
Nay more, to be drunk.

229. us?] *Gifford¹*; ~, 36   230. Within] *36*; Which, in *Mason*   239-40. Yes./
Nay] *McIlwraith*; *undivided 36*

Carolo.   I had rather see her buried.   240
Cozimo. Dare you trust your own eyes, if you finde her now
More then distemper'd?
Carolo.   I will pull them out Sir,
If your Grace can make this good. And if you please
To grant me liberty, as she is I'll fetch her,
And in a moment.
Cozimo.   Looke you doe, and faile not,   245
On the perill of your head.
Carolo.   Drunk. She disdaines it. *Exit* CAROLO.
Cozimo. Such contrarieties were never reade of.
Charomonte is no foole, nor can I think
His confidence built on sand. We are abus'd,
'Tis too apparent.

                    Enter CAROLO *and* LIDIA.

Lidia.   I am indispos'd Sir,   250
And that life you tender'd once, much indanger'd
In forcing me from my Chamber.
Carolo.   Here she is Sir,
Suddainly sick I grant, but sure not drunk,
Speake to my Lord the Duke.
Lidia.   All is discover'd.   *Kneeles.*
Cozimo. Is this your onely daughter?
Carolo.   And my heire Sir,   255
ᵣ Nor keepe I any woman in my house
(Unlesse for sordid offices) but one,
I doe maintaine trimm'd up in her cast habits,
To make her sport. And she indeede loves wine,
And wil take too much of it. And perhaps for mirth   260
She was presented to you.
Cozimo.   It shall yeeld
No sport to the contrivers, 'tis too plaine now;
Her presence does confirme what Contarino
Deliver'd of her, nor can sicknesse dimme
The splendor of her beauties, being her selfe then   265
She must exceede his praise.
Lidia.   Will your Grace heare me?
I am faint and can say little.
Cozimo.   Here are accents,

Whose every syllable is musicall!
Pray you let me raise you, and a while rest here;
False Sanazarro, trecherous Giovanni!   270
But stand we talking?
   Carolo.   Here's a storme soone rais'd.
   Cozimo. As thou art our Subject, Charomonte, sweare
To act what we command.
   Carolo.   That is an oath
I long since tooke.
   Cozimo.   Then by that oath we charge thee
Without excuse, deniall, or delay   275
To apprehend, and suddainly, Sanazarro,
And our ingratefull Nephew. We have said it.
Doe it without reply, or we pronounce thee,
Like them, a traytor to us. See them guarded
In severall lodgings, and forbid accesse   280
To all, but when we warrant. Is our will
Heard, sooner then obay'd?
   Carolo.   These are strange turnes,
But I must not dispute 'em.   *Exit* CAROLO.
   Cozimo.   Be severe in't.
O my abused lenity! from what height
Is my power falne?
I1ᵛ *Lidia.*   O me most miserable!   285
That being innocent, make others guilty.
Most gracious Prince!
   Cozimo.   Pray you rise, and then speake to me.
   Lidia. My knees shal first be rooted in this earth,
And Mirrha-like I'll grow up to a tree,
Dropping perpetuall teares of sorrow, which   290
Hardned by the rough winde, and turn'd to amber,
Unfortunate virgins like my selfe shall weare,
Before I'll make Petition to your Greatnesse
But with such reverence, my hands held up thus,
As I would doe to heaven. You Princes are   295
As gods on earth to us, and to be su'd too
With such humility, as his Deputies
May chalenge from their vassalls.
   Cozimo.   Here's that forme
Of language I expected; pray you speake,

What is your suit?

Lidia.   That you would looke upon me   300
As an humble thing, that millions of degrees
Is plac'd beneath you. For what am I dread sir?
Or what can fall in the whole course of my life,
That may be worth your care, much lesse your trouble?
As the lowly shrub is to the lofty Cedar,   305
Or a molehill to Olympus, if compar'd,
I am to you Sir. Or suppose the Prince,
(Which cannot finde beliefe in me,) forgetting
The greatnesse of his birth and hopes, hath throwne
An eye of favour on me, in me punnish,   310
(That am the cause) the rashnesse of his youth.
Shall the Queene of the inhabitants of the ayre,
The Eagle that beares thunder on her wings,
In her angry mood destroy her hopefull young,
For suff'ring a Wren to perch too neere 'em?   315
Such is our disproportion.

Cozimo.   With what fervour
She pleades against her selfe!

Lidia.   For me poore Mayde,
I know the Prince to be so farre above me,
That my wishes cannot reach him. Yet I am
So much his creature, that to fix him in   320
Your wonted grace and favour, I'll abjure
His sight for ever, and betake my selfe
To a religious life (where in my prayers
I may remember him) and ne're see man more
But my ghostly father. Will you trust me Sir?   325
In truth I'll keepe my word; or if this faile,
A little more of feare what may befall him,
Will stop my breath for ever.

Cozimo.   Had you thus argu'd   *Raises her.*
As you were your selfe, and brought as advocates
Your health and beauty, to make way for you,   330
No crime of his could put on such a shape,
But I should looke with the eyes of mercy on it.
What would I give to see this diamond
In her perfect lustre, as she was before
The clouds of sicknesse dimm'd it! yet take comfort,   335

And as you would obtaine remission for
His trecherie to me, cheere your drooping spirits,
And call the blood againe into your cheekes,
And then pleade for him. And in such a habit
As in your highest hopes you would put on,   340
If we were to receive you for our Bride.
    Lidia. I'll doe my best Sir.
    Cozimo.   And that best will be
A crowne of all felicity to me.   *Exeunt.*

The end of the fourth Act.

[V. i]   *Actus quinti Scæna prima.*

SANAZARRO *above.*

    Sanazarro. TIS prov'd in me, the curse of humane frailty
(Adding to our afflictions) makes us know
What's good, and yet our violent passions force us
To follow what is ill. Reason assur'd me
It was not safe to shave a Lyons skinne,   5
And that to trifle with a Soveraigne, was
I2ᵛ To play with lightning: yet imperious beauty
Treading upon the neck of understanding,
Compell'd me to put off my naturall shape
Of loyall duty, to disguise my selfe   10
In the adulterate, and cobweb masque
Of disobedient trecherie. Where is now
My borrowed Greatnesse? or the promis'd lives
Of following Courtiers ecchoing my will?
In a moment vanish'd? Power that stands not on   15
Its proper base, which is peculiar onely
To absolute Princes, falls, or rises, with
Their frowne, or favour. The great Duke my Master
(Who almost chang'd me to his other selfe)
No sooner takes his beames of comfort from me,   20
But I as one unknowne, or unregarded,
Unpittied suffer! who makes intercession
To his mercy for me now? who does remember
The service I have done him? not a man;
And such as spake no language, but my Lord,   25

The favorite of Tuskanies grand Duke,
Deride my madnesse. Ha! What noise of horses? *Looks backwards.*
A goodly troope! This back-part of my prison
Allowes me liberty to see and know them.
Contarino! Yes, 'tis he, and Hippolito;   30
And the Dutchesse Fiorinda; Urbins heire,
A Princesse I have slighted; yet I weare
Her favours. And to teach me what I am,
She whom I scorn'd can onely mediate for me.
This way she makes, yet speake to her I dare not,   35
And how to make suit to her, is a taske
Of as much difficulty; yes; thou blessed pledge   *Takes off the*
Of her affection ayde me. This supplies   *ring, and a pane*
The want of penne and ink, and this of paper.   *of glasse.*
It must be so, and I in my Petition   40
Concise and pithie.

> *Enter* CONTARINO *leading in* FIORINDA, ALPHONSO,
>   HIPPOLITO, HIERONIMO, CALAMINTA.

Fiorinda.   'Tis a goodly pile this.
Hieronimo. But better by the owner.
Alphonso.   But most rich
In the great States it covers.
Fiorinda.   The Dukes pleasure
Commands us hither.
Contarino.   Which was laid on us
To attend you to it.
Hippolito.   Signior Charomonte,   45
To see your Excellence his guest, will think
Himselfe most happy.
Fiorinda.   Tye my shooe. What's that?
                                    The pane thrown down.
A pane throwne from the window no winde stirring?
Calaminta. And at your feet too falne, there's somthing writ on't.
Contarino. Some Courtier belike would have it known   50
He wore a Diamond.
Calaminta.   Ha; it is directed:
To the Princesse Fiorinda.

Fiorinda.   We will reade it.

                The inscription.

He whom you pleas'd to favour, is cast downe,
Past hope of rising, by the great Dukes frowne,
If by your gracious meanes, he cannot have   55
A pardon. And that got, he lives your slave.

                The subscription.

Of men the most distressed, Sanazarro.

Of me the most belov'd, and I will save thee,
Or perish with thee. Sure thy fault must be
Of some prodigious shape, if that my prayers   60
And humble intercession to the Duke
Prevaile not with him.

                Enter COZIMO *and* CAROLO.

                        Here he comes, delay
Shall not make lesse my benefit.
        Cozimo.   What we purpose
Shall know no change, and therefore move me not,
We were made as properties, and what we shall   65
Determine of 'em, cannot be call'd rigour,
But noble justice. When they prov'd disloyall,
They were cruell to themselves. The Prince that pardons
The first affront offer'd to majestie,
13ᵛ Invites a second, rend'ring that power   70
Subjects should tremble at, contemptible.
Ingratitude is a monster, Carolo,
To be strangl'd in the birth, not to be cherish'd.
Madame, you are happily met with.
        Fiorinda.   Sir, I am
An humble Suitor to you; and the rather   75
Am confident of a grant, in that your Grace
When I made choyce to be at your devotion,
Vow'd to denie me nothing.
        Cozimo.   To this minute
We have confirm'd it, what's your boone?
        Fiorinda.   It is Sir,
That you in being gracious to your servant,   80

The ne're sufficiently prais'd Sanazarro,
(That now under your heavy displeasure suffers)
Would be good unto your selfe. His services
So many, and so great (your storme of fury
Calm'd by your better judgment) must inform you,   85
Some little slip (for sure it is no more)
From his loyall duty, with your justice cannot
Make foule his faire deservings. Great Sir, therefore
Looke backward on his former worth, and turn
Your eye from his offence (what 'tis I know not)   90
And I am confident, you will receive him
Once more into your favour.
 Cozimo.   You say well,
You are ignorant in the nature of his fault,
Which when you understand (as we'll instruct you)
Your pitty will appeare a charity   95
(It being conferr'd on an unthankfull man)
To be repented. He's a traytor Madame
To you, to us, to gratitude, and in that
All crimes are comprehended.
 Fiorinda.   If his offence
Aym'd at me onely, what so e're it is   100
'Tis freely pardon'd.
 Cozimo.   This compassion in you
Must make the colour of his guilt more ugly:
The honors we have hourely heap'd upon him,
The titles, the rewards, to the envie of
The old Nobility, as the common people,   105
We now forbeare to touch at, and will onely
Insist on his grosse wrongs to you. You were pleas'd
Forgetting both your selfe and proper Greatnesse,
To favour him, nay, to court him to embrace
A happinesse, which on his knees with joy   110
He should have su'd for. Who repin'd not at
The grace you did him? yet in recompence
Of your large bounties, the disloyall wretch
Makes you a stale; and what he might be by you
Scorn'd, and derided, gives himselfe up wholly   115
To the service of another. If you can

Beare this with patience, we must say you have not
The bitternesse of spleene, or irefull passions
Familiar to women. Pause upon it,
And when you seriously have waigh'd his cariage,   120
Move us againe, if your reason will allow it,
His trechery knowne: and then if you continue
His advocate for him, we perhaps, because
We would denie you nothing, may awake
Our sleeping mercy. Carolo!

  Carolo.   My Lord.   *They whisper.*

  Fiorinda. To endure a rivall, that were equall to me,   126
Cannot but speake my poverty of spirit,
But an inferiour more; yet true love must not
Know, or degrees, or distances. Lidia may be
As farre above me in her forme, as she   130
Is in her birth beneath me, and what I
In Sanazarro lik'd, he loves in her.
But if I free him now, the benefit
Being done so timely, and confirming too
My strength and power, my soules best faculties being   135
Bent wholly to preserve him, must supply me
With all I am defective in, and binde him
My creature ever. It must needes be so,
14ᵛ Nor will I give it o're thus.

  Cozimo.   Does our Nephew
Beare his restraint so constantly, as you   140
Deliver it to us?

  Carolo.   In my judgement Sir
He suffers more for his offence to you,
Then in his feare of what can follow it.
For he is so collected and prepar'd
To welcome that, you shall determine of him,   145
As if his doubts and feares were equall to him.
And sure he's not acquainted with much guilt,
That more laments the telling one untruth
Under your pardon still (for 'twas a fault Sir)
Then others that pretend to conscience, doe   150
Their crying secret sinnes.

  Cozimo.   No more, this Glosse

137. defective in] *Coxeter*; defective *36*

Defends not the corruption of the text,
Urge it no more.   CAROLO *and the others whisper.*
    Fiorinda.   I once more must make bold Sir
To trench upon your patience. I have
Consider'd my wrongs duly. Yet that cannot   155
Divert my intercession for a man
Your Grace like me, once favour'd. I am still
A suppliant to you, that you would vouchsafe
The hearing his defence, and that I may
With your allowance see, and comfort him.   160
Then having heard all that he can alleadge
In his excuse, for being false to you,
Censure him as you please.
    Cozimo.   You will o're-come,
There's no contending with you. Pray you enjoy
What you desire. And tell him, he shall have   165
A speedy tryall. In which we'll forbeare
To sit a Judge, because our purpose is
To rise up his accuser.
    Fiorinda.   All encrease
Of happines wait on Cozimo.   *Exeunt* FIORINDA, CALAMINTA.
    Alphonso.   Was it no more?
    Carolo. My Honor's pawn'd for it.
    Contarino.   I'll second you.   170
    Hippolito. Since it is for the service and the safety
Of the hopefull Prince, fall what can fall, I'll runne
The desperate hazard.
    Hieronimo.   He's no friend to vertue
That does decline it.   *They all kneele.*
    Cozimo.   Ha; what sue you for?
Shall we be ever troubl'd? doe not tempt   175
That anger may consume you.
    Carolo.   Let it Sir,
The losse is lesse, though Innocents, we perish,
Then that your sisters sonne should fall unheard
Under your fury. Shall we feare to entreate
That grace for him, that are your faithfull servants,   180
Which you vouchsafe the Count, like us a subject?
    Cozimo. Did not we vowe, till sicknesse had forsooke

171. *Hippolito.*] *Gifford; Lodovi. 36*

Thy daughter Lidia, and she appear'd
In her perfect health and beauty to pleade for him,
We were deafe to all perswasion?
    Carolo.   And that hope Sir   185
Hath wrought a miracle. She is recover'd,
And if you please to warrant her, will bring
The penitent Prince before you.
    Cozimo.   To enjoy
Such happines, what would we not dispense with?
    Alphonso. ⎫
    Hippolito. ⎬ We all kneele for the Prince.
    Hieronimo. ⎭
    Contarino.   Nor can it stand   190
With your mercy, that are gracious to Strangers,
To be cruell to your owne.
    Cozimo.   But art thou certaine
I shall behold her at the best?
    Carolo.   If ever
She was hansome, as it fits not me to say so,
She is now much better'd.
    Cozimo.   Rise, thou art but dead   195
If this prove otherwise. Lidia appeare,
And feast an appetite almost pin'd to death
K1ᵛ With longing expectation to behold
Thy excellencies; thou as beauties Queene
Shalt censure the detractors. Let my Nephew   200
Be led in triumph under her command,
We'll have it so; and Sanazarro tremble
To think whom he hath slander'd; we'll retire
Our selves a little, and prepare to meete
A blessing, which imagination tells us   205
We are not worthy of; and then come forth
But with such reverence, as if I were
(My selfe the Priest, the sacrifice my heart)
To offer at the Altar of that goodnesse
That must or kill or save me.   *Exit* COZIMO.
    Carolo.   Are not these   210

190. *Alphonso.* ⎫
     Hippolito. ⎬ *after Gifford*; *Al. Ludo. Hie. 36*
     Hieronimo. ⎭

Strange gambols in the Duke?
Alphonso.   Great Princes have
Like meaner men their weaknesse.
Hippolito.   And may use it
Without controule or check.
Contarino.   'Tis fit they should,
Their priviledge were lesse else, then their Subjects.   214
Hieronimo. Let them have their humors, there's no crossing 'em.
                                        [*Exeunt.*]

i]   *Actus quinti Scæna ultima.*

                FIORINDA, SANAZARRO, CALAMINTA.

Sanazarro. And can it be your bounties should fall down
In showers on my ingratitude? or the wrongs
Your Greatnesse should revenge, teach you to pittie?
What retribution can I make? what service
Pay to your goodnesse, that in some proportion   5
May to the world expresse, I would be thankfull?
Since my engagements are so great, that all
My best endevours to appeare your creature
Can but proclaime my wants, and what I owe
To your magnificence.
Fiorinda.   All debts are discharg'd   10
2ʳ In this acknowledgement: yet since you please
I shall impose some termes of satisfaction
For that which you professe your selfe oblig'd for,
They shall be gentle ones, and such as will not
I hope afflict you.
Sanazarro.   Make me understand   15
Great Princesse, what they are, and my obedience
Shall with all cheerefull willingnesse subscribe
To what you shall command.
Fiorinda.   I will binde you to
Make good your promise. First, I then enjoyne you
To love a Lady, that a Noble way   20
Truly affects you, and that you would take
To your protection and care the Dukedome

212. *Hippolito.*] *Gifford; Lodovico. 36*   215 SD. *Exeunt.*] *Gifford; not in 36*

Of Urbin, which no more is mine, but yours.
And that when you have full possession of
My person, as my fortunes, you would use me   25
Not as a Princesse, but instruct me in
The duties of an humble wife, for such
(The priviledge of my birth no more remembred)
I will be to you. This consented to,
All injuries forgotten, on your lips   30
I thus signe your quietus.

    Sanazarro.   I am wretched
In having but one life to be imploy'd
As you please to dispose it. And believe it,
If it be not already forfeited
To the furie of my Prince, as 'tis your gift,   35
With all the faculties of my soule, I'll study
In what I may to serve you.

    Fiorinda.   I am happy
In this assurance.

          Enter GIOVANNI *and* LIDIA.

          What sweet Lady's this?
    Sanazarro. 'Tis Lidia Madame, she—
    Fiorinda.   I understand you:
Nay, blush not, by my life she is a rare one!   40
And if I were your Judge I would not blame you,
To like and love her. But Sir you are mine now,
And I presume so on your constancie,
That I dare not be jealous.

    Sanazarro.   All thoughts of her
Are in your goodnesse buried.

    Lidia.   Pray you Sir   45
Be comforted, your innocence should not know
What 'tis to feare, and if that you but looke on
The guards that you have in your selfe, you cannot.
The Duke's your Uncle Sir, and though a little
Incens'd against you, when he sees your sorrow   50
He must be reconcil'd. What rugged Tartar,
Or Canniball, though bath'd in humane gore,
But, looking on your sweetnesse, would forget

V. ii. 38. *rearranged by Gifford*[2]; In . . . What / Sweet *36*

His cruell nature, and let fall his weapon,
Though then aym'd at your throat?
    Giovanni.   O Lidia,   55
Of Mayds the honor, and your sexes glory.
It is not feare to die, but to loose you
That brings this Feaver on me. I will now
Discover to you, that which till this minute
I durst not trust the ayre with. Ere you knew   60
What power the magique of your beauty had,
I was inchanted by it, lik'd, and lov'd it,
My fondnesse still encreasing with my yeares:
And flatter'd by false hopes, I did attend
Some blessed oportunity to move   65
The Duke with his consent to make you mine.
But now, such is my starre-cross'd destinie,
When he beholds you as you are, he cannot
Denie himselfe the happinesse to enjoy you.
And I as well in reason may entreat him   70
To give away his Crowne, as to part from
A jewell of more value, such you are:
Yet howsoever, when you are his Dutchesse,
And I am turn'd into forgotten dust,
Pray you love my memory. I should say more   75
But I am cut off.

      Enter COZIMO, CAROLO, CONTARINO *and others.*

    Sanazarro.   The Duke? that countenance once,
When it was cloth'd in smiles, shew'd like an Angels,
But now 'tis folded up in clouds of fury,
'Tis terrible to looke on.   *The* DUKE *admiring* LIDIA.
    Lidia.   Sir.
    Cozimo.   A while
Silence your musicall tongue, and let me feast   80
My eyes with the most ravishing object that
They ever gaz'd on. There's no miniature
In her faire face, but is a copious theme
Which would (discours'd at large of) make a volume.
What cleare arch'd browes! what sparkling eyes! the Lillies   85
Contending with the Roses in her cheekes,
Who shall most set them off! what ruby lips!

Or unto what can I compare her neck,
But to a rock of christall? every limb
Proportion'd to loves wish, and in their neatnesse   90
Add lustre to the riches of her habit,
Not borrow from it.

Lidia.   You are pleas'd to shew Sir
The fluencie of your language, in advancing
A Subject much unworthy.

Cozimo.   How unworthy?
By all the vowes which Lovers offer at   95
The Cyprian Goddesse Altars, eloquence
It selfe presuming, as you are, to speake you,
Would be struck dumb. And what have you deserv'd then?
(Wretches you kneele too late) that have endevour'd
To spout the poyson of your black detraction   100
On this immaculate whitenesse? was it malice
To her perfections? or—

Fiorinda.   Your Highnesse promis'd
A gracious hearing to the Count.

Lidia.   And Prince too;
Doe not make voyde so just a grant.

Cozimo.   We will not,
Yet since their accusation must be urg'd,   105
And strongly, ere their weak defence have hearing,
We seat you here as Judges to determine

Ladies in the chaires of State.

K3ᵛ Of your grosse wrongs and ours. And now remembring
Whose Deputies you are, be neither sway'd,
Or with particular spleene, or foolish pittie,   110
For neither can become you.

Carolo.   There's some hope yet
Since they have such gentle Judges.

Cozimo.   Rise, and stand forth then,
And heare with horror to your guilty soules
What we will prove against you. Could this Princesse
(Thou enemie to thy selfe) stoope her high flight   115
Of towring greatnesse to invite thy lownesse
To looke up to it, and with nimble wings
Of gratitude, couldst thou forbeare to meet it?
Were her favours boundlesse in a noble way,

And warranted by our allowance, yet   120
In thy acceptation there appear'd no signe
Of a modest thankfulnesse?
    Fiorinda.   Pray you forbeare
To presse that farther, 'tis a fault we have
Already heard, and pardon'd.
    Cozimo.   We will then
Passe over it, and briefly touch at that   125
Which does concern our selfe. In which both being
Equall offenders, what we shall speake, points
Indifferently at either. How we rais'd thee
(Forgetfull Sanazarro) of our Grace
To a full possession of power, and honors,   130
It being too well knowne, we'll not remember.
And what thou wert (rash youth) in expectation
(And from which headlong thou hast throwne thy selfe)
Not Florence, but all Tuskany can witnesse
With admiration. To assure thy hopes,   135
We did keepe constant to a widdowed bed,
And did deny our selfe those lawfull pleasures,
Our absolute power and height of blood allow'd us.
Made both, the keyes that open'd our hearts secrets,
And what you spake believ'd as Oracles.   140
But you in recompence of this to him
That gave you all, to whom you ow'd your being
With trecherous lies endevour'd to conceale
This jewell from our knowledge, which our selfe
Could onely lay just clayme too.
    Giovanni.   'Tis most true Sir.   145
    Sanazarro. We both confesse a guilty cause.
    Cozimo.   Looke on her,
Is this a beauty fit to be imbrac'd
By any Subjects armes? Can any tyre
Become that forhead, but a Diadem?
Or should we grant your being false to us   150
Could be excus'd, your trechery to her
In seeking to deprive her of that greatnesse
(Her matchless forme consider'd) she was born too,
Must ne're finde pardon! We have spoken Ladies

Like a rough Orator, that brings more truth   155
Then rhetorique to make good his accusation,
And now expect your sentence.   *The Ladies descend from the State.*
    Lidia.   In your birth Sir
You were mark'd out the Judge of life, and death,
And we that are your Subjects to attend
With trembling feare your doome.
    Fiorinda.   We doe resigne   160
This Chaire as onely proper to your selfe.
    Giovanni. And since in justice we are lost, we flie
Unto your saving mercie.   *All kneeling.*
    Sanazarro.   Which sets off
A Prince much more then rigour.
    Carolo.   And becomes him
When 'tis express'd to such as fell by weaknesse   165
(That being a twin-borne brother to affection)
Better then wreathes of conquest.
    Hieronimo, Hippolito, Contarino, Alphonso. We all speake
Their language mighty Sir.
    Cozimo.   You know our temper,
And therefore with more boldnesse venter on it.
And would not our consent to your demands   170
Deprive us of a happinesse hereafter
Ever to be despair'd of, we perhaps
Might hearken neerer to you, and could wish
With some qualification or excuse
You might make lesse the mountaines of your crimes,   175
And so invite our clemencie to feast with you.
But you that knew with what impatiencie
Of griefe we parted from the faire Clarinda
Our Dutchesse, (let her memory still be sacred)
And with what imprecations on our selfe   180
We vow'd, not hoping e're to see her equall,
Ne're to make triall of a second choyce,
If Nature fram'd not one that did excell her,
(As this Mayds beauty prompts us that she does)
And yet with oathes then mix'd with teares, upon   185
Her monument we swore our eye should never
Againe be tempted, 'tis true, and those vowes

      167. *Hippolito.*] *Gifford*; *Lod.* 36

K4ᵛ

Are registred above, something here tells me.
Carolo thou heardst us sweare.
  Carolo.   And sweare so deeply,
That if all womens beauties were in this   190
(As she's not to be nam'd with the dead Dutchess,)
Nay, all their vertues bound up in one story
(Of which mine is scarce an Epitome)
If you should take her as a wife, the waight
Of your perjuries would sink you. If I durst   195
I had told you this before.
  Cozimo.   'Tis strong truth Carolo,
And yet what was necessity in us
Cannot free them from treason.
  Carolo.   There's your error.
The Prince in care to have you keepe your vowes
Made unto heaven, vouchsaf'd to love my daughter. 200
  Lidia. He told me so indeed Sir.
  Fiorinda.   And the Count
Averr'd as much to me.
  Cozimo.   You all conspire
To force our mercy from us.
  Carolo.   Which giv'n up,
To after-times, preserves you unforsworne,
An Honor, which will live upon your Tombe   205
When your Greatnesse is forgotten.
  Cozimo.   Though we know
All this is practise, and that both are false,
Such reverence we will pay to dead Clarinda,
And to our serious oathes, that we are pleas'd
With our owne hand to blinde our eyes, and not 210
Know what we understand. Here Giovanni
We pardon thee, and take from us in this,
More then our Dukedome, love her. As I part
With her, all thoughts of women flie fast from us.
Sanazarro, we forgive you. In your service   215
To this Princesse merit it. Yet let not others
That are in trust and grace, as you have beene,
By the example of our lenity,
Presume upon their Soveraignes clemencie. *A showt.*
  All. Long live great Cozimo.

Enter CALANDRINO, PETRONELLA.

Calandrino.   Sure the Duke is   220
In the giving vaine they are so lowd. Come on Spouse,
We have heard all, and we will have our boone too.
Cozimo. What is't?
Calandrino.   That your Grace, in remembrance of
My share in a dance, and that I play'd your part
When you should have drunk hard, would get this Signiors grant 225
To give this Damsell to me in the Church,
For we are contracted; in it you shall doe
Your Dukedome pleasure.
Cozimo.   How?
Calandrino.   Why the whole race
Of such as can act naturally fooles parts,
Are quite worne out, and they that doe survive,   230
Doe onely zanie us; and we will bring you,
If we die not without issue, of both sexes
Such chopping mirth-makers, as shall preserve
Perpetuall cause of sport, both to your Grace,
L1ᵛ And your posterity, that sad melancholly   235
Shall ne're approach you.
Cozimo.   We are pleas'd in it,
And will pay her portion. May the passage prove
Of what's presented, worthy of your love,
And favour, as was aym'd, and we have all   239
That can in compasse of our wishes fall.   [*Exeunt.*]

The end.

240 SD. *Exeunt.*] *Gifford; not in* 36

THE PICTURE

INTRODUCTION

(a) *Date*

According to Malone, *The Picture* was licensed for performance on 8 June 1629: '*The Picture*, by Philip Massinger, licensed for the King's Company.'[1]

There is some evidence to suggest that the play was completed shortly before its first production. A satirical reference (II. ii. 17–20) to the training of the gentry at

> An Academie erected, with large pensions
> To such as in a table could set downe
> The congees, cringes, postures, methods, phrase,
> Proper to euery Nation

may have to do with the proposals for an 'Academ Roial or College of Honor', first mooted in 1617 by Edmond Bolton. Bolton was still vainly but hopefully soliciting royal support for his Academy at least as late as October 1627.[2] It is also worth noting that in Jonson's *The New Inn*, first performed in January 1629, the Host criticizes the education of the gentry at some length (I. iii. 52–88), and laments the passing of the days 'when the nourceries selfe, was noble, / And only vertue made it . . . Euery house became / An Academy of honour, and those parts— / We see departed, in the practise, now, / Quite from the institution.'

Eubulus's eloquent protest against the neglect of soldiers in peace time (II. ii. 80–119) is one of Massinger's set pieces in praise of the military profession, repeating several stock themes and expressions from earlier plays.[3] Its material may be too commonplace to provide firm evidence for a particular date of composition, but in 1629 such

---

[1] Adams, *Herbert*, p. 32.

[2] 'The Academ Roial of King James I', E. M. Portal, *Proceedings of the British Academy*, vii (1915–16), 189–208.

[3] See *The Duke of Milan*, III. i. 1–43, and *The Unnatural Combat*, III. iii. 54–106. The comparison Eubulus draws between the soldier and the physician is also found in Gosson's *The School of Abuse* (1579); see the note to II. ii. 84 ff.

a speech would have been apposite enough. England had signed the Treaty of Susa with France on 24 April; on the Continent the Peace of Lubeck, signed on 7 June, confirmed a temporary lull in the Thirty Years War; and the war with Spain (already virtually at an end) was to be formally concluded in November 1630 by the Treaty of Madrid.

(b) *Sources*

The sources of *The Picture* have been studied by Emil Koeppel, Alfred Merle, Arpad Steiner, and G. E. Dawson.[1] Their researches established that one of Massinger's chief sources for the play was the story 'A Lady of Boeme', which is the twenty-eighth tale in the second volume of William Painter's *The Palace of Pleasure* (1580).

The story tells how a knight, Sir Ulrico, went to the court of King Mathias of Hungary, 'to seke meanes for ability to sustaine his wife and himselfe.'[2] With him he took a magic 'Image', given him by Pollacco, 'a very cunning enchaunter', who told him: 'If the wife doe not breake hir maryage faith, you shall still see the same so fayre and wel coloured as it was at the first making, and seeme as though it newly came from the painter's shop, but if perchaunce she meane to abuse her honesty the same wil waxe pale, and in deede committing that filthy Fact, sodainly the colour will be blacke . . . but at times when she is attempted or pursued, the colour will be so yealow as Gold.' In battle with the Turks the knight soon won the name of 'a most valiant soldier and prudent Captaine, whereby he merueylously gayned the fauor and grace of the king.' When Ulrico talked at court of the beauty of his wife, two Hungarian barons made a wager that they could seduce her within the space of five months. First one, then the other, went to Ulrico's castle, but his wife, Lady Barbara, realizing what they intended, sent each in turn into a room whose lock they could not open from inside. Acting through 'a lyttle girle' (Massinger's Corisca), Lady Barbara reduced each of the barons to spinning and reeling, then sent 'one of hir Seruants in poast to the Court to advertise hir husband of all that

---

[1] *Quellen-Studien*, pp. 124–6; *Massingers 'The Picture' und Painter II, 28*, Halle, 1905; 'Massinger's *The Picture*, Bandello, and Hungary', *MLN*, xlvi (1931), 401–3; 'Massinger's "The Picture"', unpublished doctoral dissertation, Cornell University, 1931, pp. xvii–lv.

[2] Quotations are taken from the edition by J. Jacobs, 3 vols., 1890; the complete text is printed in volume 3, pp. 195–221.

which chaunced'. Several court officials were sent to see the barons, 'whom a little before the arriuall of these Commissioners, the Lady had caused to be put together, that by Spinning and Reeling they might comfort one another'. According to the terms of their wager, Ulrico was awarded the barons' wealth and estates, 'the Queene taking the Ladies' part, and fauoring the knight', whereupon he brought his wife to court to live with him.

Massinger has largely invented the characters of Baptista, Corisca, and Hilario, and, in Dawson's words, 'shifts the whole emphasis to a psychological development of the two principal characters' (p. xxxi) under the stress of real moral temptation. It is typical of his treatment, for instance, that Sophia is deeply moved by the report of her husband's behaviour at court (III. vi. 126 ff.), where Painter's heroine remains quite unaffected by her suitors' prattle. The narrative sequence is followed fairly closely (with some compression of events), but, in keeping with his much less solemn treatment of the whole story, Massinger softens the close, ending his play with 'mercy' and 'peace', rather than with the original punishments and rewards.

Painter's 'The Lady of Boeme' is a close translation of a *novella* by Bandello,[1] which itself is derived from a fourteenth-century French epic. There are many other Eastern and European versions of what was originally a Buddhist story dating from about the third century B.C.,[2] and Dawson (pp. xxxix–xlvii) gathers some evidence to suggest that Massinger (who always seems to have read widely in preparation for a new play) knew at least two other English versions: George Whetstone's 'The Arbour of Vertue', a free poetic rendering of Bandello, in his *The Rock of Regard* (1576), and Adam of Cobsam's independent poem, *The Wright's Chaste Wife*.[3] (The latter is the only version in which the importunate suitors are precipitated into a dungeon through a trapdoor, as are Ubaldo and Ricardo in Massinger's play). Massinger may also have come across Spenser's modification of the tale, in *The Faerie Queene*, V. v; there

[1] 'Mirabil Beffa fatta da una Gentildonna a dui Baroni del Regno d'Ongaria', *Novelle* (1554), I. xxi. There is a modern translation (1890) by John Payne for the Villon Society.

[2] A full but not exhaustive account of sources and analogues will be found in *The Ocean of Story* (C. H. Tawney's translation of Somadeva's *Katha Sarit Sagara*), edited by N. M. Penzer, 1924, i. 42–4, and 165–8.

[3] *The Wright's Chaste Wife*, written about 1460, was not printed until 1865, when F. J. Furnivall edited the manuscript for the Early English Text Society, but manuscript or oral versions may have been available in Massinger's time.

are several Spenserian echoes in Hilario's buffoonery in II. i (see notes to II. i. 91–2 and 140).

As I have shown elsewhere,[1] the second main source for *The Picture* was *The Theater of Honour and Knight-hood, or A Compendious Chronicle and Historie of the whole Christian World* (1623), a translation by 'I. W.' of a French work by André Favyn, published at Paris in 1620.

Working freely from genealogies of the Kings of Hungary and Poland, Massinger created his doting ruler, the imperious Honoria, and her blunt critic, Eubulus. There too, in inchoate form, he found the material for the Honoria–Mathias plot, which he shaped as a counterpart to the story of Sophia and the courtiers. The controlling moral themes of *The Picture* were also found in the genealogies:

> The History of this Prince, is (as others of the same nature are) a Mirrour or depicted Table of humaine inconstancie: whereto Great men are a thousand times more subiect, then those that are made of meaner temper, that climbe not, but walke contentedly on plaine ground . . . all men (euen by naturall instinct as it were) doe ill endure the commaund of a woman. For, they will be commaunded by their like, and not by a woman; whom all Lawes, both diuine and humaine haue subiected to Man.[2]

Far from preaching such maxims, Massinger explores their validity in his play, turning Painter's romance of a complaisant husband and a preternaturally loyal wife into a realistic and often amusing picture of human claims to constancy and superiority.

Always meticulous over local detail, Massinger appears to have consulted Knolles's *General History of the Turks* (the third edition was printed in 1621), for the background of the Turkish Wars. There he learned of the presence of Timariot horsemen in Hungary (cf. *The Picture*, I. i. 3–6), while Knolles's account of the battles of Huniades lies behind Ferdinand's long description of the battle in which Mathias wins his fame (II. ii. 128 ff.) Finally, as Koeppel pointed out,[3] Ubaldo and Ricardo's attempt to seduce Sophia, by slandering Mathias and inciting her to revenge herself by cuckolding her husband (with their assistance), imitates the approach used by Iachimo, in his attempted seduction of Imogen (*Cymbeline*, I. vi).

[1] 'Massinger's Hungarian History', *The Yearbook of English Studies*, ii. (1972), 89–92.   [2] *The Theater of Honor and Knight-hood*, ii. 227.
[3] *Quellen-Studien*, pp. 125–6.

(c) *Text*

The only seventeenth-century edition of *The Picture* was published in 1630 by Thomas Walkley. The printer was 'I. N.', identified by his initials and by the ornaments he used as the second John Norton, who kept a press from 1621 to 1640.[1]

There is no entry for this edition in the Stationers' Register, but there is a later record, dated 8 August 1634, of a transfer of the publishing rights to the play to John Waterson.[2]

> M[r]. Io: Waterson. Assigned ouer vnto him by vertue of a Note vnder the hand & seale of Thomas Walkeley & subscribed by M[r]. Rothwell warden all his estate right Title & interest in a Tragi-Comedy called the Picture written by M[r] Messinger   vj[d].

Waterson acquired rights over four other Massinger plays, *The Renegado* (1630), *The Emperor of the East* and *The Maid of Honour* (1632), and *The Unnatural Combat* (1639).

The 1630 quarto is mentioned in booksellers' lists and catalogues in 1656, 1661, 1663, and 1671.[3] It will be referred to from now on as *30*; the title-page exists in two states, the earliest of which is reproduced on page 193.[4]

30 is in quarto, A–M⁴, N² (50 unnumbered leaves); see Greg, *Bibliography*, no. 436 (iii. 586–7). Signatures are in roman, with the

---

[1] H. Jenkins gives a general account of Norton in 'The 1631 Quarto of *The Tragedy of Hoffman*', *The Library*, 5th Series, vi (1951), 88–99, and G. W. Miller provides a catalogue of his ornaments in 'A London Ornament Stock: 1598–1683', *Studies in Bibliography*, vii (1955), 125–51. The device on the title-page corresponds to Miller's Ornament 4, that on A3[r] to Decorative Initial I5, and those on B1[r] to Ornament 26 and Decorative Initial S8. When Norton printed *The Fatal Dowry* in 1632, he used Ornament 26 again on B1[r]; the type ornaments in the two quartos are composed of the same elements, and the running title in *The Fatal Dowry* is in the same fount as that of sheets B to K in *The Picture*.

[2] Register D 298; Greg, *Bibliography*, i. 43; Arber, iv. 324.

[3] Greg, *Bibliography*, iii. 1325, 1335, 1348, and iv. 1659.

[4] Only the upper portion of the title-page was reset, retaining the wording, but changing the layout, the capitalization, and the spelling of '*TRAGÆCOMÆDJE*': 'THE / PICTVRE. / *A* / TRAGECOMEDIE, / As it was often presented with good / allowance, at the *Globe*, and *Blacke-* / *Friers* Play-houses, by the Kings / Maiesties seruants.' The priority of the state reading '*A TRAGÆCOMÆDJE*' is established by two misprints on other pages of the same forme (Dedication, l. 23, Verse, l. 1), which were later corrected. '*TRAGÆCOMÆDJE*' is a spelling characteristic of Massinger (it occurs again in the heading of the commendatory verses on A4[r], and cf. the press corrections from 'TRAGEDIE' to 'TRAGÆDIE' and from 'Trage-Comedy' to 'Tragæ-Comedy' on the title-page of *The Duke of Milan*, and on B1[r] of *The Maid of Honour* respectively), so the variant must be due to the printer's anxiety to give the quarto title-page an attractive appearance.

exception of A3; Signature G2 is misprinted G3, and in some copies E2 is misplaced on E4. The contents are: A1, *blank*; A2^r, *title*; A2^v, 'Dramatis personæ. The Actors names.'; A3^r, *dedication begins*, 'To my Honored, and selected friends of the Noble society of the Inner Temple.'; A3^v, *dedication ends, signed 'Philip Massinger.'*; A4^r, *poem*, 'To his worthy friend M^r. *Philip Massinger*, vpon his *Tragæcomædie* stiled, *The Picture*.'; A4^v, *poem ends, signed 'Thomas Iay.'*; B1^r, 'THE PICTVRE, *A true Hungarian History*.', *text begins*; N2^v, *text ends*, '*FINIS*.' The text is set in roman, 20 lines measuring approximately 80 mm. There are normally 36 lines to the page (B–I), rising to 38 in sheet K (39 on K3^v), and to 39 in sheets L–N. A. K. McIlwraith, in 'Some Bibliographical Notes on Massinger', *The Library*, 4th Series, xi (1931), 85, has shown that in this way the printer was able to save a final half sheet.

In sheets B–I, two sets of running titles regularly alternate between the inner and outer formes, but in sheet K two titles from both sets appear in each forme, and for sheets L–N three new sets of running titles were composed in a smaller type. McIlwraith has given a detailed account of the shuffling about of these titles, in the article mentioned above (pp. 85–6). The change in type corresponds to an increase in the number of lines per page, but no satisfactory explanation of the distribution of running titles in the last three sheets has been found.

There are manifold signs of haste (or extreme carelessness) in the composition of the text. Turned letters and literal misprints are common, and the punctuation is totally inadequate by any standards; there are also many instances of foul case, mixed founts, broken type, frisket cuts, and so on. On the other hand, there are no signs of extensive textual corruption, though a few individual words have been misread. It is reasonably certain that two compositors set up the text; compositor A's stint was sheets B–E, while compositor B was responsible for sheet A, and F–N. Compositor A sets important names in roman in stage directions, where B uses only italic; he uses the spelling *Ile*, against B's *I'll*. In his share of the play there is a strong preference for *-ess(e)* and *-(e)y* endings to *-es* and *-ie* endings (16 :1, and 5 :1), while in B's share of the play *-es* endings are almost as common as those in *-ess(e)* (the figures are 9 :11), and the preference for *-y* to *-ie* endings is less strong (3 :1).

McIlwraith found press corrections in eight out of the twenty-six formes: A, C, M (o) and (i); L (i), and N (o). Most of the corrections are of simple mechanical errors, such as turned letters or literal misprints, though the two lines lost from the foot of M4ᵛ by some accident at the press are restored in the corrected state of sheet M (o). It is unlikely that Massinger assisted in the work of correction; there are none of his characteristic alterations of spelling or punctuation, and none of the compositors' misreadings is set right. At least three copies of *30* contain a fresh setting of sheet I,¹ a degenerate reprint of the original issue rather than the product of another reading of the printer's manuscript. The few copies found, and the badness of the composition and press-work, support McIlwraith's theory that sometime after the original printing the publisher found that he needed a fresh stock of sheet I to put together more copies of the play, and was supplied with a hastily composed reprint.

There is ample spelling evidence, distributed throughout the text, that the printer's copy was a manuscript in Massinger's own hand. Where the dramatist's preferred spelling is one of several widely accepted alternatives, it is generally his which the compositors use: *ghests*, *guifts*, *hard* (heard), *honor*, *lipps*, *lowd*, *perfit*, *sute*. Endings in *-all*, and medial *y* for *i*, are extremely common. Then there are instances of Massinger's more unusual spellings: *atchieuement*, *buisnesse*, *fower* (four), *gieue*, *ijggobobs*, *Phœnix*, *prologe*, *tertij*, *titely*, *threasourer*, *yow*. Both *h* and *c* are unnecessarily capitalised on occasion, and it is evident that, in the manner of the *Believe As You List* manuscript, the printer's copy gave no indications for italics, and lacked marginal capitals. There are a few signs of alteration and addition in the manuscript (see the textual notes to II. ii. 98–9, 309–11; III. vi. 93–5, 113–14).

The stage directions are numerous and often very full, but there is practically no evidence of annotation by a book-keeper. Some directions for music specify an instrument ('*a trumpet.*'; '*A horne.*'), but more often they indicate in general terms the kind of song or musical effect which the author had in mind: '*Loud musicke as they passe, a song in the praise of war*'; '*Musicke aboue, a song of pleasure*'. There are Latinate directions, in Massinger's manner—'*Exeunt omnes præter Eubulum.*'—and frequent permissive directions for groups of minor characters: '*Hilario with other seruants.*'; '*attendants with perfumes.*'; '*Captaines*'; '*fower, or fiue with vizards.*' There is some positive evidence that the manuscript was not used in the

¹ See Greg, *Bibliography*, iii. 586–7, and McIlwraith's article cited in the text, pp. 86–7.

theatre, in the frequent carelessness about bringing minor characters on and off stage (as at I. i. 108, II. ii. 46, 423, IV. ii. 192). Many directions refer to properties, actions, costume, and appearance, in considerable detail, but there is nothing beyond the author's range, and the phrasing often suggests his presence: '*Sophia hauing in the interime redd the letter and opend the Casket.*'; '*Lowd musicke,* Honoria *in state vnder a Canopy, her traine borne vp by* Siluia *and* Acanthe.'; '*Enter* Hilario, *with a long white hayre and beard, in an anticke armour, one with a horne before him.*'; '*Ricardo entring with a great noyse aboue, as fallen.*' In short, the printer's manuscript is likely to have been the author's fair copy of his play, a copy without annotations for use in the theatre.

There are copies of 30 in the following libraries and institutions: the University of Arizona; Bamburgh Castle Library; the Bodleian Library (2 copies); the Boston Public Library; the British Museum (3 copies); the Clark Library, University of California; Cambridge University Library; the Chapin Library; the University of Chicago; the Library of Congress; Cornell University; the Folger Shakespeare Library (3 copies); Glasgow University; Harvard University; the Henry E. Huntington Library (2 copies); the University of Illinois; the University of Leeds; the University of London; Merton College, Oxford; the Pierpont Morgan Library; the Newberry Library; the University of Pennsylvania; Princeton University; the Royal Library, The Hague; the John Rylands Library; the National Library of Scotland; the University of Sheffield; the University of Texas; the Victoria and Albert Museum (2 copies); Worcester College, Oxford; and Yale University.

The present text has been prepared from the Bodleian Library copy, Malone 236 (6).

In the Harbord copy of *The Picture*, now in the Folger Shakespeare Library (Gosse 5297), there are nearly sixty autograph corrections, confined to sheets A–F.[1] Massinger gives most of his attention to punctuation, making the sense of the lines as unambiguous as possible, but he also touches up indistinct letters, and corrects misprints and spellings. There are thirteen substantive corrections, three of them made in the text of Jay's commendatory poem.

The Picture was first reprinted by Dodsley, in volume viii of

---

[1] For the provenance of this copy see vol. i, p. xxxii. The corrections have been studied by Greg, Gray, and McIlwraith; see above, p. 7.

A Select Collection of Old Plays (1744). It was later included in the collected editions of Coxeter, Mason, Gifford, Coleridge, and Cunningham. A bowdlerized text was given in the second volume of *The Plays of Philip Massinger, Adapted for Family Reading*, edited by W. Harness for Murray in 1830; an American edition followed in 1831. Critical editions of the play were prepared in 1931 by G. E. Dawson, unpublished doctoral thesis, Cornell University, Ithaca, New York, and by A. K. McIlwraith, as part of his unpublished Oxford doctoral thesis, 'The Life and Works of Philip Massinger'. The present editor is very much indebted to the thorough work of both these scholars.

For the adaptation by Henry Bate, *The Magic Picture*, published in 1783, see page 190.

Excerpts from *The Picture* were printed in T. Hayward's *The British Muse*, 1738 (reissued in 1740 as *The Quintessence of English Poetry*), and in Charles Lamb's *Specimens of English Dramatic Poets*, 1808. The first scene of the play, and other short passages, were printed in *Beauties of Massinger*, published by John Porter in 1817. Ernest Lafond translated *The Picture* into French, in *Contemporains de Shakspeare: Massinger*, Paris, 1864, as did M. Mélèse, in the first volume of *Les Contemporains de Shakespeare*, Paris, 1934. M. Horn-Monval, *Répertoire bibliographique des traductions et adaptations françaises du théâtre étranger*, Paris, i (1963), no. 281[1, 2], records one adaptation for Radiodiffusion Française by Paul Castan, and another by Madeleine Mélèse and Jacques Dapoigny.

(d) *Stage History*

Most of the information we have about the original performances of the play is contained in Herbert's licence, dated 8 June, 1629 (see p. 181), and the title-page of the 1630 quarto, which says that *The Picture* 'was often presented with good allowance, at the *Globe*, and *Blackefriers* play-houses, by the Kings Maiesties seruants'. Bentley (iv. 809) points out that the release of the text for publication so soon after the original production suggests that the play met with no great success. However, in his dedication to 'my Honored, and selected friends of the Noble society of the Inner Temple', Massinger declares that 'The Play in the presentment found such a generall approbation, that it gaue mee assurance of their fauour to whose protection it is now sacred.' If the dramatist was referring only to a particular performance enjoyed by the Templars, no record of the occasion has survived.¹ The names of twelve of the actors are known from the Cast List printed in *30*.

In his edition of *The Picture*, pp. lvii–lviii, G. E. Dawson endorses the view of several earlier scholars that Heywood borrowed from Massinger in his *A Challenge for Beauty*, probably written in 1634 or 1635.² In both dramas there is a haughty and beautiful queen, married to an uxorious husband, who sends two licentious courtiers to seduce a rival; there are also verbal parallels. In his edition of Simon Baylie's *The Wizard* (*Materials for the Study of the Old English Drama*, N.S. 4, 1930), lvi–lvii, De Vocht listed a number of ideas and expressions which he thought Massinger had culled from Baylie's play. Some of the parallels are clear enough, but it is more than likely that the imitator was Baylie rather than Massinger; *The Wizard* may have been written at any time between 1620 and 1640, and practically nothing is known of its author. R. J. Kaufman found traces of *The Picture* in Brome's *The Queen's Exchange*,³ which may have been written in 1631. The closest parallels occur in the first scene of Brome's play, where an outspoken old courtier criticizes an imperious Queen, just as Eubulus does in *The Picture*, I. ii, and in the language of II. i, in which an ambassador describes the Queen of the doting King Osric, who is thrown into a melancholic fit by a fancied insult to her picture.

There have been occasional revivals of *The Picture*. Sybil Rosenfeld found a record of a production of the play by William Smith's provincial company at Canterbury in February 1763, 'revived after nine years' absence for the benefit of Miss Seymour.' The company then travelled to Sittingbourne, giving *The Picture* there for the first time in April and May.⁴

In his 1805 edition of Massinger, Gifford referred to an attempted revival of *The Picture* by Kemble, but in the 1813 edition he corrected the name to that of Henry Bate (later Sir Henry Bate Dudley), who in 1783 did write an adaptation of the play, called *The Magic Picture*. This was produced at Covent Garden on 8 November, and

---

¹ From 1629 to 1641 the 'Blackfriars Players' performed the two plays given each year in the Inner Temple hall, one at Allhallows and the other at Candlemas, but titles of plays are seldom mentioned in the existing records; see *A Calendar of the Inner Temple Records*, ed. F. A. Inderwick and R. A. Roberts (5 vols., 1896–1936), ii. pp. xlix–liv.
² See Bentley, iv. 563.　　　　　　³ *Richard Brome*, 1961, p. 179.
⁴ *Strolling Players and Drama in the Provinces* (*1660–1765*), 1939, pp. 262–3.

The London Stage (*1660–1800*), Part 5, ed. C. B. Hogan, Carbondale, Illinois, 1968, i, records six more performances, the last on 2 January 1784.[1] The play was introduced by no less a character than the Ghost of Massinger:

> Regardless of your bell, which strikes mine ear,
> I, troubled shade of *Massinger*, appear!
> What frenzy cou'd impel the daring thought,
> To seize the PIECE my lab'ring fancy wrought?
> The PICTURE glowing with selected *dies*?—
> O 'tis a deed to make a *Spirit* rise!
> But why should I meet favour from an age,
> That marks even Shakespeare in its rage?

The cast included Wroughton (Eugenius), Whitfield (Ladislaus), Clarke (Eubulus), Hull (Baptista), Davies (Ferdinand), Edwin (Ubaldo), Wilson (Ricardo), Quick (Hilario), Mrs. Bates (Honoria), Mrs. Wilson (Corisca), Miss Platt (Acanthe), and Miss Younge (Sophia). Aickin spoke the prologue, and music written by Shields was 'sung by almost all the musical powers of the house'.

Bate's play was published soon after its first performance,[2] and in an Advertisement dated 17 November 1783, he describes his own adaptation. 'After giving a different turn to the drama, by making the changes of the Picture, the effects of *Eugenius's* jealousy, instead of the magic art of *Baptista*, and expunging the gross indelicacies which overran the play, it was found that most of the characters required a little fresh modelling to complete the design of the present undertaking. Hence the necessity of new-writing no inconsiderable part of the dialogue, in imitation of the old Dramatist. . . . The same kind of irregular and broken measure still prevails, except where the language could be reduced to the heroic verse without impairing the spirit of the dialogue' (A3ʳ). Bate scarcely altered the plot, but the play was 'lightened' by the insertion of four songs (including

---

[1] There are reviews in *The London Magazine*, Nov. 1783, 457, *The British Magazine and Review*, iii (Nov. 1783), 382, *The Town and Country Magazine*, xv (1783), 603–4, and *The London Chronicle*, Nov. 8–11, 1783. Comment was generally favourable: the critic in *The Town and Country Magazine* wrote, 'The comedy was received with great applause, and it will probably, in its new garb, turn out a stock play.' However, a review of the published play in *The English Review*, ii (1783), 471, strongly objected to 'some nasty allusions to a disorder not fit to be mentioned in decent company.'

[2] The prologue is among the Larpent manuscripts (Larpent 637); it was printed, together with three of the songs from the play, in *The London Magazine*, issue cited, p. 607.

a Gilbertian dialogue sung by Ricardo and Ubaldo in their imprisonment!), the comic parts of Hilario and Corisca were developed,
and the dialogue was cavalierly cut or rewritten in the interests of
clarity, brevity, and decorum. A reviewer observed that 'the
principal objection to the play is, that there is too much farce in it,
an objection that dies away before the *Gods*.'

No later performance of *The Picture* is known.

THE PICTVRE

A TRAGÆCOMÆDIE,

As it was often presented with good
allowance, at the *Globe*, and
Blackefriers play-houses, by
the Kings Maiesties
seruants.

Written by Philip Massinger.

LONDON.

Printed by *I. N.* for *Thomas Walkley* and are
to be sould at his shoppe at the *Eagle* and
Child in Brittains Burse. 1630.

Dramatis personæ.	The Actors names.	
Ladislaus King of Hungarie.	*Robert Benfield.*	
Eubulus an old Counsaylor.	*Iohn Lewin.*	
Ferdinand Generall of the army.	*Richard Sharpe.*	
Mathias a knight of *Bohemia.*	*Ioseph Taylor.*	5
Vbaldo,	*Thomas Pollard.*	
Ricardo, 2. wild courtiers.	*Eylardt Swanstone.*	
Hilario seruant to *Sophia.*	*Iohn Shanucke.*	
Iulio Baptista a great scholler.	*William Pen.*	
Honoria the Queene.	*Iohn Tomson.*	10
Acanthe a maid of honor.	*Alexander Goffe.*	
[*Siluia* a maid of honor.]		
Sophia wife to *Mathias.*	*Iohn Hunnieman.*	
Corisca, Sophias woman.	*William Trigge.*	

6. Masquers.   15
6. Seruants to the Queene.
   Attendants.
[2. Posts.]
[2. Captaines.]
[2. Boyes.]   20
[A Guide.]

12. *Siluia* . . . honor.] *Gifford*; *not in 30*   18–21. 2. Posts . . . Guide.] *Gifford*;
not in 30

To my Honored, and selected friends of the Noble society of the Inner Temple.

I T may bee obiected, my not inscribing their names, or tittles, to whom I dedicate this Poem, proceedeth either from my diffidence of their affection to me, or their vnwillingnes to be publishde the 5 Patrons of a trifle. To such as shall make so strict an inquisition of mee, I truely answere. The Play in the presentment found such a generall approbation, that it gaue mee assurance of their fauour to whose protection it is now sacred, and they haue profes'd they so sincerely allow of it, and the maker, that they would haue freely 10 granted that in the publication, which for some reasons, I denide my selfe. One, and that is a maine one: I had rather inioy (as I haue donne) the reall proofes of their friendship, then mountebancke like boast their numbers in a Catalogue. Accept it noble gentlemen as a confirmation of his seruice who hath nothing else to assure you, 15 and witnes to the world how much he stands ingagd for your soe frequent bounties, and in your charitable opinion of me beleeue, that you now may, and shall euer command,

Your seruant

Philip Massinger. 20

To his worthy friend M.ʳ *Philip Massinger,*
vpon his *Tragæcomædie*
stiled, *The Picture.*

ME thinkes I heere some busy Criticke say
Who's this that singly vshers on this Play?
'Tis boldnes I confesse, and yet perchance
It may be constur'd loue, not arrogance.
I do not heere vpon this leafe intrude   5
By praysing one, to wrong a multitude.
Nor do I thinke that all are tyed to be
(Forc'd by my vote) in the same creed with me.
Each man hath liberty to iudge; free will,
At his owne pleasure to speake good, or ill.   10
But yet your Muse alreadie's knowne so well
Her worth will hardly find an infidell.
Heere she hath drawne a picture, which shall lye
Safe for all future times to practisse by.
What ere shall follow are but Coppies, some   15
Preceding workes were types of this to come.
'Tis your owne liuely image, and setts forth
When we are dust the beauty of your worth.
He that shall dully read and not aduance
Ought that is heere betrayes his ignorance.   20
Yet whosoeuer beyond desert commends
Errs more by much then he that reprehends,
For prayse misplac'd, and honor set vpon
A worthlesse subiect is detraction.
I cannot sin so heere, vnlesse I went   25
About, to stile you only excellent.
Apollo's guifts are not confind alone
To your dispose, He hath more heires then one,
And such as do deriue from his blest hand

1. thinkes] *30²*; thinges *30¹*

A large inheritance in the Poets land   30
As well as you, nor are you I assure
My selfe so enuious, but you can endure
To heere their praise, whose worth long since was knowne
And iustly to, prefer'd before your owne.
I know you would take it for an iniury,   35
(And 'tis a well becomming modesty)
To be paraleld with *Beaumont*, or to heare
Your name by some to partiall friend writt neere
Vnequal'd *Ionson*: being men whose fire
At distance, and with reuerence you admire.   40
Do so and you shall find your gaine will bee
Much more by yeelding them prioritie
Then with a certainety of losse to hould
A foolish competition; Tis to bould
A tasque, and to be shunde, nor shall my prayse   45
With to much waight ruine, what it would rayse.

Thomas Iay.

---

34. iustly] *Coxeter*; lustly *30*   35. you] *30²*; yon *30¹*   37. or] *Massinger MS*; or *defective 30*   38. writt] *Massinger MS*; write *30*   40. admire] *Massinger MS*; admir'd *30*

The Picture

A true Hungarian History

Actus primi, Scena prima.

Enter MATHIAS *in armour,* SOPHIA *in a riding sute,* CORISCA, HILARIO, *with other Seruants.*

Mathias. SINCE we must part *Sophia*, to passe further
Is not alone impertinent but dangerous.
We are not distant from the *Turkesh* campe
Aboue fiue leagues, and who knowes but some partie
Of his Timariots that scoure the countrey   5
May fall vpon vs. Be now as thy name
Truely interpreted hath euer spoke thee,
Wise, and discreete, and to thy vnderstanding
Marrie thy constant pacience.
   Sophia.   Yow put me Sir,
To the vtmost triall of it.
   Mathias.   Nay noe melting,   10
Since the necessity that now seperates vs,
We haue long since disputed, and the reasons
Forcing me to it, too oft wash'd in teares.
I grant that you in birth were farre aboue mee,
And great men my superiours riualls for you,   15
But mutuall consent of hearts as hands
Ioynde by true loue hath made vs one, and equall;
Nor is it in me meere desire of fame,
Or to be cride vp by the publike voyce
For a braue souldier that puts on my armour,   20
Such aerie tumours take not me. You know
How narrow our demeanes are, and whats more,
Hauing as yet no charge of children on vs

I. i. 13. teares.] *Dodsley*; teates, *30*   16. hearts] *McIlwraith*; heart, *30*

We hardly can subsist.
   Sophia.   In you alone sir
I haue all abundance.
   Mathias.   For my minds content   25
In your owne language I could answere you.
You haue beene an obedient wife, a right one,
And to my power, though short of your desert
I haue beene euer an indulgent husband.
We haue long inioyd the sweets of loue, and though   30
Not to Satietie, or lothing, yet
We must not liue such dotardes on our pleasures
As still to hugge them to the certaine losse
Of profit, and preferment; competent meanes
Maintaines a quiet bed, want breeds dissention   35
Euen in good women.
   Sophia.   Haue you found in me sir
Any distast, or signe of discontent
For want of whats superfluous?
   Mathias.   No *Sophia.*
Nor shalt thou euer haue cause to repent
Thy constant course in goodnes (if heauen blesse   40
My honest vndertakings); 'tis for thee
That I turne souldier, and put forth deerest
Vpon this sea of action as a factor
To trade for rich materialls to adorne
Thy noble parts, and show 'em in full lustre.   45
I blush that other ladies lesse in beauty
And outward forme, but in the harmonie
Of the soules rauishing musicke the same age
Not to be nam'd with thee, should so out shine thee
In iewels, and variety of wardrobes,   50
B2r While you (to whose sweet innocence both Indies
Compar'd are of no value) wanting these
Passe vnregarded.
   Sophia.   If I am so rich sir
In your opinion, why should you borrow
Additions for me?

---

26. you.] *Massinger MS*; ~∧ 30   31. Satietie] *Massinger MS*; satisfie 30
40–1. (if . . . vndertakings);] *Massinger MS* (vndertakings)); if . . . vndertakings; 30
53. sir] *Massinger MS* (s^r.); or 30

Mathias.　　　　Why? I should be censur'd　　　55
Of ignorance, possessing such a Iewell
Aboue all price, if I forbeare to giue it
The best of ornaments. Therefore *Sophia*
In few words know my pleasure and obey me,
As you haue euer done. To your discretion,　　60
I leaue the gouerment of my family
And our poore fortunes, and from these command
Obedience to you as to my selfe.
To the vtmost of what's mine liue plentifully,
And ere the remnant of our store be spent,　　65
With my good sword I hope I shall reape for you
A haruest in such full abundance, as
Shall make a merry winter.
　　Sophia.　　　　　Since you are not
To be diuerted Sir from what you purpose
All arguments to stay you heere are vselesse.　　70
Goe when you please Sir; Eyes I charge you waste not
One drop of sorrow, looke you hoord all vp
Till in my widdowed bed I call vpon you,
But then be sure you faile not. You blest Angels,
Guardians of humane life, I at this instant　　75
Forbeare t'inuoke you, at our parting 'twere
To personate deuotion. My soule
Shall goe along with you, and when you are
Circl'd with death and horrour seeke and finde you:
And then I will not leaue a Saint vnsu'd to　　80
For your protection. To tell you what
I will doe in your absence, would shew poorely,
My actions shall speake me; 'twere to doubt you
To begge I may heere from you, where you are,
You cannot liue obscure nor shall one post　　85
By night, or day passe vnexamined by me.
If I dwell long vpon your lips, consider
After this feast the griping fast that followes
And it will be excusable. Pray turne from mee.
All that I can is spoken.　　　　　*Exit* SOPHIA.
　　Mathias.　　　　Follow your mistrisse.　　90

60. done.] *Massinger MS*; ~ ∧ *30*　　　84. you,] *30*; ~; *Gifford*　　are,] *30*; ~;
Dodsley　　90. mistrisse] *Massinger MS*; mistersse *30*

B2ᵛ

Forbeare your wishes for me, let mee finde 'em
At my returne in your prompt will to serue her.
   Hilario. For my part sir I will grow leane with study
To make her merry.
   Corisca.   Though you are my Lord,
Yet being her gentlewoman, by my place   95
I may take my leaue; your hand or if you please
To haue me fight so high, ile not be coy
But stande a tiptoe for't.
   Mathias.   O farewell gyrle.
   Hilario. A kisse well begg'd *Corisca.*
   Corisca.   Twas my fee,
Loue how he melts! I cannot blame my ladies   100
Vnwillingnesse to part with such marmulade lips.
There will be scrambling for 'em in the campe,
And were it not for my honesty I could wish now
I were his leager landresse. I would finde
Sope of mine owne, enough to wash his linnen   105
Or I would straine hard for't.
   Hilario.   How the mammet twitters!
Come, come my ladie staies for vs.
   Corisca.   Would I had beene
Her ladiship the last night.
   Hilario.   Noe more of that, wench.
          Exeunt HILARIO[, CORISCA, *and Seruants*].
   Mathias. I am strangely troubled: yet why should I nourish
A furie heere, and with imagind foode,   110
Hauing no reall grounds on which to raise
A building of suspition, she was euer
B3ʳ Or can be false heereafter? I in this
But foolishly inquire the knowledge of
A future sorrow, which if I find out,   115
My present ignorance were a cheape purchase
Though with my losse of beeing. I haue already
Dealt with a friend of mine, a generall scholler,
One deepely read in natures hidden secrets,
And though with much vnwillingnesse haue woone him   120

---

108 SD. CORISCA ... *Seruants*] *after Gifford*; *not in 30*   109. should I] *Dodsley*;
I should *30*   112. building] *Dodsley*; buildings *30*   120. woone] *Massinger*
MS; wone *30*

To doe asmuch as Art can to resolue me
My fate that followes—to my wish, Hee's come.

Enter BAPTISTA.

Iulio Baptista, now I may affirme
Your promise, and performance walke together.
And therefore without circumstance to the point, 125
Instruct me what I am.
    Baptista.   I could wish you had
Made triall of my loue some other way.
    Mathias. Nay this is from the purpose.
    Baptista.   If you can
Proportion your desire to any meane
I do pronounce you happy. I haue found 130
By certaine rules of Art your matchlesse wife
Is to this present hower from all pollution
Free and vntainted.
    Mathias.   Good.
    Baptista.   In reason therefore
You should fixe heere, and make no farther search
Of what may fall heereafter.
    Mathias.   O *Baptista* 135
Tis not in me to master so my passions,
I must know farther, or you haue made good
But halfe your promise. While my loue stood by,
Holding her vpright, and my presence was
A watch vpon her; her desires being met to 140
With equall ardor from me; what one proofe
Could she giue of her constancy, being vntempted?
But when I am absent, and my comming backe
Vncertaine, and those wanton heates in women
Not to be quench'd by lawfull meanes, and shee 145
The absolute disposer of her selfe,
Without controule, or curbe, nay more inuited
By opportunity and all strong temptations,
If then she hold out—
    Baptista.   As no doubt she will.
    Mathias. Those doubts must be made certainties *Baptista* 150
By your assurance, or your boasted Art

122. followes—] *Massinger MS*; ∼ₐ *30*   138. promise.] *Massinger MS*; ∼ₐ *30*

Deserues no admiration. How you trifle,
And play with my affliction! I am on
The racke till you confirme mee.
    Baptista.   Sure *Mathias,*
I am no God, nor can I diue into   155
Her hidden thoughts, or know what her intents are.
That is deni'd to art, and kept conceald
Euen from the diuels themselues: they can but guesse
Out of long obseruation what is likely,
But positiuely to foretell that this shall be   160
You may conclude impossible. All I can
I will doe for you, when you are distant from her
A thousand leauges as if you then were with her
You shall know truly when she is solicited,
And how far wrought on.
    Mathias.   I desire no more.   165
    Baptista. Take then this little modell of *Sophia*
With more then humane skill limde to the life;
Each line, and linament of it in the drawing
Soe punctually obserued that had it motion
In so much 'twere her selfe.
    Mathias.   It is indeede   170
An admirable peece, but if it haue not
Some hidden vertue that I cannot guesse at
In what can it aduantage me?
    Baptista.   Ile instruct you.
Carry it still about you and as oft
B4ʳ As you desire to know how shee's affected   175
With curious eyes peruse it. While it keepes
The figure it now has intire, and perfit,
She is not onely innocent in fact
But vnattempted: but if once it varie
From the true forme, and what's now white, and red   180
Incline to yellow, rest most confident
Shees with all violence courted but vnconquerd.
But if it turne all blacke 'tis an assurance
The fort by composition, or surprize

---

152. admiration.] *Massinger MS*; ~, *30*   trifle,] *Massinger MS*; ~ₐ *30*
154. racke] *Massinger MS*; wracke *30*   162. you,] *Massinger MS*; ~ₐ *30*
177. perfit,] *Massinger MS*; ~ₐ *30*   181. yellow,] *Massinger MS*; ~ₐ *30*

Is forc'd or with her free consent surrenderd.   185
     Mathias. How much you haue ingag'd me for this fauour,
The seruice of my whole life shall make good.
     Baptista. We will not part so, Ile along with you,
And it is needfull. With the rising Sun
The armies meete, yet ere the fights begun   190
In spite of oposition I will place you
In the head of the Hungarian Generals troope
And neere his person.
     Mathias.   As my better Angel
You shall direct and guide mee.
     Baptista.   As we ride   194
Ile tell you more.
     Mathias.   In all things Ile obey you.   *Exeunt.*

Actus primi, scæna secunda.

Enter VBALDO, RICARDO.

Ricardo. When came the post?
Vbaldo.   The last night.
Ricardo.   From the campe?
Vbaldo. Yes as 'tis said, and the letter writ and signd
By the generall *Ferdinand.*
     Ricardo.   Nay then sans question
It is of moment.
     Vbaldo.   It concernes the liues
Of two great armies.
     Ricardo.   Was it cherfully   5
Receiued by the King?
     Vbaldo.   Yes, for being assured
The armies were in view of one another,
Hauing proclaimed a publicke fast, and prayer
For the good successe, dispatch'd a gentleman
Of his priuy chamber to the generall   10
With absolute authority from him
To trie the fortune of a day.

188. you,] *Massinger MS*; ~ₐ *30*   189. needfull.] *Massinger MS*; ~ₐ *30*
190. fights] *Massinger MS*; fight *30*   I. ii. 6. for] *30*; for he *McIlwraith*   9. the]
30; his *McIlwraith*   dispatch'd] *30*; he dispatch'd *Dodsley*

    Ricardo.   No doubt then
The Generall will come on and fight it brauelye.
Heauen prosper him, this militarie art
I grant to be the noblest of professions   15
And yet I thanke my stars for't I was neuer
Inclin'd to learne it, since this bubble honour,
(Which is indeede the nothing souldiers fight for
With the losse of limbes, or life) is in my iudgement
Too deare a purchase.
    Vbaldo.   Giue me our Court-warfare,   20
The danger is not great in the encounter
Of a faire Mistresse.
    Ricardo.   Faire and sound together
Doe very well *Vbaldo.* But such are
With difficulty to be found out, and when they know
Their value prizde too high. By thy owne report   25
Thou wast at twelue a gamester, and since that
Studied all kinds of females, from the night-trader
I'the streete, with certaine danger to thy pocket,
To the great Lady in her Cabinet,
That spent vpon thee more in cullises   30
To strengthen thy weake backe, then would maintaine
Twelue Flanders mares, and as many running horses:
Besides Apothecaries and Chirurgeons bills
Payd vpon all occasions, and those frequent.
   C1ʳ   *Vbaldo.* You talke *Ricardo,* as if yet you were   35
A nouice in those misteries.
    Ricardo.   By no meanes.
My Doctor can assure the contrary,
I loose no time, I haue felt the paine and pleasure,
As he that is a gamester, and playes often
Must sometimes be a looser.
    Vbaldo.   Wherefore then   40
Doe you enuy me?
    Ricardo.   It growes not from my want,
Nor thy abundance, but being as I am
The likelier man, and of much more experience,
My good parts, are my curses; there's no beauty

---

13. brauelye.] *Massinger MS* (brauely,e); brauely, *30 (defective* y)   38. time,]
Massinger MS; ~. *30*   44. curses] *Massinger MS*; cursies *30*

But yeeldes ere it be summon'd, and as nature 45
Had sign'd me the monopolie of maidenheads,
There's none can buy till I haue made my market.
Satiety cloyes me; as I liue I would part with
Halfe my estate, nay trauaile ore the world
To finde that onely Phænix in my search 50
That could hold out against me.
    Vbaldo.   Be not rapp'd so:
You may spare that labour, as she is a woman
What thinke you of the Queene?
    Ricardo.   I dare not aime at
The petticoate royall, that is still excepted:
Yet were she not my Kings, being the abstract 55
Of all that's rare, or to be wish'd in woman,
To write her in my catalogue, hauing inioy'd her,
I would venter my necke to a halter. But we talke of
Impossibilities; as she hath a beauty
Would make old *Nestor* young, such maiesty 60
Drawes foorth a sword of terrour to defend it,
As would fright *Paris*, though the Queene of loue
Vow'd her best furtherance to him.
    Vbaldo.   Haue you obseru'd
The grauity of her language mix'd with sweetnesse?
    Ricardo. Then at what distance she reserues her selfe 65
When the King himselfe makes his approaches to her.
    Vbaldo. As she were still a virgine, and his life
But one continued wooing.
    Ricardo.   She well knowes
Her worth, and values it.
    Vbaldo.   And so farre the King is
Indulgent to her humors, that he forbeares 70
The duety of a husband, but when she calles for't.
    Ricardo. All his imaginations and thoughts
Are buried in her, the lowd noyse of warre
Cannot awake him.
    Vbaldo.   At this very instant,
When both his life and Crowne are at the stake, 75
He onely studies her content, and when
She's pleas'd to shew her selfe, musicke and masques

71. but] *Massinger MS*; bxt 30

Are with all care and cost prouided for her.
Ricardo. This night she promis'd to appeare.
Vbaldo.   You may
Beleeue it by the diligence of the King   80
As if he were her harbinger.

Enter LADISLAUS, EUBULUS, *and Attendants with perfumes.*

Ladislaus.   These roomes
Are not perfum'd as we directed.
Eubulus.   Not Sir?
I know not what you would haue, I am sure the smoke
Cost treble the price of the whole weekes prouision
Spent in your Maiesties kitchins.
Ladislaus.   How! I scorne   85
Thy grosse comparison. When my *Honoria*,
Th'amazement of the present time, and enuy
Of all succeeding ages does descend
To sanctifie a place, and in her presence
Makes it a Temple to me, can I be   90
C2ʳ Too curious, much lesse prodigall to receiue her?
But that the splendour of her beames of beauty
Hath strucke thee blinde—
Eubulus.   As dotage hath done you.
Ladislaus. Dotage, O blasphemy! is it in me
To serue her to her merit? is she not   95
The daughter of a King?
Eubulus.   And you the sonne
Of ours I take it, by what priuiledge else
Doe you reigne ouer vs? for my part I know not
Where the dispairity lyes.
Ladislaus.   Her birth old man,
Old in the Kingdomes seruice which protects thee,   100
Is the least grace in her: and though her beauties
Might make the thunderer a riuall for her,
They are but superficiall ornaments
And faintly speake her; from her heauenly mind
Were all antiquity and fiction lost   105
Our moderne Poets could not in their fancie
But fashion a *Minerua* farre transcending

79–80. may / Beleeue] *Gifford*; *undivided 30*   93. you] *Dodsley*; yon *30*

Th'imagin'd one, whom *Homer* onely dreamt of.
But then adde this, she's mine, mine *Eubulus*,
And though she know one glance from her faire eyes   110
Must make all gazers her idolaters,
Shee is so sparing of their influence
That to shun superstition in others,
Shee shootes her powerfull beames onely at me.
And can I then, whom she desires to hold   115
Her Kingly captiue aboue all the world,
Whose Nations and Empires if she pleas'd
Shee might command as slaues, but gladly pay
The humble tribute of my loue and seruice?
Nay if I sayd of adoration to her   120
I did not erre.
    Eubulus.   Well, since you hugge your fetters
In loues name weare'em. You are a King, and that
Concludes you wise. Your will a powerfull reason,
Which we that are foolish Subiects must not argue.
And what in a meane man I should call folly,   125
Is in your Maiesty remarkable wisedome.
But for me I subscribe.
    Ladislaus.   Doe, and looke vp:
Vpon this wonder.

Lowd musicke, HONORIA *in state vnder a Canopy, her traine
        borne vp by* SILVIA *and* ACANTHE.

    Ricardo.   Wonder? it is more Sir.
    Vbaldo. A rapture, an astonishment.
    Ricardo.   What thinke you Sir?
    Eubulus. As the King thinkes, that is the surest guard   130
We Courtiers euer lie at. Was Prince euer
So drownd in dotage? Without spectacles
I can see a hansome woman, and she is so:
But yet to admiration looke not on her.
Heauen how he fawnes; and as it were his duty,   135
With what assured grauity she receiues it!
Her hand againe! O she at length vouchsafes
Her Lip, and as he had suck'd Nectar from it
How he's exalted! Women in their natures
Affect command, but this humility   140

2ᵛ

In a husband and a King markes her the way
To absolute tyranie. So, *Iuno's* plac'd
In *Ioues* Tribunall, and like *Mercurie*,
Forgetting his owne greatnesse, he attends
For her imployments. She prepares to speake,   145
What Oracles shall we heare now?
    Honoria.   That you please Sir,
With such assurances of loue and fauour,
To grace your handmaid, but in being yours Sir,
A matchlesse Queene, and one that knowes her selfe so,
Bindes me in retribution to deserue   150
The grace conferd vpon me.
    Ladislaus.   You transcend
In all things excellent, and it is my glory,
Your worth weigh'd truly, to depose my selfe
From absolute command, surrendring vp
My will and faculties to your disposure: 155
And heere I vow, not for a day or yeere,
But my whole life, which I wish long to serue you:
That whatsoeuer I in iustice may
Exact from these my subiects, you from me
May boldly challenge. And when you require it,   160
In signe of my subiection, as your vassall,
Thus I will pay my homage.
    Honoria.   O forbeare Sir,
Let not my Lips enuie my Robe: on them
Print your alegiance often. I desire
No other fealtie.
    Ladislaus.   Gracious Soueraigne,   165
Boundlesse in bounty!
    Eubulus.   Is not heere fine fooling?
He's questionlesse bewitch'd. Would I were gelt,
So that would disenchant him. Though I forfeit
My life for it I must speake. By your good leaue sir,
I haue no sute to you, nor can you grant one   170
Hauing no Power. You are like me a subiect,
Her more then serene Maiesty being present.
And I must tell you, 'tis ill manners in you,
Hauing depos'd your selfe to keepe your hat on,
And not stand bare as we doe, being no King,   175

C3ʳ

But a fellow subiect with vs. Gentlemen vshers
It does belong to your place, see it reform'd,
He has giuen away his Crowne, and cannot challenge
The priuiledge of his bonnet.
Ladislaus. Doe not tempt me.
Eubulus. Tempt you, in what? in following your example? 180
If you are angry question me heereafter,
As *Ladislaus* should do *Eubulus*
On equall termes. You were of late my soueraigne
But weary of it, I now bend my knee
To her diuinity, and desire a boone 185
From her more then magnificence.
Honoria. Take it freely.
Nay be not mou'd, for our mirth sake let vs heare him.
Eubulus. 'Tis but to aske a question, haue you ne're read
The story of *Semiramis* and *Ninus*?
Honoria. Not as I remember.
Eubulus. I will then instruct you, 190
And tis to the purpose: this *Ninus* was a King,
And such an impotent louing King as this was
But now hee's none; this *Ninus* (pray you obserue me)
Doted on this *Semiramis*, a smiths wife,
(I must confesse there the comparison holdes not, 195
You are a Kings daughter, yet vnder your correction
Like her a woman); this *Assirian monarch*
(Of whom this is a patterne) to expresse
His loue, and seruice, seated her as you are,
In his regall throne, and bound by oth his Nobles 200
Forgetting all alleageance to himselfe
One day to be her subiects, and to put
In execution what euer shee
Pleas'd to impose vpon 'em. Pray you command him
To minister the like to vs and then 205
You shall heare what follow'd.
Ladislaus. Well sir to your story.
Eubulus. You haue no warrant, stand by. Let me know
Your pleasure Goddesse.
Honoria. Let this nod assure you.
Eubulus. Goddesse like indeede, as I liue a pretty Idoll!

179. not] *Dodsley*; no *30*   180. example?] *Massinger MS* (example); examp *30*

She knowing her power, wisely made vse of it 210
And fearing his inconstancy, and repentance
Of what he had granted (as in reason Madam,
You may doe his) that hee might neuer haue
C4^r Power to recall his grant, or question her
For her short gouernment, instantly gaue order 215
To haue his head strucke off.
    Ladislaus.   I'st possible?
    Eubulus. The story sayes so and commends her wisedome
For making vse of her authority:
And it is worth your imitation Madam,
He loues subiection, and you are no Queene 220
Vnlesse you make him feele the waight of it.
You are more then all the world to him, and that
He may be soe to you, and not seeke change,
When his delights are sated, mew him vp
In some close prison, if you let him liue, 225
(Which is no policy) and there dyet him
As you thinke fit to feede your appetite
Since there ends his ambition.
    Vbaldo.   Diuelish counsaile.
    Ricardo. The King's amaz'd.
    Vbaldo.   The Queene appeares too full
Of deepe imaginations, *Eubulus* 230
Hath put both to it.
    Ricardo.   Now she seemes resolu'd;
I long to know the issue.   HONORIA *descends.*
    Honoria.   Giue me leaue,
Deare sir to reprehend you for appearing
Perplex'd with what this old man, out of enuy
Of your vnequal'd graces showr'd vpon me, 235
Hath in his fabulous story sawcily
Applide to me: sir that you onely nourish
One doubt *Honoria* dares abuse the power
With which shee is inuested by your fauour,
Or that she euer can make vse of it 240
To the iniury of you the great bestower,
Takes from your iudgement. It was your delight

   223. soe] *conj. Coxeter;* foe *30;* true *Mason*   225. liue,] *Massinger MS;* ∼ₐ *30*
   234. man,] *Massinger MS;* ∼ₐ *30*

To seeke to me with more obsequiousnesse,
4ᵛ Then I desir'd. And stood it with my duety
Not to receiue what you were pleas'd to offer?   245
I doe but act the Part you put vpon me,
And though you make me personate a Queene,
And you my subiect, when the play your pleasure
Is at a period, I am what I was
Before I enter'd, still your humble wife,   250
And you my royall Soueraigne.
 Ricardo.   Admirable!
 Honoria. I haue heard of Captains taken more with dangers
Then the rewards, and if in your approches
To those delights which are your owne, and freely,
To heighten your desire, you make the passage   255
Narrow and difficult, shall I prescribe you?
Or blame your fondnesse? Or can that swell me
Beyond my iust proportion?
 Vbaldo.   Aboue wonder!
 Ladislaus. Heauen make me thankefull for such goodnesse.
 Honoria.   Now Sir,
The state I tooke to satisfie your pleasure   260
I change to this humility, and the oath
You made to me of homage, I thus cancell,
And seate you in your owne.
 Ladislaus.   I am transported
Beyond my selfe.
 Honoria. And now to your wise Lordship,
Am I prou'd a *Semiramis*? or hath   265
My *Ninus*, as maliciously you made him,
Cause to repent th'excesse of fauour to me,
Which you call dotage?
 Ladislaus.   Answere wretch.
 Eubulus.   I dare Sir,
And say how euer the euent may pleade
In your defence, you had a guilty cause;   270
Nor was it wisedome in you (I repeate it)
To teach a Lady, humble in her selfe,
1ʳ With the ridiculous dotage of a louer
To be ambitious.
 Honoria. *Eubulus,* I am so,

Tis rooted in me, you mistake my temper.   275
I do professe my selfe to be the most
Ambitious of my sex, but not to hould
Command ouer my Lord, such a proud torrent
Would sincke me in my wishes; not that I
Am ignorant how much I can deserue   280
And may with iustice challenge.
   Eubulus.   This I look'd for;
After this seeming humble ebbe I knew
A gushing tide would follow.
   Honoria.   By my birth,
And liberall giftes of nature, as of fortune,
From you, as things beneath me, I expect   285
What's due to maiesty, in which I am
A sharer with your soueraigne.
   Eubulus.   Good againe!
   Honoria. And as I am most eminent in place,
In all my actions I would appeere so.
   Ladislaus. You need not feare a riuall.
   Honoria.   I hope not;   290
And till I finde one, I disdaine to know
What enuie is.
   Ladislaus.   You are aboue it Madam.
   Honoria. For beauty without art, discourse, and free
From affectation, with what graces else
Can in the wife and daughter of a King   295
Be wish'd, I dare prefer my selfe.
   Eubulus.   As I
Blush for you lady. Trumpet your owne prayses?
This spoken by the people had beene heard
With honour to you; does the court afford
No oyle-tongu'd parasite, that you are forc'd   300
To be your owne grosse flatterer?
D1ᵛ   *Ladislaus.*   Bee dumbe,
Thou spirit of contradiction.
   Honoria.   The wolfe
But barkes against the Moone, and I contemne it.
The masque you promis'd.

   296. selfe. / As I] *30*; selfe, as— / I *Gifford*   297. lady. Trumpet] *Gifford*;
lady, trumpet *30*; lady, trumpet not *Dodsley* prayses?] *30*; ~! *Dodsley*

A horne. *Enter a* POST.

Ladislaus.   Let 'em enter. How!
Eubulus. Heere's one, I feare vnlook'd for.
Ladislaus.   From the Campe?
Post. The Generall victorious in your fortune,   306
Kisses your hand in this Sir.
   Ladislaus.   That great Power,
Who at his pleasure does dispose of battailes,
Be euer prais'd for't. Read sweet, and pertake it:
The *Turke* is vanquish'd, and with little losse   310
Vpon our part, in which our ioy is doubl'd.
   Eubulus. But let it not exalt you, beare it Sir
With moderation, and pay what you owe for't.
   Ladislaus. I vnderstand thee *Eubulus.* Ile not now
Enquire particulars. Our delights deferr'd,   315
With reuerence to the Temples; there wee'l tender
Our Soules deuotions to his dread might,
Who edg'd our swords, and taught vs how to fight. *Exeunt omnes.*

The end of the first Act.

Actus secundi, Scæna prima.

Enter HILARIO, CORISCA.

Hilario. YOU like my speech?
Corisca.   Yes, if you giue it action
In the deliuerie.
   Hilario.   If? I pitty you.
I haue plaide the foole before, this is not the first time,
Nor shall be I hope the last.
   Corisca.   Nay I thinke so to.
   Hilario. And if I put her not out of her dumps with laughter, 5
Ile make her howle for anger.
   Corisca.   Not too much
Of that, good fellow *Hilario.* Our sad Lady
Hath dranke too often of that bitter cup,
A pleasant one must restore her. With what patience
Would she indure to heare of the death of my Lord,   10

That meerely out of doubt he may miscary
Afflicts her selfe thus?
  Hilario.   Vm, 'tis a question
A widdow onely can resolue. There be some
That in their husbands sicknesses haue wep'd
Their pottle of teares a day: but being once certaine   15
At midnight he was dead, haue in the morning
Dri'd vp their handkerchers, and thought no more on't.
  Corisca. Tush, shee is none of that race; if her sorrow
Be not true and perfit, I against my sex
Will take my oath woman nere wep'd in earnest.   20
She has made her selfe a prisoner to her chamber,
Darke as a dungeon, in which no beame
Of comfort enters. She admits no visits;
Eates little, and her nightly musicke is
Of sighes and groanes tun'd to such harmonie   25
D2ᵛ Of feeling greefe, that I against my nature
Am made one of the consort. This houre onely
She takes the aire, a custome euery day
She sollemnly obserues, with greedy hopes
From some that passe by to receiue assurance   30
Of the successe, and safety of her Lord:
Now if that your deuice will take—
  Hilario.   Nere feare it:
I am prouided cap a pe, and haue
My properties in readinesse.
  Sophia within.   Bring my vaile there.
  Corisca. Be gone, I heare her comming.
  Hilario.   If I doe not   35
Appeare, and what's more, appeare perfit, hisse me.
              Exit HILARIO.

      Enter SOPHIA.

  Sophia. I was flatter'd once I was a Star, but now
Turn'd a prodigious meteor, and like one
Hang in the aire betweene my hopes, and feares,
And euery howre, the little stuffe burnt out   40
That yeelds a waning light to dying comfort,
I doe expect my fall and certaine ruine.

   II. i. 40. howre,] *Massinger MS*; ~ˏ *30*

In wretched things more wretched is delay,
And hope, a parasite to me, being vnmasqu'd
Appeares more horrid then despaire, and my   45
Distraction worse then madnesse: eu'n my prayers
When with most zeale sent vpward, are pull'd downe,
With strong imaginary doubts and feares,
And in their suddaine precipice orewhelme me.
Dreames, and phantasticke visions walke the round   50
About my widdowed bed, and euery slumber
Broken with lowd alarms: can these be then
But sad presages girle?
    Corisca.   You make 'em so,
And antedate a losse shall ne're fall on you.
Such pure affection, such mutuall loue,   55
A bed, and vndefil'd on either part,
A house without contention, in two bodies
One will, and Soule like to the rod of concord,
Kissing each other, cannot be short liu'd
Or end in barrennesse: if all these deare Madam   60
(Sweet in your sadnesse) should produce no fruite,
Or leaue the age no models of your selues,
To witnesse to posterity what you were,
Succeeding times frighted with the example,
But hearing of your story, would instruct   65
Their fairest issue to meete sensually,
Like other creatures, and forbeare to raise
True loue, or *Himen* Altars.
    Sophia.   O *Corisca,*
I know thy reasons are like to thy wishes,
And they are built vpon a weake foundation,   70
To raise me comfort. Ten long dayes are past,
Ten long dayes my *Corisca,* since my Lord
Embarqu'd himselfe vpon a Sea of danger,
In his deare care of me. And if his life
Had not beene shipwrack'd on the rocke of war,   75
His tendernesse of me (knowing how much
I languish for his absence) had prouided
Some trusty friend from whom I might receiue
Assurance of his safety.
    Corisca.   Ill newes Madam,

D3ʳ

Are swallow-wing'd, but what's good walkes on crutches: 80
With patience expect it, and ere long
No doubt you shall heare from him.   *A sowgelders horne blowne.*
Sophia.   Ha! What's that?
Corisca. The foole has got a sowgelders horne.—A post   *Aside.*
As I take it Madam.
Sophia.   It makes this way still,
Neerer and neerer.
Corisca.   From the Campe I hope.   85

D3ᵛ *Enter* HILARIO, *with a long white hayre and beard, in an anticke*
     armour, one with a horne before him.

Sophia. The messenger appeares, and in strange armour.
Heauen if it be thy will!
Hilario.   It is no boote
To striue, our horses tir'd let's walke on foot,
And that the Castle which is very neere vs,
To giue vs entertainment may soone heare vs,   90
Blow lustily my Lad, and drawing nigh a,
Aske for a Lady which is clep'd *Sophia.*
Corisca. He names you Madam.
Hilario.   For to her I bring,
Thus clad in armes, newes of a pretty thing,
By name *Mathias.*   [*Exit Post.*]
Sophia.   From my Lord? O Sir,   95
I am *Sophia,* that *Mathias* wife.
So may *Mars* fauour you in all your battailes,
As you with speede vnloade me of the burthen
I labour vnder, till I am confirm'd
Both where, and how you left him.
Hilario.   If thou art   100
As I beleeue, the pigs-ney of his heart,
Know hee's in health, and what's more, full of glee,
And so much I was will'd to say to thee.
Sophia. Haue you no letters from him?
Hilario.   No more words.
In the Campe we vse no pens, but write with swords: 105

82 SD. *blowne.*] *Massinger MS*; *blowne. A Post.* 30   83. *horne . . . Aside.*] *Mas-*
singer MS (horne. aside. A post); horne. *30*   95 SD. *Exit Post.*] *after Gifford*; *not*
in 30   102. more,] *Massinger MS*; ∼ₐ *30*   104. more] *30*; mere *Coxeter*

Yet as I am inioyn'd, by word of mouth
I will proclaime his deeds from North to South.
But tremble not while I relate the wonder,
Though my eyes like lightning shine, and my voyce thunder.
Sophia. This is some counterfeit bragart.
Corisca.   Heare him Madam. 110
Hilario. The Reere march'd first, which follow'd by the Van,
And wing'd with the Battalia, no man
D4ʳ Durst stay to shift a shirt or louze himselfe;
Yet ere the armies ioyn'd, that hopefull elfe,
Thy deere, my dainty duckling, bold *Mathias*   115
Aduanc'd, and star'd like *Hercules* or *Golias*.
A hundred thousand *Turkes*, it is no vaunt,
Assail'd him, euery one a Termagaunt,
But what did he then? with his keene edgde speare
He cut, and carbonadode 'em, heere, and there,   120
Lay leggs and armes, and as 'tis sayd truely
Of *Beuis*, some he quarter'd all in three.
Sophia. This is ridiculous.
Hilario.   I must take breath
Then like a Nightingale i'le sing his death.
Sophia. His death?
Hilario.   I am out.
Corisca.   Recouer dunder-head.   125
Hilario. How he escap'd I should haue sung, not dide;
For, though a knight, when I said so, I lide.
Weary he was, and scarse could stand vpright
And looking round for some couragious Knight
To reskue him, as one perplex'd in woe   130
He cald to me, helpe, helpe *Hilario*,
My valiant seruant helpe.
Corisca.   He has spoyld all.
Sophia. Are you the man of armes then? ile make bold
To take of your martiall beard, you had fooles hayre
Enough without it. Slaue, how durst thou make   135
Thy sport of what concernes me more then life,
In such an anticke fashion? am I growne
Contemptible to those I feed? you mignion

---

115. deere,] *Massinger MS*; ∼ₐ *30*   my] *30*; thy *Coxeter*   119. edgde] *editor*;
edge *30*   127. so,] *Massinger MS*; ∼ₐ *30*

Had a hand in it to, as it appeares;
Your petticote serues for bases to this warrior.   140
   Corisca. We did it for your mirth.
   Hilario.   For my selfe I hope
I haue spoke like a souldier.
   Sophia.   Hence you rascall.
D4ᵛ I neuer but with reuerence name my Lord
And can I heere it by thy tongue prophain'd
And not correct thy folly? but you are   145
Transform'd, and turnd Knight errant, take your course
And wander where you please, for heere I vow
By my Lords life (an oath I will not breake)
Till his returne, or certainty of his safety,
My doores are shut against thee.   *Exit* SOPHIA.
   Corisca.   You haue made   150
A fine peece of worke on't: how do you like the quality?
You had a foolish itch to be an actor,
And may strowle where you please.
   Hilario.   Will you buy my share?
   Corisca. No certainely, I feare I haue already
Too much of mine owne, I'le onely as a damsell   155
(As the bookes say) thus far helpe to disarme you,
And so deere *Don Quixote* taking my leaue,
I leaue you to your fortune.   *Exit* CORISCA.
   Hilario.   Haue I sweate
My braines out for this quaint and rare inuention,
And am I thus rewarded? I could turne   160
Tragœdian, and rore now, but that I feare
'Twould get me too great a stomacke, hauing no meat
To pacifie Colon. What will become of me?
I cannot begge in armor, and steale I dare not:
My end must bee to stand in a corne feild   165
And fright away the crowes for bread, and cheese,
Or finde some hollow tree in the high way,
And there vntill my Lord returne sell switches.
No more *Hilario*, but *Dolorio* now
Ile weepe my eyes out, and bee blind of purpose   170
To moue compassion, and so I vanish.   *Exit* HILARIO.

168. switches.] *Massinger MS*; ∼ₐ 30

[ɪ^r
ii]

Actus secundi, Scæna secunda.

Enter EUBULUS, VBALDO, RICARDO, *and others.*

Eubulus. Are the gentlemen sent before as it was order'd
By the Kings direction to entertaine
The Generall?
Ricardo.   Long since, they by this haue met him,
And giu'n him the bienvenue.
Eubulus.   I hope I neede not
Instruct you in your parts.
Vbaldo.   How! vs my Lord!   5
Feare not, we know our distances and degrees
To the very inch where we are to salute him.
Ricardo. The state were miserable if the Court had none
Of her owne breede, familiar with all garbes
Gracious in *England, Italie, Spaine* or *France*,   10
With forme, and punctuallity to receiue
Stranger Embassadours. For the Generall
Hee's a meere natiue, and it matters not
Which way we doe accost him.
Vbaldo.   'Tis great pitty
That such as sit at the helme prouide no better   15
For the training vp of the Gentry. In my iudgement
An Academie erected, with large pensions
To such as in a table could set downe
The congees, cringes, postures, methods, phrase,
Proper to euery Nation—
Ricardo.   O it were   20
An admirable piece of worke!
Vbaldo.   And yet rich fooles
Throw away their charity on Hospitals
For beggers, and lame souldiers, and nere study
The due regard to complement and court-ship,
Matters of more import, and are indeed   25
The glories of a Monarchie.
Eubulus.   These no doubt
Are state points, gallants, I confesse, but sure,
Our court needs no aydes this way, since it is

II. ii. 9. garbes] *Gifford;* ~. 30

A schoole of nothing else: there are some of you
Whom I forbeare to name, whose coyning heads   30
Are the mints of all new fashions, that haue donne
More hurt to the Kingdome by superfluous brauerie
Which the foolish gentry imitate then a war
Or a long famine; all the treasure by
This foule excesse, is got into the marchants,   35
Embroiderers, silkemans, Iewellers, Taylors hand,
And the third part of the land to, the nobility
Ingrossing titles onely.
 Ricardo.   My lord you are bitter.   *A trumpet.*

     Enter a SERVANT.

 Seruant. The Generall is alighted, and now entred.
 Ricardo. Were he ten Generals I am prepard   40
And know what I will doe.
 Eubulus.   Pray you what *Ricardo*?
 Ricardo. Ile fight at complement with him.
 Vbaldo.   Ile charge home to.
 Eubulus. And thats a desperate seruice if you come off well.

 Enter FERDINAND, MATHIAS, BAPTISTA, *two Captaines.*

 Ferdinand. Captaine, command the officers to keepe
The souldier as he march'd in ranke, and file,   45
Till they heare farther from me. [*Exeunt Captaines.*]
 Eubulus.   Heer's one speakes
In another keye, this is no canting language
Taught in your Academie.
 Ferdinand.   Nay I will present you
To the King my selfe.
 Mathias.   A grace beyond my merit.
 Ferdinand. You vndervalew what I cannot set   50
Too high a price on.
 Eubulus.   With a friends true heart
I gratulate your returne.
E2ʳ *Ferdinand.*   Next to the fauour
Of the great King I am happy in your friendship.
 Vbaldo. By courtship, course on both sides.

38 SD. *A trumpet.*] *Gifford*; *follows* SERVANT. *30* 45. ranke, and file,] *Massinger MS*; ranke and file *30* 46 SD. *Exeunt Captaines.*] *Gifford*; *not in 30*

Ferdinand.   Pray you receiue
This stranger to your knowledge, on my credit   55
At all parts hee deserues it.
    Eubulus.   Your report
Is a strong assurance to mee, sir most welcome.
    Mathias. This sayd by you, the reuerence of your age
Commands mee to beleeue it.
    Ricardo.   This was pretty.
But second mee now, I cannot stoope too lowe   60
To doe your excellence that due obseruance
Your fortune claimes.
    Eubulus.   Hee nere thinks on his vertue.
    Ricardo. For beeing, as you are, the soule of souldiers,
And bulwarke of *Bellona*,
    Vbaldo.   The protection
Both of the court and King,
    Ricardo.   And the sole mignion   65
Of mighty *Mars*,
    Vbaldo.   One that with iustice may
Increase the number of the worthies.
    Eubulus.   Hoye day.
    Ricardo. It beeing impossible in my armes to circle
Such giant worth.
    Vbaldo.   At distance wee presume
To kisse your honored gauntlet.
    Eubulus.   What replie now   70
Can he make to this fopperie?
    Ferdinand.   You haue sayd
Gallants, so much, and hitherto done soe little,
That till I learne to speake, and you to doe
I must take time to thanke you.
    Eubulus.   As I liue,
Answer'd as I could wish. How the fops gape now!   75
    Ricardo. This was harsh, and scuruie.
    Vbaldo.   We will be reueng'd
When he comes to court the ladies, and laugh at him.
    Eubulus. Nay doe your offices gentlemen, and conduct
The Generall to the presence.
    Ricardo.   Keepe your order.
    Vbaldo. Make way for the Generall. *Exeunt omnes præter* EUBULUM.

2ᵛ

Eubulus. What wise man 80
That with iudicious eyes lookes one a souldier
But must confesse that fortunes swinge is more
Ore that profession, then all kinds else
Of life pursu'd by man. They in a state
Are but as chirurgions to wounded men 85
Euen desperate in their hopes, while paine and anguish
Make them blaspheme, and call in vaine for death;
Their wiues and children kisse the chirurgions knees,
Promise him mountaines, if his sauing hand
Restore the tortur'd wretch to former strength. 90
But when grimme death by *Æsculapius* art
Is frighted from the house, and health appeares
In sanguin colours on the sicke mans face,
All is forgot, and asking his reward
Hee's payd with curses, often receaues wounds 95
From him whose woundes hee curde: so souldiers
Though of more worth and vse, meete the same fate,
As it is too apparent. I haue obseru'd
When horrid *Mars* the touch of whose rough hand
With Palsies shakes a kingdome, hath put on 100
His dreadfull Helmet, and with terror fills
The place where he like an vnwelcome guest
Resolues to reuell, how the Lords of acres,
The tradesman, marchant, and litigious pleader
(And such like *Scarabes* bred 'ith dung of peace) 105
In hope of their protection humbly offer
E3ʳ Their daughters to their beds, heyres to their seruice,
And wash with teares, their sweate, their dust, their scars;
But when those clouds of war that menaced
A bloudy deluge to th'affrighted state, 110
Are by their breath dispers'd, and ouer blowne,
And famine, bloud, and death, *Bellona's* pages,
Whip'd from the quiet continent to Thrace,
Souldiers, that like the foolish hedge sparrow
To their owne ruine hatch this Cucckow peace, 115

87. death;] *30*; ∼, *Gifford*   89. sauing] *Dodsley*; saning *30*   96–8. so . . .
apparent.] *30*; *omitted Gifford*¹   98–9. obseru'd / When] *Massinger MS*; obseru'd
/ In one hue. / When *30*   103. Resolues] *Massinger MS*; Resolue *30*   acres,]
Massinger MS (acres); her, like *30*

Are straight thought burdensome, since want of meanes
Growing from want of action breedes contempt,
And that the worst of ills fall to their lot,
Their seruice with the danger soone forgot.

Enter a SERVANT.

Seruant. The Queene, my Lord, hath made choyce of this roome
To see the masque.
Eubulus.　　　Ile be a looker on,　　　121
My dancing dayes are past.

Loud musicke as they passe, a song in the praise of war. VBALDO,
RICARDO, LADISLAUS, FERDINAND, HONORIA, MATHIAS,
SILVIA, ACANTHE, BAPTISTA, *and others.*

Ladislaus.　　　This courtesie
To a stranger my *Honoria*, keepes faire ranke
With all your rarities. After your trauaile
Looke on our court delights; but first from your　　　125
Relation, with erected eares i'll heare
The musicke of your war which must be sweet,
Ending in victory.
Ferdinand.　　　Not to trouble
Your maiesties with description of a battaile
To full of horror for the place, and to　　　130
Avoyd perticulers, which should I deliuer
I must trench longer on your pacience then
My manners will gieue way to, in a word sir
It was well fought on both sides, and almost
With equall fortune. It continuing doubtfull　　　135
Vpon whose tents plum'd victory would take
Her glorious stande, impatient of delay,
With the flower of our prime gentlemen I charg'd
Their maine Battalia, and with their assistance
Brake in, but when I was almost assur'd　　　140
That they were routed, by a Stratagem
Of the subtill *Turke*, who opening his grosse body,
And ralijng vp his troopes on either side,

121. be a] *Mason*; be *30*　　123. keepes] *Dodsley*; keepe *30*　　125. delights;]
Massinger MS; ~, *30*　　131. perticulers, which should I] *Massinger MS*; perticulers
which I should *30*　　133. manners] *Massinger MS*; manner *30*　　137. stande]
Dodsley; stands *30*

I found my selfe so far ingag'd (for I
Must not conceale my errors) that I knew not   145
Which way with honor to come off.
    Eubulus.   I like
A Generall that tells his faults, and is not
Ambitious to ingrosse vnto himselfe
All honour as some haue, in which with iustice
They could not claime a share.
    Ferdinand.   Being thus hem'd in   150
Their Cimitars rag'd among vs, and my horse
Kil'd vnder me, I euery minute look'd for
An honourable end, and that was all
My hope could fashion to me. Circl'd thus
With death and horror, as one sent from heauen   155
This man of men with some choise horse that followed
His braue example, did pursue the tract
His sword cut for 'em, and but that I see him
Already blush to heare what he being present,
I know would wish vnspoken, I should say sir   160
By what hee did, we bouldly may beleeue
All that is writ of *Hector.*
    Mathias.   Generall
Pray spare these strange Hyperboles.
    Eubulus.   Do not blush
To heare a truth, heere are a payre of Monsieurs
Had they beene in your place would haue run away   165
And nere chang'd countenance.
    Vbaldo.   We haue your good word still.
    Eubulus. And shall while you deserue it.
    Ladislaus.   Silence, on.
    Ferdinand. He as I sayd, like dreadfull lightning throwne
From *Iupiters* shield dispersd the armed Gire
With which I was enuirond, horse and man   170
Shruncke vnder his strong arme, more with his lookes
Frighted, the valiant fled, with which encourag'd
My souldiers (like young Eglets praying vnder
The wings of their fierce damne) as if from him

E4^r

---

154. hope] *30*; hopes *McIlwraith*   170. enuirond,] *Massinger MS*; ∼ ∧ *30*
171. arme,] *Massinger MS*; ∼ ∧ *30*   172. fled,] *Massinger MS*; ∼ ∧ *30*
174. damne] *Massinger MS*; dame *30*; damme *conj. Greg*

They tooke both spirit, and fire brauely came on.   175
By him I was remounted, and inspir'd
With trebble courage, and such as fled before
Bouldly made head againe, and to confirme 'em
It suddainely was apparent, that the fortune
Of the day was ours, each souldier and commander   180
Performd his part; but this was the great wheele
By which the lesser mou'd, and all rewards
And signes of honour, as the Ciuicke garland,
The murall wreath, the enemies prime horse,
With the Generals sword, and armour (the old honors   185
With which the Romans crown'd their seuerall leaders)
To him alone are proper.
   Ladislaus.   And they shall
Deseruedly fall on him; sit, tis our pleasure.
   Ferdinand. Which I must serue, not argue.
   Honoria.   You are a stranger,
But in your seruice for the King, a natiue.   190
And though a free Queene, I am bound in duty
To cherish vertue wheresoere I find it:
This place is yours.
   Mathias.   It were presumption in me
To sit so neere you.
   Honoria.   Not, hauing our warrant.
   Ladislaus. Let the masquers enter: by the preparation   195
Tis a French brawle, an apish imitation
Of what you really performe in battaile,
And *Pallas* bound vp in a little volume,
Apollo with his lute attending on her,   199
Serue for the induction.   *Song and dance.*

Enter [Masquers and] the two Boyes, one with his lute, the other like
Pallas. *A song in the prayse of souldiers, especially being victorious:*
    the song [and dance] ended the King goes on.

Song by Pallas.

Though we contemplate to expresse
The glory of your happinesse,

---

186. Romans] *Dodsley*; Roman *30*   crown'd] *Mason*; crowne *30*   188. sit]
30; sir *Dawson*   194. Not,] *Massinger MS*; ~ʌ *30*   200 SD. *Song . . . dance.*]
Mason; follows her (l. 199) *30*   200 SD. *Masquers and*] *after Gifford; not in 30*
and dance] *editor; not in 30*

That by your powerfull arme haue binne
　So true a victor, that no sinne
Could euer taint you with a blame　　　　　205
　To lessen your deserued fame.

Or though we contend to set
　Your worth in the full height, or get
Cælestiall singers (crownd with bayes)
　With florishes to dresse your praise,　　210
You know your conquest, but your story
　Liues in your triumphant glory.

Ladislaus.　Our thanks to all.
To the banquet thats prepard to entertaine 'em;

[Exeunt Masquers, Boyes.]

What would my best *Honoria*?
　Honoria.　　　　　　　May it please　　215
My King that I, who by his suffrage euer
Haue had power to command, may now intreat
An honor from him.
　Ladislaus.　　　　Why should you desire

Fɪʳ What is your owne? what ere it be you are
The mistris of it.
　Honoria.　　　I am happy in　　　　220
Your grant: my sute sir is, that your commanders,
Especially this stranger, may as I
In my discretion shall thinke good, receiue
What's due to their deserts.
　Ladislaus.　　　　　What you determine
Shall know no alteration.
　Eubulus.　　　　　The souldier　　225
Is like to haue good vsage when he depends
Vpon her pleasure! are all the men so bad
That to giue satisfaction we must haue
A woman threasourer, heauen helpe all?
　Honoria.　　　　　　With you sir
I will begin, and as in my esteeme　　　　230
You are most eminent expect to haue,
What's fit for me to giue, and you to take;

---

214 SD. *Exeunt . . . Boyes.*] *after Gifford; not in 30*　　216. I,] *Massinger MS;*
～ᴧ *30*　　　　228. must haue] *Massinger MS*; must *30*

The fauour in the quicke dispatch being doubld,
Goe fetch my casket, and with speed.   *Exit* ACANTHE.
    Eubulus.   The Kingdome
Is very bare of mony, when rewards   235
Issue from the Queenes iewell house: giue him gold
And store, no question the gentleman wants it.
Good Madam what shall he doe with a hoop ring,
And a sparke of diamond in it? though you tooke it

              Enter ACANTHE.

For the greater honor from your maiesties finger,   240
'Twill not increase the value. He must purchase
Rich suites, the gay comparison of court-shipp,
Reuell, and feast, which, the war ended, is
A souldiers glory, and tis fit that way
Your bountie should prouide for him.
    Honoria.   You are rude,   245
And by your narrow thoughts proportion mine.
What I will doe now, shall be worth the enuie
Of *Cleopatra.* Open it; see heere   HONORIA *descends.*
The Lapidaries Idol, gold is trash
And a poore salarie fit for groomes, weare these   250
As studded stars in your armour, and make the Sun
Looke dimme with iealousie of a greater light
Then his beames guild the day with: when it is
Expos'd to view, call it *Honorias* guift,
The Queene *Honorias* guift that loues a souldier,   255
And to giue ornament, and lustre to him
Parts freely with her owne. Yet not to take
From the magnificence of the King, I will
Dispence his bounty to, but as a page
To wait on mine; for other trifles take   260
A hundred thousand crownes, your hand deere sir,
And this shall be thy warrant.   *Takes of the Kings signet.*
    Eubulus.   I perceiue
I was cheated in this woman: now she is

233. doubld,] *Massinger MS* (~.); ~ₐ *30*   235. mony,] *Massinger MS*; ~: *30*
242. comparison] *30*; caparison *Dodsley*   248. *Cleopatra.*] *Massinger MS*; ~ₐ *30*
it;] *Massinger MS*; ~, *30*   249. Idol,] *Massinger MS*; ~ₐ *30*   255. souldier,]
Massinger MS (souldier); soulder, *30*   260. trifles] *Massinger MS*; tosses *30*

I th' gieuing veine to souldiers, let her be proud
And the King dote, soe she goe on, I care not.   265
    Honoria. This done, our pleasure is that all arrearages
Be payd into the Captaines, and their troopes
With a large donatiue to increase their Zeale
For the seruice of the kingdome.
    Eubulus.   Better still,
Let men of armes be vsd thus, if they do not   270
Charge desperately vpon the Cannons mouth
Though the Diuell ror'd, and fight like dragons, hang me.
Now they may drinke sacke, but small beere, with a pasport
To begge with as they trauaile, and no money,
Turnes their red blood to buttermilke.
    Honoria.   Are you pleas'd sir   275
With what I haue done?
    Ladislaus.   Yes, and thus confirme it,
With this addition of mine owne; you haue sir
From our lou'd Queene receaued some recompence
For your life hazarded in the late action,
F2r And that we may follow her great example   280
In cherishing valor without limit, aske
What you from vs can wish.
    Mathias.   If it be true,
Dread sir as 'tis affirmd, that euery soyle
Where he is well, is to a valiant man
His naturall country, reason may assure me   285
I should fix heere, where blessings beyond hope
From you the spring like riuers flow vnto me.
If wealth were my ambition, by the Queene
I am made rich already, to the amazment
Of all that see, or shall hereafter read   290
The story of her bounty; if to spend
The remnant of my life in deedes of armes,
No region is more fertill of good knights
From whom my knowledg that way may be beterd
Then this your warlike Hungary; if fauour,   295
Or grace in court could take me, by your grant
Far far beyond my merrit, I may make
In yours a free election, but alas sir
I am not mine owne, but by my destiny

(Which I cannot resist) forc'd to prefer　　　　　300
My countries smoke before the glorious fire
With which your bounties warme me. All I aske sir,
Though I cannot be ignorant it must rellish
Of foule ingratitud, is your gracious licence
For my departure.
　　Ladislaus.　　　Whether?
　　Mathias.　　　　　　To my owne home sir　　　305
My owne poore home, which will at my returne
Grow rich by your magnificence. I am heere
But a body without a soule, and till I finde it
In the embraces of my constant wife,
And, to set of that constancy, in her beauty　　　310
And matchlesse excellencies without a riuall,
I am but halfe my selfe.
　　Honoria.　　　And is she then
So chast, and faire as you infer?
　　Mathias.　　　　　　O Madam
Though it must argue weakenes in a rich man
To show his gold before an armed thiefe,　　　315
And I in praysing of my wife, but feed
The fire of lust in others to attempt her,
Such is my full sayld confidence in her vertue.
Though in my absence she were now beseeg'd
By a strong army of lasciuious wooers,　　　320
And euery one more expert in his art,
Then those that tempted chast *Penelope,*
Though they raisd batteries by Prodigall guiftes,
By amorous letters, vowes made for her seruice,
With all the Engins wanton appetite　　　325
Could mount to shake the fortresse of her honor,
Heere, heere is my assurance she holdes out　　*Kisses the picture.*
And is impregnable.
　　Honoria.　　　What's that?
　　Mathias.　　　　　　Her faire figure.
　　Ladislaus. As I liue an excellent face!
　　Honoria.　　　　　　You haue seene a better.
　　Ladislaus. I euer except yours, nay frowne not sweetest,　　　330

309–11. *conjecturally rearranged by Coxeter*; 30 *reads* In . . . constancy / in . . . riuall
327 SD. *Kisses*] Dodsley; *kisse* 30

The Cyprian Queene compard to you, in my
Opinion is a *Negro*. As you orderd
I'll see the souldier payd, and in my absence
Pray you vse your powerfull arguments to stay
This gentleman in our seruice.
    Honoria.   I will doe   335
My parts.
    Ladislaus. On to the campe.
            Exeunt LADISLAUS, FERDINAND, EUBULUS,
                BAPTISTA, *Captaines*[, SERVANT].
    Honoria.   I am full of thoughts.   [*Aside.*]
And something there is heere I must giue forme to
Though yet an *Embrion*—you *Signiers*
Haue no businesse with the souldier, as I take it,
F3ʳ You are for other warfare, quit the place,   340
But be within call.
    Ricardo.   Imployment on my life boy.
    Vbaldo. If it lie in our road we are made foreuer.
              Exeunt VBALDO, RICARDO.
    Honoria. You may perceiue the King is no way tainted
With the disease of iealousie, since he leaues mee
Thus priuate with you.
    Mathias.   It were in him Madam   345
A sinne vnpardonable to distrust such purenesse,
Though I were an *Adonis*.
    Honoria.   I presume
He neither does, nor dares: and yet the story
Deliuered of you by the Generall
With your Heroick courage (which sinckes deepely   350
Into a knowing womans heart) besides
Your promising presence might beget some scruple,
In a meaner man, but more of this heereafter.
I'll take another Theme now and coniure you
By the honors you haue woone, and by the loue   355
Sacred to your deere wife, to answere truely
To what I shall demand.
    Mathias.   You need not vse
Charmes to this purpose Madam.

336 SD. SERVANT] *editor*; *not in 30*   *Aside.*] *Gifford*; *not in 30*   350. Heroick]
Dodsley; *Herc'nk 30*

Honoria.   Tell me then
Being your selfe assur'd 'tis not in man
To sully with one spott th'immaculate whitenes   360
Of your wifes honor, if you haue not since
The Gordion of your loue was tide by marriage
Playd false with her?
   Mathias.   By the hopes of mercy neuer.
   Honoria. It may be, not frequenting the conuerse
Of handsome ladies, you were neuer tempted   365
And so your faith's vntride yet.
   Mathias.   Surely Madam,
I am no woman hater; I haue beene
F3ᵛ Receiued to the society of the best,
And fairest of our climate, and haue met with
No common entertainement, yet nere felt   370
The least heat that way.
   Honoria.   Strange; and doe you thinke still
The earth can show no beauty that can drench
In *Lethe* all remembrance of the fauour
You now beare to your owne?
   Mathias.   Nature must find out
Some other mold to fashion a new creature   375
Fairer then her *Pandora*, ere I proue
Guilty or in my wishes, or my thoughts,
To my *Sophia*.
   Honoria.   Sir consider better;
Not one in our whole sex?
   Mathias.   I am constant to
My resolution.
   Honoria.   But dare you stand   380
The oposition, and bind your selfe
By oath for the performance?
   Mathias.   My faith else
Had but a weake foundation.
   Honoria.   I take hold
Vpon your promise, and inioyne your stay
For one month heere.
   Mathias.   I am caught.
   Honoria.   And if I do not   385

360. spott] *Dodsley*; sport *30*   374. You] *Dodsley*; Your *30*

Produce a lady in that time that shall
Make you confesse your error I submit
My selfe to any pennaltie you shall please
T'impose vpon me; in the meane space write
To your chast wife, acquainte her with your fortune.   390
The iewells that were mine you may send to her,
For better confirmation, I'll prouide you
Of trusty messengers, but how far distant is she?
    Mathias. A dayes hard riding.
F4ʳ   *Honoria.*   Thers no retiring,
I'll bind you to your word.
    Mathias.   Wel since there is   395
Noe way to shun it I will stand the hazard
And instantly make ready my dispatch.
'Till then, I'll leaue your maiesty.   *Exit* MATHIAS.
    Honoria.   How I burst
With enuie that there liues besides my selfe
One faire, and loyall woman; 'twas the end   400
Of my ambition to be recorded
The onely wonder of the age, and shall I
Giue way to a competitor? nay more
To adde to my affliction, the assurances
That I plac'd in my beautie haue deceau'd me: 405
I thought one amorous glance of mine could bring
All hearts to my subiection, but this stranger
Vnmoud as rockes contemnes me. But I cannot
Sit downe so with my honor, I will gaine
A double victory by working him   410
To my desire, and tainte her in her honor
Or loose my selfe. I haue read that sometime poyson
Is vsefull. To suplant her ile imploy
With any cost *Vbaldo*, and *Ricardo*,
Two noted courtiers of approued cunning   415
In all the windings of lusts labirinthe,
And in corrupting him I will out goe
Neros Poppæa. If he shut his eares,
Against my Siren notes, Ile boldly sweare
Vlysses liues againe, or that I haue found   420
A frozen Cynike, cold in spite of all

412. sometime] *30*; sometimes *McIlwraith*

Allurements, one, whom beauty cannot moue
Nor softest blandishments entice to loue.

           Exeunt HONORIA [, SILVIA, ACANTHE].

        The end of the second Act.

'4ᵛ

 i]

Actus tertij, Scæna prima.

Enter HILARIO.

Hilario. THINNE, thinne prouision, I am dieted
Like one set to watch hawkes, and to keepe me waking
My croaking guts make a perpetuall larum.
Heere I stand centinell, and though I fright
Beggers from my ladies gate, in hope to haue   5
A greater share, I find my commons mend not.
I lookt this morning in my glasse the riuer
And there appeard a fish cald a poore Iohn
Cut with a lenten face in my owne likenesse,
And it seemd to speake and say goodmorrow cousen: 10
No man comes this way but has a fling at me,
A Chirurgion passing by ask'd at what rate
I would sell my selfe, I answered for what vse?
To make sayd he a liueing Anatomy
And set thee vp in our hall, for thou art transparent   15
Without dissection, and indeede he had reason,
For I am scourd with this poore purge to nothing.
They say that hunger dwels in the campe, but till
My Lord returnes, or certaine tidings of him,
He will not part with me; but sorrowes drie   20
And I must drinke howsoeuer.

      Enter VBALDO, *and* RICARDO, GUIDE.

  Guide.   That is her castle
Vpon my certaine knowledge.
    Vbaldo.   Our horses held out
To my desire: I am a fire to be at it.
    Ricardo. Take the iades for thy reward; before I part hence,

---

    423 SD. SILVIA, ACANTHE] *editor*; *not in 30*   III. i. 21 SD. *Enter . . .* GUIDE.]
Coxeter; *follows* castle *30*

I hope to be better carried, giue me the Cabinet.   25
Soe leaue vs now.
    Guide.   Good fortune to you Gallants.   *Exit* GUIDE.

G1ʳ   *Vbaldo.* Being ioynt Agents, in a designe of trust to,
For the seruice of the Queene, and our owne pleasure,
Let vs proceed with iudgement.
    Ricardo.   If I take not
This fort at the first assault, make me an Euenuche,   30
So I may haue precedence.
    Vbaldo.   On no termes.
We are both to play one prize. He that workes best
I'the searching of this mine shall carry it
Without contention.
    Ricardo.   Make you your aproaches
As I directed.
    Vbaldo.   I need no instruction,   35
I worke not on your anuile; I'll giue fire
With my owne linstocke, if the powder be dancke
The Diuell rend the touch-hole. Who haue we heere?
What skelliton's this?
    Ricardo.   A ghost! or the image of famine!
Where doest thou dwell?
    Hilario.   Dwell sir? my dwelling is   40
I'th high way; that goodly house was once
My habitation, but I am banished.
And cannot be cald home 'till newes arriue
Of the good knight *Mathias*.
    Ricardo.   If that will
Restore thee thou art safe.
    Vbaldo.   We come from him   45
With presents to his Lady.
    Hilario.   But are you sure
Hee is in health?
    Ricardo.   Neuer so well, conduct vs
To the lady.
    Hilario.   Though a poore snake I will leape
Out of my skine for ioy, breake picher breake,
And wallet late my cubbard I bequeath thee   50
To the next begger, thou red herring swimme

33. searching of] *Gifford*; searching *30*

G1ᵛ To the red sea againe; me thinckes I am already
Knuckle deepe in the flesh potts, and though waking, dreame
Of wine and plenty.
    Ricardo.   What's the mistery
Of this strange passion?
    Hilario.   My belly gentlemen,   55
Will not gieue me leaue to tell you. When I haue brought you
To my ladies presence I am disenchanted,
There you shall shall know all. Follow, if I outstrip you
Know I run for my belly.
    Vbaldo.   A mad fellow.   *Exeunt.*

[. ii]

Actus tertij, Scæna secunda.

Enter SOPHIA, CORISCA.

    Sophia. Do not againe delude me.
    Corisca.   If I doe,
Send me a grasing with my fellow *Hilario.*
I stood as you commanded in the turret
Obseruing all that pas'd by, and euen now
I did diserne a payre of Caualiers,   5
For such their outside spoke them, with their guide
Dismounting from their horses; they said something
To our hungry Centinell that made him caper
And frisk 'ith ayre for ioy, and to confirme this
See Madam they're in view.

Enter HILARIO, VBALDO, RICARDO.

    Hilario.   Newes from my Lord!   10
Tidings of ioy, these are no counterfaites,
But Knights indeed, deere Madam signe my pardon
That I may feed againe, and picke vp my crumes;
I haue had a long fast of it.
    Sophia.   Eate, I forgiue thee.
    Hilario. O comfortable wordes; eate, I forgiue thee,   15
G2ʳ And if in this I doe not soone obey you
And ramne in to the purpose billet me againe

54. mistery] *Dodsley*; misery *30*   III. ii. 1–2. doe, / Send] *Gifford*; *undivided 30*
10. they're] *after Dodsley*; they *30*

I'the high way. Butler and Cooke be ready
For I enter like a tyrant.   *Exit* HILARIO.
  Vbaldo.   Since mine eies
Were neuer happy in soe sweete an obiect,   20
Without enquiry I presume you are
The ladie of the house, and so salute you.
  Ricardo. This letter with these iewels from your Lord
Warrant my boldnes Madam.
  Vbaldo.   In being a seruant
To such rare beauty you must needes deserue   25
This courtesie from a stranger.
  Ricardo.   You are still
Before hand with me, pretty one I descend
To take the height of your lippe, and if I misse
In the altitude, heereafter if you please
I will make vse of my *Iacobs* staffe.

                    SOPHIA *hauing in the interime redd the letter*
                              and opend the Casket.
  Corisca.   These gentlemen   30
Haue certainely had good breeding, as it appeares
By their neat kissing, they hit me so pat on the lipps
At the first sight.
  Sophia.   Heauen in thy mercy make mee
Thy thankfull handmaid for this boundles blessing
In thy goodnesse showr'd vpon me.
  Vbaldo.   I do not like   35
This simple deuotion in her, it is seldome
Practisd among my mistresses.
  Ricardo.   Or mine.
Would they kneele to I know not who for the possession
Of such inestimable wealth before
They thank'd the bringers of it? the poore lady   40
Does want instruction, but I'll be her tutor
G2ᵛ And read her another lesson.
  Sophia.   If I haue
Showne want of manners gentlemen in my slownes
To pay the thankes I owe you for your trauaile
To doe my Lord, and me (howere vnworthy   45

    21. enquiry] *Coxeter*; eniury *30*; injury *Dodsley*   30 SD. *opend*] *Dodsley*; *gend
30*   32. pat] *Dodsley*; bat *30*   43. slownes] *Dodsley*; showes *30*

Of such a benifit) this noble fauour,
Impute it in your clemencie to the excesse
Of ioy that ouer whelm'd me.
   Ricardo.   She speakes well.
   Vbaldo. Polite, and courtly.
   Sophia.   And howere it may
Increase th'offence to trouble you with more   50
Demandes touching my Lord, before I haue
Inuited you to rest, such as the coursenesse
Of my poore house can offer, pray you conniue
On my weake tendernesse though I intreate
To learne from you something hee hath it may bee   55
In his letter left vnmention'd.
   Ricardo.   I can onely
Giue you assurance that he is in health,
Grac'd by the King, and Queene.
   Vbaldo.   And in the court
With admiration look'd on.
   Ricardo.   You must therefore
Put off these widdowes garments, and appeere   60
Like to your selfe.
   Vbaldo.   And entertaine all pleasures
Your fortune markes out for you.
   Ricardo.   There are other
Perticular priuacies which on occasion
I will deliuer to you.
   Sophia.   You oblige me
To your seruice euer.
   Ricardo.   Good! your seruice, marke that.   65
   Sophia. In the meane time by your good acceptance make
My rusticke entertainement rellish of
The curiousnesse of the court.
   Vbaldo.   Your lookes sweete Madam
Cannot but make each dish a feast.
   Sophia.   It shall be
Such in the freedome of my will to please you.   70
I'll show you the way; this is to great an honor
From such braue ghests to me so meane an hostesse.   *Exeunt.*

G3^r

---

52. rest] *30*; taste *Dodsley*   53. conniue] *Dodsley*; conuine *30*   62. fortune]
Dodsley; fortunes *30*

Actus tertij, Scæna tertia.

Enter ACANTHE, *to fower, or fiue with vizards.*

Acanthe. You know your charge, giue it action, and expect
Rewards beyond your hopes.

1.   If we but eye 'em,
They are ours I warrant you.

2.   May we not aske why
We are put vpon this.

Acanthe.   Let that stop your mouth,
And learne more manners groome. Tis vpon the hower   5
In which they vse to walke heere; when you haue 'em,
In your power, with violence carry them to the place
Where I appointed, there I will expect you.
Be bold, and carefull.   *Exit* ACANTHE.

Enter MATHIAS *and* BAPTISTA.

1.   These are they.

2.   Are you sure?

1. Am I sure I am my selfe?   10

2. Cease on him strongly. If he haue but means
To draw his sword, 'tis ten to one we smart for't.
Take all aduantages.

Mathias.   I cannot guesse
What her intents are, but her carriage was
As I but now related.

G3ᵛ   *Baptista.*   Your assurance   15
In the constancie of your lady is the armor
That must defend you, whers the picture?

Mathias.   Heere.
And no way alter'd.

Baptista.   If she be not perfit,
There is no truth in art.

Mathias.   By this I hope
She hath receiu'd my letters.

Baptista.   Without question   20
These courtiers are rancke riders, when they are
To visit a handsome lady.

III. iii. *tertia*] *Dodsley; prima* 30   o SD. *to*] *Dodsley; two* 30; *and Gifford*; &
McIlwraith   11. means] *Coxeter*; meant 30

Mathias. Lend me your eare.
One peece of her entertainment will require
Your deerest priuacy.
    1. Now they stand faire,
Vpon 'em.
    Mathias. Villaines.
    1. Stop their mouths. We come not   25
To trie your valures; kill him if he offer
To open his mouth. We haue you, tis in vaine
To make resistance, mount 'em and a way.   *Exeunt.*

Actus tertij, Scæna quarta.

Enter Seruants with lights, LADISLAUS, FERDINAND, EUBULUS.

Ladislaus. 'Tis late; go to your rest, but doe not enuy
The happinesse I draw neere to.
    Eubulus. If you inioy it
The moderate way the sport yeelds I confesse
A pretty titillation, but to much oft
Will bring you on your knees. In my yonger daies   5
I was my selfe a gamster, and I found
By a sad experience, there is no such soker
As a yonge spongie wife; she keepes a thousand
Horseleches in her box, and the thieues will sucke out
Both bloud, and marrow: I feele a kind of crampe   10
In my ioynts when I thinke on't, but it may bee Queenes
And such a Queene as yours is, has the art—
    Ferdinand. You take leaue
To talke my Lord.
    Ladislaus. He may since he can do nothing.
    Eubulus. If you spend this way to much of your royall stock
Ere long we may be puefellowes.
    Ladislaus. The doore shut?   15
Knocke gentlie, harder. So, heere comes her woman,
Take of my gowne.

Enter ACANTHE.

Acanthe. My Lord, the Queene by me
This night desires your pardon.

Ladislaus.   How *Acanthe*!
I come by her appointment, 'twas her grant,
The motion was her owne.
    Acanthe.   It may be sir   20
But by her Doctors since she is aduis'd
For her health sake to forbeare.
    Eubulus.   I do not like
This phisicall lecherie, the old downe right way
Is worth a thousand on't.
    Ladislaus.   Prethe *Acanthe*,
Mediate for me.
    Eubulus.   O the fiends of hell!   25
Would any man bribe his seruant to make way
To his owne wife? if this be the court state
Shame fall on such as vse it.
    Acanthe.   By this iewell
This night I dare not moue her, but to morrow
I will watch all occasion.
    Ladislaus.   Take this   30
G4ᵛ To be mindfull of me.   *Exit* ACANTHE.
    Eubulus.   Slight, I thought a king
Might haue tooke vp any woman at the Kings Price
And must he buy his owne at a deerer rate
Then a stranger in a brothell?
    Ladislaus.   What is that
You mutter sir?
    Eubulus.   No treason to your honor.   35
I'll speake it out though it anger you: if you pay for
Your lawfull pleasure in some kind great sir,
What do you make the Queene? cannot you clicket
Without a fee? or when she has a suit
For you to grant?
    Ferdinand.   O hold sir.
    Ladislaus.   Off with his head.   40
    Eubulus. Do when you please, you but blow out a taper
That would light your vnderstanding, and in care of't
Is burnt downe to the socket. Be as you are sir

---

24. on't] *Coxeter*; out *30*; of't *Dodsley*   25. Mediate] *Dodsley*; Meditate *30*
30. occasion] *30*; occasions *Gifford*   31. thought] *Dodsley*; though *30*   39–40. suit /
For *Gifford*; *undivided 30*

An absolute monarch, it did show more Kinglike
In those libidinous Cæsars that compeld   45
Matrons, and virgins of all rankes to bow
Vnto their rauenous lusts, and did admit
Of more excuse then I can vrge for you,
That slaue your selfe to th'imperious humor
Of a proud beauty.
   Ladislaus.   Out of my sight.
   Eubulus.   I will sir   50
Giue way to your furious passion, but when reason
Hath got the better of it I much hope
The counsaile that offends now, will deserue
Your royall thankes. Tranquillity of mind
Stay with you sir. I do begin to doubt   55
Ther's something more in the Queenes strangnes, then
Is yet disclosd, and i'll find it out
Or loose my selfe in the serch.
   Ferdinand.   Sure He is honest,
ʳ And from your infancy hath truely seru'd you;
Let that plead for him, and impute this harshnes   60
To the frowardnes of his age.
   Ladislaus.   I am much troubled
And do begin to stagger. *Ferdinand* good night,
To morrow visit vs. Backe to our owne lodgings.   *Exeunt.*

Actus tertij, Scæna quinta.

Enter ACANTHE, *the vizarded Seruants,* MATHIAS, BAPTISTA.

   Acanthe. You haue donne brauely, locke this in that roome,
There let him ruminate, I'll anon vnhood him.
                     They carry of BAPTISTA.
The other must stay heere. As soone as I
Haue quit the place giue him the liberty,
And vse of his eies; that donne disperse your selues   5
As priuately as you can, but on your liues
No word of what hath pas'd.   *Exit* ACANTHE.
   1.   If I doe, sell
My tongue to a tripe wife; come vnbind his armes.
You are now at your owne disposure and howeuer

We vs'd you roughly, I hope you will find heere　　　　10
Such entertainment, as will giue you cause
To thanke vs for the seruice, and so I leaue you. *Exeunt Seruants.*
　　Mathias. If I am in a prison 'tis a neat one,
What *Oedipus* can resolue this riddle? Ha!
I neuer gaue iust cause to any man　　　　　　　　　15
Basely to plot against my life; but what is
Become of my true friend? for him I suffer
More then my selfe.
　　Acanthe [*within*]. Remoue that idle feare,
Hee's safe as you are.
　　Mathias.　　　　　　Whoso'ere thou art
For him I thanke thee. I cannot imagine　　　　　20
Where I should be, though I haue read the table

Of errant knighthood, stuff'd, with the relations
Of magicall enchantments, yet I am not
So sottishly credulous, to beleeue the diuell
Hath that way power, Ha? musicke!　　　　　　　25

　　　　Musicke aboue, a song of pleasure.

　　The blushing rose and purple flower,
　　　　Let grow to long are soonest blasted.
　　Dainty fruites, though sweete, will sower
　　　　And rot in ripenes, left vntasted.
　　Yet here is one more sweete then these;　　　30
　　　　The more you tast, the more shee'l please.

　　Beauty though inclos'd with ice,
　　　　Is a shadow chast as rare,
　　Then how much those sweetes intice,
　　　　That haue issue full as faire.　　　　　35
　　Earth cannot yeeld from all her powers
　　　　One equall, for Dame Venus *bowers.*

A song too, certainely be it he, or she
That owes this voyce, it hath not bene acquainted
With much affliction. Whosoere you are　　　　　40

III. v. 18. *within*] *Gifford*; *not in 30*　　21. table] *30*; tales *Gifford*² 　　22. Of]
Dodsley; Or *30*　　28. *fruites*] *30*; fruitt *Gamble*　　32. though] *Dodsley, Gamble*;
thotgh 30; that's *Gifford*　　inclos'd] *30*; Compard *Gamble*　　33. *Is] 30*; tis *Gamble*
34. Then] *30*; yett *Gamble*

That doe inhabit heere, if you haue bodies
And are not meere aeriall formes appeare

Enter HONORIA.

And make me know your end with me. Most strange!
What haue I coniur'd vp? sure if this be
A spirit 'tis no damn'd one. What a shapes heere;　　　45
Then with what maiesty it moues. If *Iuno*
Were now to keepe her state among the Gods,
And *Hercules* to be made againe her ghest
She could not put on a more glorious habit
Though her handmaid *Iris* lent her various colours　　　50
Or ould *Oceanus* rauishd from the deepe
All iewels shipwrack'd in it. As you haue
Thus far made knowne your selfe, if that your face
Haue not too much diuinity about it
For mortall eies to gaze on, perfit what　　　55
You haue begun with wonder, and amazement
To my astonish'd senses.　　　*Kneeles. She puls of her masque.*
　　　　　　How! the Queene!

　Honoria. Rise sir, and heare my reasons in defence
Of the rape, for so you may conceaue, which I
By my instruments made vpon you. You perhaps　　　60
May thinke, what you haue suffer'd for my lust
Is a common practise with me, but I call
Those euer shining lamps, and their great maker
As witnesses of my inocence, I nere look'd on
A man but your best selfe, on whom I euer　　　65
(Except the King) vouchsaf'd an eie of fauour.

　Mathias. The King indeed, and onely such a King
Deserues your rarities Madam, and but hee
'Twere gyant like ambition in any
In his wishes onely to presume to tast　　　70
The nectar of your kisses; or to feed
His appetite with that ambrosia, due
And proper to a prince, and what binds more,
A lawfull husband: for my selfe great Queene
I am a thing obscure, disfurnish'd of　　　75
All merit, that can rayse me higher then

73. binds more,] *Dodsley*; bind mores 30

In my most humble thankefulnes for your bounty
To hazard my life for you, and that way
I am most ambitious.
    Honoria.   I desire no more
Then what you promise; if you dare expose   80
Your life as you professe, to doe me seruice,
How can it better be imployd, then in
Preseruing mine? which onely you can doe,
And must doe with the danger of your owne.

H2ᵛ A desperate danger to: if priuate men   85
Can brooke no riuals in what they affect,
But to the death pursue such as inuade
What law makes their inheritance, the King
To whom you know I am deerer then his crowne,
His health, his eies, his after-hopes with all   90
His present blessings, must fall on that man
Like dreadfull lightning, that is won by prayers,
Threates, or rewards to staine his bed, or make
His hop'd for issue doubtfull.
    Mathias.   If you aime
At what I more then feare you doe, the reasons   95
Which you deliuer should in iudgement rather
Deter me, then invite a grant, with my
Assured ruine.
    Honoria.   True if that you were
Of a cold temper, one whom doubt, or feare,
In the most horrid formes they could put on   100
Might teach to be ingratefull; your deniall
To me, that haue deseru'd so much, is more
If it can haue addition.
    Mathias.   I know not
What your commandes are.
    Honoria.   Haue you fought so well
Among arm'd men, yet cannot ghesse what lists   105
You are to enter when you are in priuate
With a willing ladie, one, that to inioye
Your company this night deni'd the King
Accesse, to what's his owne. If you will presse me
To speake in playner language—

          107. willing] *Dodsley*; willingly *30*

Mathias.　　　　　　　　　Pray you forbeare,　110
I would I did not vnderstand too much
Already; by your words I am instructed
To credite that, which not confirmd by you,
Had bred suspition in me of vntruth
Though an Angell had affirm'd it. But suppose　115
3ʳ That cloyd with happines (which is euer builte
On vertuous chastity) in the wantonnesse
Of appetite, you desire to make triall
Of the false delights propos'd by vitious lust:
Among ten thousand euery way more able　120
And apter to be wrought on, such as owe you
Obedience being your subiects, why should you
Make choice of me, a stranger?
　Honoria.　　　　　　　Though yet reason
Was nere admitted in the court of loue,
I'll yeeld you one vnanswerable. As I vrg'd　125
In our last priuate conference, you haue
A pretty promising presence, but there are
Many in limbes, and feature who may take
That way the right hand file of you; besides
Your May of youth is pas'd, and the blood spent　130
By woundes, though brauely taken, render you
Disabld for loues seruice, and that valour
Set off with better fortune, which it may be
Swels you aboue your boundes, is not the hooke
That hath caught me good sir. I need no champion　135
With his sword to guard my honor, or my beauty,
In both I can defend my selfe, and liue
My owne protection.
　Mathias.　　　　　If these aduocates
(The best that can plead for me) haue no power,
What can you find in me else, that may tempt you　140
With irrecouerable losse vnto your selfe
To be a gayner from me?
　Honoria.　　　　　You haue Sir
A iewell of such matchlesse worth and lustre,
As does disdaine comparison, and darkens
All that is rare in other men, and that　145

126. last] *30*; late *Dodsley*　131. render] *30*; renders *Gifford*

I must or win, or lessen.

    Mathias.   You heape more

Amazement on me, what am I posses'd of

H3ᵛ That you can couet? make me vnderstand it,

If it haue a name!

    Honoria.   Yes an imagin'd one,

But is in substance nothing, being a garment   150

Worne out of fashion, and long since giuen ore

By the court and country; tis your loyalty,

And constancy to your wife, 'tis that I dote on,

And does deserue my enuy, and that iewell

Or by faire play, or foule, I must winne from you.   155

    Mathias. These are meere contraries: if you loue me Madam

For my constancy, why seeke you to destroy it?

If my keeping it preserue me worth your fauour,

Or if it be a iewell of that value,

As you with labour'd rhetorick would perswad me,   160

What can you stake against it?

    Honoria.   A Queenes fame,

And equall honor.

    Mathias.   So whoeuer wins

Both shall be loosers.

    Honoria.   That is that I aime at

Yet on the by I lay my youth, my beauty,

This moist palme, this soft lippe, and those delights   165

Darkenesse should onely iudge of. Do you find 'em

Infectious in the tryall, that you start

As frighted with their touch?

    Mathias.   Is it in man

To resist such strong temptations?

    Honoria.   He begins

To wauer.

    Mathias. Madam as you are gracious   170

Grant this short nights deliberation to me,

And with the rising sun from me you shall

Receiue full satisfaction.

    Honoria.   Though extreames

---

    146. You] *Dodsley*; Yon *30*   158. If] *Mason*; In *30*   keeping it preserue] *30*;
keeping, it preserues *Dodsley*   164. by] *30*; die *Coxeter*   172. sun] *Dodsley*;
sum *30*

Hate all delay, I will denie you nothing.
This key will bring you to your friend; you are safe both   175
H4ʳ And all things vsefull that could be prepar'd
For one I loue and honor waite vpon you.
Take counsaile of your pillow, such a fortune
(As with affections swiftest wings flies to you)
Will not be often tendred.   *Exit* HONORIA.
    Mathias.   How my blood   180
Rebels! I now could call her backe and yet
Ther's something stayes me: if the King had tenderd
Such fauours to my wife 'tis to be doubted
They had not bene refus'd, but being a man
I should not yeeld first, or proue an example   185
For her defence of fraylty. By this sans question
She's tempted too, and heere I may examine   *Lookes on the picture.*
How shee holds out. She's still the same, the same
Pure Christal rocke of chastity! perish all
Allurements that may alter me, the snow   190
Of her sweete coldnes, hath extinguished quite
The fire that but euen now began to flame!
And I by her confirm'd, rewards, nor titles,
Nor certaine death from the refused Queene
Shall shake my faith, since I resolue to be   195
Loyall to her, as she is true to me.   *Exit* MATHIAS.

vi]   *Actus tertij, Scæna sexta.*

Enter VBALDO, RICARDO.

    Vbaldo. What we spake on the voley begins to worke,
We haue layd a good foundation.
    Ricardo.   Build it vp
Or else tis nothing: you haue by lot the honor
Of the first assault, but as it is condition'd
Obserue the time proportion'd, I'll not part with   5
I4ᵛ My share in the atchieuement; when I whistle,
Or hemme fall off.

187 SD. *Lookes*] Dodsley; *looke* 30   III. vi. *sexta*] Coxeter; *secunda* 30

Enter SOPHIA.

Vbaldo.   She comes. Stand by, I'll watch
My oportunity.
          Sophia.   I find my selfe
Strangely distracted with the various stories
Now well, now ill, then doubtfully by my ghests   10
Deliuer'd of my Lord: and like poore beggers
That in their dreames find treasure, by reflection
Of a wounded fancie, make it questionable
Whither they sleepe, or not; yet teickl'd with
Such a phantasticke hope of happinesse,   15
Wish they may neuer wake, in some such measure,
Incredulous of what I see, and touch
As 'twere a fading apparition, I
Am still perplex'd, and troubled, and when most
Confirm'd tis true, a curious iealousie   20
To be assur'd, by what meanes, and from whom
Such a masse of welth, was first deseru'd, then gotten,
Cunningly steales into me. I haue practis'd
For my certaine resolution with these courtiers,
Promising priuate conference to either,   25
And at this hower, if in search of the truth
I heare or say more, then becomes my vertue
Forgiue me my *Mathias*.
          Vbaldo.   Now I make in.
Maddam as you commanded I attend
Your pleasure.
          Sophia.   I must thanke you for the fauour.   30
          Vbaldo. I am no ghostly father, yet if you haue
Some scruples, touching your Lord, you would be resolu'd of,
I am prepar'd.
          Sophia.   But will you take your oath
To answere truely?
          Vbaldo.   On the hemme of your smocke if you please,
11ʳ A vow I dare not breake, it beeing a booke   35
I would gladly swere on.
          Sophia.   To spare sir that trouble
I'll take your word which in a gentleman
Should be of equall value. Is my Lord then

16. wake,] *Dodsley*; ∼ₐ *30*   23. steales] *Dodsley*; steale *30*   36. on] *30*¹; on't *30*²

In such grace with the Queene?
   Vbaldo.   You should best know
By what you haue found from him, whether he can   40
Deserue a grace or noe.
   Sophia.   What grace do you meane?
   Vbaldo. That speciall grace (if you'l haue it) he laboured so hard for
Betweene a paire of sheets on your wedding night
When your Ladiship lost you know what.
   Sophia.   Fie be more modest
Or I must leaue you.
   Vbaldo.   I would tell a truth   45
As cleanely as I could, and yet the subiecte
Makes me run out a little.
   Sophia.   You would put now
A foolish ielousie in my head my Lord
Hath gotten a new mistris.
   Vbaldo.   One? a hundred!
But vnder seale I speake it, I presume   50
Vpon your silence, it being for your profit.
They talke of *Hercules* backe for fifty in a night;
'Twas well, but yet to yours he was a pidler.
Such a souldier, and a courtier neuer came
To Alba regalis, the ladies run mad for him,   55
And there is such contention among 'em
Who shall ingrosse him wholy, that the like
Was neuer hard of.
   Sophia.   Are they handsome women?
   Vbaldo. Fie noe, course mammets, and whats worse they are old to,
Some fifty, some threescore, and they pay deere for't,   60
Beleeuing, that he carries a powder in his breeches
1ᵛ Will make 'em young againe, and these sucke shrewdly.
   Ricardo. Sir I must fetch you off.   *Whistles.*
   Vbaldo.   I could tell you wonders
Of the cures he has done, but a buisnesse of import
Calls me away, but that dispatch'd I will   65
Be with you presently.   *Steps aside.*
   Sophia.   There is something more
In this then bare suspition.

39. You] *30²*; Yon *30¹*   42–3. *rearranged by McIlwraith; 30 reads* That . . . it)/
He . . . sheets / On . . . night   52. backe for] *30; omitted Gifford*

[*Enter* RICARDO.]

Ricardo.   Saue you lady,
Now you looke like your selfe! I haue not look'd on
A lady more compleat, yet haue seene a Madam
Weare a garment of this fashion, of the same stuffe to,   70
One iust of your dimensions,—sate the wind there boy.
   Sophia. What lady sir?
   Ricardo.   Nay nothing, and me thinkes
I should know this rubie: very good! tis the same.
This chaine of orient pearle, and this diamond to
Haue beene worne before, but much good may they do you.   75
Strength to the gentlemans backe! he toyld hard for 'em,
Before he got 'em.
   Sophia.   Why? how were they gotten? VBALDO *hemms.*
   Ricardo. Not in the feeld with his sword, vpon my life!
He may thanke his close stilletto, plage vpon it
Run the minutes so fast? pray you excuse my manners,   80
I left a letter in my chamber window,
Which I would not haue seene on any termes, fye on it
Forgetfull as I am, but I strayt attend you.   RICARDO *steps aside.*
   Sophia. This is strange! his letters sayd these iewels were
Presented him by the Queene, as a reward   85
For his good seruice, and the trunckes of clothes
That followd them this last night, with hast made vp
By his direction.

I2ʳ   *Enter* VBALDO.

Vbaldo.   I was telling you
Of wonders Maddam.
   Sophia.   If you are soe skilfull,
Without premeditation answere me,   90
Know you this gowne, and these rich iewels?
   Vbaldo.   Heauen,
How things will come out! but that I should offend you,
And wrong my more then noble friend your husband,
For we are sworne brothers, in the discouery
Of his neerest secrets I could—
   Sophia.   By the hope of fauour   95

  67 SD. *Enter* RICARDO.] *after Gifford; not in 30*   71. sate] *30*; sat *Dodsley*
93-4. friend your husband,] *Gifford;* friend / Your husband *30*

That you haue from me out with it.

  Vbaldo.   Tis a potent spell
I cannot resist; why I will tell you Madam,
And to how many seuerall women you are
Beholding for your brauerie. This was
The Wedding gowne of *Paulina* a rich strumpet,   100
Worne but a day when she married ould *Gonzago*,
And left of trading.
  Sophia.   O my hart.
  Vbaldo.   This chaine
Of pearle was a great widdowes, that inuited
Your Lord to the masque, and the wether prouing foule
He lodg'd in her house all night, and merry they were, 105
But how he came by it I know not.
  Sophia.   Periurd man!
  Vbaldo. This ring was *Iuliettas*, a fine peece
But very good at the sport; this diamond
Was Madam *Acanthes* giuen him for a song
Prick'd in a priuate arbor, as she sayd   110
When the Queene askd for it, and she hard him sing to,
And danc'd to his hornepipe or there are lyers abroad.
There are other toyes about you the same way purchas'd
But paraleld with these not worth the relation.
You are happy in a husband, neuer man   115
Made better vse of his strength; would you haue him wast
His body away for nothing? If he holds out,
Thers not an Embrodered peticote in the court
But shall be at your seruice.
  Sophia.   I commend him,
It is a thriuing trade, but pray you leaue me   120
A little to my selfe.
  Vbaldo.   You may command
Your seruant madam.   [*Steps aside.*]
      She's stung vnto the quicke ladd.
  Ricardo. I did my part; if this potion worke not hang me!
Let her sleepe as well as she can to night, to morrow
Wee'll mount new batteries.

101. Worne] *30²*; Worme *30¹* *Gonzago,*] *McIlwraith*; *Gonzage,* *30¹*; *Gonzage.*
30²; *Gonzaga, Gifford*   113–14. *rearranged by Gifford*; *30 reads* There . . . you
/ The . . . paraleld / With . . . relation. 116. you] *30¹*; yon *30²* 122. She's]
Dodsley; she *30* SD. *Steps aside.*] *after Gifford*; *not in 30*

Vbaldo.   And till then leaue her.   125
                                    Exeunt VBALDO, RICARDO.
   Sophia. You powers that take into your care the gard
Of inocence ayd me, for I am a creature
Soe forfeyted to dispaire, hope cannot fancie
A ransome to redeeme me. I begin
To wauer in my faith and make it doubtfull   130
Whither the Saints that were canoniz'd for
Their holines of life sind not in secret,
Since my *Mathias* is falne from his vertue
In such an open fashion. Could it be else
That such a husband so deuoted to me,   135
So vow'd to temperance, for laciuious hire
Should prostitute himselfe to common harlots
Ould, and deform'd to? wast for this he left me?
And in a faind pretence for want of meanes
To giue me ornament? or to bring home   140
Diseases to me? suppose these are false,
And lustfull goates; if he were true and right
Why stayes he so long from me? being made rich,
And that the onely reason why he left me.
No he is lost; and shall I weare the spoiles   145
13ʳ And Salaries of lust? they cleaue vnto me
Like *Nessus* poyson'd shirt! no in my rage
I'll teare 'em of, and from my body wash
The venome with my teares. Haue I no spleene
Nor anger of a woman? shall he build   150
Vpon my ruins and I vnreueng'd
Deplore his falshood? no! with the same trash
For which he hath dishonor'd me, I'll purchase
A iust reuenge. I am not yet so much
In debt to yeares, nor so misshap'd that all   155
Should flie from my Embraces. Chastity
Thou onely art a name, and I renounce thee,
I am now a seruant to voluptuousnesse,
Wantons of all degrees and fashions welcome,
You shall be entertain'd, and if I stray   160
Let him condemne himselfe, that lead the way.   *Exit.*
                    The end of the third Act.

          130. make] *Dodsley*; marke *30*

Actus quarti, Scæna prima.

Enter MATHIAS, BAPTISTA.

Baptista. WE are in a desperat straight, ther's no euasion
Nor hope left to come of, but by your yeelding
To the necessity; you must faine a grant
To her violent passion, or—
Mathias.   What my *Baptista*?
Baptista. We are but dead else.
Mathias.   Were the sword now heau'd vp,
And my necke vpon the blocke, I would not buy   6
An howers repriue with the losse of faith and vertue
To be made immortall heere. Art thou a scholler,
Nay almost without paralell, and yet feare
To dye, which is ineuitable? you may vrge   10
The many yeeres that by the course of nature
We may trauaile in this tedious pilgrimage,
And hould it as a blessing, as it is
When innocence is our guide, yet know *Baptista*
Our vertues are preferr'd before our yeeres   15
By the great iudge. To dye vntaynted in
Our fame, and reputation is the greatest,
And to loose that can we desire to liue?
Or shall I for a momentary pleasure
Which soone comes to a period, to all times   20
Haue breach of faith and periury remembred
In a still liuing Epitaph? no *Baptista*,
Since my *Sophia* will go to her graue
Vnspotted in her faith, I'll follow her
With equall loyalty; but looke on this   25
Your owne great worke, your masterpeese, and then
She being still the same, teach me to alter.   *The picture altred.*
Ha! sure I doe not sleepe! or if I dreame,
This is a terrible vision! I will cleare
My eiesight, perhaps melancholly makes me   30
See that which is not.

IV. i. 4. passion, or] *30¹*; passion. *30²*   15. preferr'd] *Dodsley*; preseru'd *30*
22. no] *30¹*; on *30²*   *Baptista*] *30²*; Baptist *30¹*   27 SD. The . . . altred.] *editor*;
follows dreame, (l. 28) *30*

    Baptista.   It is to apparent.
I grieue to looke vpon't; besides the yellow
That does assure she's tempted there are lines
Of a darke colour, that disperse themselues
Ore euery miniature of her face, and those   35
Confirme—
    Mathias. She is turnd whore.
    Baptista.   I must not say so.
Yet as a friend to truth if you will haue me
Interpret it, in her consent, and wishes
She's false but not in fact yet.
    Mathias.   Fact *Baptista*?
Make not your selfe a pandar to her loosenes,   40
In labouring to palliate what a vizard
Of impudence cannot couer. Did e're woman
In her will decline from chastety, but found meanes
To giue her hot lust fuell? it is more
Impossible in nature for grosse bodies   45
Descending, of themselues, to hang in the ayre,
Or with my single arme to vnderprop
A falling tower, nay in its violent course
To stoppe the lightning, then to stay a woman
Hurried by two furies, lust and falshood,   50
In her full carier to wickednes.
    Baptista.   Pray you temper
The violence of your passion.
    Mathias.   In extreames
Of this condition, can it be in man
To vse a moderation? I am throwne
From a steepe rocke headlong into a gulph   55
Of misery, and find my selfe past hope
In the same moment that I apprehend
That I am falling; and this the figure of
My Idoll few howers since, while she continued
In her perfection, that was late a mirror   60
In which I saw miracles, shapes of duty,
Stayd manners, with all excellency a husband
Could wish in a chast wife, is on the suddaine

14ʳ

---

47. arme] *30¹*; armes *30²*   50. by] *30*; by the *conj. McIlwraith*   51. temper]
Dodsley; tempter *30*   61. miracles,] *30²*; miracules *30*; miraculous *Dodsley*

Turnd to a magicall glasse, and does present
Nothing but hornes, and horror.
   Baptista.   You may yet   65
And 'tis the best foundation, build vp comfort
On your owne goodnes.
   Mathias.   Noe, that hath vndone me
For now I hold my temperance a sinne
Worse then excesse, and what was vice a vertue.
Haue I refus'd a Queene, and such a Queene   70
Whose rauishing beauties at the first sight had tempted
A hermit from his beades, and chang'd his prayers
To amorous Sonets, to preserue my faith
Inuiolate to thee, with the hazard of
My death with torture, since she could inflict   75
No lesse for my contempt, and haue I made
Such a returne from thee? I will not curse thee,
Nor for thy falshood raile against the sex,
'Tis poore, and common; Ile onely with wise men
Whisper vnto my selfe, howere they seeme,   80
Nor present, nor past times, nor the age to come
Hath heeretofore, can now, or euer shall
Produce on constant woman.
   Baptista.   This is more
Then the Satirists wrot against 'em.
   Mathias.   Ther's no language
That can expresse the poyson of these Aspicks,   85
These weeping Crocadiles, and all to little
That hath beene sayd against 'em; but I'll mould
My thoughts into another forme, and if
She can out-liue the report of what I haue donne
This hand when next she comes within my reach   90
Shall be her executioner.

Enter HONORIA.

   Baptista.   The Queene sir.
   Honoria. Wait our command at distance; sir you haue to
Free liberty to depart.

76. made] *30*; met *Dodsley*   86. all] *30*; all's *conj. McIlwraith*   87. beene]
Dodsley; beeing *30¹*; being *30²*   91 SD. HONORIA] *30*; HONORIA *and* ACANTHE
Gifford   92. distance] *30*; distance: *Exit Acanthe Gifford*   haue to] *30*; too have
Gifford

8118945.3   K

Baptista. I know my manners
And thanke you for the fauour. *Exit* BAPTISTA.
  Honoria.   Haue you taken
Good rest in your new lodgings? I expect now 95
Your resolute answere, but aduise maturely
Before I heare it.
  Mathias. Let my actions Madam,
For no words can dilate my ioy in all
You can command with cherefulnes to serue you,
Assure your highnes, and in signe of my 100
Submission, and contrition for my error,

Ki^r My lipps, that but the last night shund the touch
Of yours as poyson, taught humility now,
Thus on your foot, and that too great an honor
For such an vndeseruer, seales my duty. 105
A cloudy mist of ignorance equall to
Cimmerian darkenes, would not let me see then
What now with adoration, and wonder,
With reuerence I looke vp to: but those foggs
Dispersd and scatterd by the powerfull beames 110
With which your selfe, the Sun of all perfection,
Vouchsafe to cure my blindnes, like a suppliant
As low as I can kneele I humbly begge
What you once pleasd to tender.
  Honoria.   This is more
Then I could hope! what find you so attractiue 115
Vpon my face in so short time to make
This suddaine Metamorphosis? pray you rise;
I for your late neglect thus signe your pardon.
I now you kisse like a louer, and not as brothers
Coldly salute their sisters.
  Mathias. I am turnd 120
All spirit and fire.
  Honoria. Yet to giue some allay
To this hot feruor 'twere good to remember
The King, whose eies and eares are euery where,
With the danger to that followes, this discouer'd.
  Mathias. Danger? a buggebeare Maddam! let ride once 125
Like *Phaeton* in the Chariot of your fauour,

125. let] *30*; let me *Coxeter*; let's *Dodsley*

And I contemne *Ioues* thunder. Though the King
In our embraces stood a looker on,
His hang-men and with studied cruelty ready
To dragge me from your armes, it should not fright me   130
From the inioying that, a single life is
Too poore a price for. O that now all vigour
Of my youth were recollected for an hower
That my desire might meete with yours and draw
The enuy of all men in the Encounter   135
Vpon my head! I should, but we loose time,
Be gratious mighty Queene.
 Honoria.   Pause yet a little.
The bounties of the King, and what weighs more,
Your boasted constancie to your machlesse wife,
Should not so soone be shaken.
 Mathias.   The whole fabricke   140
When I but looke on you, is in a moment
Oreturnd, and ruind, and as riuers loose
Their names, when they are swallowed by the *Ocean*
In you alone all faculties of my soule
Are wholy taken vp, my wife, and King   145
At the best as things forgotten.
 Honoria.   Can this be?   [*Aside.*]
I haue gaynd my end now.
 Mathias.   Wherefore stay you Madam?
 Honoria. In my consideration what a nothing
Mans constancy is.
 Mathias. Your beauties make it so,
In my sweet lady.
 Honoria. And it is my glory: 150
I could be coy now as you were, but I
Am of a gentler temper; howsoeuer,
And in a iust returne of what I haue suffer'd
In your disdaine, with the same measure graunt me
Equall deliberation. I ere long   155
Will visite you againe and when I next
Appeare, as conquerd by it, slauelike wayt
On my triumphant beauty.   *Exit* HONORIA.
 Mathias.   What a change

140. so soone] *Gifford*; soone *30*   146 SD. *Aside.*] *Coxeter*; *not in 30*

Is heere, beyond my feare, but by thy falshood
Sophia not her beauty. Is it deni'd me   160
To sinne but in my wishes? what a frowne
In scorne at her departure she threw on me!
I am both waies lost; stormes of Contempt, and scorne
Are ready to breake on me, and all hope
Of shelter doubtfull. I can neither be   165
Disloyall, nor yet honest, I stand guilty
On either part; at the worst death will end all,
K2ʳ And he must be my iudge to right my wrong,
Since I haue lou'd too much and liu'd too long.   *Exit* MATHIAS.

[IV. ii]   *Actus quarti, Scæna secunda.*

Enter SOPHIA *sola with a booke and a note.*

Sophia. Nor custome nor example, nor vast numbers
Of such as doe offend make lesse the sinne;
For each particular crime a strict accompt
Will be exacted, and that comfort which
The damnd pretend, fellowes in misery,   5
Takes nothing from their torments. Euery one
Must suffer in himselfe the measure of
His wickednes; if so, as I must grant
It being vnrefutable in reason,
Howere my Lord offend, it is no warrant   10
For me to walke in his forbidden paths.
What penance then can expiate my guilte
For my consent (transported then with passion)
To wantonnesse? the woundes I giue my fame
Cannot recouer his, and though I haue fedd   15
These courtiers with promises and hopes
I am yet in fact vntainted, and I trust
My sorrow for it with my purity
And loue to goodnes for it selfe, made powerfull
Though all they haue alleadg'd proue true or false,   20
Will be such exorcismes as shall command
This furie iealousie from me. What I haue

Determind touching them I am resolu'd
To put in execution, Within there!

    Enter HILARIO, CORISCA, *with other* SERVANTS.

Where are my noble ghests?
  Hilario.   The elder, Maddam,   25
Is drinking by himselfe to your Ladiships health
In Muskadine and egges, and for a rasher
To draw His liquor downe he hath got a pie
Of marrow-bones, Potatos and Eringos,
With many such ingredients, and tis sayd   30
He hath sent his man in post to the next towne,
For a pound of Amber gris, and halfe a pecke
Of fishes cald Cantharides.
  Corisca.   The younger
Prunes vp himselfe as if this night he were
To act a bridegroomes part, but to what purpose   35
I am ignorance it selfe.
  Sophia.   Continue so.   *Giues a paper.*
Let those lodgings be prepard as this directs you,
And fayle not in a circumstance, as you
Respect my fauour.
  1 *Seruant.*   We haue our instructions.
  2 *Seruant.* And punctually will follow 'em.   *Exeunt* SERVANTS.

    Enter VBALDO.

  Hilario.   Heere comes Madam
The Lord *Vbaldo.*
  Vbaldo.   Pretty on, thers gould,   41
To buy thee a new gowne, and ther's for thee,
Grow fat, and fit for seruice. I am now
As I should be, at the height and able to
Beget a gyant. O my better Angell   45
In this you show your wisdome when you pay
The lecher in his owne coyne; shall you sit puling,
Like a patient *Grissell,* and be laught at? no!
This is a fayre reueng, shall we to it?
  Sophia.   To what sir?
  Vbaldo. The sport you promisd.

    IV. ii. 24 SD. *Enter . . .* SERVANTS.] *Gifford; following* ghests? (l. 25) 30

Sophia.   Could it be donne with safety—

Vbaldo. I warant you, I am sound as a bell, a tough   51
Old blade, and steele to the backe, as you shall find me
In the triall on your anuill.

Sophia.   So, but how sir
Shall I satisfie your friend to whom by promise
I am equally ingag'd?

Vbaldo.   I must confesse   55
The more the merier, but of all men liuing
Take heed of him: you may safer run vpon
The mouth of a cannon, when it is vnlading,

K3ʳ And come off colder.

Sophia.   How! is he not holsome?

Vbaldo. Holsome? I'll tell you for your good, he is   60
A spittle of diseases and indeed
More lothsome and infectious; the tubbe is
His weekely bath; He hath not dranke this seauen yeare
Before he came to your house, but compositions
Of Sassafras, and Guacum, and drie mutton   65
His daily portion; name what scratch soeuer
Can be got by women and the Surgeons will resolue you
At this time or at that *Ricardo* had it.

Sophia. Blesse me from him.

Vbaldo.   'Tis a good prayer Lady,
It being a degree vnto the pox   70
Onely to mention him; if my tongue burne not hange me
When I but name *Ricardo.*

Sophia.   Sir this caution
Must be rewarded.

Vbaldo.   I hope I haue marrd his market.
But when?

Sophia. Why presently. Follow my woman,
She knowes where to conduct you, and will serue   75
To night for a page, let the wastcote I apointed
With the cambricq shirt perfumd, and the rich cappe
Be brought into his chamber.

Vbaldo.   Excellent Lady.

50. safety—] *McIlwraith*; ∼. *30*; ∼? *Coxeter*
fections, *30*   65. mutton] *30*; mutton's *Coxeter*
74. presently.] *after Dodsley*; ∼ˏ *30*
62. infectious;] *Dodsley*; in-
72. name] *Dodsley*; namd *30*

And a caudle too in the morning.
 Corisca.   I will fit you.
      Exeunt VBALDO *and* CORISCA.

    Enter RICARDO.

 Sophia. So hot on the scent here comes the other beagle. 80
 Ricardo. Take purse and all.
 Hilario.   If this company would come often
I should make a pretty terme on't.   [*Aside.*]
 Sophia.   For your sake
I haue put him off, he only begd a kisse,
I gaue it and so parted.
 Ricardo.   I hope better.
He did not touch your lipps?
 Sophia.   Yes. I assure you 85
There was no danger in it.
 Ricardo.   No? eate presently
These lozenges, of forty crownes an ounce,
Or you are vndone.
 Sophia.   What is the vertue of 'em?
 Ricardo. They are preseruatiues against stinking breath
Rising from rotten lungs.
 Sophia.   If so your carriage 90
Of such deere antidotes in my opinion
May render yours suspected.
 Ricardo.   Fie no I vse 'em
When I talke with him, I should be poysond else.
But i'll be free with you. Hee was once a creature
It may be of Gods making, but long since 95
He is turnd to a druggists shoppe; the spring and fall
Hold all the yeere with him, that he liues he owes
To art not nature, she has giuen him ore.
He moues like the faery King, on scrues and wheeles
Made by his Doctors recipes, and yet still 100
They are out of ioynt, and euery day reparing.
He has a regiment of whores he keepes
At his owne charge in a lazar house but the best is
There's not a nose among 'em: Hee's acquainted

 80. scent] *30;* ~! *Coxeter* 82 SD. *Aside.*] *editor; not in 30* 85. you] *editor;*
~. *30* 86. it.] *30;* ~? *Dodsley*

With the greene water and the spitting pill's   105
Familiar to him, in a frosty morning
You may thrust him in a pottle pot, his bones
Rattle in his Skinne like beanes tos'd in a bladder,
If he but heere a coche the fomentation,
The Friction with fumigation cannot saue him   110
From the chine euill, in a word he is
Not on disease but all; yet being my friend
I will forbeare his caracter, for I would not
Wrong him in your opinion.

   Sophia.   The best is
The vertues you bestow on him to me   115
Are misteries I know not, but howeuer
I am at your seruice. Sirrha let it be your care
T'vncloth the gentleman, and with speed, delay
K4ʳ Takes from delight.

   Ricardo.   Good, there's my hat, sword, cloke,
A vengeance on these buttons, off with my dublet,   120
I dare show my Skinne, in the touch you will like it better,
Prethe cut my codpeese poynt, and for this seruice
When I leaue them off they are thine.

   Hilario.   I'll take your word sir.

   Ricardo. Deere lady stay not long.

   Sophia.   I may come too soone sir.

   Ricardo. No, no I am ready now.

   Hilario.   This is the way sir.   125

                  Exeunt HILARIO *and* RICARDO.

   Sophia. I was much too blame to credit their reports
Touching my Lord that so traduce each other
And with such virulent malice, though I presume
They are bad enough, but I haue studied for 'em
A way for their recouerie.

    The noyse of clapping a doore, VBALDO *aboue in his shirt.*

   Vbaldo.   What dost thou meane wench?   130
Why dost thou shut the doore upon me? ha!
My cloths are taine away to! shall I starue heere?
Is this my lodging? I am sure the lady talkd of
A rich cappe, a perfum'd shirt, and a wastcote

    105. pill's] *Dodsley*; pill *30*   122. poynt] *30*; poynts *Gifford*

But heere is nothing but a little fresh straw, 135
A pettycote for a couerlet and that torne to,
And an ould womans biggen for a night cappe,

Enter CORISCA.

Slight tis a prison, or a pigstie, ha!
The windows grated with Iron; I cannot force 'em
And if I leape downe heere I breake my necke. 140
I am betrayd, rogues, villaines let me out!
I am a Lord, and that's no common tittle,
And shall I be vsd thus?
　　Sophia.　　　　　Let him raue, Hee's fast.
I'll parley with him at leasure.

　　　RICARDO *entring with a great noyse aboue, as fallen.*

　　Ricardo.　　　　　Zoones haue you trap doores?
　　Sophia. The other birds i'th cage too, let him flutter. 145
　　Ricardo. Whither am I falne? into Hell?
4ᵛ　　*Vbaldo.*　　　　　Who makes that noyse there?
Helpe me if thou art a friend!
　　Ricardo.　　　　　A friend? I am where
I cannot helpe my selfe; let me see
Thy face.
　　Vbaldo. How! *Ricardo!* prethe throw me
Thy cloke, if thou canst to couer me; I am almost 150
Frozen to death.
　　Ricardo.　　My cloke? I haue no breeches,
I am in my shirt as thou art, and heer's nothing
For my selfe but a clownes cast suite.
　　Vbaldo.　　　　　We are both vndone.
Prethe rore a little, Madam!

　　　Enter HILARIO *in* RICARDO'S *suite.*

　　Ricardo.　　　　　Lady of the house!
　　Vbaldo. Groomes of the chamber!
　　Ricardo.　　　　　Gentlewomen, milkemaydes!
　　Vbaldo. Shall we be murthered?
　　Sophia.　　　　　Noe but soundly punish'd 156
To your diserts.

　　　148-9. see | Thy] *editor*; *undivided 30*

Ricardo.　　　You are not in earnest Madam?
Sophia. Iudge as you find, and feele it, and now heere
What I irreuocablie purpose to you.
Being receau'd as ghests into my house　　　160
And with all it afforded entertaind
You haue forgot all hospitable duties,
And with the defamation of my Lord
Wrought on my woman weakenesse in reuenge
Of his iniuries, as you fashiond 'em to me,　　　165
To yeeld my honor to your lawlesse lust.
　　Hilario. Marke that poore fellowes.
　　Sophia.　　　　　　　And so far you haue
Transgres'd against the dignity of men
(Who should, bound to it by vertue, still defend
Chast ladies honors) that it was your trade　　　170
To make 'em infamous; but you are caught
In your owne toiles like lustfull beasts, and therfore
Hope not to find the vsage of men from me.
Such mercie you haue forfeited, and shall suffer
Liᶠ Like the most slauish women.
　　Vbaldo.　　　　　　How will you vse vs?　　　175
　　Sophia. Ease and excesse in feeding made you wanton;
A plurisie of ill blood you must let out
By labour, and spare diet, that way got to,
Or perish for hunger. Reach him vp that distaffe
With the flax vpon it; though no *Omphale*　　　180
Nor you a second *Hercules*, as I take it,
As you spinne well at my command, and please me
Your wages in the coursest bread, and water,
Shall be proportionable.
　　Vbaldo.　　　　I will starue first.
　　Sophia. That's as you please.
　　Ricardo.　　　　What will become of me now?　185
　　Sophia. You shall haue gentler worke. I haue oft obseru'd
You were proud to show the finenesse of your hands,
And softnes of your fingers; you should reele well
What he spins if you giue your mind to it, as i'll force you.
Deliuer him his materialls. Now you know　　　190
Your penance fall to worke, hunger will teach you,

　　　　　　189. i'll] *Dodsley*; ill 30

And so as slaues to your lust, not me, I leaue you.

                   Exeunt SOPHIA, [CORISCA,] *and* SERVANTS.

Vbaldo. I shall spinne a fine thred out now!

Ricardo.   I cannot looke

On these deuices but they put me in mind

Of rope-makers.

Hilario.   Fellow thinke of thy taske.   195

Forget such vanities, my liuery there

Will serue the to worke in.

Ricardo.   Let me haue my clothes yet,

I was bountifull to thee.

Hilario.   They are past your wearing

And mine by promise, as all these can witnes.

You haue no holydaies comming, nor will I worke   200

While these, and this lasts, and so when you please

You may shut vp your shoppe windowes.   *Exit* HILARIO.

Vbaldo.   I am faint

And must lye downe.

Ricardo.   I am hungry to, and could.

O cursed women!

Vbaldo.   This comes of our whoring.

But let vs rest aswell as we can to night   205

But not ore sleepe our selues, least we fast to morrow.

                     They draw the curtaines.

Actus quarti, Scæna tertia.

Enter LADISLAUS, HONORIA, EUBULUS, FERDINAND,
ACANTHE, *Attendants.*

Honoria. Now you know all sir, with the motiues why

I forc'd him to my lodging.

Ladislaus.   I desire

No more such trials Lady.

Honoria.   I presume sir

You do not doubt my chastity.

Ladislaus.   I would not,

But these are strange inducements.

192 SD. SOPHIA . . . SERVANTS.] *editor*; *Sophia.* | *and seruants. 30*; *Sophia and Corisca.
Gifford*   206 SD. *draw*] *Dodsley*; *drew 30*   IV. iii. *tertia*] *McIlwraith*; *tertij 30*
SD. *Attendants*] *Coxeter*; *attendance 30*

 Eubulus.   By no meanes sir.   5
Why though he were with violence ceasd vpon,
And still detaynd, the man sir being no souldier
Nor vsd to charge his pike when the breach is open
There was no danger in't: you must conceiue sir,
Being relligious, she chose him for a Chaplaine 10
To read old Homelies to her in the darke,
Shee's bound to it by her Cannons.
 Ladislaus.   Still tormented
With thy impertinence.
 Honoria.   By your selfe deere sir.
I was ambitious onely to ouer throw
His boasted constancy in his consent,   15
But for fact I contemne him. I was neuer
Vnchast in thought, I laboured to giue proofe
What power dwels in this beauty you admire so,
And when you see how soone it hath transform'd him,
And with what superstition hee addores it, 20
Determine as you please.
 Ladislaus.   I will looke on
This pageant but—
 Honoria.   When you haue seene and hard sir,
The passages, which I my selfe discouer'd,
And could haue kept conceal'd had I meant basely
L2ʳ Iudge as you please.
 Ladislaus.   Well I'll obserue the issue. 25
 Eubulus. How had you tooke this, Generall, in your wife?
 Ferdinand. As a strange curiosity, but Queenes
Are priuiledgd aboue subiects, and tis fit sir.   *Exeunt.*

[IV. iv]   *Actus quarti, Scæna quarta.*

      Enter MATHIAS, BAPTISTA.

 Baptista. You are much alterd sir since the last night
When the Queene left you, and looke cheerefully,
Your dulnesse quite blowne ouer.
 Mathias.   I haue seene a vision
This morning makes it good, and neuer was

   13. sir.] *30*; ~, *Coxeter*   IV. iv. *quarta*] *McIlwraith*; *quarti 30*

In such security as at this instant,   5
Fall what can fall, and when the Queene appeares
Whose shortest absence now is tedious to me,
Obserue 'th incounter.

Enter HONORIA [*below*]. LADISLAUS, EUBULUS, FERDINAND,
        ACANTHE, *with others aboue.*

Baptista.   She already is
Entred the lists.
Mathias.   And I prepard to meete her.
Baptista. I know my duty.
Honoria.   Not so, you may stay now   10
As a witnes of our contract.
Baptista.   I obey
In all things Madam.
Honoria.   Wher's that reuerence,
Or rather superstitious addoration,
Which captiue like to my triumphant beauty
You payd last night? no humble knee? nor signe   15
Of vassall duty? sure this is the foote,
To whose proud couer, and then happy in it,
Your lipps were glewd; and that the necke then offer'd,
To witnes your subiection, to be trod on.
Your certaine losse of life in the Kings anger   20
Was then to meane a price to buy my fauour.
And that false gloweworme fire of constancie
To your wife, extinguished by a greater light
Shot from our eyes; and that, it may be (being
To glorious to be look'd on) hath depriu'd you   25
Of speech, and motion: but I will take off
A little from the splendor, and descend
From my owne height, and in your lownesse heere you
Plead as a suppliant.
Mathias.   I do remember
I once saw such a woman.
Honoria.   How!
Mathias.   And then   30
She did appeare a most magnificent Queene

8 SD. *below*] *after Coxeter; not in 30*

And, what's more, vertuous though somewhat darkned
With pride and selfe oppinion.
    Eubulus.   Call you this courtship?
    Mathias. And she was happy in a royall husband,
Whom enuie could not tax, vnlesse it were   35
For his too much indulgence to her humors.
    Eubulus. Pray you sir obserue that touch, tis to the purpose;
I like the play the better for't.
    Mathias.   And she liu'd
Worthy her birth, and fortune; you retayne yet
Some part of her angelicall forme, but when   40
Enuie to the beauty of another woman
Inferior to hers, (one she neuer
Had seene but in her picture) had dispers'd
Infection through her veines, and loyaltie
Which a great Queene as shee was should haue nourish'd   45
Grew odious to her—
    Honoria.   I am thunderstrocke.
    Mathias. And lust in all the brauery it could borrow
From maiesty, howere disguisde, had tooke
Sure footing in the kingdome of her heart
(The throne of chastity once,) how in a moment   50
All that was gratious, great, and glorious in her
And woone vpon all hearts, like seeming shadowes
Wanting true substance vanish'd!
    Honoria.   How his reasons
Worke on my Soule.
    Mathias.   Retire into your selfe,
L3ʳ Your owne strengths Madam, strongly man'd with vertue,   55
And be but as you were, and there's no office
So base beneath the slauery, that men
Impose on beasts, but I will gladly bow to.
But as you play, and iuggle with a stranger,
Varying your shapes like *Thetis*, though the beauties   60
Of all that are by Poets raptures sainted
Were now in you vnited, you should passe
Pittied by me perhaps, but not regarded.
    Eubulus. If this take not I am cheated.

42. (one] *30*; one that *Gifford*; (& one *McIlwraith*   56. office] *Dodsley*;
offence. *30*   61. sainted] *30*; painted *Coxeter*

Mathias.   To slip once
Is incident, and excusde by humane fraylty,   65
But to fall euer damnable. We were both
Guilty I grant in tendering our affection,
But, as I hope you will doe, I repented.
When we are growne vp to ripenesse, our life is
Like to this picture. While we runne   70
A constant race in goodnesse, it retaines
The iust proportion. But the iourneye being
Tedious, and sweet temptations in the way,
That may in some degree diuert vs from
The rode that we put forth in, ere we end   75
Our pilgrimage, it may like this turne yellow
Or be with blacknesse clouded. But when we
Finde we haue gone astray, and labour to
Returne vnto our neuer fayling guide
Vertue, contrition with vnfained teares,   80
The spots of vice wash'd off, will soone restore it
To the first purenesse.
Honoria.   I am disenchanted!
Mercy, O mercy heauens!   *Kneeles.*
Ladislaus.   I am rauished with
What I haue seene and hard.
Ferdinand.   Let vs descend and heere
The rest below.
Eubulus.   This hath falne out beyond   85
My expectation.   *They descend.*
Honoria.   How haue I wandred
Out of the tract of piety, and misled
By ouerweening pride, and flattery
Of fawning sycophants (the bane of greatnes)
Could neuer meete till now a passenger   90
That in his charity would set me right,
Or stay me in my precipice to ruine.
How ill haue I return'd your goodnes to me!
The horror in my thought of't turnes me marble.
But if it may be yet preuented,

70. picture] *30*; magic picture *Gifford*   72. iourneye] *Dodsley*; iourneyes *30*
84–6. Let . . . expectation.] *30*; Let . . . descend, / And . . . below. / This . . . out /
Beyond . . . expectation. *Gifford*   94. of't] *Coxeter*; oft *30*; on't *Dodsley*

Enter the King and others.

O sir,   95
What can I do to shew my sorrow or
With what brow aske your pardon?
    Ladislaus.   Pray you rise.
    Honoria. Neuer, till you forgiue me, and receiue
Vnto your loue, and fauour a chang'd woman.
My state, and pride turn'd to humillity henceforth   100
Shall waite on your commands, and my obedience
Steer'd only by your will.
    Ladislaus.   And that will proue
A second and a better marriage to me.
All is forgot.
    Honoria. Sir I must not rise yet
Till with a free confession of a crime,   105
Vnknowne to you yet, and a following suite
Which thus I beg be granted.
    Ladislaus.   I melt with you.
Tis pardon'd, and confirm'd thus.
    Honoria.   Know then sir,
In malice to this good knights wife I practis'd
Vbaldo, and *Ricardo*, to corrupt her.   110
    Baptista. Thence grew the change of the picture.
    Honoria.   And how far
They haue preuaild I am ignorant. Now if you sir
For the honor of this goodman, may be intreated
To trauaile thither, it being but a dayes iourney,
To fetch 'em off,
    Ladislaus.   We will put on to night.   115
    Baptista. I if you please your harbinger.
    Ladislaus.   I thanke you.
Let me embrace you in my armes, your seruice
Donne on the *Turke* compard with this waighs nothing.
    Mathias. I am still your humble creature.
    Ladislaus.   My true friend.
    Ferdinand. And so you are bound to hold him.
    Eubulus.   Such a plante

L4ʳ

---

95 SD. *Enter . . . others.*] *Gifford*; *follows* l. 94 *30*   103-4. me. / All] *Gifford*;
undivided 30   107. beg] *30*; ~, *Dodsley*   113. For] *Coxeter*; Or *30*

Imported to your Kingdome, and heere grafted　　121
Would yeeld more fruit then all the idle weedes
That sucke vp your raigne of fauour.
 Ladislaus.   In my will
I'll not be wanting; prepare for our iourney.
In acte be my *Honoria* now, not name,　　125
And to all after times preserue thy fame. *Exeunt.*

The end of the fourth Act.

i]　　*Actus quinti, Scæna prima.*

SOPHIA, CORISCA, HILARIO.

Sophia. ARE they then so humble?
 Hilario.   Hunger and hard labour
Haue tamde 'em Madam; at the first they below'd
Like staggs tane in a toyle and would not worke
For sullennesse, but when they found without it
There was no eating, and that to starue to death　　5
Was much against their stomachs, by degree
Against their wills they fell to it.
 Corisca.   And now feed on
The little pittance you allow with gladnesse.
 Hilario. I do remember that they stop'd their noses
At the sight of beefe, and mutton as course feeding　　10
For their fine palats, but now their worke being ended
They leape at a barley crust and hold chese parings
With a spoonefull of pal'd wine pour'd in their water,
For festiuall excedings.
 Corisca.   When I examine
My spinsters worke hee trembles like a prentice,　　15
And takes a box on the eare when I spie faults
And botches in his labour, as a fauour
From a curst mistrisse.
 Hilario.   The other to reeles well
4ᵛ For his time, and if your ladiship would please
To see 'em for your sport, since they want ayring,　　20
It would do well in my iudgement: you shall heere

V. i. 6. degree] *30*; degrees, *Dodsley*　　18. reeles] *Dodsley*; reele *30*

Such a hungry dialoge from 'em.

Sophia.   But suppose
When they are out of prison they should grow
Rebellious?

Hilario.   Neuer feare't. I'll vndertake
To lead 'em out by the nose with a course thred   25
Of the ones spinning and make the other reele after
And without grumbling, and when you are weary of
Their company as easily returne 'em.

Corisca. Deere Madam it will helpe to driue away
Your melancholy.

Sophia.   Well on this assurance   30
I am content, bring 'em hither.

Hilario.   I will do it
In stately Equipage.   *Exit* HILARIO.

Sophia.   They haue confessed then
They were set on by the Queene to taynt mee in
My loyalty to my Lord?

Corisca.   Twas the maine cause,
That brought 'em hither.

Sophia.   I am glad I know it   35
And as I haue begun, before I end
I'll at the height reuenge it. Let vs steppe aside,
They come; the obiects so ridiculous
In spight of my sad thoughts I cannot but
Lend a forc'd smile to grace it.

        Enter HILARIO, VBALDO *spinning*, RICARDO *reeling.*

Hilario.   Come away.   40
Worke as you go, and loose no time; 'tis precious,
You'll find it in your Commons.

Ricardo.   Comons call you it?
The word is proper. I haue graz'd so long
Vpon your commons I am almost staru'd heere.

Hilario. Worke harder and they shall be better'd.

Vbaldo.   Better'd?   45
Worser they cannot be: would I might lye
Mı^r Like a dogge vnder her table and serue for a footstoole
So I might haue my belly full of that

        39-40. but / Lend a] 30; but lend / A *Gifford*

Her Island curr refuses.
Hilario.   How do you like
Your ayring? is it not a fauour?
Ricardo.   Yes,   50
Iust such a one as you vse to a brace of gray-houndes
When they are ledd out of their kennels to scumber.
But our case is ten times harder, we haue nothing
In our bellies to be vented; if you will bee
An honest yeoman pheuterer, feed vs first,   55
And walke vs after!
Hilario.   Yeoman pheuterer?
Such another word to your Gouernor, and you goe
Supperlesse to bed for't.
Vbaldo.   Nay euen as you please.
The comfortable names of breake-fasts, dinners,
Collations, supper, beuerage, are words   60
Worne out of our remembrance.
Ricardo.   O for the steame
Of meat in a cookes shoppe!
Vbaldo.   I am so drie
I haue not spittle enough to wett my fingers
When I draw my flax from my distaffe.
Ricardo.   Nor I strength
To raise my hand to the top of my reeler. Oh!   65
I haue the crampe all ouer me.
Hilario.   What do you thincke
Were best to apply to it? a crampstone as I take it
Were very vsefull.
Ricardo.   Oh no more of stones,
We haue beene vsd to long like hawkes already.
Vbaldo. We are not so high in our flesh now to need casting;   70
We will come to an empty fist.
Hilario.   Nay that you shall not.
So hoe birdes, how the eyasses scratch, and scramble!
Take heed of a surfet, do not cast your gorges,
This is more then I haue commission for, be thankefull.
Sophia. Were all that studie the abuse of women   75
Vsd thus, the citty would not swarme with Cuccholds

11ᵛ

55. An] *Dodsley*; And *30*   pheuterer] *Mason*; phenterer *30*   56. Yeoman]
Dodsley; Yeomen *30*   pheuterer] *Mason*; phenterer *30*

Nor so many trads-men breake.
 Corisca.   Pray you appeare now
And marke the alteration.
 Hilario.   To your worke,
My Lady is in presence, show your duties
Exceeding well.
 Sophia.   How do your scollers profite? 80
 Hilario. Hold vp your heads demurely. Prettily
For young beginners.
 Corisca.   And will do well in time
If they be kept in awe.
 Ricardo.   In awe? I am sure
I quake like an aspen leafe.
 Vbaldo.   No mercy Lady?
 Ricardo. Nor intermission?
 Sophia.   Let me see your worke. 85
Fie vpon't what a thredds heere, a poore coblers wife
Would make a finer to sow a clounes rent start vp,
And heere you reele as you were druncke.
 Ricardo.   I am sure
It is not with wine.
 Sophia. O take heade of wine,
Could water is far better for your healths 90
Of which I am very tender; you had foule bodies
And must continue in this phisicall diet
Till the cause of your disease be tane away
For feare of a relaps and that is dangerous.
Yet I hope alredy that you are in some 95
Degree recouerd and that way to resolue me
Answer me truely, nay what I propound
Concernes both, neerer, what would you now giue
If your meanes were in your hands to lye all night
With a fresh and hansume ladie?
 Vbaldo.   How! a lady? 100
O I am pasd it, hunger with her razor
Hath made me an euenuch.
 Ricardo.   For a messe of porridge
Well sop'd with a bunch of raddish and a carret
I would sell my barronrie, but for women—oh

M2^r Noe more of women! not a doyte for a doxeie   105
After this hungry voyage.
    Sophia.   These are truly
Good symptomes, let them not venture to much in the ayre
Till they are weaker.
    Ricardo.   This is tyranie.
    Vbaldo. Scorne vpon scorne.
    Sophia.   You were so
In your malitious intents to me   110

Enter a SERVANT.

And therefore tis but iustice. Whats the busnesse?
    Seruant. My Lords great frend signior *Baptista*, Madam,
Is newly lighted from his horse with certaine
Assurance of my Lords arriuall.
    Sophia.   How?
And stand I trifling here? hence with the mungrells   115
To there seuerall kennels, there let them houle in priuat,
Ile bee no farther troubled.   *Exeunt* SOPHIA *and* SERVANT.
    Vbaldo.   O that euer
I saw this fury!
    Ricardo.   Or look'd one a woman
But as a prodigie in nature.
    Hilario.   Silence!
Noe more of this.
    Corisca.   Me thincks you haue noe cause   120
To repent your being heere.
    Hilario.   Haue you not learnt
When your states are spent your seuerall trades to liue by,
And neuer charge the hospitall?
    Corisca.   Worke but titely
And wee will not vse a dishe-cloute in the house
But of your spinning.
    Vbaldo.   O I would this hempe   125
Were turnd to a halter!
    Hilario.   Will you march?
    Ricardo.   A soft one
Good generall I beseech you!
    Vbaldo.   I can hardly
Draw my legs after me.

　　Hilario.　　　　　　　For a crouch you may vse
M2ᵛ Your distaffe, a good wit makes vse of all things.　　　*Exeunt.*

　　　　　Actus quinti, Scæna secunda.

　　　　　　　　Enter SOPHIA, BAPTISTA.

　Sophia. Was he iealous of me?
　Baptista.　　　　　　　Ther's no perfite loue
Without some touch of't Madam.
　Sophia.　　　　　　And my picture
Made by your diuelish art, a spie vpon
My actions? I neuer sate to be drawne,
Nor had you sir comision for't.
　Baptista.　　　　　　Excuse me,　　　　　　5
At his earnest sute I did it.
　Sophia.　　　　　　Very good,
Was I growne so cheape in his opinion of me?
　Baptista. The prosperous euents that cround his fortunes
May qualifie the offence.
　Sophia.　　　　Good! the euents,
The sanctuary fooles and madmen flie to,　　　　　10
When their rash and desperat vndertakings thriue well;
But good, and wisemen are directed by
Graue counsailes, and with such deliberation
Proceed in their affaires that chance has nothing
To do with 'em. Howsoere, take the paynes sir　　　15
To meete the honor in the King, and Queenes
Approches to my house, that breakes vpon mee:
I will expect them with my best of care.
　Baptista. To entertaine such royall ghests—
　Sophia.　　　　　　　　I know it;
Leaue that to me sir.　　　　　　　*Exit* BAPTISTA.
　　　　　What should moue the Queene　　　20
So giuen to ease and pleasure, as fame speakes her,
To such a iourney? or worke on my Lord
To doubt my loyalty? nay more to take
For the resolution of his feares, a course

That is by holy writ denide a christian?   25
'Twas impious in him, and perhaps the welcome
He hopes in my embraces may deceiue
His expectation! the trumpets speake
The Kings arriuall, helpe a womans wit now,   29
To make him know his fault and my iust anger.   *Exit* SOPHIA.

Actus quinti, scæna vltima.

Loud musicke. Enter MATHIAS, EUBULUS, LADISLAUS,
FERDINAND, HONORIA, BAPTISTA, ACANTHE, *with Attendants.*

Eubulus. Your maiesty must be weary.
Honoria.   No my Lord,
A willing mind makes a hard iourney easie.
Mathias. Not *Ioue* attended on by *Hermes*, was
More welcome to the cottage of *Philemon*,
And his poore *Baucis*, then your gratious selfe,   5
Your matchlesse Queene, and all your royall traine
Are to your seruant and his wife.
Ladislaus.   Where is she?
Honoria. I long to see her as my now lou'd riuall.
Eubulus. And I to haue a smack at her, 'tis a cordiall
To an old man, better then sacke, and a tost   10
Before he goes to supper.
Mathias.   Ha! is my house turnd
To a wildernesse? nor wife nor seruants ready
With all rites due to maiesty to receiue
Such vnexpected blessings? you assurd me
Of better preparation; hath not   15
Th'excesse of ioy transported her beyond
Her vnderstanding?
Baptista.   I now parted from her,
And gaue her your directions.
Mathias.   How shall I begge
Your maiesties patience? sure my famelie's druncke
Or by some witch in enuie of my glory   20
A dead sleepe throwne vpon 'em.

V. iii. 8. lou'd] *Dodsley*; loud *30*   13. With all] *Dodsley*; Withall *30*

Enter HILARIO, *and Seruants.*

  1 *Seruant.*   Sir.
  Mathias.   But that
The sacred presence of the King forbids it,
My sword should make a massacre among you.
Where is your mistris?
  Hilario.   First you are welcome home sir,
Then know she saies shee's sicke sir—there's no notice   [*Aside.*]
Taken of my brauery.

M3ᵛ *Mathias.*   Sicke at such a time!   26
It cannot be! though she were on her death bed,
And her spirit euen now departed heere stand they
Could call it backe againe, and in this honor
Giue her a second being; bring me to her,   30
I know not what to vrge, or how to redeeme
This morgage of her manners.   *Exeunt* MATHIAS *and* HILARIO.
  Eubulus.   Ther's no climate
On the world I thinke where on iades tricke or other
Raignes not in women.
  Ferdinand.   You were euer bitter
Against the Sex.
  Ladislaus.   This is very strange.
  Honoria.   Meane women   35
Haue their faults as well, as Queenes.
  Ladislaus.   O shee appeares now.

Enter MATHIAS, SOPHIA.

  Mathias. The iniury that you conceiue I haue done you
Dispute heereafter, and in your peruersenes
Wrong not your selfe, and me.
  Sophia.   I am pasd my childhood,
And need no tutor.
  Mathias.   This is the great King.   40
To whom I am ingag'd till death for all
I stand posess'd of.
  Sophia.   My humble roofe is proud sir,
To be the canopie of so much greatnes,
Set off with goodnes.

Ladislaus. My owne prayses flying
In such pure ayre, as your sweete breath faire Lady,   45
Cannot but please me.
    Mathias. This is the Queene of Queenes,
In her magnificence to me.
    Sophia. In my duty
I kisse her highnes robe.
    Honoria. You stoope to low
To her whose lipps would meete with yours.
    Sophia. Howere
It may appeare preposterous in women   50
Soe to encounter, 'tis your pleasure Madam
And not my proud ambition; do you heere sir?
Without a magicall picture, in the touch,
I find your printe of close and wanton kisses
On the Queenes lipps.
    Mathias. Vpon your life be silent.   55
And now salute these Lords.
    Sophia. Since you'll haue me,
You shall see I am experienc'd at the game
And can play it titely. You are a braue man sir
And do deserue a free and harty welcome;
Be this the prologe to it.
    Eubulus. An old mans turne   60
Is euer last in kissing, I haue lipps too,
Howeuer cold ones Madam.
    Sophia. I will warme 'em.
With the fire of mine.
    Eubulus. And so she has. I thanke you:
I shall sleepe the better all night for't.
    Mathias. You expresse
The boldnes of a wanton courtezan,   65
And not a matrons modesty, take vp,
Or you are disgrac'd foreuer.
    Sophia. How? with kissing
Feelingly as you tought mee? would you haue me
Turne my cheeke to 'em, as proud ladies vse
To their inferiors, as if they intended   70
Some businesse should be whisperd in their eare
And not a salutation? what I doe

I will do freely, now I am in the humor
I'll flie at all, are there any more?
    Mathias.   Forbeare.
Or you will rayse my anger to a height,   75
That will descend in fury.
    Sophia.   Whie? you know
How to resolue your selfe what my intents are,
By the helpe of *Mephostophiles*, and your picture,
Pray you looke vpon't againe. I humbly thanke
The Queenes great care of me, while you were absent.   80
M4ᵛ She knew how tedious 'twas for a young wife,
And being for that time a kind of widdow,
To passe away her melancholly howers
Without good company, and in charity therefore
Prouided for me: out of her owne store   85
She culd the Lords *Ubaldo*, and *Ricardo*,
Two principall courtiers for Ladies seruice,
To do me all good offices, and as such
Imployd by her. I hope I haue receaud,
And entertaind 'em, nor shall they depart   90
Without the effect arising from the cause
That brought 'em hither.
    Mathias.   Thou dost be-lye thy selfe,
I know that in my absence thou wer't honest,
Howeuer now turnd monster.
    Sophia.   The truth is
We did not deale like you in speculations   95
On cheating pictures; we knew shadowes were
No substances and actuall performance
The best assurance; I will bring 'em hither
To make good in this presence so much for me.
Some minutes space I begge your maiesties pardon.   100
You are mou'd now; champe vpon this bit a little,
Anon you shall haue another, waite me *Hilario*.
                   Exeunt SOPHIA, *and* HILARIO.
    Ladislaus. How now? turnd statue sir?
    Mathias.   Flie, and flie quicklie
From this cursed habitation, or this Gorgon
Will make you all as I am; in her tongue   105
Millions of adders hisse, and euery hayre

Vpon her wicked head a snake more dreadfull
Then that *Tisiphon*, threw on *Athamas*,
Which in his madnes forc'd him to dismember
His proper issue. O that euer I   110
Repos'd my trust in magicke, or beleeud
Impossibilities, or that charmes had power
To sincke and serch into the bottomlesse hell,
Of a false womans heart.
   Eubulus.   These are the fruites
Of marriage; an old batchelor, as I am,   115
And what's more will continue so, is not troublde
With these fine fagaries.
   Ferdinand.   Till you are resolu'd sir,
Forsake not hope.
   Baptista.   Vpon my life this is
Dissimulation.
   Ladislaus.   And it sutes not with
Your fortitude and wisdome to be thus   120
Transported with your passion.
   Honoria.   You were once
Deceaud in me sir as I was in you,
Yet the deceipte pleasd both.
   Mathias.   She hath confes'd all,
What further proofe should I aske?
   Honoria.   Yet remember
The distance that is interpos'd betweene   125
A womans tongue, and her hart, and you must grant
You build vpon no certaineties.

     Enter SOPHIA, CORISCA, HILARIO, VBALDO, *and*
            RICARDO, *as before.*

   Eubulus.   What haue we heere?
   Sophia. You must come on and show your selues.
   Vbaldo.   The King!
   Ricardo. And Queene too! would I were as far vnder the earth
As I am aboue it.
   Vbaldo.   Some Poet will   130

113–14. To . . . heart.] *30²*; *omitted 30¹*   114. Of] *Mason*; For *30²*   115. an]
Dodsley; and *30*   117. fagaries] *30*; vagaries *Dodsley*   123. pleasd] *Dodsley*;
please *30*   128. your] *Dodsley*; you *30*

From this relation, or in verse, or proose,
Or both together blended, render vs
Ridiculous to all ages.
    Ladislaus.   I remember
This face when it was in a better plight:
Are not you *Ricardo* ?
    Honoria.   And this thing I take it   135
Was once *Vbaldo.*
    Vbaldo.   I am now I know not what.
    Ricardo. We thanke your maiesty for imploying vs
To this subtill *Circe.*
    Eubulus.   How my Lord ? turnd spinster ?
Do you worke by the day or by the great ?
    Ferdinand.   Is your Theorbo
Turnd to a distaffe Signior, and your voyce   140
With which you chanted rome for a lusty gallant
Turnd to the note of lacreymæ ?
    Eubulus.   Prethee tell me
For I know thou art free, how often and to the purpose
Haue you beene merry with this lady ?
    Ricardo.   Neuer, neuer.
    Ladislaus. Howsoeuer you should say so, for your credit,   145
Being the only court-bull.
    Vbaldo.   O that euer
I saw this kicking heyfer !
    Sophia.   You see Madam
How I haue curd your seruants, and what fauours
They with their rampant valour haue woone from me.
You may as they are phisickd, I presume,   150
Trust a faire virgine with 'em; they haue learnd
Their seuerall trades to liue by, and payd nothing
But cold, and hunger for 'em, and may now
Set vp for them selues for heere I giue 'em ouer.
And now to you sir, why doe you not againe,   155
Peruse your picture ? and take the aduice
Of your learned consort ? these are the men, or none
That made you, as the Italian sayes, a beco.
    Mathias. I know not which way to intreat your pardon
Nor am I worthy of it my *Sophia,*   160
My best *Sophia* ! heere before the king,

The Queene, these Lords, and all the lookers on
I do renounce my error, and embrace you
As the great example to all after times
For such as would dye chast, and noble wiues   165
With reuerence to immitate.
    Sophia.   Not so sir.
I yet hold of, howeuer I haue purg'd
My doubted innocence; the foule aspertions
In your vnmanly doubts cast on my honor
Cannot so soone be washd of.
    Eubulus.   Shall we haue   170
More ijggobobs yet?
    Sophia.   When you went to the warrs
I set no spie vpon you to obserue
Which way you wandred: though our sex by nature
Is subiect to suspitions and feares,
My confidence in your loyalty freed me from 'em.   175
But to deale as you did gainst your religion
With this inchanter to suruey my actions
Was more then womans weaknes, therefore know
And tis my boone vnto the King, I doe
Desire a seperation from your bed,   180
For I will spend the remnant of my life
In prayer, and meditation.
    Mathias.   O take pitty
Vpon my weake condition, or I am
More wretched in your innocence, then if
I had found you guilty! haue you showne a iewell   185
Out of the cabinet of your rich mind
To locke it vp againe? She turnes away,
Will none speake for me? shame, and sinne hath robd me
Of the vse of my tongue.
    Ladislaus.   Since you haue conquerd Maddam
You wrong the glory of your victory   190
If you vse it not with mercy.
    Ferdinand.   Any penance
You please to impose vpon him I dare warrant
He will gladly suffer.
    Eubulus.   Haue I liu'd to see
But on good woman, and shall we for a trifle

Haue her turne nun? I will first pull downe the cloyster!   195
To the ould sport againe with a good lucke to you!
'Tis not alone enough that you are good,
We must haue some of the breed of you; will you destroy
The kind, and race of goodnesse? I am conuerted
And aske your pardon Madam for my ill opinion   200
Against the sex, and show me but two such more,

N2ᵛ I'll marry yet, and loue em.
  Honoria.   She that yet
Nere knew what 'twas to bend but to the King
Thus begges remission for him.
  Sophia.   O deere Madam
Wrong not your greatnesse so.
  Omnes.   We all are sutors.   205
  Vbaldo. I do deserue to bee hard among the rest.
  Ricardo. And we haue sufferd for it.
  Sophia.   I perceiue
Thers no resistance, but suppose I pardon
What's past, who can secure me, He'll be free
From iealousie heereafter?
  Mathias.   I will be   210
My owne security, go ride where you please,
Feast, reuele, banquet, and make choise with whom,
I'll set no watch vpon you, and for proofe of't,
This cursed picture I surrender vp
To a consuming fire.
  Baptista.   As I abiure   215
The practise of my art.
  Sophia.   Vpon theis termes
I am reconcil'd, and for these that haue payd
The price of their folly, I desire your mercy.
  Ladislaus. At your request they haue it.
  Vbaldo.   Hang all trades now.
  Ricardo. I will find a new one, and that is to liue honest.   220
  Hilario. These are my fee's.
  Vbaldo.   Pray you take 'em with a mischeefe.
  Ladislaus. So all ends in peace now

195. turne] *Dodsley*; returne *30* 204. begges] *Dodsley*; begge *30* 211. you]
Dodsley; yon *30* 213. proofe of't,] *Dodsley*; proofe, oft *30* 216. theis]
Dodsley; this *30*

And to all married men be this a caution
Which they should duly tender as their life: 224
Neither to dote to much nor doubt a wife. *Exeunt Omnes.*

FINIS.

APPENDIX: MUSIC

THE BLUSHING ROSE

Music for the song 'The Blushing Rose' (III. v. 25 ff.) is found in MS. *ZB–216 in the Music Division (Special Collections) of the New York Public Library. The setting, by an unnamed composer, is number 78 in a commonplace book of songs belonging to the theatre musician John Gamble. It is for two treble voices, above an unfigured bass line. There is a modern edition of the complete collection of songs by Vincent Duckles, *John Gamble's Commonplace Book: A Critical Edition of New York Public Library MS Drexel 4257*, unpublished doctoral dissertation, University of California, Berkeley, 1953.

In the present edition, a realization of the accompaniment has been supplied, with a keyboard instrument in mind. The original time-signature ₵ is modernized as $\frac{4}{4}$. The manuscript text is reproduced in substance and accidentals, except that long *s* has been modernized. In bar 17, stave 1, the textual underlay erroneously reads 'shee'. In the fourth line of the second stanza of the text the word 'issue' has been supplied from 30, where the scribe left a blank space in the New York manuscript.

The blush - inge _ rose, & pur - ple

flower, lett grow to Longe are soonestt blas - ted

dain - tie fruitt though sweett   will sower   &

10

itt hear is one,

rott in rip - - - nes leftt untasted;   itt heare is

itt hear is hear   is   one;   more sweett   then

one   itt hear is   one;   more sweett   then

these;   the   more you tastt y^e more   sheell please; y^e

these;   the   more you tastt y^e more   sheell please; y^e

more — you — tastt yᵉ more sheell please.

more — you — tastt yᵉ more sheell please.

Verse 2

Bewtie though Compard with Ice
tis a shaddow Chastt as rare
yett how much those sweets Intice
thatt haue [issue] full as faire
    Earth Cannott yeild
    earth Cannott yeild
Earth Cannott Cannott yeild
    from all her powers
one equall equall from dame uenus bowers
one equall equall from dame uenus bowers / :

BELIEVE AS YOU LIST

INTRODUCTION

(a) *Date*

Two entries in Sir Henry Herbert's office-book determine the exact date of composition of *Believe As You List*. In January 1631 Herbert noted that 'This day being the 11 of Janu. 1630, I did refuse to allow of a play of Messinger's, because itt did contain dangerous matter, as the deposing of Sebastian king of Portugal, by Philip the [Second,] and ther being a peace sworen twixte the kings of England and Spayne'.[1] Four months later, Herbert wrote his licence for performance on folio 27^v of the manuscript of *Believe As You List*: 'This Play, called Beleiue as you liste, may bee acted. this 6. of May. 1631. Henry Herbert.'

Malone's transcript and comment on the appropriate office-book entry reads, 'Believe as you list, May 7, 1631. Acted by the king's company. This play is lost',[2] and the discrepancy in date between the licence on the manuscript and the transcript of the office-book entry has been variously explained. Greg suggested that Herbert licensed the play on the 6th and received his fee on the 7th; Adams and McIlwraith suggested that Herbert took the play home to read and license it on the evening of the 6th, and made a book entry at his office on the following day.

There can be no doubt that *Believe As You List* is a rewriting of the play which Herbert refused to license on January 11. In several places names belonging to the story of Sebastian were copied from the original draft before the transcriber thought to alter them to their new counterparts,[3] and the Malone Society editor, C. J. Sisson,[4] further points out (pp. xix–xx) that wherever possible Massinger found new names that were the metrical equivalents of the old ones.

---

[1] Adams, *Herbert*, p. 19. The Treaty of Madrid between England and Spain had been concluded on 5 Nov. 1630.   [2] *Variorum Shakspeare*, 1821, iii. 230.
[3] Clear instances occur at I. i. 28, II. i. 50, II. ii. 328, III. i. 20, IV. iii. 0 SD., V. ii. 60.
[4] See p. 300 below.

The majority of the slips and corrections in the manuscript are characteristic of a transcript, rather than of fresh composition. The original play was completed, then, by the end of 1630; the present manuscript of *Believe As You List* was written between 11 January and 6 May 1631.[1]

(b) *Sources*

So much of the original version of *Believe As You List* survives in Massinger's revision of the play that a discussion of the sources must take into account two groups of material. The first version of the tragedy was based on various accounts purporting to describe the life of Don Sebastian, King of Portugal, after his disastrous defeat in Morocco in 1578. For the rewritten tragedy Massinger drew largely on accounts of the life and times of Antiochus the Great (241–187 B.C.), which he conflated with episodes from the later life of Hannibal. The principal sources are well established, but a full study of the dramatist's interweaving of material from his multiple sources is still to be written.[2]

A. *The Don Sebastian Story.* The death of Sebastian in the battle of Alcacer-el-Kebir, and the subsequent appearance of several pretenders claiming to be the king, attracted much attention in England and gave rise to many books, plays, and pamphlets, some of them now lost.[3] Neither *Captain Thomas Stukely* (1596) nor Peele's *The Battle of Alcazar* (1598–9) gave Massinger anything, but Chettle and Dekker's lost play *King Sebastian of Portugal* (1601) may have been used, as may two ballads, now known only from their entry in the Stationers' Register, *Strange newes of the Retourne of Don Sebastian Kinge of Portugall* (1599) and *The Wonder of the world of Don Sebastian the King of Portugall that lost him selfe in the battell of*

---

[1] During part of this time Massinger may have been working on *The Emperor of the East*, which was licensed for performance on 11 Mar. 1631, and *The Unfortunate Piety* was licensed only one month later than *Believe As You List*, on 13 June 1631. See p. 391.

[2] The principal studies are by Koeppel, *Quellen-Studien*, 151–65; C. J. Sisson, in his Malone Society edition of the play, pp. xvii–xx; and by P. M. Smith, 'Massinger's Use of Sources, with special reference to "The Duke of Milan" and "Believe as You List"', unpublished University of Birmingham dissertation, 1963.

[3] See E. W. Bovill, *The Battle of Alcazar*, 1952; H. V. Livermore, *History of Portugal*, 1947, pp. 270–4; M. d'Antas, *Les Faux Don Sébastien*, Paris, 1866; S. C. Chew, *The Crescent and the Rose*, 1937, pp. 527–30; *The Dramatic Works of George Peele*, ed. F. S. Hook and J. Yoklavich (vol. ii of *The Life and Works of George Peele*, General Editor C. T. Prouty), 1961, pp. 226–79.

Affrick (1601).[1] However, so much of *Believe As You List* can be traced to the known sources that these works cannot have contributed very much to Massinger's play.

As Koeppel demonstrated in 1897, the dramatist's major source for the narrative of Sebastian's life was P. V. P. Cayet's *Chronologie septenaire de l'histoire de la paix entre les roys de France et d'Espagne*, Paris, 1605.[2] Cayet alone supplied in the form of a consecutive narrative the story of Sebastian's wanderings after his defeat, his association with a hermit, his arrival at Venice after being robbed by his own servants, and his recognition by some of his countrymen —the material of Massinger's first Act. From the same source came the arrival of the persecuting Spanish ambassador, and Sebastian's examination before the Venetian Senate (the substance of Act II), his flight to sanctuary in Florence and the Spanish diplomatic pressure which compelled his protector, the Grand Duke, to surrender him (Act III), his imprisonment and condemnation at Naples (Act IV), and his interview with the Duke and Duchess of Medina Sidonia at St. Lucar de Barrameda (Act V).

Massinger filled out and coloured Cayet's objective narrative with material from three pamphlets which probably originated among the followers of the Portuguese Pretender, Don Antonio, who lived for a time in England and France.[3] These were (1) Anthony Munday's translation, as *The Strangest Adventure that ever happened: either in the ages passed or present* (1601), of a French version (*Aduenture admirable par dessus toutes autres*) of a Spanish compilation by José Teixeira; (2) *The true history of the late and lamentable adventures of Dom Sebastian*, an anonymous translation of *Histoire veritable des dernieres et piteuses aduentures de Don Sebastian* (1602), printed by Simon Stafford and James Shaw in the same year; and (3) *A Continuation of the Lamentable and Admirable Adventures of Don Sebastian*, a translation (possibly by Munday)[4] from *Suyte dun discours intitulé aduenture admirable* (1602), printed for James Shaw in 1603.

In these pamphlets Massinger found Don Sebastian treated

---

[1] *Henslowe's Diary*, ed. R. A. Foakes and R. T. Rickert, 1961, pp. 168–70; Arber, iii. 137, 182.

[2] There were later editions of 1606, 1607, 1608, and 1609.

[3] See 'English Translations of Portuguese Books before 1640', H. Thomas, *The Library*, 4th Series, vii (1926), 1–30.

[4] The reader of the *Continuation* is frequently exhorted to consult 'the Book called *Admirable Adventures*'.

sympathetically as a noble martyr to the ruthless machinations of Castilian agents. Father Sampayo (Massinger's Berecinthius), who is mentioned only briefly in Cayet, is depicted more fully in *The Strangest Adventure* as a loyal and diligent servant; the merchants who accompany him and finally betray the king (V. i) come from the same source. The 1602 pamphlet, an unabridged translation of the same original from which Cayet freely excerpted material, supplied many pathetic details (such as the 'slavishe habit' and the weeping spectators) in Massinger's account of Sebastian's degradation (IV. iv). There is mention of a 'gross and corpulent gentleman' in the 1603 pamphlet, and an episode in the same work in which Don Sebastian is confronted at Naples by 'Paula Catizzone, with her daughter . . . being shipped from Messina by the Catholick King's agents' probably suggested Massinger's temptation scene (IV. ii). The dramatist found source material for Don Sebastian's noble courtship of the Duchess of Medina Sidonia (the Cornelia of *Believe As You List*) in both the 1602 and 1603 pamphlets.

Massinger himself may have invented the scenes in the original version of the play corresponding to the putting to death of the King's treacherous servants (II. i), the imprisonment of Berecinthius (IV. iii), as a comic parallel to the imprisonment of Sebastian, and Flaminius' dealings with the politician Philoxenus (III. ii–iii).

B. *The Antiochus–Hannibal Story.* Massinger's chief source for the second version of his tragedy was Ralegh's *History of the World* (1614), Book 5, chapters 2–6,[1] in which he discovered classical parallels to Don Sebastian's career in the lives of Antiochus the Great and the defeated Hannibal. In Ralegh the dramatist found the theme of Roman greed for the Asian territories of Antiochus, and a king who suffered a serious defeat in Greece (though Massinger conflated the battle of Thermopylae (191 B.C.) with the greater disaster for Antiochus at Magnesia in 190 B.C.). Antiochus' expedition to the East before his invasion of Greece served as a rough equivalent of Sebastian's wanderings after his defeat in Morocco. Roman diplomatic pressure against Hannibal after Zama, his defence before the Carthaginian Senate, and his flight by night to Tyre provided a parallel to Sebastian's examination by the Venetians, and Hannibal's persecution by Titus Flaminius at the court of the friendly Prusias of Bithynia replaced Sebastian's betrayal by the Duke of Florence.

---

[1] Later editions were published in 1617, 1621, and 1628. Massinger's borrowings are concentrated in chapter 5, sections 2–8, and chapter 6, section 2.

In addition to Ralegh, Massinger read Plutarch's life of Flaminius; the Greek writer's account of Flaminius' unpopularity over the death of Hannibal probably suggested the fate of Massinger's character. The dramatist further drew on Livy's account of Antiochus' negotiations with Prusias, broken off under Roman diplomatic pressure (*History of Rome*, V. xxxvii. 25) and Justin's description of Hannibal's conduct before the Carthaginian Senate (*Epitome*, xxxi).[1] Roma Gill has also drawn attention to the influence of Machiavellian ideas on the formation of the character of Flaminius.[2]

S. R. Gardiner found in *Believe As You List* a transparent commentary on the fortunes of Frederick, the dispossessed Elector Palatine and King of Bohemia.[3] According to Gardiner, Bithynia represents England, Carthage the Dutch States from which Frederick sought assistance, Rome is Spain; Antiochus stands for Frederick, Prusias for Charles I, his consort for Henrietta Maria, Philoxenus for Weston, the leader of the pro-Spanish faction at court, and Flaminius for the Spanish ambassador, Gondomar. Like *The Bondman* and *The Maid of Honour*, in Gardiner's view the play is to be read as an expression of the anti-Spanish policy of the Herberts, and as a gesture of sympathy for the exiled Frederick.

There are too many discrepancies for *Believe As You List* to be read as a sustained political allegory, and the application of the tragedy is far from unambiguous.[4] The play can stand alone as 'the trewe relation of [a] remarkable storie'; it offers moving dramatic images of the sufferings of a fallen king in 'the shoppe of policie'. But Sir Henry Herbert's refusal to license the original play, the Prologue's artless explanation that

> yf you finde what'ę Roman here,
> *Grecian*, or *Asiaticqe*, drawe to nere
> a late, & sad example, tis confest
> hee's but an English scholler at his best,

[1] English versions of each of these classical texts were available to Massinger: Plutarch was translated by North in 1579, Livy by Holland in 1600, and Justin by 'G. W.' in 1606.

[2] '"Necessitie of State": Massinger's *Believe As You List*', *English Studies*, xlvi (1965), 407–16.

[3] 'The Political Element in Massinger', *Contemporary Review*, xxviii (1876), 495–507. For the political background, see C. V. Wedgewood, *The Thirty Years War*, 1938.

[4] See 'Contemporary Politics in Massinger', A. Gross, *Studies in English Literature*, vi (1966), 279–90.

a stranger to *Cosmographie*, and may erre
in the cuntries names, the shape, & character
of the person he presente

as well as Massinger's apparent invention of Philoxenus, the
'knoweinge man in politicɑ̣ designes', all suggest that the play-
wright was at least willing to exploit English sympathy for the
fortunes of Frederick, an interest given impetus in 1630 by the
appearance of Gustavus Adolphus as Protestant champion in
the Thirty Years War.

(c) *Text*

Believe As You List was first entered in the Stationers' Register on
9 September 1653.

M^r. Mosely.   Entred also for his Copies the severall Playes following.
$$xx^s. \ vj^d$$
The Widdowes Prize. by M^r. W^m. Samson

. . . .

The Iudge, or Beleiue, as yo^u list. by Phill: Massinger.[1]

(Register E 285–6; Greg, *Bibliography*, i. 60–1; Eyre and Rivington, i.
428–9.)

There is a second entry on 29 June 1660.

Mr Hum: Moseley.   Entred for his Copies (vnder the hand of M^r
Thrale Warden) the severall Plays following. That is to say
The Faithfull Friend. a Comedy. by ffrancis Beamont & Iohn ffletcher

. . . .

Believe as you list. a Tragedy. by Phillip Massinger.

(Register F 196; Greg, *Bibliography*, i. 68; Eyre and Rivington, ii. 271.)

However, the play was never printed. It survives only in the form
of an autograph manuscript now in the British Museum (Egerton
2828).[2] This is the author's fair copy, prepared for the prompter's
use in performance at the playhouse by the company's book-keeper.

The autograph of *Believe As You List* is a folio manuscript of
29 leaves, measuring 12$\frac{3}{8}$ by 7$\frac{1}{2}$ inches. Folio 1 is of modern paper,

---

[1] *The Judge* is certainly a separate play now lost, since it was licensed by Herbert for
the King's company on 6 June 1627 (Adams, *Herbert*, p. 31). On Humphrey Moseley's
coupling of the two titles, probably in an attempt to save a registration fee, see Greg,
Bibliography, ii. 979–80, and Bentley, iv. 793–4.

[2] Greg, *Bibliography*, no. Θ 79 (ii. 985–6). For the history of the manuscript see
C. J. Sisson's edition, pp. v–x.

folios 2 and 3 of vellum (the original wrapper), and folios 4–29 of seventeenth-century paper. A tankard watermark appears in folios 4, 7, 9, 10, 13, 15, 16, 18, 21, 22, 24, and 26. There is a fleur-de-lis watermark in folio 29, a separate sheet added to Massinger's manuscript after its licensing. Folio 5 has been torn from the manuscript, leaving only a narrow strip of the inner margin, and fraying of the paper has caused some loss of text at the bottom of folios 4, 6, 7, 23–7, and at the top of folios 4, 6, 26, 27, and 29. The foliation used for reference in this edition is modern. Massinger himself numbered folios 4–27 from 1 to 12, in the upper left-hand corner of the recto of the first leaf of each sheet.

The contents of the manuscript are as follows: 1ʳ, *note by J. O. Halliwell-Phillips*; 1ᵛ, *blank*; 2ʳ, *title*, 'A new playe / Call'd: / Beleeue as you / List: / Written By Mʳ Massenger / May 6ᵗʰ / 1631 / A Tragedy'; 2ᵛ, *indenture dated 7 October 1595, concerning a lease running until 1625*; 3ʳ, *indenture continued*; 3ᵛ, *blank*; 4ʳ, *text begins*, 'Actus primi, Scæna prima.'; 27ᵛ, *text ends*, 'The Ende.'; 28ʳ, *blank*; 28ᵛ, *Prologue*; 29ʳ, *Epilogue*; 29ᵛ, *notes on stage properties*.

The body of the play is written in Massinger's own hand, a distinctive mixture of English and Italian forms, identified as the author's by Sir George Warner in 1901.[1] Massinger's own work is indicated in the textual apparatus by the siglum *MS*. A second hand found throughout the manuscript is that of Edward Knight, the book-keeper of the King's men.[2] Knight wrote out the title-page (with the exception of the words 'A Tragedy', which are a modern addition), the Prologue and Epilogue, and the list of properties. He also made various alterations and additions to the text, using in general an English hand for changes made in the dialogue, and a heavy Italian hand for alterations to stage directions etc. His work is indicated in the textual apparatus by the siglum *Knight*. The third hand present is that of Sir Henry Herbert (siglum *Herbert*), whose signed licence is at the foot of folio 27ᵛ, and who made at least one correction or direction in the margin of folio 5ʳ. Apart from Halliwell-Phillips's note and the addition to the title-page, there are occasional substantive and accidental corrections made in Massinger's text by

---

[1] 'An Autograph Play of Philip Massinger', *The Athenaeum*, 3821 (19 Jan. 1901), 90–1. See also C. J. Sisson's edition, pp. xii–xv.

[2] See W. W. Greg, 'Prompt Copies, Private Transcripts, and "the Playhouse-Scrivener"', *The Library*, 4th Series, vi (1926), 148–56; and *The Honest Man's Fortune*, ed. J. Gerritsen, Groningen, 1952, xxi–xxviii, xxxi–xxxiv.

an unidentified modern hand (or hands). These are distinguished in
the textual apparatus by the siglum *corrector*.

Believe As You List was first published by T. C. Croker (assisted
by F. W. Fairholt) for the Percy Society in 1849. There followed
*The Plays of Philip Massinger from the Text of William Gifford with
the Addition of the Tragedy 'Believe As You List'*, edited by Cunningham in 1868, and *The Best Plays of the Old Dramatists: Philip
Massinger*, edited by Symons, with S. W. Orson as textual editor,
1887–9. J. S. Farmer published a collotype facsimile under the title
Believe As Ye List in 1907, and L. A. Sherman included the play
among the four texts in *Philip Massinger*, New York, 1912. C. J.
Sisson edited *Believe As You List* for the Malone Society in 1928;
the present edition is greatly indebted to his scrupulously careful
account of the manuscript. W. W. Greg supplied a facsimile and
transcription of IV. ii. 45–96 (folio 20ʳ) in *Dramatic Documents from
the Elizabethan Playhouses*, 1931, and in the same year A. K. Mc-
Ilwraith edited the play for his Oxford thesis.

M. Horn-Monval, *Répertoire bibliographique des traductions et
adaptations françaises du théâtre étranger*, Paris, 1963, records an
undated translation in manuscript by Joseph de Smet, and Maurice
Chelli printed his own translation of Act two, Scene two, in *Le
Drame de Massinger*, Lyons, 1923.

The present text is printed from A. K. McIlwraith's transcript of
Massinger's manuscript, checked against the original and against
Sisson's Malone Society reprint (siglum *Sisson*), and collated with
the editions of Croker (siglum *Croker*), Cunningham, Sherman, and
Symons. Three textual studies of the play have also been consulted:
(1) J. P. Collier, 'On Massinger's "Believe as you List", a newly
discovered manuscript Tragedy, printed by the Percy Society', *The
Shakespeare Society's Papers*, iv (1849), 133–9 (siglum *Collier*); (2)
A. H. Cruickshank, *Philip Massinger*, 1920 (siglum *Cruickshank*); and
S. A. Tannenbaum, 'Corrections to the Text of *Believe As You List*',
PMLA, xlii (1927), 777–81 (siglum *Tannenbaum*). In the textual
apparatus, square brackets indicate a deletion in the manuscript, by
Massinger unless otherwise noted. (As reported in the apparatus,
Croker used square brackets to indicate a conjectural reading.)
Mutilations of the text in the manuscript are indicated by pointed
brackets thus ⟨ ⟩. Only traces of those letters or words printed
within such brackets are now visible.

No attempt has been made to reproduce in every respect the

present physical appearance of the whole manuscript, but Massinger's work is faithfully reproduced, with the following exceptions: (1) Massinger's foliation is silently omitted; (2) his boxes enclosing stage directions, the short lines marking off successive speeches, and all other lines are not reproduced; (3) as noted in the textual apparatus, there is some relineation of text, stage directions, and scene headings; (4) as noted in the apparatus also, there is a minimum of editorial emendation. Lines too long to fit the present text-page are turned over silently.

The title-page, Prologue and Epilogue, and list of properties are supplied from Knight's manuscript in an appropriate position, and the book-keeper's corrections are occasionally accepted into the text. Otherwise, what Knight and Herbert added to Massinger's manu-script is recorded in the textual apparatus, and not in its original place in the text. Knight's distinction between an italic and a roman script has not been preserved.

In accordance with the general style of the present edition of Massinger's plays, lines are numbered marginally in fives, beginning afresh at each new scene, and Act and Scene indications are inserted marginally at the head of each scene. The folio number of each page of the original is inserted marginally against the first line of the original page.

(d) *Stage History*

Little is known of contemporary performances of *Believe As You List*, other than the fact that Sir Henry Herbert licensed Massinger's play on 6 May 1631, and that the manuscript was carefully prepared by the King's men's book-keeper for use in the theatre.[1] The completion-date of the first version of the tragedy suggests that it was intended for performances at the Blackfriars theatre rather than at the Globe,[2] and Knight's annotations make it possible to reconstruct much of the original cast list. Antiochus was played by Joseph Taylor, Chrysalus by Elyard Swanston, Berecinthius by Thomas Pollard, the three merchants by John Honyman, William Penn, and Curtis Greville, Flaminius by John Lowin, Calistus by

---

[1] Knight's work has been studied in detail by W. W. Greg, *Dramatic Documents from the Elizabethan Playhouses*, 1931, ii. 293–300.

[2] See Bentley, vi. 14–16. The second version of the play may also have been intended for the Blackfriars theatre; it is not known precisely when the King's men shifted to their summer playhouse, the Globe, though it seems to have been usually during May.

both Richard Baxter and Thomas Hobbes, Demetrius (successively) by William Pattrick, Francis Balls, and 'Rowland'.[1] William Mago, 'Nick', and 'Rowland' played the parts of Carthaginian officers and (with Francis Balls) Prusias's attendants. Lentulus was played by Richard Robinson, Titus by Richard Baxter, the jailor by William Penn, Marcellus by Robert Benfeild, a Roman Captain by William Pattrick, a jailor's assistant by 'Rowland', and Marcellus's attendants by 'Rowland', Francis Balls, 'Nick', and Richard Baxter. Henry Wilson played the lute for the song in IV. ii, performed by an anonymous 'Boy'.

Both Bentley and Ure have raised the question of a connection between Massinger's play and Ford's *Perkin Warbeck*, produced by Queen Henrietta's men at the Phoenix theatre.[2] Each play gives a sympathetic account of a royal pretender, and Ford's work, like his friend Massinger's, seems to have been subjected to censorship. It is quite possible that these plays were put on in competition by the rival companies, or perhaps both dramatists intended to exploit contemporary interest in an international affair, but in the absence of a firm dating for *Perkin Warbeck*[3] nothing more than speculation is possible.

Believe As You List has not been acted since such performances as may have been given before 1642.

---

[1] See the commentary for notes on the actors named.

[2] Bentley, iii. 456; *The Chronicle History of Perkin Warbeck: A Strange Truth*, ed. P. Ure, 1968, pp. 181–3. See also Philip Edwards, 'The Royal Pretenders in Massinger and Ford', *Essays and Studies 1974*, pp. 18–36.

[3] The limits are 1625–34, and the traditional placing is about 1633; see Ure's edition, pp. xxviii–xxxv.

The manuscript of *Believe As You List* in Massinger's hand, with the alterations and marginal additions of Edward Knight, book-keeper to the King's men. The middle portion of Fol. 8 verso (I. ii. 208—II. i. 15)

The manuscript of *Believe As You List*. The upper portion of Fol. 20 recto (IV. ii. 49–69)

Believe As You List

[THE PERSONS PRESENTED

Antiochus, King of Lower Asia.
A Stoic.
Chrysalus ⎫
Syrus ⎬ bondmen of *Antiochus*.   5
Geta ⎭
Berecinthius, Archflamen of Cybele.
3 Asian merchants.
Titus Flaminius, a Roman ambassador to Carthage.
Calistus ⎫ freemen of *Flaminius*.   10
Demetrius ⎭
Amilcar, leader of the Carthaginian senate.
Hanno ⎫
Asdrubal ⎬ Carthaginian senators.
Carthalo ⎭   15
Carthaginian officers.
Lentulus, a Roman ambassador to Carthage.
Titus, an agent of *Flaminius*.
Prusias, King of Bithynia.
The Queen of Bithynia.   20
Philoxenus, tutor to *Prusias*.
Attendants.
Bithynian Guard.
A. Metellus, a Roman Proconsul.
Sempronius, a Roman Centurion under *Metellus*.   25
A jailor and his assistants.
A Corinthian courtesan.
Marcellus, Proconsul of Sicily.
Cornelia, his wife.
Zanthia, a Moorish woman attending *Cornelia*.   30
A Roman Captain under *Marcellus*.
Roman soldiers.
Servants.
A Guard.]

1–34. THE PERSONS PRESENTED . . . Guard.] *after Croker and Sisson; not in MS*

Prologue:

⟩ author is from arrogance,
that he craves pardon for his Ignorance
in storie, yf you finde what'ę Roman here,
Grecian, or *Asiaticqe,* drawe to nere
a late, & sad example, tis confest   5
hee's but an English scholler at his best,
a stranger to *Cosmographie,* and may erre
in the cuntries names, the shape, & character
of the person he presentę, yet he is bolde
in me to promise, be it new, or olde,   10
the tale is worth the hearinge, & may move
compassion, perhaps deserve yoʳ love,
and approbation, he dares not boast
his paynes, & care, or what bookes he hath tost
& turnde to make it vp, the rarietie   15
of the eventę in this strange historie
now offerd to you, by his owne confession
must make it good, & not his weake expression.
you sit his Iudges, & like Iudges bee
from favour to his cause, or malice free,   20
then whether hee hath hit the white or mist,
as the title speakes, beleeve you as you list.

Title. *Prologue:*] *Croker* ([Pr]ologue.); ⟨ *gu*⟩*e: MS*   1. ⟩ author] *MS*; [Soe] far
our author *Croker*

[Believe As You List]

Actus primi, Scæna prima.

Antiochus: stoicꝙ. in philosophers habits. Chrysalus. Syrus.
Geta. bondemen.

Stoicꝙ:　You are now in sight of Carthage, that greate Cittie
wch in Her empires vastnesse rivalls Rome
at her prowde height. two howers will bringe you
thither.
make vse of what you haue learnde in your longe
travayles,
and from the golden principles read to you　　5
in th'Athenian Academie; stand resolude
for either fortune. you must now forget
the contemplations of a private man
and put in action that wch may complie
with the maiestie of a monarch.

Antiochus:　How that title,　　10
that glorious attribute of maiestie
that troublesome, thowgh most trivmphant robe
designde mee in my birth, wch I haue worne
with terror, and astonishement to others
affrights mee now! o memorie! memorie!　　15
of what I was once! when the easterne worlde
with wonder in my may of youth look'd on mee.
embassadors of the most potent kinges
with noble æmulation contendinge
to court my freindship, their faire daughters
offer'd　　20
as pledges to assure it, with all pompe
and circumstance of glorie. Rome her selfe,
and Carthage æmulous, whose side I showlde

Title. Believe . . . List] *editor*; *not in MS*　　I. i. prima.] *Croker* (PRIMA.);
p⟨ ⟩ma. *MS*　o SD. bondemen.] *conj. Sisson*; ⟨b⟩ondeme⟨ *MS*　*Knight over-writes Massinger's stops with upright bars. He inserts after* Chrysalus. *above a caret* (wth a
writing ⟨&⟩ pen⟨y　15. affrights] *a superfluous minim follows* ff *in MS*

confirme in my protection. o remembrance
with what ingenious crueltie, and tortures   25
out of a due consideration of
my present, lowe, and desperate condition
do'st thou afflicte mee now!

[Hermit:] Stoicꝗ: you must oppose
(for soe the stoicꝗ discipline com̃andes you)
that wisdome, with your pacyence fortefi'd   30
wᶜh holdes dominion over fate, against
the torrent of your passion.

Antiochus: I showlde,
I doe confesse I showlde yf I cowlde drincke vp
that river of forgetfullnesse Poets dreame of.
But still in dreadfull formes, (Philosophie wantinge
power to remoue 'em) all those innocent spirits   36
borroweinge againe their bodies gash'de with
        woundes
(wᶜh strowde Achaias bloodie plaines, and made
rivoletts of gore) appeare to mee, exactinge
a stricte accompte of my ambitions follye   40
for the exposinge of twelue thowsande soules
(whoe fell that fatall day) to certaine ruine.
neither the counsaile of the Persian kinge
prevaylinge with mee, nor the graue advice
of my wise enemie Marcus Scaurus hindringe   45
my desperate enterprise to late repented.
mee thinckes I now looke on my butcherd armie.

Stoicꝗ: this is meere melancholye.

Antiochus: o 'tis more sʳ
heere, there, and every where they doe pursue mee.
The Genivs of my cuntrie, made a slaue   50
like a weepinge mother seemes to kneele before mee
wringeinge her manacled handes; the hopefull youth,
and braverie of my kingedome in their pale,
and ghastlye lookes lamentinge that they were
to soone by my meanes forc'd from theire sweete
        beeinge.   55
olde men with siluer ⟨lockes   ⟩ in vain

---

28. thou] u *altered from* w *or* m *in MS*   Stoicꝗ:] *Knight, who deletes Massinger's*
Hermit: 40. ambitions] *Croker* (ambition's); ambitious *Sisson*

⟨th   ⟩

4ᵛ   trayn⟨e   n⟩ all delights, or sacred to
the cha⟨ste⟩ Dianas rites, compelde to bowe to
the souldiers [greedie] lusts, or at an outcrie solde 60
vnder the speare, like beasts, to bee spurnde, and
    trod on
by their prowde mistrisses the Roman matrons.
o sʳ consyder [sir] then yf it can bee
in the constancie of a stoicꜫ to indure
what nowe I suffer.

[Antiochus:] stoicꜫ: two and twentye yeares   65
travaylinge ore the worlde you haue pay'd the
    forfeite
of this ingagement, [and] & shed a sea of teares
in your sorrowe for it; and now beeinge call'd from
the rigour of a stricte philosophers life
by the cries of your poore cuntrie, you are bounde 70
with an obedient cheerefullnesse to follow
the path that you are enter'd in: wᶜh will
guide you out of a wildernesse of horror
to the flourishinge plaines of safetie, the iust gods
smoothinge the way before you.

Antiochus: thowgh I grant   75
that all impossibilities are easie
to their omnipotence, gieue mee leaue to feare
the more then doubtfull issue. can it fall
in the compasse of my hopes the lordlye Romans
soe longe possessde of Asia, [his] their plea   80
made good by conquest, and that ratefide
with their relligious authoritie
the propagation of the cõmon welth
to whose increase they are sworne to, will ere part
    with
a pray soe pretious, and deerelye purchasde,   85
A Tigresse circlde with her famishd whelpes
will sooner yeelde a lambe snatchde from the flocke
to the dumbe oratorie of the ewe
then Rome restore one foote of earth that may

57. ⟨th ⟩] *MS*; Their olives and . . . *Croker*   58. trayn⟨e n⟩] *MS*; traynde up
in *Croker*

<table>
<tr><td></td><td>diminishe her vast empire</td><td></td></tr>
<tr><td>Stoicꝗ:</td><td>In her will</td><td>90</td></tr>
</table>

	diminishe her vast empire	
Stoicꝗ:	In her will	90
	this may bee granted: but you haue a title	
	soe stronge, and cleare, that there's noe colour left	
	to varnishe Romes pretences. ad this sᵣ.	
	the Asian princes warn'd by your example	
	and yet vnconque'rd, never will consent	95
	that such a foule example of iniustice	
	shall to the scandall of the present age	
	hereafter bee recorded. they in this	
	are equallie ingag'd with you, and must	
	thowgh not in loue to iustice for their safetie	100
	in policie assist, garde, and protecte you	
	and you may rest assur'd neither the kinge	
	of Parthia, the Gauls, nor big bonde Germans	
	nor this greate Carthage growne alreadie iealous	
	of Romes incrochinge empire will crie aime	105
	to such an vsurpation, wᶜh must	
	take from their owne securitie. besides	
	your mother was a Roman for her sake	
	and the famelies from wᶜh shee is deriud	
	you must finde favour	
Antiochus:	For her sake alas sᵣ	110
	ambition knowes noe kinred, right, and lawfull	
	was never yet founde as a marginall note	
	in the blacke booke of profit. I am suncke	
	to lowe to bee bouyde vp, it beeinge helde	
	a foolishe weakenesse, and disease in statists	115
	in favour of a weakeman to provoke	
	such as are mightie; the imperious waues	
	⟨f ⟩ callamities ⟨ ⟩e alreadie swolne	
	⟩ a will	

5ᵣ   [*10 lines missing*]   120

---

102. kinge] *altered from* kings *in MS*   118. ⟨f . . . alreadie] *MS*; Of my callamities [hav]e alreadie *Croker*   swolne] *conj. Sisson*; sw⟨ ⟩lne *MS*; fallne *Croker*
119. ⟩ a will] *MS*; [wi]ll unravell *Croker*   120–251. *Folio 5 has been torn out,*
leaving an irregular inner strip. The estimates of lines lost follow McIlwraith

125

Antiochus: [*5 lines missing*]   130

Chrysalus: [*2 lines missing*]   135

Geta: [*4 lines missing*]

     140

Syrus: [*5 lines missing*]

     145

Geta: [*2 lines missing*]

Syrus: [*1 line missing*]

Geta: [*2 lines missing*]

     150

Chrysalus: [*7 lines missing*]

     155

       w⟨

Syrus: hau⟨

       a k⟨   160

130. Antiochus:] *editor*; An⟨ *MS*   135. Chrysalus:] *editor*; Chry⟨ *MS*
137. Geta:] *editor*; Get⟨ *MS*   141. Syrus:] *Croker* (*Syrus.*); Syru⟨ *MS*
146. Geta:] *editor*; Get⟨ *MS*   148. Syrus:] *editor*; Syru⟨ *MS*   149. Geta:]
Croker (*Geta.*); Geta⟨ *MS*   151. Chrysalus:] *Croker* (*Chrysalus.*); Chrysalus⟨ *MS*
157. *Croker reads an* O *at the beginning of this line*

Chrysalus:	a ki⟨
	alas ⟨
	[buri]⟨ buri
	all ⟨
	in tr⟨
	to m⟨e
	this is ⟨
Geta:	wee kn⟨
Chrysalus:	but wh⟨
	to bee ⟨
	noe soon⟨
	shall for⟨g
	Hee's pr⟨
	all that ⟨
Syrus:	Humph. ⟨
Chrysalus:	and wher⟨
	your bu⟨
Geta:	I am in ⟨
	& feele my⟨
Chrysalus:	a bulls [pi]⟨
	when you ⟨
	make the cur⟨
Syrus:	what woulde y⟨
Geta:	or what doe yo⟨
Chrysalus:	to saue my se⟨
	and what is m⟨
	not one in supp⟨
	bee wantinge s⟨

165

170

175

180

185

5ᵛ   [*37 lines missing*]

190

195

163–6. *In the l.h. margin, Herbert marks the beginning and end of the passage with crosses, underlines the beginning of lines 163, 165, and 166, and writes* buried = *against line 164*   175. Syrus:] *MS; Knight adds the speech heading* Geta: *beneath, joining it to this line by a rule*   188. s⟨] *MS; so* Croker

200

205

210

215

220

225

⟩ more

[*5 lines missing*]

230

[Stoicꝗ.]

226. ⟩ more] *MS*; ⟩e more *Croker*
lines, the sixth ending with a t
deleted, perhaps by Knight

227–31. *Croker estimates the loss of seven*
232. Stoicꝗ.] *Croker* ([S]toicque.); ⟩toicꝗ. *MS*,

[*1 line missing*]

⟩y forth

[*5 lines missing*]   235

⟩nd malice   240
⟩nde you   exit stoicǫ
⟩rms

[*3 lines missing*]

245

⟩anishde !

[*1 line missing*]

⟩yrus.

⟩s mischief.

⟩y open   250

⟩e torne booke

6ʳ   ⟩opes, despaire with sable winges

⟩ore my head; the golde with wᶜh

⟩ans furnish'd mee to supplie my wants

⟩ made my first apparence like my selfe 255

⟩ disloyall villaines ravish'd from mee !

⟩ch that I was to tempt their abiect mindes

⟩h such a purchase. can I in this weede

& without gold to fee an advocate

to pleade my royall title nourishe hope   260

of a recoverie? forlorne maiestie

wantinge the outward glosse, and cerimonie

to gieue it lustre, meetes noe more respecte

then knowledge with the ignorant. Ha ! what is

containde in this wast paper? 'tis indor'sde 265

234. ⟩y] *Sisson*; ⟩h *Croker*   235-9. *Croker estimates a loss of six lines, the fourth
ending with an* e   242. ⟩rms] *Sisson*; ⟩-ums *Croker*; ⟩ims *McIlwraith*   243. *Croker
reads an* e *at the end of the line*   245. *Croker reads* lse *at the end of the line*
246. ⟩anishde!] *MS*; vanishde! *Croker*   248. ⟩yrus.] *MS*; Syrus. *Croker*   249. ⟩s]
MS; is *Croker*   251. ⟩e] *MS*; the *Croker*   256. disloyall] *MS*; ⟩s disloyall
Croker   257. ⟩ch] *MS*; [Wr]etch *Croker*   258. ⟩h] *MS*; [Wi]th *Croker*
259. & without] *conj. McIlwraith*; ⟩ithout *MS*; [Wi]thout *Croker*; And without *Symons*
260. to pleade] *conj. Croker* ([To] pleade); ⟩pleade *MS*   261. of] *conj. Croker*
([O]f); ⟩f *MS*

to the noe kinge Antiochus. and subscribde
noe more thy servant but superior. Chrysalus.
what am I falne to? there is somethinge writ more.
why this small peece of silver? what I read may

reads:— reveale the misterie—forget thow wert ever　270
calld kinge Antiochus, with this charitie
I enter thee a begger—to towgh Heart
will nothinge breake thee? o that now I stood
on some high Pyramid from whence I might
bee seene by the whole worlde, & with a voice　275
lowder then thunder, pierce the eares of prowd,
and secure greatenesse with the trewe relation
of my remarkeable storie, that my fall
might not bee fruitlesse, but still liue the greate
example of mans frayletie. I that was　280
borne, and bred vp a kinge, whose frowne, or smile
spake death, or life, my will a law; my person
environde with an armie; now exposde
to the contempt, and scorne of my owne slaue
whoe in his pride, as a god compar'd with mee　285
bids mee become a begger. but complaynts
are weake, and womanishe. I will like a palme tree
growe vnder my huge waight: nor shall the feare
of death, or torture, that deiection bringe
to make mee liue, or dye, lesse then a kinge.　exit.

ii] Actus primi, scæna secunda.
Berecinthivs a flamen. 3 Asian marchants.

1 marchant: wee are growne soe contemptible, hee disdaines
to gieue vs hearinge.

2.marchant: keepes vs of at such distance
and with his Roman gravitie declines
our sude for conference, as with much more ease
wee might make our approches to the Parthian　5
without a present, then worke hym to haue
a feelinge of our grievances.

266. *In the l.h. margin, Knight writes* reads:—　270, 272. *Knight's dashes oblite-*
rate Massinger's punctuation　288. waight] gh *altered from* te *in MS*　290. to
make mee] *MS*; make mee to *conj. editor*; make mee *or Cunningham*　I. ii. Actus . . .
marchants.] *one line in MS*　*In l.h. margin, Knight writes* Ent: Berecinthius: /
(wᵗʰ.3. papers: & / .3. Marchant*e*　5. Parthian] i *altered, probably from* a *in MS*

3 marchant: a statesman?
                the divell I thincke, whoe onlye knowes hym truelye
                can gieue his character. when Hee is to determine
                a poynt of iustice, His wordes fall in measure   10
                like plum̃ets of a clocke, observinge time
                and iust proportion.

1 marchant: but when Hee is
                to speake in any cawse concernes hym selfe
                or Romes republicꝗ, like a gushinge torrent
                not to bee stopp'd in it's full course, his reasons   15
                deliverd like a seconde mercurie,
                breake in and beare downe w⟨hats⟩oever is
6ᵛ   oppos'd against 'em.

2 marchant: when Hee smiles, let such
                beware, as haue to doe with hym, for then
                sans doubt Hee's bent to mischeife.

Berecinthius: as I am   20
                Cybeles flamen, whose most sacred image
                drawne thus in pompe I weare vpon my brest,
                I am priveledgde, nor is it in his power
                to doe mee wronge, and hee shall finde I can
                chant, and alowd to when I am not at   25
                her altar kneelinge. mother of the gods what is hee.
                at his best but a Patritian of Rome,
                His name Titus flaminivs, and speake mine
                Berecinthivs Archflamen to Cybele[s] it makes as
                    greate a sownde.

3 marchant: trewe but his place sʳ   30
                and the power it carries in it, as Romes legate
                gieues hym preheminence ore you.

Berecinthius: not an atome.
                when morall honestie, and ius gentium faile
                to lende reliefe to such as are oppresd
                relligion must vse her strength. I am perfit   35
                in theis notes you gaue mee. doe they contayne at
                full

---

9. character.] *MS*; ~ₐ *Sisson*   10. iustice,] *MS*; ~. *Sisson*   17. breake]
Croker (Breake); bre⟨ ⟩ke *MS*   beare downe] *Cunningham*; b⟨ ⟩e d⟨ ⟩e *MS*; b[reak]
d[owne] *Croker*   18. against] *Croker*; agai⟨ ⟩st *MS*   31. legate] l *altered from*
a *in MS*   36. contayne] a *altered from* e *in MS*

	your grievances, and losses.
1 marchant	woulde they were
	as well redre'sd, as they are punctuallie
	deliver'd to you.
Berecinthius:	say noe more, they shall
	& to the purpose.
2 marchant:	Heere hee comes.
Berecinthius:	haue at hym. Enter Titus flaminivs. Calistus.
	Demetrius. 2 freedmen.
flaminius:	blowe away theis troublesome & importunate drones
	I haue embrions of greater consequence 42
	in my imaginations to w^{ch}
	I must gieue life, and forme, not now vouchsafinge
	to heare their idle buzzes.
1 marchant:	note you that. 45
Berecinthivs:	yes I doe note it. but the flamen is not
	soe light to bee remou'd by a groomes breath
	I must, and will speake, and I thus confront hym.
flaminivs:	but that the image of the goddesse w^{ch}
	thow wearst vpon thy brest protects thy rudenesse,
	it had forfeyted thy life. dost thou not tremble 51
	when an incensed Roman frownes.
Berecinthivs:	I see
	noe Gorgon in your face.
flaminivs:	must I speake in thunder
	before thow wilt bee awde?
Berecinthivs:	I rather looke
	for reverence from thee, yf thow respectest 55
	the goddesse power and in her name I charge thee
	to gieue mee hearinge. yf theis lyons rore
	for thy contempt of her expecte a vengeance
	sutable to thy pride.
flaminivs:	thow shalt orecome.
	theres noe contendinge with thee.
3 marchant:	hitherto 60
	the flamen hath the better
1 marchant.	but I feare

---

37. *In l.h. margin, Knight writes* Ent: fflaminius: / Calistus: Demetri: 40 SD.
Enter ... freedmen.] *MS; deleted by Knight*   48. hym.] *Croker; a large blot on
the MS covers any punctuation*   53. flaminivs] iv *altered from* us *in MS*

Hee will not keepe it.

Berecinthivs: knowe you theis mens faces?

flaminivs: yes yes poore Asiaticqs.

Berecinthivs: Poore they are made soe
by your Roman tyrannie & oppression.

flaminivs: take heede   65
yf arrogantly you presume to tax
the Roman governement [youll finde and feele] your
goddesse cannot
gieue priveledge to it, and youl finde and feele
'tis litle lesse then treason flamen.

Berecinthius: truth
in your pride is soe interpreted. theis poore men, 70
theis Asiaticq marchants whom you looke [vp]on
with such contempt, and scorne, are they to whom
Rome owes her braverie; their industrious serch
to the farthest Inde with danger to them selues
bringes home securitie to you, to you vnthanckefull;
your magazines are from their sweat supplide;   76
the legions with wch you fright the worlde
are from their labour pay'd; the Tirian fishe
whose blood dies your prowde purple, in the colour
distinguishinge the senators garded robe   80
from a plebeian habit, their nets catch;
the diamonde hewde from the rocke, the pearle
diude for in to the bottome of the sea;
the saphir, rubie, Iacinth, amber, currall,
and all rich ornaments, of your Latian dames   85
are Asian spoyles; they are indeede the nurses,
and sinnewes of your war, and without them
what cowlde you doe? your handkercher.

flaminivs: wipe your face

7^r

---

64. Berecinthivs:] *Croker* (*Berecinthius.*); B⟩er⟨ ⟩int⟨h⟩ivs: *MS*   they] y *altered from* i *in MS*   65. flaminivs:] *conj. Croker*; *MS damaged*   take heede] *conj. Sisson*; ⟨ k⟩e he⟨ ⟩d⟨e⟩ *MS*; deeds *Croker*   66. tax] x *altered from* k *in MS*   67. cannot] *Croker*; canno⟨ *MS*   69. Berecinthius:] *Croker* (*Berecinthius.*); ⟨ ⟩thius: *MS*   71. theis] *Croker*; ⟨ eis⟩ *MS*   Asiaticq *altered from* Asiaticqs *in MS*   marchants] *interlined above a caret, the caret duplicated by Knight*   72. with] *conj. Croker* ([W]ith); ⟨ ⟩ith *MS*   73. Rome] *conj. Croker* ([Ro]me); ⟨ ⟩me *MS*   braverie] br *altered from* ba *in MS*   74. to] *conj. Croker* ([T]o); ⟨ ⟩o *MS*   farthest] s *altered from* r *in MS*   80. garded] *altered from* gaudie *in MS*

	you are in a sweat. the weather's hot take heede	
	of meltinge your fat kidneys	
Berecinthivs:	there's noe heate	90
	can thaw thy frozen conscience.	
flaminivs:	to it againe now	
	I am not mou'd.	
Berecinthivs:	I see it yf you had	
	the feelinge of a man, you wowlde not suffer	
	theis men, whoe haue deserv'd soe well to sincke	
	vnder the burthen of their wronges. yf they	95
	are subiects, why inioy they not the right[s]	
	and priveledge of subiects? what defence	
	can you alleage for your connivence to	
	the Carthaginian gallies whoe forcd from em	
	the prize they tooke belongeinge not to them,	100
	nor their confæderates?	
flaminivs:	with reverence	
	to your soe sacred goddesse, I must tell you	
	you are growne presumptuous, and in your demandes	
	a rash, and sawcie flamen. meddle with	
	your [s] iuglinge misteries, and keepe in awe	105
	your gelded ministers. Shall I yeelde accompe	
	of what I doe to you?	
1.marchant:	Hee smiles in scorne.	
2.marchant	nay then I knowe what followes.	
3.marchant:	in his lookes	
	a tempest rises.	
flaminivs:	how dare you complayne?	
	or in a looke repine? our governement	110
	hath bene to easie, and the yoke wᶜh Rome	
	in her accustomde lenitie ⟨im⟩po'sd	
	vpon your stubborne neckes begets contempt.	
	hath our familiar com̃erce, and tradinge	
	almost as with our æqualls, tought you to	115
	dispute our actions? haue you quite forgot	
	what wee are, and you ought to bee? shall vassalls	
	capitulate with their lordes?	
2 marchant:	I now hee speakes	

	in his owne Dialecte.	
flaminivs:	'tis to frequent wretches	
	to haue the vanquishd hate the conqueror,	120
	and from vs needes noe answer. doe not I knowe	
	how odious the lordlye Roman is	
	to the despised Asian? and that	
	to gaine your libertie you woulde pull downe	
	the altars of your gods, and like the gyants	125
	rayse a newe war 'gainst heaven.	
1 marchant:	terrible.	
flaminivs:	did you not gieue assurance of this when	
	giddie Antiochus died? and rather then	
	accept vs guardians of your orphan kingedome,	
	when the victorious Scaurus with his sword	130
	pleaded the Roman title, with one vote	
	you did exclaime against vs as the men	
	that sought to lay an vniust gripe vpon	
	your territories? nere remembringe that	
	in the brasse leau'd booke of fate it was set downe	
	the earth showlde know noe soueraigne but Rome.	
	yet you repinde, and rather chose to pay	137
	homage, and fealtie to the Parthian,	
	th' Ægiptian Ptolomee, or indeede any	
	then bow vnto the Roman.	
Berecinthivs:	& perhaps	140
	our gouernement in them had bene more gentle	
	since yours is insupportable.	
flaminivs:	yf thow wer't not	
	in a free state the tongue that belcheth forth	
	theis blasphemies showlde bee seard. for you presume	
	not	
	to trouble mee heereafter. yf you doe	145
	you shall with horror to your prowdest hopes	
	feele reallie that wee haue iron hamers	
	to pulverize rebellion, and that	
	wee dare vse you as slaues. bee you to warnd s^r	
	since this is my last caution. I haue seene	150

---

129. guardians] u *altered, probably from* a *in MS*   139. Ægiptian] ip *altered, probably from* y *in MS*   145. heereafter] *second* e *altered from* a *in MS*
148. pulverize] l *altered, probably from* t *in MS*

a murmurer like your selfe for his attemptinge
to rayse sedition in Romes provinces
hangd vp in such a habit.   ex flaminivs cum suis.

Berecinthivs: I haue tooke
poyson in at my eares; & I shall burst
yf it come not vp in my replie.

1 marchant: Hee's gone s[r]   155
Berecinthivs: Hee durst not stay mee. yf hee had, had founde
I woulde not swallowe my spettle.

2 marchants: as wee must
our wronges and our disgraces.

3 marchant. o the wretched
condition that wee liue in! made the anvile
on w[c]h Romes tyrannies, are shap'd, and fashionde.

8[r] 1 marchant. But our callamities there is nothinge left vs   161
w[c]h wee can call our owne.

2 marchant: our wiues, and daughters
lye open to their lusts, and such as showlde bee
our iudges dare not right vs.

3 marchant: O Antiochus
thrice happie were the men whom fate appointed
to fall with thee in Achaia.

2 marchant: they haue set   166
a period to their miseries.

1 marchant: wee surviue
to linger out a tædious life, and death,
wee call in vaine for flies vs.

Berecinthivs: yf relligion
bee not [b] a meere worde only, and the gods   170
are iust wee shall finde a deliverie
when least expected.

1 marchant: 'tis beyonde all hope s[r].   enter Antiochus.
Berecinthivs: Ha whoe is this?
Antiochus: your charitie to a poore man
as you are Asians.

2 marchant: pray you obserue hym.
3 marchant: I am amazde.
1 marchant: I thunderstrooke.

---

169. for] *MS*; *deleted by corrector*, what *interlined above*   170. *In l.h. margin,*
Knight writes Ent: Antiochus   172 SD. enter Antiochus.] *MS*; *deleted by Knight*

Berecinthivs:	what are you?	175
Antiochus:	the kinge Antiochus.	
1 marchant:	or some deitie	
	that hath assumde his shape.	
Berecinthivs:	Hee only differs	
	in the colour of his haire, and age.	
Antiochus:	consider	
	what two, and twentye yeares of miserie	
	can worke vpon a wretch that longe time spent to	
	vnder distant zeniths, and the change you looke on	
	will not deserue your wonder.	
1 marchant:	His owne voice!	182
2 marchant:	His verye countenance! his forhead! eies!	
3 marchant:	His nose! his German lippe!	
Berecinthivs:	His stature! speech	
1 marchant:	His arme, hand, legge, and foote, on the lefte side	
	shorter then on the right.	
2 marchant:	the moles vpon	186
	his face, and handes.	
3 marchant:	the scarres causde by his hurts	
	on his right browe, & head.	
Berecinthivs:	the hollownesse	
	of his vnder iawe occasiond by the losse	
	of a tooth pulld out by his chirurgion.	
1 marchant	to confirme vs	190
	tell vs his name when hee seru'd you.	
Antiochus:	you all knewe hym	
	as I doe you Demetrivs Castor.	
2 marchant:	strange.	
3 marchant.	but most infalliblie trew.	
Berecinthivs:	soe many markes	
	confirminge vs wee sinne in our distrust	
	a sacrifice for his safetie.	
8ᵛ 1 marchant:	may Rome sincke	195
2 marchant:	& Asia once more flourishe.	
3 marchant:	you the meanes sʳ.	
Antiochus:	silence your showtes. I will gieue stronger proofes	

184. German] G *altered, probably from* f *in* MS; *word deleted by Knight, who writes* very *above the deletion*   185–6. His . . . right.] MS; *deleted by Knight*   191. his] MS; *deleted by Knight, who writes* yoʳ chirurgions *above the deletion*

then theis exterior markes when I appeare
before the Carthaginian Senators
with whom I haue helde more intelligence   200
and private counsailes, then with all the kinges
of Asia, or Affricɋ Ile amaze them
with the wonder of my storie.

Berecinthivs: yet vntill
your maiestie bee furnishde like your selfe
to a neighbour village.

Antiochus: where you please the omen   205
of this encounter promises a good issue
and our gods pleasd oppressed Asia
when ayde is least expected may shake of
th' insultinge Roman bondage, and in mee
gayne, and inioy her pristine libertie.   exevnt.

I. i]   Actus secundi, scæna prima.
flaminivs. Calistus.

flaminivs: A man that stiles hym selfe Antiochus say you?
Calistus: not alone stil'de soe but as such receaud
and honor'd by the Asians.

flaminivs: two impostors
for their pretension to that fatall name
alreadie haue pay'd deere nor shall this third   5
escape vnpunnish'd.

Calistus: 'twill exact your wisdome
with an Herculean arme (the cause requires it)
to strangle this new monster in the birth.
for on my life hee hath deliverd to
the credulous multitude such reasons why   10
they showlde beleeue Hee is the trewe Antiochus
that with their gratulations for his safetie,
& wishes for his restitution many
offer the hazarde of their liues, and fortunes
to doe hym service.

205. neighbour] r *altered from* re *in MS*   209. th'] *altered from* the *in MS*
II. i. Actus ... Calistus.] *one line in MS   In l.h. margin, Knight writes* Act: 2: /
Long / Ent:—. *He deletes* Actus ... prima. *and alters* flaminivs. Calistus. *to* flam-
inivs. | & Calistus: R: Bax   2. alone] *MS*; aloud *Sisson*

flaminivs: poore seduced fooles.   15
                     However 'tis a buisnesse of such waight
                     I must not sleepe in't. is hee now in Carthage?
Calistus: noe s^r remou'd to a Grange some two miles of
                     and there the malecontents, and such whose wants,
                     with forfeyted credits make em wish a change   20
                     of the Roman governement in troopes flocke to hym.
flaminivs: with one puffe thus I will disperse, and scatter
                     this heape of dust. heere take my ringe. by this
                     intreate my freinde Amilcar to procure
                     a mandate from the Carthaginian senate   25
                     for the apprehension of this impostor
                     & with all possible speede. how ere I knowe
                                              exit Calistus.
                     the Rumor of Antiochus death vncertaine
                     it much imports the safetie of great Rome
                     to haue it soe beleeude.   enter Demetrivs.
Demetrivs: there waite withowt   30
                     three fellowes I nere sawe before, whoe much
                     importune their accesse. they sweare they bringe
                     buisnesse alonge with em that deserues your eare
                     it beeinge for the safetie of the republicq̅
                     and quiet of the provinces. they are full   35
                     of golde, I haue felt their bountie
flaminivs: such are welcome.
                     gieue them admittance. in this various play
                                    [Exit Demetrius.]
                     of state, and policie, theres noe propertie   Enter
                            Demetrius. Chrysalus. Geta Syrus.
                     but may bee vsefull—. now freindes what designe[s]
                     carries you to mee?
Geta: my most Honor'd lord   40
Syrus: may it please your mightinesse.
flaminivs: let one speake for all

    29. *In l.h. margin,* Knight *writes* Ent: Demetrius / Wm Pattrick   30 SD. enter
Demetrivs.] *MS; deleted by Knight*   36. flaminivs] vs *altered from* us *in MS*
37 SD. Exit Demetrius.] *Sherman; not in MS*   38 SD. Enter . . . Syrus.] (*as
one line*) *Croker;* Enter Calistus. / Chrysalus. Geta / Syrus. *MS*   Demetrius]
Knight, who deletes Calistus. *then strikes out the whole SD. and writes in the l.h. margin*
Ent: chrisalus / Geta: Syrus: / Demetrius: 41. mightinesse] *altered from* might-
ines *in MS*

I cannot brooke this discorde.

Chrysalus: as our duties
coṁandes vs noble Roman, havinge discover'd
a dreadfull danger with the nimble winges
of speede approchinge to the state of Rome   45
wee houlde it fit you shoulde haue the first [honor]
    notice
that you may haue the honor to prevent it.

flaminivs: I thancke you. but instruct mee what forme weares
the danger that you speake of.

Chrysalus: it appeares
in the shape of [Dom Sebastian] King Antiochus:

flaminivs: how! is hee   50
rose from the dead?

Chrysalus: alas hee never died sʳ
Hee at this instant liues the more the pittie
Hee showlde surviue to the disturbance of
Romes close, and politicꝗ counsailes, in the gettinge
possession of his kingedome wᶜh hee woulde   55
recover, simple as hee is, the playne
and downe right way of iustice.

flaminivs: very likelye.
but how are you assur'd this is Antiochus
and not a counterfaite? answer that?

Chrysalus: I serude hym
in the Achaian war. where his armie routed   60
& the warlike Romans hot in their execution
to shun their furye Hee and his mignions were
havinge cast of their glorious armor, [we] forcd
to hide them selues as dead with feare and horror
amonge the slawghterd carkases. I lay by them   65
and rose with them at midnight. then retiringe
vnto their shippes wee sayld to Corinth, thence
to India, where hee spent many yeares
with their gymnosophists. there I wayted on hym,
and came thence with hym. but at length tyr'd out
with an vnrewarded service, and affrighted   71

50. King Antiochus:] *Knight, who deletes Massinger's* Dom Sebastian   64. as] s
altered from d *in MS*   66. *In l.h. margin, Knight writes* Table ready: /& .6. chaires
/ to sett out   67. sayld] (d *altered from* e) *McIlwraith*; sayled *Sisson*

in my imagination with the dangers,
or rather certaine ruines in pursuinge
his more then desperate fortunes wee forsooke hym.

flaminivs: a wise, and politicɋ fellow. gieue mee thy hande.
thow art sure of this?

Chrysalus: as of my life.

flaminivs: and this is   76
knowne only to you three?

Chrysalus: there's noe man liues els
9ᵛ   to witnesse it.

flaminivs: the better. but informe mee,
and as you woulde oblige mee to you, truelye
where did you leaue hym?

Syrus: for the payment of   80
our longe, and tædious travaile wee made bolde
to rifle hym.

flaminivs: good.

Geta: & soe disablinge hym
of meanes to claime his right, wee hope despaire
hath made hym hange hymselfe.

flaminivs: it had bene safer
yf you had donne it for hym. but as 'tis   85
you are honest men. you haue reveald this secret
to noe man but my selfe.

Chrysalus: nor ever will.

flaminivs: I will take order that you never shall.   (aside
and since you haue bene trew vnto the state
Ile keepe you soe. I am evn now consyderinge   90
how to advance you.

Chrysalus: what a pleasant smile
his honor throwes vpon vs.

Geta: wee are made.

flaminivs: and now 'tis founde out. that noe danger may
come neere you, showlde the robberie bee discover'd
wᶜh the Carthaginian lawes you knowe call death   95
my howse shall bee your sanctuarie.

Syrus: there's a favour.

flaminivs: and that our entertainment come not short

73. *In l.h. margin, Knight writes* Mʳ Hobs: calld / vp   82. flaminivs:] flam
altered from Geta *in MS*   91. Chrysalus] y *altered from* u *in MS*

	of your deservinges I comĩt you to
	my secretaries care. see that they want not
	amonge their other delicates.
Chrysalus:	marke that.
flaminivs	a sublimated pill of mercurie
	for sugar to their wine.
Demetrivs:	I vnderstande you.
flaminivs:	attende theis honest men as yf they were

of your deservinges I comĩt you to
my secretaries care. see that they want not
amonge their other delicates.

Chrysalus: marke that.   100

flaminivs a sublimated pill of mercurie
    for sugar to their wine.

Demetrivs: I vnderstande you.

flaminivs: attende theis honest men as yf they were
    made Roman Cittizens.—and bee sure at night
    I may see 'em well lodg'd—dead in the vault I
     meane   105
    their golde is thy rewarde.

Demetrivs: beleeue it donne s^r.

flaminivs: and when 'tis knowne how I haue recompencd
    (thowgh you were trecherous to your owne kinge)
    the service donne to Rome I hope that others
    will followe your example. enter freindes. 110
    Ile soe provide, that when you next come forth
    you shall not feare who sees you

Chrysalus: was there ever
    soe sweete a temperd Roman?   exevnt.

flaminivs: you shall finde it.
    Ha ! what's the matter? doe I feele a stinge heere
    for what is donne to theis poore snakes? my reason
    will easilie remoue it. that assures mee 116
    that as I am a Roman to preserue
    and propagate her empire, thowgh they were
    my fathers sonnes they must not liue to witnesse
    Antiochus is in beeinge. the relation 120
    the villaine made, in everie circumstance
    appeerd soe like to truth that I began
    to feele an inclination to beleeue
    what I must haue noe faith in. by my birth 124
    I am bounde to serue thee Rome, and what I doe
    necessitie of state compells mee to.   exit

10^r

---

102. Demetrivs:] *Knight* (Demet:), *who deletes Massinger's* Calistus: 106. Demetrivs:] *Knight* (Demet:), *who deletes Massinger's* Calistus:

Actus secundi, scæna secunda.

Amilcar. Hanno. Asdrubal. Carthalo. officers.

Amilcar: To steere a middle course twixt theis extreames
exacts our serious care.

Hanno: I knowe not wch way
I showlde incline.

[Asdrubal] Amilcar: the reasons this man vrges
to proue hymselfe Antiochus are soe pregnant
and the attestation of his cuntriemen   5
in every circumstance soe punctuall
as not to showe hym our compassion were
a kinde of barbarous crueltie.

Carthalo: vnder correction
gieue mee leaue to speake my thowghts. wee are
bounde to waigh
not what wee showlde doe in the poynt of honor,
swayde by our pittie, but what may bee donne   11
with the safetie of the state.

Asdrubal: wch is indeede
the maine consyderation. for, grant
this is the trewe Antiochus, without danger
nay almost certaine ruine to our selues   15
wee cannot yeelde hym favour or protection.

Hanno: wee haue fear'd and felt the Roman power, and must
expecte yf wee provoke hym a returne
not limitted to the qualitie of the offence
but left at large to his interpretation   20
wch seldome is confind. whoe knowes not that
the tribute Rome receiues from Asia, is
her chiefe supportance. other provinces
hardlye defray the charge by wch they are
kepd in subiection, they in name perhaps   25
render the Roman terrible, but his strength
and power to doe hurt without quæstion is
deriud from Asia. and can wee hope then
that such as lende their aydes to force it from em

II. ii. Actus . . . officers.] *one line in MS*   *In l.h. margin, Knight writes* Ent:
and deletes Actus . . . secunda. *He overwrites Massinger's stops after the first four names
with upright bars; and writes* w^m Mago: Nick: *beneath* Hanno. Asdrubal. *and* Rowland:
on top of officers.   23. supportance] c *altered from* t *in MS*

will bee helde for lesse then capitall enemies 30
and as such pursude, and punnishde?

Carthalo: I cowlde wishe
wee were well rid of hym.

Asdrubal: the surest course
is to deliver hym into the handes
of bolde flaminivs.

Hanno: and soe oblige
Rome for a [na] matchlesse benefit.

Amilcar: yf my power 35
were absolute, as 'tis but titular
and that confinde to, beeinge by you elected
prince of the senate onlye for a yeare
I woulde oppose your counsailes, and not labour
with arguments to confute em. yet however 40
thowgh a fellow patriot with you let it not savour
of vsurpation thowgh in my opinion
I crosse your abler iudgements. call to minde
our grandsires glories (thowgh not seconded
with a due imitation) and remember 45
with what expence of coyne, as blood they did
maintaine their [nat] libertie, and kepde the scale
of empire evn 'twixt Carthage, and prowd Rome.
And thowgh the Punicꝗ faith is branded by
[Her] our enemies, our confæderates, and freindes
founde it as firme as fate. are seaventeene kinges
our fædaries, our strengths [at sea superior] vpon
the sea 52
exceedinge theirs, and our lande sowldiers
in number far aboue theirs, thowgh inferior
in armes, and discipline (to our shame wee speake it)
and then for our cavallerie [how often] in the
champaigne 56
howe [they brak] often haue they brake their piles,
& routed
theyr coward legions.

Hanno: this I grant sᵣ is not
to bee contradicted.

Amilcar: yf soe, as wee finde it
in our recordes, and that this state hath bene 60

the sanctuary to w^c^h mightie kinges
haue fled to for protection, and founde it
let it not to posteritie bee tolde
that wee soe far degenerate from the race
wee are deriu'd as in a servile feare   65
of the Roman power in a kinde to play the bawdes
to their ravenous lusts [in a kinde to play the b] by
   yeeldinge vp a man
that weares the shape of our confæderate
to their devouringe gripe whose stronge assurance
of our integritie, and impartiall doome   70
hath made this seate his altar.

Carthalo: I ioine with you
in this opinion but noe farther then
it may bee donne with safetie.

Asdrubal: in his ruines
to burye our selues you needes must grant ro bee
an inconsyderate pittie noe way suitinge   75
with a wisemans reason.

Carthalo: let vs face to face
heare the accuser, and accusd, and then
as eithers arguments worke on vs determine
as the respecte of our securitie,
or honor shall invite vs.

Amilcar: from the senate   80
intreate the Roman Titus flaminivs
 ·to assist vs with his counsaile.

Hanno: & let the prisoner
bee brought into the court.

Amilcar: the gods of Carthage   Enter flaminivs.
directe vs to the right way.

Asdrubal: with what gravitie
Hee does approch vs

Carthalo: as hee woulde comãnde   85
not argue his desires.

Amilcar: may it please your lordship
to take your place.

11^r^

83 SD. Enter flaminivs.] *deleted by Knight. In l.h. margin he writes* Ent: fflaminius / m^r^
Hobs: / ⟨&⟩ Rowland; *in the r.h. margin, above Massinger's direction he writes* Ent:
fflaminius: m^r^ Hobs: / Rowland: ffan Balls:

flaminivs: in civill courtesie
                  as I am Titus flaminivs I may thancke you.
                  but sittinge heere as Romes embassador
                  in wᶜh you are honor'd, to instruct you in   90
                  Her will, wᶜh you are bounde to serue not argue
                  I must not borrow that were poore, but take
                  as a tribute due to her, that's iustlye stilde
                  the mistrisse of this earthlye globe the boldnesse
                  to reprehende your slowe progression in   95
                  doeinge her greatnesse right. that shee beleeues
                  in mee, that this impostor was subornde
                  by the conquer'd Asiaticꝗs [this impost] in their
                    hopes
                  of future libertie to vsurpe the name
                  of dead Antiochus, shoulde satisfie   100
                  your scrupulous doubts, all proofes beyonde this
                    beeinge
                  meerelye superfluous.
Carthalo: my lord, my lord.
                  you trench to much vpon vs.
Asdruball: wee are not
                  lead by an implicite faith
Hanno: nor though wee woulde
                  preserue Romes amitie, must not yeelde vp   105
                  the freedome of our wills, & iudgements, to
                  quit, or condemne, as wee shall bee appointed
                  by his imperious pleasure.
Carthalo: wee confesse not
                  nor ever will shee hath a power aboue vs
                  Carthage is still her æquall.
Amilcar: yf you can   110
                  proue this man an impostor, Hee shall suffer
                  as hee deserues, yf not you shall perceiue
                  you haue noe empire heere.
Hanno: call in the prisoner
                  then as you please confront hym.
flaminivs: this neglecte
                  heereafter will be thowght on.
Amilcar: wee shall stand   115

98. Asiaticꝗs] A *altered from long* s *in MS*

	the danger howsoever. when wee did
	his cause vnheard, at your request comīt
	this kinge, or this impostor, you receau'd
	more favour then wee owde you
officer:	roome for the prisoner. Enter officers.
	Antiochus (Habited like a kinge)
	Berecinthivs. the three marchants.
Antiochus:	this shape that you haue put mee in suites ill 120
	with the late austerenesse of my life.
Berecinthivs:	faire glosse
	wrongs not the richest stuffe but sets it of.
	& let your language high and stately speake you
	as you were borne a kinge.
Antiochus:	Health to the senate
	wee doe suppose your duties donne, sit still 125
	Titus flaminivs wee remember you
	as you are a publicꝗ minister from Rome
	you may sit cover'd.
flaminivs:	How!
Antiochus:	but as wee are
	a potent kinge, in whose court you haue waited
	and sought [my] our favour, you betray your pride,
	and the more then sawcie rudenesse of your manners.
	a bended knee remembringe what wee are 132
	much better would become you.
flaminivs:	Ha!
Antiochus:	wee sayd it.
	but fall from our owne height to holde discourse
	with a thinge soe far beneath vs.
Berecin:	admirable! 135
Amilcar:	The Roman lookes as hee had seene the wolfe
	how his confidence awes hym.
Asdruball:	bee hee what hee will
	Hee beares hym selfe like a kinge, and I must tell you
	I am amazd to.

11ᵛ (margin)

119. officer:] *MS*; *Knight prefixes* wᵗʰin: 119 SD. Enter . . . marchants.] *MS*
reads Enter . . . Antiochus / (Habited . . . kinge) / Berecinthivs . . . three / marchants.
Knight prefixes —Ent— *to Massinger's direction, deletes* officers., *adds* Garde *after*
marchants., *and marks off the characters with upright bars.*   120. *In l.h. margin,*
Knight writes Ent: / Berecinthius: / .3. Marchantᵉ: / Garde   125. suppose] *Croker*;
s⟨ ⟩ppose *MS*

Antiochus: Are wee soe transformde
from what wee were, since our disaster in   140
the Græcian enterprise that you gaze vpon vs
as some strange prodegie never seene in [Cartha]
Affricq̃.
Antiochus speakes to you, the kinge Antiochus
and challenges a retribution in
his entertainment, of the loue, and favours   145
extended to you. call to memorie
your trewe freinde, and confæderate, whoe refusde
in his respect to you the profferd amitie
of the Roman people. Hath this vile inchanter
inviron'd mee with such thicke clowdes in your   150
erroneous beleefe, from his report
that I was longe since dead, that beeinge present
the beames of maiestie cannot breake throwgh
the foggie mists raysde by his wicked charmes
to lende you light to knowe mee? I cite you   155
my lord Amilcar, now I looke on you
as prince of the senate, but when you were lesse
I haue seene you in my court assisted by
graue Hanno, Asdrubal, and Carthalo
the pillars of the Carthaginian greatenesse   160
I knowe you all. Antiochus nere deseru'd
to bee thus sleighted.

Amilcar: not soe. wee in you
looke on the figure of the kinge Antiochus,
but without stronger proofes then yet you haue
producd to make vs thincke soe cannot heare you
but as a man suspected.

Antiochus: of what guilt?   166

flaminivs: of subornation, and imposture.

Antiochus: Silence
this fellowes sawcie tongue. o maiestie
how soone a short eclipse hath made thy splendor
as it had never shinde on theis forgotten.   170
but you refuse to heare mee as a kinge
denie not yet in iustice what you grant
to com̃on men, free libertie without
his interruption, (havinge heard what Hee

12ʳ

	obiects against mee) to acquit my selfe	175
	of that wch in his malice I am chargd with
Amilcar:	you haue it.
Antiochus:	as my present fortune wills mee
	I thancke your goodnesse. rise thow cursed agent
	of mischiefe, and accumulate in one heape
	all engins by the divell thy tutor fashiond	180
	to ruine innocence; in poyson steepe
	thy bloudied tongue, and let thy wordes as full
	of bitternes, as malice labour to
	seduce theis noble hearers. make mee in
	thy coyned accusation guiltie of	185
	such crimes, whose names my innocence nere knewe.
	Ile stande the charge; and when that thow hast shot
	all arrowes in thy quiver fether'd with
	sclanders, and aimde with crueltie in vaine.
	my truth thowgh yet conceald, the mountaines of
	thy glossed fictions in her strength remou'd	191
	shall in a glorious shape appeare, and showe
	thy paynted mistrisse falshood, when strippd bare
	of borrowed, and adulterate colours in
	her owne shape, and deformitie.
Berecinthivs:	I am ravishde!	195
1 marchant:	o more then royall s^r!
Amilcar:	forbeare.
2 marchant:	the monster
	prepares to speake.
Berecinthivs:	& still that villainous smile
	vshers his followeinge mischiefes.
flaminivs	since the assurance
	from one of my place, qualitie, and rancke,
	is not sufficient with you to suppresse	200
	this bold seductor, to acquit our state
	from the least tyrannous imputation
	I will forget awhile I am a Roman,
	whose arguments are warranted by his sworde
	and not filde from his tongue. this creature heere	205
	that stiles hymselfe Antiochus, I knowe
	for an Apostata Iew, thowgh others say

203. *In l.h. margin,* Knight *writes* the great booke: / of Accompt*e* / ready.

Hee is a cheatinge Greeke calld Pseudolus,
and [hath] keepes a whore in Corinth but Ile come
to reall proofes, reports, and rumors beeinge   210
subiects vnsutable with my gravitie
to speake, or yours to heare. 'Tis most apparent
the kinge Antiochus was slaine in Greece,
his bodie at his subiects suite deliverd,
his ashes from the funerall pile rakd vp   215
and in a golden vrne preserud, and kepd
in the royall monument of [his] the Asian kinges
such was the clemencie of marcus scaurus
the Roman conqueror, whose trivmphe was
grac'd only with his statue. but suppose   220
Hee had surviud (wch is impossible)
can it fall in the compasse of your reason
that this impostor (yf hee were the man
wch hee with impudence affirmes Hee is,
woulde haue wanderd two, and twenty tædious
      yeares   225
like a vagabond ore the worlde, and not haue tried
Romes mercie as a suppliant.

Hanno: shrowde suspitions.
flaminivs: a mason of Callipolis heretofore
presumde as far, and was like this impostor
by slavishe Asians follow'd, and a second   230
a Cretan, of a base condition did
maintaine the like. all ages haue bene furnish'd
with such as haue vsurpd vpon the names
and persons of deade princes. is it not
...as evident as the day, this wretch instructed   235
by theis poore Asians (sworne enemies
to the maiestie of Rome but personates
the dead Antiochus? hir'd to it by theis
to stirre vp a rebellion, wch they call
[rebellion] deliverie or restoringe. & will you   240
whoe for your wisdome are esteemd the sages
and oracles of Affricke, meddle in
th'affaires of this affronter, wch noe monarch
lesse rashe, and giddie then Antiochus was

      210. beeinge] in *altered from* n *in MS*

◀2^v

would vndertake.

Antiochus: would I were dead indeede   245
rather then heare this livinge.

flaminivs: I confesse
Hee hath some markes of kinge Antiochus, but
the most of em artificiall. then obserue
what kinde of men they are that doe abett hym.
proscribd, and bannishd persons, the ringe leader
of this seditious troope a turbulent flamen   251
growne fat with idlenes

Berecinthivs: that's I.

flaminivs: & puffd vp
with the winde of his ambition.

Berecinthivs: [settinge aside] with reverence to
[thy place] the state thow liest, I am growne to this
bulke
by beeinge libde, and my disabilitie   255
to deflowre thy sisters.

Amilcar: thancke [thy] your goddesse. shee
defendes you from a whippinge.

Hanno: take hym of
Hee does disturbe the court.

Berecinthivs: I shall finde a place yet
where I will rore my wronges out.   exevnt
officers with Berecinthivs.

flaminivs: as you haue
in the removinge of that violent foole,   260
gieun mee a tast of your severitie
make it a feast, and perfit your greate iustice
in the surrendringe vp this false pretender
to the correction of the law, & let hym
vndergoe the same punnishement wch others   265
haue iustlye sufferd that preceded hym
in the same machination.

Antiochus: as you wishe
a noble memorie to after times
reserue one eare for my defence and let not
for your owne wisdomes, let not that beleefe   270

255. libde] *altered from* libbe *in MS*   256. sisters] *Cruickshank*; sister *Sisson*
259 SD. exevnt . . . Berecinthivs.] *MS reads* exevnt . . . with / Berecinthivs.

3ʳ

this subtle fiende woulde plant, bee rooted in you
till you haue heard mee. woulde you know the truth
and reall cause why poore Antiochus hath
soe longe conceald hymselfe ? thowgh in the openinge
a wounde in some degree by time closde vp   275
I shall poure scaldinge oyle, and sulphur in it.
I will in the relation of my
to bee lamented storye punctualie
confute my false accuser. pray you conceaue
as far as your compassion will permit   280
how greate the griefe, and agonie of my soule was
when I consyderd that the violence
of my ill reynd ambition had made Greece
the fatall sepulchre of soe many thousands
of braue, and able men that mighte haue stood   285
in opposition for the defence
of mine owne kingedom, and a readie ayde
for my confæderates. after wᶜh route
& my retraite in a disguise to Athens
the shame of this disgrace thowgh I then had   290
the forheade of this man woulde haue deterd mee
from beeinge ever seene where I was knowne
and such was then my resolution.

Amilcar: this granted, whither went you ?

Antiochus: as a punnishement
imposde vpon my selfe and æquall to   295
my wilfull follie gievinge ore the worlde
I went into a desert.

flaminivs: this agrees
with the dead slaues report but I must contemne it.

Amilcar: what drewe you from that austere life ?

Asdrubal: cleere that.

Antiochus: the counsayle of a graue Philosopher   300
wrought on mee to make knowne my selfe the man
that I was borne. and of all potentates
in Affricꝗ to determine of the truth
of my life and condition I preferd
the coṁon welth of Carthage.

flaminivs: as the fittest   305

285–6. that . . . opposition] *one line, interlined with a caret after* men *in MS*

	to bee abusde.	
Antiochus:	this is not faire.	
Amilcar:	my lord	
	yf not intreat I must comande your silence	
	or absence wᶜh you please.	
flaminivs:	soe peremptorie.	
Antiochus:	to vindicate my selfe from all suspition	
	of forgerie, and imposture. in this scrowle	310
	writ with my royall hande you may pervse	
	a true memoriall of all circumstances,	
	answers, despatches, doubts, & difficulties,	
	betwene my selfe, and your embassadors	
	sent to negotiate with mee.	
Amilcar:	fetch the recordes.	315
Antiochus:	'tis my desire you shoulde truth seekes the light.	
	and when you haue compar'd 'em yf you finde em	
	in any poynt of moment differinge	
	conclude mee such a one, as this false man	
	presents mee to you. but yf you perceiue	320
the recordes	those private passages in my cabinet argude	
brought in	and but to your embassadors, and my selfe	
	conceald from all men, in each poynt agreeinge.	
	iudge yf a cheatinge Greeke a Pseudolus	
	or an Apostata Iewe coulde ere arriue at	325
	such deepe, and waightie secrets.	
Hanno:	to a sillable	
	they are the same.	
Amilcar:	it cannot bee but this is	
	the trew [Sebastian.] Antiochus:	
flaminivs:	a magitian rather	
	& hath the spirit of Pithon.	
Carthalo:	theis are toyes.	
Antiochus:	you see hee will omit noe trifle that	330
	his malice can lay holde of to divert	
	your loue, and favour to mee. now for my death	
	(the firmest base on wᶜh hee buildes the strength	
	of his assertions, yf you please to waigh it	

13ᵛ

318. *In l.h. margin, Knight writes* Ent: / Rowland: wᵗʰ / the booke of / records; *in the r.h. margin* Ent: Rowland / wᵗʰ the Records: 324. Greeke] *second* e *altered from* a *in MS*   328. Antiochus:] *Knight, who deletes Massinger's* Sebastian.

    with your accustomd [clemencie] wisdome youle
      perceiue 335
    tis meerely fabulous. had they meant fairely
    and as a truth woulde haue it soe confirmde
    to the doubtfull Asians. why did they not
    suffer the carkase they affirmd was mine
    to bee viewd by such men as were interressed 340
    in the greate cause, that were bred vp with mee
    and were familiar with the marks I carried
    vpon my bodie, and not relye vpon
    poore prisoners taken in the war, from whom
    in hope of libertie, and rewarde, they drewe 345
    such depositions as they [pleasd] knewe woulde
      make
    for their darke endes. was any thinge more easie
    then to suppose a bodie, and that plac'd on
    a sollemne herse with funerall pompe to inter it
    in a rich monument, and then proclaime 350
    this is the bodye of Antiochus
    kinge of the lower Asia.
flaminivs: Romes honor
    is taxd in this of practise, and corruption.
    Ile heare noe more. in your determinations
    consyder what it is to holde and keepe her 355
    your freinde or enemie.   [exit flaminivs.]
Amilcar: wee wishe wee coulde
    receaue you as a kinge, since your relation
    hath wrought soe much vpon vs that wee doe
    incline to that beleefe. but since wee cannot
    as such protecte you but with certaine danger 360
    vntill you are by other potent nations
    proclaimde for such. our fittinge caution
    cannot bee censur'd thowgh wee doe intreate
    you would elswhere seeke iustice.
Antiochus: where? when 'tis
    frighted from you by power.
Amilcar: and yet take comfort 365
    not all the threates of Rome shall force vs to

356 SD. exit flaminivs.] *Cunningham*; *not in MS*   364. iustice] *Croker* (justice);
iustie *MS*

deliver you. the short time that you stay
in [Venice] Carthage you are safe. noe more a
  prisoner
you are inlargd. with full securitie
consult of your affaires, in what wee may   370
wee are your freindes. breake vp the court.   exevnt
                                   Carthaginians.

1 marchant: deere s^r
take courage in your libertie the worlde
lyes open to you.

2 marchant: wee shall meete with comfort
when most despaird of by vs.

Antiochus.   never. never.
poore men thowgh falne may rise. but kings like mee
yf once by fortune slaude are nere set free.   376
            exevnt   the ende of ye seconde Act

[III. i]   Act 3^d. Scæne first
            Ent: flaminivs. Calistus. Demetrivs

fla: you gaue hym store of gold with the instructions
that I prescribde hym.

Calistus: yes my lord, and on
the forfeiture of my credit with your [hono] honor
Titus will doe his parts and diue into
their deepest secrets.

flaminivs: men of place pay deere   5
for their intelligence it eates out the profit
of their imployment. but in a designe
of such waight prodigalitie is a vertue.

14^r   the fellowe was of trust that you despatchd
to Rome with the packet?

Demetrivs: yes s^r Hee flies not rides.   10
by this yf his accesse answer his care

368. Venice] *conj. Sisson*; ⟨V i e⟩ *MS, deleted by Massinger and by Knight*
376. yf . . . Act] *MS reads* yf . . . y^e / seconde Act   *In l.h. margin, Knight writes* Act: 3:
III. i. Act . . . first] *MS reads* Act 3^d. / Scæne first *in l.h. margin against the SD.*
SD. Ent . . . Demetrivs] *MS*; *Knight writes* Ent: *in l.h. margin, on top of Massinger's*
Act 3^d. *He deletes Massinger's* Ent: *and interlines* wth .2. *letters above a caret after*
flaminivs. *He inserts an upright bar before* Calistus *and writes* Mr Hobs: & Rowland
on top of Massinger's Calistus. Demetrivs   9. you despatchd] *Croker* (you dispatch'de); yo⟨ ⟩espatchd *MS*

	Hee is vpon returne.
flaminivs:	I am on the stage
	and yf now in the scæne imposd vpon mee
	soe full of change, nay a meere labirinth
	of politicꝗ windinges I showe not my selfe 15
	a Protean actor varijnge everie shape
	with the occasion, it will hardlye poyze
	the expectation. Ile soe place my nets
	that yf this birde want winges to carrye hym
	at one flight out of [Europe] Affricꝗ I shall catch
	hym. 20
	Calistus.
Calistus:	sʳ
flaminivs	gieue theis at Siracusa
	to the [good kinge Hiero.] proconsull Marcellus.
	let another post
	to Sardinia with theis. you haue the picture
	of the impostor?
Demetrivs:	drawne to the life my lord.
flaminivs	take it alonge with you. I haue comãnded 25
	in the senates name that they man out their gallies,
	and not to let one vessell passe without
	a stricte examination. the sea
	shall not protecte hym from mee. I haue chargd to
	the garrisons that keepe the passages 30
	by lande, to let none scape, that come from Carthage
	without a curious serch.
Lentulus:	I will excuse Enter Lentulus.
	my visit without preparation, feare not.
flaminivs	whoe haue wee heere?
Lentulus:	when you haue viewd mee better
	you will resolue your selfe.
flaminivs	my good Lord Lentulus. 35
Lentulus:	you name mee right. the speed that brought mee
	hither
	as you see accoutred, and without a trayne
	sutable to my rancke, may tell your lordship

15. windinges] *MS*; ~, *corrector*   16. actor] *MS*; ~, *corrector*   18. nets] *Sisson*; netes *Croker*   22. proconsull Marcellus.] *Knight, who deletes Massinger's good kinge Hiero.*   31. *In l.h. margin, Knight writes* Ent: / Lentulus: mʳ Rob: / (wᵗʰ a letter.

that the designe admits noe vacant time
for complement. your advertisements haue bene read
in open court. the consulls, and the senate   41
are full of wonder, and astonishement
at the relation. your care is much
coɱended, and will finde a due rewarde
when what you haue soe well begun, is ended.   45
in the meane time with their perticular thanckes
they thus salute you. you shall finde there that
their good opinion of mee (far aboue
my hopes, or meritts,) haue appointed mee
your successor in Carthage, and coɱit   50
vnto your abler trust the prosecution
of this impostor.

flaminivs: as their creature ever
I shall obey, and serue em. I will leaue
my freed man to instructe you in the course
of my proceedinges. you shall finde hym able   55
& faithfull on my honor.

Lentulus: I receaue hym
at his due valewe. can you ghesse yet whither
this creature tendes? by some passengers I met
I was tolde howere the state denies to yeelde hym
to our dispose they will not yet incense vs   60
by gievinge hym protection.   Enter Titus.

flaminivs: ere longe
I hope I shall resolue you. to my wishe
heere comes my trew discoverer. bee briefe,
& labour not with circumstance to indeere
the service thou hast donne mee.

Titus: as your lordship   65
coɱanded mee in this Carthaginian habit
I made my first approches, and deliverd
the golde was giun mee as a private present
sent from the lord Amilcar, for his viaticum
to another cuntrie. for I did pretende   70
I was his mæniall servant.

flaminivs: very well.

---

60. *In l.h. margin, Knight writes* Ent: Titus: / R. Baxt: 61 SD. Enter Titus.]
MS; *deleted by Knight*   62. resolue] *Croker*; re⟨s   ⟩ue *MS*

(left margin) 14ᵛ

Titus:
    'twas entertaind almost with sacrifice
    and I as one most welcome was admitted
    into their turbulent counsaile. many meanes
    were there propounded, whither, and to whom   75
    their kinge Antiochus (for soe they stile hym)
    shoulde flie for safetie. one vrgd to the Parthian,
    a seconde into Egipt, and a thirde
    to the Batavian. but in conclusion
    the corpulent flamen that woulde governe all,   80
    & in his nature woulde not gieue allowance
    to any proposition that was not
    the childe of his owne brayne resolud to carry
    their may game prince, coverd with a disguise
    to Prusias kinge of Bithinia. his opinion   85
    carried it, and thither without pause, or stay
    to thancke my lord for his bountie, they are gone
    vpon my certaine knowledge for I rid
    two dayes, and nights alonge that I might not builde
    vpon suppositions. by this they are   90
    at their iourneys ende.

flaminivs:
    with my thanckes [take] theres thy rewarde.
    I will take little rest vntill I haue
    sowrd his sweete entertainment. you haue bene
    in the court of this Prusias, of what temper is hee?

Lentulus:
    a well disposd, and noble gentleman,   95
    and very carefull to preserue the peace
    & quiet of his subiects.

flaminivs:
    I shall finde hym
    the apter to bee wrought on. doe you knowe whoe is
    his spetiall favorite?

Lentulus:
    one that was his tutor.   100
    a seeminge polititian, and talkes often
    the ende of his ambition is to bee
    a gentleman of Rome.

flaminivs:
    I shall fit hym, feare not
    your travayles ended. mine begins, and therefore
    [sans ceremonie] I will take my leaue   105
    formalitie of manners now is vselesse.

---

91. flaminivs] iv *altered from* us *in MS*   thy] *altered from* this *in MS*
106. formalitie . . . vselesse.] *added by Massinger after* leaue (l. 105)

                I longe to bee a horsebacke.

Lentulus: you haue my wishes
                for a faire successe.

flaminivs: my care shall not bee wantinge.   exevnt

[III. ii]   Actus tertij, scæna secunda.
                  Antiochus. the .3. marchants.

1 marchant: This tædious iourney from your maiesties
                longe discontinuance of ridinge hard
                with wearinesse hath dulld your spirits.

2 marchant: the flamen
                his corpulencie consyderd hath helde out
                beyonde imagination

3 marchant: as often   5
                as hee rodd downe a hill I did expect
                the chininge of his horse.

15ʳ Antiochus: I wonder more
                how mine sustaind his burthen. since the waight
                that sitts on my more heavie heart woulde cracke
                the sinewes of an elephant.

2 marchant: tis sayd   10
                that beast hath strength to carry syx arm'd men
                in a turret on his backe.

Antiochus: trewe but the sorrowe
                of a wretched, and forsaken kinge like mee
                is far more ponderous.

1 marchant: o part not sʳ
                from your owne strength by yeeldinge to despaire
                I am most confident Berecinthivs will   16
                from the greate kinge Prusias, in his goodnesse greate
                bringe comfort to you.

Antiochus: I am prepar'd however
                lower I cannot fall.

flourishe   3 mar: Ha! theis are signes
                of a glorious entertainment, not contempt.   Enter
                                           Berecinthivs.

III. ii. Actus . . . marchants.] *one line in MS*; *deleted by Knight, who writes in l.h. margin* Ent: Antiochus / & .3. Marchant*ę*   5–6. often / as] *Cunningham*; *undivided in MS*   18. *In l.h. margin, Knight writes* fflorish   19 SD. flourishe] *MS*; *deleted by Knight, who interlines* Ent: Berecinthi   20 SD. Enter Berecinthivs.] *MS*; *deleted by Knight*

Berecinthivs:	beare vp s^r. I haue donne you simple service, 21
	I thancke my eloquence, and boldnesse for it.
	when would a modest, silent foole effect
	what I haue donne, but such men are not borne
	for great employments. The fox that woulde confer
	with a lyon, without feare, must see hym often. 26
	o for a dozen of rubbers, and a bath
	and yet I neede noe tubbe since I drench my selfe
	in mine owne balsum.
1 marchant:	balsamum? it smells
	like a tallow chandlers shoppe.
Berecinthivs:	does it soe you thinnegut? 30
	thow thinge without moysture. but I haue noe time
	to answer thee. the greate kinge (by my meanes s^r
	ever remember that) in his owne person
	with his faire consort, and a gallant trayne
	are come to entertaine you.
[Antiochus:	Ioue yf thow art 35
	pleasd that it shall bee soe.
Berecinthivs:	change not you Ioues purpose
	in your slownesse to receaue it. in your carriage
	expresse your selfe. they come.]
Prusias:	the stronge assurance Enter Prusias.
	Queene, Philoxenus. attendants.
	you gaue at Carthage to confirme you are
	the kinge Antiochus (for soe much from 40
	my agent there I haue heard) comandes mee to
	beleeue you are soe. & however they
	awde by the Roman greatenesse durst not lende you
	aide or protection; in mee you shall finde
	a surer gard. I stande on mine owne bases: 45
	nor shall or threates, or prayers deter mee from
	doeinge a good deed in it selfe rewarded.
	you are welcome to my bosome.
Antiochus:	all that yet
	I can returne [is] you s^r is thanckes, expre'sd

---

37. *In l.h. margin, Knight writes* fflorish *and deletes a second* fflorish *beneath it. In r.h. margin, Knight writes* Ent: Prusius: Queene / Philoxenes: Rowl: Wm Mag⟨o⟩ / m^r Balls: Nick: & Lady: 38 SD. Enter . . . attendants.] *MS reads* Enter . . . Philoxenus. / attendants. *Knight deletes this SD.*

	in teares of ioy, to find heere that compassion	50
	hath not forsooke the earth.	
Queene:	alas good kinge	
	I pittie hym.	
Prusias:	this ladye s^r your servant	
	presents her dutye to you.	
. . . Antiochus:	pray you forgieue mee	
	callamitie my to longe rude companion	
	hath taught mee gratious madam to forget	55
	civilitie, & manners.	
Queene:	I nere touchd	
	but the kinge my husbands lipps, & as I liue	
	hee kisses very like hym.	
Prusias:	heere is one	
	I dare present to you for a knoweinge man	
	in politicꝗ designes but hee is present	60
	I shoulde say more els.	
. . . Antiochus:	your assistance s^r	
	to rayse a [k] trod downe kinge will well become you	
Philoxenus:	what man can doe that is familiar with	
	the [d] deepe directions of [Xemophon] Xenophon,	
	or Aristotles politicꝗs, besides	65
	mine owne collections, wch some prefer	
	& with good reason as they say before em.	
	your highnes may expecte	
Prusias:	wee will at leasure	
	consyder of the manner, and the meanes	
	how to restore you to your owne.	
Queene:	& till then	70
	suppose your selfe in your owne court.	
Antiochus:	the gods	
	bee sureties for the payment of this debt	
flourishe	I stande ingagde. your bounties overwhelme mee.	

15^v

exevnt. Prusias. Antiochus Queene.
Philoxenus attendants.

| Berec: | I marrie this is as it shoulde bee. ha? |

64. Xemophon] X *altered from* x *in MS*   65. Aristotles] A *altered from* a *in MS*
70. Queene] u *altered from* e *in MS*   73 SD. flourishe] *MS*; *Knight writes* fflorish:
on top of Massinger's direction   exevnt . . . attendants.] *MS reads* exevnt . . .
Antiochus / Queene. Philoxenus / attendants.

after theis stormes raysde by this Roman divell   75
Titus flaminivs, you knowe whom I meane
are wee got into the port once. I must purge.

1 marchant: not without cause.

Berecinthivs: or my increasinge bellie
will metamorphose mee into the [shape] shape
of a greate tortoyse, and I shall appeare   80
a cypher, a rounde man, or what you will
now ieere at my bulke, and spare not.

1 marchant: you are pleasant.

Berecinthivs: farce thy leane ribbes with hope, and thow wilt
                   growe to
another kinde of creature. when our kinge is
restor'd, let mee consyder, as hee must bee   85
and I the principall meanes, Ile first growe rich,
infinite rich, and builde a strange newe temple
to the goddesse that I worship, and soe binde her
to prosper all my purposes.

2 marchant: bee not rapd soe.

Berecinthivs: prethee doe not trouble mee. first I will expell   90
the Romans out of Asia. and soe breakinge
their reputation in the worlde, wee will
renewe our league wth Carthage. then drawe [in]to
our partye, the Ægiptian Ptolomee,
and greate Arsaces issue. I will bee   95
the Generall, and marche to Rome, wch taken
Ile fill prowd Tiber with the carkases
of men, woemen, & children. doe not persuade mee
Ile showe noe mercie.

3 marchant: haue the power to hurt first.

Berecinthivs: then by the senators whom Ile vse as horses,   100
I will bee drawne in a chariot made for my bulke
in trivmph to the Capitoll more admir'd
then Bacchus was in India. Titus flaminivs
our enemie lead like a dogge in a chaine
as I descende, or reascende in state   105
shall serue for my footestoole. [I will coniure hym

---

79. the shape] sha *altered from* sla *in MS*   97. Tiber] T *altered from* t *in MS*
101. chariot] o *altered from* t *in MS*   105. *In l.h. margin, Knight writes* Ent:
fflaminius / & R: Baxter:

yf revenge hath any spells.]

flaminivs: comande the Captaine   Enter flaminivs. &
                                                        Demetrivs.
                to waite mee with his galley at the next port
                I am confident I shall fraught hym. exit Demetrivs.

1 marchant: you are coniuringe
                & see what you haue raysde.

Berecinthivs: Cybele saue mee.   110
                I doe not feare thee Pluto thowgh thou hast
16ʳ   assum'd a shape not to bee matchde in Cocytus.
                why dost thou followe mee?

flaminivs: art thow mad?

Berecinthivs: thow comest
                to make mee soe. how my iellie quakes! avant
                what haue I to doe with thee.

flaminivs: you shall know at leasure.   115
                the time is nowe to pretious.   exit flaminivs.

Berecyⁿᵗ: 'tis vanish'd.
                sure 'twas an apparition

1 marchant: I feare
                a fatall one to vs.

2 marchant: wee may easilie ghesse at
                the cause that bringes hym hither.

3 marchant: now yf ever
                confirme the kinge.

1 marchant: against this batterie   120
                new workes are to bee raysd, or wee are ruinde.

Berecinthivs: what thincke you of this rampire? 'twill holde out,
                and hee shall shoote throwgh, and throwgh it but
                    Ile crosse hym.   exevnt.

[III. iii]   Actus tertij scæna tertia.
                            flaminivs. Philoxenus.

flaminivs: what wee haue sayd the Consulls will make good
                and the glad senate ratefie.

Philoxenus: they haue soe

107 SD. Enter . . . Demetrivs.] *MS reads* Enter . . . & / Demetrivs. *Knight prefixes*
Titus: *to* Demetrivs. *and then deletes the whole* S D.   123. crosse] r *altered, prob-
ably from* o *in MS*   III. iii. Actus . . . Philoxenus.] *one line in MS. Knight deletes*
Massinger's *heading, and writes in the l.h. margin* Ent: fflaminius / & Philoxenus

obligde mee for this favor, that there is not
a service of that difficultie from w^{ch}
I woulde decline. in this rest confident   5
I am your owne, and sure.

flaminivs: you shall doe s^r
a noble office in it. and however
wee thancke you for the courtesie, the profit
& certaine honors, the worldes terror Rome
in thanckefulnesse cannot but shower vpon you,   10
are whoelye yours. how happie I esteeme
my selfe in this imployment to meete with
a wise, and provident statesman.

Philoxenus: my good lord.

flaminivs: I flatter not in speakinge truth. you are soe
& in this prompt alacritie, confirme it.   15
since a wise forecast in the managing
worldlye affaires is the trewe wisdome, rashnesse
the schoolemistrisse of idiots. you well knowe
charitie begins at home, and that wee are
neerest vnto our selves. fooles builde vpon   20
imaginarie hopes, but wisemen ever
on reall certainties. a tender conscience
like a gloweworme showes a seeminge fire in
    darkenesse,
but set neere to the glorious light of honor
it is invisible. as you are a statseman,   25
and a master in that art, you must remoue
all rubbs (thowgh[g] with a little wronge, sometimes)
that may put by the bias of your counsailes,
from the faire marke they aime at.

Philoxenus: you are read well
in worldlye passages.

flaminivs: I barter with you   30
such trifles as I haue. but yf you pleasde
you could instruct mee, that Philosophie,
and policie in states are not such strangers
as men ore curious and precise would haue em.
but to the poynt. with speede get mee accesse   35

---

16. managing] *Knight*; managine *Massinger*   27. *Massinger's brackets delete and*
replace commas

	to the kinge your pupil, and tis well for hym
	that Hee hath such a tutor. rich Bithinia

16ᵛ

was never soe indebted to a patriot,
& vigilant watchman for her peace, and safetie
as to your selfe.

Philoxenus: without boast[e]e I may whisper   40
I haue donne somethinge that way.

flaminivs: all, in all.
fame fillinge her lowde trompe with truth proclaimes
it.
but when it shall bee vnderstood you are
the principall meanes, by wᶜh a dangerous serpent
warmde in your soveraignes bosome, is deliverd, 45
to haue his stinge, and venemous teeth pulld out
and the ruine in a willinge grant avoyded,
wᶜh in detayninge hym falls on the kingedome
not Prusias alone, but his sau'd people
will rayse your providence altars

Philoxenus: let mee intreate   50
your pacyence some few minutes, Ile bringe the kinge
in person to you.

flaminivs: doe, and this effected
thincke of the ringe you are priveledgde to weare
when a Roman gentleman, and after that
of provinces, and purple. I must smile now   55
                        exit Philoxenus.
in my consideration, with what glibnesse
my flatteries oyld with hopes of future greatenesse
are swallow'd by this dull pate. but it is not
worth 'thobservation. most of our seeminge statse-
men
are cought in the same [nooze] nooze. retur'nd soe
      soone   Enter Prusias, & Philoxenus.
& the kinge with hym? but his angrie forhead   61
furrow'd with frownes, noe matter I am for hym.

46. out] *MS*; ∼; *corrector*   48. kingedome] *MS*; ∼. *corrector*   50. altars]
MS; ∼. *corrector*   52. effected] *MS*; ∼, *corrector*   56. glibnesse] *MS*; ∼,
corrector   60. same nooze] z *altered from* s *in MS*   60 SD. Enter . . . Philoxenus.] *MS, which reads* Enter . . . & / Philoxenus. *Knight deletes Massinger's direction,
and writes in the l.h. margin between ll. 58 and 59* Ent: Prusius / & Philoxenus:

Prusias: from the people of Rome? soe quicke! hath hee
       brought with hym
    letters of credence, and authoritie,
    to treate with vs?

Philoxenus: I read em.

Prusias: what can hee   65
    propounde, wch I must feare to heare? I woulde
    continewe in faire tearmes with that warlike nation,
    ever provided I wronge not my selfe
    in the least poynt of honor.

Philoxenus: to the full
    Hee will instructe your maiestie.

flaminivs: soe may   70
    fælicitie as a page attende your person
    as you embrace the freindly counsaile sent you
    from the Roman senate.

Prusias: with my thanckes to you
    their instrument, yf the advice bee such
    as by this preparation you would haue mee   75
    conceaue it is, I shall (and 'twill become mee)
    receaue it as a favour.

flaminivs: know then Rome
    in her pious care, that you may still increase
    the happinesse you liue in; and your subiectes
    vnder the shadowe of their owne vines eate   80
    the fruite they yeeld 'em; their soft musicall feasts
    continewinge, as they doe yet, vnaffrighted
    with the harsh noyse of war, intreates as low
    as her knowne power and maiestie can descende
    you woulde returne with due æqualitie   85
    a willingenes to preserue what shee hath conquer'd
    from change, and innovation.

Prusias: I attempt not
    to trouble her nor ever will

7^r flaminivs: fix there
    or yf for your owne good you will moue farther
    make Rome your thanckefull debtor by surrendringe
    into her handes the false impostor that   91
    seekes to disturbe her quiet.

      76. *Massinger's first bracket is written over a comma*

Prusias: this I loo'kd for
                 & that I shoulde finde mortall poyson wrapde vp
                 in your candied pills. must I because you say soe
                 beleeue, that this most miserable kinge is   95
                 a false affronter? whoe with arguments
                 vnanswerable & meere miraculous proofes
                 confirmes hym selfe the trewe Antiochus.
                 or is it not sufficient that you Romans
                 in your vnsatisfied ambition haue   100
                 seasd with an vniust gripe on halfe the worlde,
                 wch you call conquest, yf that I consent not
                 to haue my innocence soylde with that pollution,
                 you are willingelye smeard ore with.

flaminivs: pray you heare mee.

Prusias: I will bee first heard. shall I for your endes   105
                 infringe my princelye word? or breake the lawes
                 of hospitalitie? defeate my selfe
                 of the certaine honor to restore a kinge
                 vnto his owne? and what you Romans haue
                 extorted, and keepe from hym? far bee it from mee
                 I will not buy your amitie at such losse.   111
                 soe it bee to all after times remembred
                 I held it not sufficient to liue
                 as one borne only for my selfe, and I
                 desire noe other monument.

flaminivs   I grant   115
                 it is a spetious thinge to leaue behinde vs
                 a faire report, thowgh in the other world
                 wee haue noe feelinge of it, & to lende
                 a desperate, thowgh fruitlesse ayde, to such
                 as fate not to bee alterd hath markd out   120
                 examples of callamitie, may appeare
                 a glorious ornament, but heer's a man
                 the oracle of your kingedome that can tell you
                 when there's noe probabilitie it may be
                 effected 'tis meere madnesse to attempt it.   125

Philoxenus: a trewe position

flaminivs: your inclination

---

124. be] *Knight; omitted Massinger*   125. attempt] *final* t *altered, probably from*
e *in MS*

is honorable but your power deficient
to put your purposes into act.

Prusias: my power?
flaminivs: is not to bee disputed yf waighd truelye
with the pettie kinges your neighbours but when
   ballancd   130
with the globes, and scepters of my mistris Rome
will but I spare comparisons. but you builde on
your strength to iustefie the fact. alas
it is a feoble reede, & leaninge on it
will wounde your hande much sooner then support
   you.   135
you keepe in pay tis true some peace traynd troopes
wch awe your neighbours but consyder when
our egles shall display their sayle stretchde winges
hoveringe ore our legions, what defence
can you expecte from yours?

Philoxenus: vrge that poynt home.   140
flaminivs: our olde victorious bandes are ever readie,
and such as are not our confæderates, tremble
to thincke where next the storme shall fall with
   horror.
Philoxenus knowes it. will you to helpe one
you shoulde contemne, and is not worth your pittie
pull it on your owne head? your neighbour Carthage
would smile to see your error. let mee paynt   147
the danger to you ere it come, imagine
our legions, and th'auxiliarie forces
of such [such] as are our freinds, and tributaries   150
drawne vp, Bithinia cover'd with our [troopes]
   armies.
all places promisinge defence blockde vp
with our armd troopes; the siege continewinge;
famine within, and force without disablinge
all opposition; then the armie enter'd   155
(as victorie is insolent) the rapes
of virgins, and graue matrons; reverend old men
with their last grones accusinge you, your cittie,
and pallace sackd.

150. such such] *Knight deletes the second* such

Philoxenus: deere s^r

flaminivs: and you your selfe
                captiude, and after that chainde by the necke,   160
                your matchlesse queene, your children, officers
                    freindes
                waitinge as scornes of fortune to gieue lustre
                to the victors trivmph.

Philoxenus: I am in a fever
                to thincke vppon 't.

flaminivs: as a freinde I haue deliverd
                and more then my comission warrants mee   165
                [and more then my] this caution to you. but now
                    peace, or war,
                yf the first, I entertaine it, yf the later
                Ile instantlye defie you.

Philoxenus: pray you say peace s^r.

Prusias: on what conditions?

flaminivs: the deliverie
                of this seductor, & his complices   170
                on noe tearmes els, & suddainelye

Prusias: how can I
                dispense with my faith gieven.

Philoxenus: Ile yeelde you reasons.

Prusias: let it bee peace then oh. pray you call in
                the wretched man. in the meane time I'le consyder
                how to excuse my selfe.   exit Philoxenus.

flaminivs: while I in silence   175
                trivmphe in my successe, and meditate
                on the reward that crownes it. a stronge armie
                coulde haue donne noe more, then I alone, and with
                a little breath haue effected.   Enter Antiochus.
                        Queene. Philoxenus. Berecinthivs the
                        3 marchants. Demetrius. attendants.

Antiochus: goodnesse garde mee
                whom doe I look on. s^r come further from hym.   180
                hee is infectious; soe swolne with mischiefes
                and strange impieties; his language to

164. vppon] *second* p *altered from* o *in MS*   178. *In l.h. margin,* Knight *writes*
Ent: Antiochus: / Queene: Philoxenes: / Berecinth: 3: March^tę: / R: Baxt: / &
Atten^tę   179 SD. Enter ... attendants.] *MS reads* Enter ... Queene. / Philoxenus.
Berecinthivs / the 3 marchants. / Demetrius. attendants.

soe full of siren sorceries, yf you heare hym
there is noe touch of morall honestie
though rampierd in your soule but will flie from you.
the mandrakes shrieks, the Aspicqs deadly tooth
the teares of crocodiles, or the Basiliskes eie   187
kill not soe soone nor with that violence
as Hee whoe in his cruell nature holds
antipathie with mercie.

Prusias: I am sorrie.   190

Antiochus: sorrie? for what, that you had an intent
to bee a good, and iust prince? are compassion,
and charitie growne crimes?

Prusias: the gods can witnesse
how much I woulde doe for you. and but that
necessitie of state.

Antiochus: make not the gods   195
guiltie of your breach of faith, from them you
     finde not
trecherie comanded, and the state that seekes
strength from disloyaltie, in the quickesands w^ch
shee trusteth in is swallow'd. 'tis in vaine
to argue with you. yf I am condemnde   200
defences come to late. what doe you purpose
shall fall on poore Antiochus?

Prusias: for my
securitie, there beeinge noe meanes left els,
against my will I must deliver you

Antiochus: to whom?

Prusias: to Romes embassador.

Antiochus: o the furies!   205
exceede not hym in crueltie. remember
I am a kinge. your royall ghest. your right hande
the pawne, and pledge, that should defende mee from
my bloodie enemie. did you accuse
the Carthaginian Senate for denijnge   210
ayde, and protection to mee, gievinge hope
to my despairinge fortunes? or but now
rayse mee to make my fall more terrible?

18^r

197. trecherie] *first* r *altered, probably from* h *in MS*   203. *In l.h. margin, Knight*
writes Ent: Garde   209. my] m *altered from* a *in MS*

did you tax them of weakenesse, and will you
soe far transcende them in a coward feare   215
declaimde against by your owne mouth? o s^r
yf you dare not gieue mee harbor, set mee safe yet
in any desert, where this serpents hisses
may not bee heard, and to the gods Ile speake you
a prince both wise, and honorable.

Prusias: alas,   220
it is not in my power.

Antiochus: as an impostor
take of my head then, at the least soe far
proue merciefull; or with any torture ease mee
of the burthen of a life, rather then yeelde mee
to this politicꝗ state hangeman.

flaminivs: this to mee is   225
a kind of ravishinge musicꝗ.

Queene: I haue liu'd
for many yeares s^r your obedient handmayde,
nor ever in a sillable presum'd
to crosse your purposes: but now with a sorrow
(as greate almost as this poore kinges) behouldinge
your povertie of spirit (for it does   231
deserue noe better name) I must put of
obsequiousnesse, and silence, and take to mee
the warrant, and authoritie of [a wife] your Queene
and as such gieue you counsaile.

Prusias: you displease mee.   235

Queene: the phisicꝗ promisinge health is ever bitter.
Heare mee. will you that are a man, nay more
a kinge of men, doe that, forcd to it by feare
wch coṁon men woulde scorne? I am a woman,
a weake, and feoble woman, yet before   240
I woulde deliver vp my bondewoman
and haue it tolde I did it by constraynt
I would endure to haue theis hands cut of,
theis eies pull'd out.

Prusias: Ile heare noe more.

---

219. heard] e *altered, probably from* a *in MS*   220-1. alas, / it] *Cunningham*;
undivided MS   243. endure] en *altered from* in *in MS*   244. theis eies]
Collier; theis *MS*

Queene:	doe you then
	as a kinge shoulde.
Prusias:	away with her.
flaminivs:	my affaires they beare of the Queene.
	exacte a quicke despatch.
Prusias:	Hee's yours. conceaue 246

	what I would say. farwell exevnt. Prusias
	& Philoxenus.
Antiochus:	that I had bene
	borne dumbe. I will not grace thy trivmph tyranne.
	with one request of favour. exit Antiochus garded
Berecinthivs:	my good Lord.
flaminivs:	your will deere flamen?
Berecinthivs:	I perceaue you are like 250
	to drawe a greate charge vpon you. my fat bulke,
	and theis my lyons will not bee kepd for a little
	nor woulde wee bee chargeable, and therefore
	kissinge
	your honor'd handes I take my leaue.
flaminivs:	by noe meanes
	I haue bene busie, but I shall finde leasure 255
	to treate with you in another place.
Berecinthivs:	I woulde not
	put your lordship to the trouble.
flaminivs:	it will bee
	a pleasure rather. bringe em all away.
Berecinthivs:	the comfort is. whither I drowne, or hange
	I shall not bee longe about it. Ile preserue 260
	the dignitie of my famelie.
flaminivs:	'twill become you. the ende of the thirde Acte.

Actus quarti, scæna prima.

[Sempronivs.] A metellus a procunsul of [Lusitania]. Sempronivs
a Centurion.

metellus:	A revolt in Asia?
Sempronivs:	yes on the report

248. dumbe] b *altered from* e *in MS*   trivmph] *altered from* trumph *in MS*
254. *In l.h.margin, Knight writes* Ent: Garde: 255. bene] ne *altered from* nn *in MS*
IV. i. Actus . . . Centurion.] *one line in MS*.   Sempronivs.] Sem *altered from* A
m *in MS*   Centurion] Cen *altered from* Cap *in MS*   *In l.h. margin, Knight*
writes long Act: 4: / Ent: Metelus: / & Sempronius: / 2 / chaires / set out

the longe thowght dead Antiochus liues.

metellus: I heard [such]
such a one appear'd in Carthage but suppresde
by Titus flaminiυs my noble freinde.
[Hee] whoe by his letters promisd mee a visit,   5
yf his designes as I desire they may
succeeded to his wishes.

Semproniυs: till [hee arriue] you behoulde hym
I can bringe your honor yf you please, where you
may finde faire entertainment.

metellus: from whom captaine?

Semproniυs: a new riggd pinnace that put of from Corinth,   10
and is arriud amonge vs, tite, and yare
nor comes shee to pay custome for her fraught
but to impose a tax on such as dare
presume to looke on her, wᶜh [the] smocke gamsters
offer
sooner then shee demandes it.

metellus: some freshe courtezan   15
vpon mine honor.

Semproniυs: you are i'the right my lord.

metellus: & there lies your intelligence.

Semproniυs: true my good lord
'tis a discoverie will not shame a Captaine
when hee lies in garrison. since I was a trader
in such com̃odities, I never saw   20
her equall, I was ravishd with the obiect
& woulde you visit her I beleeue you woulde write
[my] your selfe of my opinion.

metellus: fye vpon thee
I am olde.

Semproniυs: and therefore haue the greater vse
of such a cordiall. all medeas drugges   25
and her charmes to boote that made old Æson younge
were nothinge to her touch. your viper wine
soe much in practise with gray bearded gallants

---

5. whoe . . . letters] *interlined above a caret before* Hee *in MS*   5–6. visit, / yf]
Cunningham; undivided MS   9. faire] i *altered from* r *in MS*   21. equall] e
altered from æ *in MS*   26. *In l.h. margin, Knight writes* Gascoine: & / Hubert /
below: / ready to open / the Trap / doore for / Mʳ Taylor

	but vappa to the nectar of her lippe.
	shee hath donne miracles since shee came. a vsurer
	full of the gowte, and more diseases then 31
	his crowches coulde support, vsd her rare phisicqȝ
	but one short night, and risinge in the morninge
	Hee dancde a lavolta.
9ʳ metellus:	prethee leaue thy foolinge
	& talke of somethinge els.
Sempronivs:	the whole world yeeldes not 35
	apter discourse. shee hath all the qualities
	conducinge to the sport; singes like a Syren;
	dances, as the grosse element of earth
	had noe part in her; her discourse soe full
	of eloquence & prevailinge, there is nothinge 40
	shee askes to bee denid her. had shee desir'd
	my captaines place I had cashierd my selfe
	and shoulde shee begge your procunsulship, yf you
	heard her
	'twere hers vpon my life.
metellus:	shee shoulde bee damnde first Enter flaminivs
	and her whole tribe. my lord flaminivs welcome 45
	I haue longe bene full of expectation
	of your greate designe, and hope a faire successe
	hath crownd your travaile, in your bringeinge in
	this dangerous impostor
flaminivs:	at the length
	I haue hym, and his complices.
metellus:	Ile not, now 50
	inquire how you atchieud hym, but woulde know
	since 'tis refer'd to you what punnishement
	shall fall vpon hym.
flaminivs:	yf you please in private
	I will acquaint you
metellus:	Captaine let mee intreate you
	to meditate on your woman in the next roome 55
	wee may haue imployment for you.
Sempronivs:	I had rather

43. *In l.h. margin, Knight writes* Ent: fflaminius   44 SD. Enter flaminivs] fla
altered from De *in MS. Knight interlines* fflaminius *above a caret after* Enter, *then deletes
his own and Massinger's direction*

	shee woulde cõmande my service.	
metellus:	pray you sit.	
flaminivs:	now my good lord I aske your graue advice	
	what course to take.	
metellus:	that in my iudgement needes not	
	longe consultation. Hee is a traytor	60
	and his processe framd must as a traytor suffer	
	a death due to his treason.	
flaminivs:	theres much more	
	to bee considerd. there beeinge a beleefe	
	dispersde almost throwgh Asia that hee is	
	the trewe Antiochus, & wee must decline	65
	the certaine scandall it will drawe vpon	
	the Roman governement, yf hee dye the man	
	Hee is by the most receaud to bee, and therefore	
	till that opinion bee remoud, wee must	
	vse some quaint practise that may worke vpon	70
	his hopes or feares to drawe a free confession	
	that hee was subornde to take on hym the name	
	Hee still maintaines.	
metellus:	that torture will wrest from hym	
	I knowe noe readier way.	
flaminivs:	yf you had seene	
	his carriage in Carthage and Bithinia	75
	you woulde not thincke soe. since I had hym in	
	my power I haue vsd all possible meanes that might	
	force hym into despaire & soe to doe	
	a violence on hym selfe. Hee hath not tasted	
	theis three dayes any sustenance, and still	80
	continewes fastinge.	
metellus:	keepe hym to that dyet	
	some few howers more	
flaminivs:	I am of opinion rather	
	some competence offerd hym and a place of rest	
	where hee might spende the remnant of his dayes	
	in pleasure & securitie might doe more	85
	then feare of death or torture.	
metellus:	it may bee	

67. *In l.h. margin, Knghit writes* Antiochus / ready: vnder / the stage   68. the]
interlined above a caret in MS   82. more] *MS*; ∼. *corrector*

there are such natures, and now I thincke vpon't.
I can helpe you to a [po] happie instrument
to motion it. your eare.

flaminivs: 'tis wondrous well
and it may proue fortunate.

metellus: tis but a triall   90
however I will sende for her.

flaminivs: pray you doe
shee shall haue my directions.

metellus: what botches
are made in the shoppe of policie.

flaminivs: soe they cover
the nakednesse wee must conceale it skills not. exe^t

ii]   Actus quarti, scæna secunda.
                Enter Iaylor. with a poniard & halter.

Iaylor: why should I feele compunction for that
wch yeeldes mee profit ha! a prisoners teares
shoulde sooner pierce flint or Ægiptian marble
then moue vs to compassion. yet I knowe not
the sufferinges of this miserable man   5
worke strangelye on mee. some say hee is a kinge
it may bee soe, but yf they holde out thus
I am sure hee is like to dye a beggers death
and starue for hunger. I am by a servant
of the lord flaminivs strictely comanded   10
before I haue raysde hym out of the dongeon
to lay theis instruments in his viewe. to what end
I am not to enquire, but I am certaine
after his longe fast they are viands that
will hardlye bee digested. doe you heare s^r?   15

Antiochus belowe   yf thou art my deathsman welcome.

Iaylor: I soe pittie you
that I wishe I had comission [as] as you rise
to free you from all future miserie
to knocke your braines out.

Antiochus: would thou hadst

IV. ii. Actus . . . halter.] *one line in MS. Knight deletes Massinger's heading, and
writes in l.h. margin* Ent: Iaylor: w^m penn / wth poniard / & halter   16. Antiochus
belowe] *Knight writes an identical direction on top of Massinger's*

Iaylor: you haue
                 the libertie to ayre your selfe, and that   20
                 is all I can affoord you. fast, and bee merrie
                 I am els where call'd on.   exit Iaylor
Antiochus: Death as far as faintnesse
                 will gieue mee leaue to chide thee I am angrie
                 thou comest not at mee. noe attendance? famine
                 thy meagre harbinger flatters mee with hope   25
                 of thy soe wishd arrivall, yet thy cominge
                 is still deferd. why? is it in thy scorne
                 to take a lodginge heere? I am a kinge
                 and thowh I knowe the reverence that waytes
                 vpon the potent scepter, nor the gardes   30
                 of faithfull subiects; neither threates, nor prayers
                 of freinds, or kinred, nor yet walls of brasse,
                 or fire, shoulde their prowde height knocke at the
                   moone
                 can stop thy passage, when thou art resolu'd
                 to force thy entrance, yet a kinge in reason   35
                 by the will of fate severd from cõmon men
                 shoulde haue the priveledge, and prerogatiue
                 when hee is willinge to disrobe hym selfe
                 of this cobweb garment life, to haue thee readie
                                Enter metellus. flaminivs. Sempronivs. aboue
                 to doe thy fatall office. what haue wee heere?   40
                 a poniard, and a halter. from the obiects
                 I am easilie instructed to what end
                 they were prepar'd. either will serue the turne   *
                 to ease the burthen of a wretched life
20^r or thus, or thus. in death I must cõmende   45
                 the Roman courtesie. how! am I growne
                 soe cheape, and vile in their opinion that
                 I am denide an executioner?
                 will not the losse of my life quit the cost?
                 o rare frugalitie! will they force mee to   50
                 bee mine owne hangman. everie slaue that's guiltie

38. hym] y *altered from* i *in MS*   39 SD. Enter . . . aboue] *MS reads* Enter . . .
flaminivs. / Sempronivs. aboue. *Knight deletes Massinger's direction*   41. *In l.h.*
margin, Knight writes Ent: Metellus / fflaminius: & / Sempronius / (Aboue)   49. *In*
l.h. margin, Knight writes Harry: / Willson: & / Boy ready for / the song at y^e / Arras:

of crimes not to bee namde receaues such favor
by the iudges doome, and is my innocence
the oppresde innocence of a star crosde kinge
helde more contemptible. my better angell   55
thowgh wantinge power to alter fate discovers
their hellishe purposes. yes, yes, 'tis soe.
my bodies death will not suffice, they aimde at
my soules perdition, and shall I to shun
a fewe howers more of miserie betray her?   60
noe shee is free still, & shall soe returne
from whence it came, & in her purenesse trivmph
their tyrannie chainde, and fetterd.   Enter aboue
                flaminivs. metellus. Sempronivs.

flaminivs: o the divell!
                thou art weake. this will not doe.
metellus: marke how Heele stand
                the seconde Charge.
Sempronivs: the honor is reserud   Enter Iaylor. with browne
                                  bread, & a woodden dishe of water.
                for the prettie [temde] temptinge fiende I brought,
                my life on't.   66
Iaylor: Here sʳ take this thowgh course it will kill hunger
                it is your daylie pittance, yet when you please
                your comõns may bee mended.
Antiochus: Showe mee the way
Iaylor: confesse your selfe to bee a cousninge knaue   70
                the matter's feasible. but yf you will bee
                still kinge of the crickets feede on this, & liue
                you shall not say wee'[ll] starue you.   exit Iaylor.
Antiochus: stay I beseech thee.
                and take thy cruell pittie backe againe
                to hym that sent it. This is a tyrannie   75
                that does transcende all presidents! my soule
                but even now this lumpe of clay her prison
                of it selfe in the want of nourishement openinge,

---

63 SD. Enter . . . Sempronivs.] *MS reads* Enter . . . flaminivs. / metellus. Sempronivs.
Knight deletes Massinger's direction Sempronivs] v *altered from* u *in MS* 64. *In
l.h. margin, Knight writes* Ent: Iaylor / (wᵗʰ bread & water) 65 SD. Enter . . .
water.] *MS reads* Enter . . . with / browne . . . a / woodden . . . of / water. Iaylor] I
altered from i *in MS* 67. Iaylor:] *Knight; not in Massinger* 77. this] t *altered,
probably from* l *in MS*

had shooke of her sicke fethers, and prepar'd
her selfe to make a noble flight, as set   80
at libertie, and now this reparation
againe im̃ures. you for whose curious palats
the elements are ransackde looke vpon
this bill of fare, by my penurious steward
necessitie, seru'd to a famishde kinge.   85
and warnde by my example, when your tables
cracke with the waight, of deere, and far fetchd
   dainties
dispute not with heavns bounties. what shall I doe?
yf I refuse to touch, & taste these course,
& homelye Cates, I hasten my owne fate,   90
& soe with willingenes embrace a sinne
I hitherto haue fled from. noe Ile eate,
& yf at this poore rate life can continewe
I will not throwe it of.

flaminivs: I pine with envie
              to see his constancie

metellus   bid your propertie enter   95
              & vse her subtlest magiccȝ

20ᵛ Sempron: I haue alreadie
              acquainted her with her cue. the musiccȝ vshers
              Her personall appearance.   musiccȝ & a songe.

Antiochus: from what hande,
              and voice doe I receaue this charitie
              it is vnvsuall at such a feast.   100

Enter Courtezan.   but I miscall it. 'tis some newe founde engin
              mounted to batter mee. Ha.

Courtezan: yf I were not
              more harsh, and rugged in my disposition
              then thy tormentors, theis eies had outstrippd
              my tongue, & with a shower of teares had tolde you
              compassion bringes mee hither.

---

87. cracke with] *conj. Cruickshank*; cracke not with *MS*   95. metellus] *MS*;
Knight deletes Massinger's SH., and inserts Metell: 96. & vse] *Knight overwrites*
Massinger's &   *In l.h. margin, Knight writes* the Lute. strikes / & then the Songe.
In r.h. margin, Knight writes: | : Sempro : | : I haue already aquainted hir wᵗʰ hir
cue, / the musique vshers hir personall / appearance.   96. Sempron:] *Knight*; *not
in Massinger*   96–8. I . . . songe.] *MS*; *deleted by Knight*   101 SD. Enter
Courtezan.] *MS*; *Knight writes* Ent: Courtezan *on top of Massinger's SD.*

Antiochus:	that I coulde	106
	beleeue soe much (as by my miseries	
	an oth I dare not breake) I gladlye would.	
	pittie mee thinckes I knowe not how appeares	
	soe louely in you.	

Antiochus: that I coulde 106
beleeue soe much (as by my miseries
an oth I dare not breake) I gladlye would.
pittie mee thinckes I knowe not how appeares
soe louely in you.
Courtezan: It beeinge spent vpon 110
a subiect in each circumstance deservinge
an vniversall sorrowe, though 'tis simple
it cannot bee deform'd. may I presume
to kisse your royall hande, for sure you are not
lesse then a kinge.
Antiochus: haue I one witnesse livinge 115
dares only thincke soe much?
Courtezan: I doe beleeue it
& will dye in that beleefe, & nothinge more
confirmes it then your pacyence, not to bee
founde in a meaner man. not all the trimme
of the maiestie you were borne to, though set of
with pompe, and glorious lustre, showde you in
such full perfection, as at this instant 122
shines rounde about you, in your constant bearinge
your adverse fortune, a degree beyonde
all magnanimitie that ever was 125
canonisde by mankinde.
[Cou] Anti: astonishement
and wonder seases on mee. pray you what are you?
Courtezan: without your pittie neerer to the graue
then the malice of prevaylinge enemies
can hurrie you.
Antio: my pittie! I will part with 130
soe much from what I haue ingrosd to mourne
mine owne afflictions, as I freelye grant it.
will you haue mee weepe before I know the cause
in wᶜʰ I may serue you.
Courtezan: you alreadie haue
spent to much of that stocke. pray you first heare mee
and wronge not my simplicitie with doubts 136

108. would.] *corrector*; ~ₐ *MS*   116. much] c *altered from* h *in MS*   126. Cou]
Massinger writes Antio *on top of* Cou[rtezan] *before deleting the SH.*   136. doubts]
MS; ~, *corrector*

	of that I shall deliver. I am a virgin.
Sempronivs:	yf I had not toyde with her my selfe I shoulde now
	beleeue her.
Courtezan:	& though not of the Egles brood descended
	from a noble famelie.
Sempronivs:	her mother solde her
	to a Corinthian lecher at thirteene
	as 'tis reported.
metellus:	bee silent I com̃ande you.
Antio:	to bee a virgin, and soe well deriu'd
	in my opinion faire one are not thinges
	to bee lamented.
Courtezan:	yf I had not falne
	from my cleere height of chastetie I confesse it
	in my to forwarde wishes ⟨&⟩ that is
	a sinne I am guiltie of. I am in loue sʳ
	impotentlye mad in loue, and my desires
	not to bee stopp'd in their careere.
Antiochus:	with whom
	are you soe taken?
Courtezan:	with your owne deere selfe sʳ.
	beholde mee not with such a face of wonder
	it is to sad a truth. the storie of
	your most deplorable fortune at the first warmde mee
	with more then modest heates, but since I saw you
	I am all fire, and shall turne cyndars, yf
	you showe not mercie to mee.
Antiochus:	foolishe creature
	yf I coulde suppose this trew, [&met] & met your
	wishes
	with equall ardor, as I am, what shadowe
	of seeminge hope is left you to arriue at
	the port you longe for.
Courtezan:	yf you will bee good
	vnto your selfe the voiage is accomplishde.
	it is but puttinge of a poysond shirt
	wᶜʰ in the wearinge eates into your flesh,

21ʳ

140

145

150

156

160

and must against your will bee soone forc'd from
    you: 165
the malice of your enemies tendringe to you
more trew securitie and safetie then
the violence of your freindes, and servants wishes
coulde heape vpon you.

Antiochus: 'tis impossible.
cleere this darke misterie for yet to mee   170
you speake in riddles.

Courtezan: I will make it easie
to your vnderstandinge. & thus sweeten it
in the deliverie. 'tis but to disclaime
                     offers to kisse hym
with the continuall cares that waite vpon it
the title[s] of a kinge.

Antiochus: Divell. flaminivs   175
I finde you heere.   aside

Courtezan: why doe you turne away?
the counsaile that I offer, yf you please
to entertaine it, as longe wishd compagnions
in her right hand bringes libertie, & a calme
after soe many stormes. & you noe sooner   180
shall to the worlde professe you were subornde
to this imposture (though I still beleeue
it is a truth) but with a free remission
for the offence, I as your better Genivs
will lead you from this place of horror, to   185
a paradise of delight, to wch compar'd
Thessalian Tempe, or that garden where
Venus, with her reviud Adonis spende
their pleasant howers, and make from their embraces
a perpetuitie of happines   190
deserue not to bee nam'd. there in an arbor
of it selfe supported ore a bublinge springe
with purple Hiacinths, and roses cover'd
wee will inioy the sweetes of life, nor shall
Arithmeticꝗ some vp the varieties of   195
our amorous dalliance. our viandes such
as not alone shall nourishe appetite

185. from this] *written on top of* to t *in MS*

but strengthen our performance. & when call'd for
the quiristers of the ayre shall gieue vs musicꝗ;
and when wee slumber, in a pleasant dreame   200
you shall beholde the mountaines of vexations
wch you haue heapd vpon the Roman tyrannes
in your free resignation of your kingdome
& smile at their afflictions.

Antiochus: Hence you syren

21^v Courtezan: are you displeasd?

Antiochus: were all your flatteries   205
aimde at this marke? will not my vertuous anger
assisted by contempt and scorne, yeelde strength
to spurne thee from mee? but thow art some whore,
some cõmon whore, and yf thou hast a soule
(as in such creatures it is more then doubted)   210
it hath its beeinge in thy wanton væines
& will with thy expence of blood become
like that of sensuall beastes.

metellus: this will not doe.

Antiochus: How did my enemies loose themselues to thincke
a painted prostitute with her charmes coulde conquer
what malice at the height coulde not subdue.   216
is all their stocke of malice soe consumde
as out of penurie they are forcde to vse
a whore for their last agent.

Courtezan: yf thou wer'et
ten times a kinge thou liest. I am a ladie   220
a gamsome ladie of the last edition
and though I phisicꝗ noblemen, noe whore.

metellus: Hee hath touchd her freehold.

Sempronivs: now let her alone
and shee will worrye him.

Courtezan: haue I liu'd to haue
my courtesies refusde? that I had leaue   225
to plucke thy eies out [I woulde sucke the holes]
are you soe coy? thou art a man of snowe
& thy father got thee in the wane of the moone
[dieted with gourd water. o the furies!]
but scorne mee not. 'tis trew I was set on   230

205. Courtezan:] *Croker* (*Courtezan.*); ⟨ ⟩urtezan: *MS*

                    by the higher powers but now for all the wealth
                    in Asia thou shalt not haue the favour
                    though prostrate on the earth, thou wouldst implore
                      it
                    to kisse my shooestringe.

flaminivs: wee loose time my lord.

Courtezan: foh how hee stinckes. I will not weare a ragge more
                    that hee hath breathd on.   exit.

metellus: without more adoe   236
                    let hym haue his sentence.

flaminivs: dragge hym hence.

Antiochus: are you there?   enter Iaylor with others
                    nay then

flaminivs: I will not heare hym speake. my anger
                    is lost why linger you?

Antiochus: death ends all however.   exe^t

iii]   Actus quarti. scæna tertia.
    officers leadinge in [Sampayo] Berecinthivs: & the first marchant
                       with halter.

Berecinthivs: what a skelliton they haue made of mee. starue
                    mee first
                    and hange mee after. is there noe conscience extant
                    to a man of my order. they haue degraded mee,
                    tane away my lyons, and to make mee rore like em
                    they haue parde the fleshe of from my fingers ends
                    and then laughd at mee. I haue been kep'd in
                    darkenesse   6
                    theis fiue longe dayes. noe visitants but divells
                    or men in shapes more horrid cõminge at mee.
                    A chafinge dishe of coles, and a butchers knife
                    I founde set my mee. and inquiringe why?   10
                    I was tolde that I had fleshe enough of [mne]
                    mine owne

---

234. *In l.h. margin, Knight writes* Ent: Iaylor: / & others Rowl: 237 SD. enter
... others] *MS*; *deleted by Knight*   IV. iii. Actus ... halter.] *MS reads* Actus ...
first / marchant ... halter. *Knight deletes* Actus ... tertia., *and* Sampayo (*already deleted
by Massinger*). *In l.h. margin he writes* Ent: Berecinthius: / & I: Hony: R: Baxt: & /
Gard: 1. Berecinthivs:] *MS*; *deleted by Knight and rewritten* Bere: 10. in-
quiringe] q *altered, probably from* c *in MS*

                 & yf that I were hungrie, I might freelye
                 eate mine owne carbonados, & bee croniclde
                 for a Canniball never read of.

officer: will you walke s^r.

22^r Berec: I shall come to soone though I creepe to such a
                 breakefast.   15
                 I ever vsd to take my portion sittinge
                 hangeinge in the ayre 'tis not phisicall.

officer: time flies away s^r

Bercy: whie let hym flie s^r. or yf you please to stay hym
                 & [to] binde vp the balde knaues winges, make vse
                   of my collar
                 there is substance in it I can assure your worship.
                 and I thancke your wisdome that you make distinc-
                   tion   21
                 betwene mee, and this staruelinge, Hee goes to it
                 like a grayhounde for killinge of sheepe in a two-
                   penny slippe
                 but heeres a cable will waigh vp an anchor.
                 and yet yf I may haue faire play ere I dye   25
                 ten to one I shall make it cracke.

officer: what woulde you haue s^r?

Beryc: my ballace about mee I shall nere sayle well els,
                 to the other worlde. [th] my barke you see wants
                   [ballance] stowage
                 but gieue mee halfe a dozen of Hens, and a loyne
                   of veale
                 to keepe it steddie, and you may spare the trouble 30
                 of pullinge mee by the leggs, or settinge the knot
                 vnder mine eare. this drũe well bracd, defies
                 such foolishe courtesies.

1 marchant: this mirth good flamen
                 is out of season let vs thincke of Elizivm
                 yf wee dye honest men, or what wee there   35
                 shall suffer from the furies.

Berecynthivs: thow art a foole
                 to thincke there are or gods, or goddesses,
                 for the later yf that shee had any power

16. vsd] *Sisson*; vse *Croker*   27. Beryc:] y *altered from* i *in MS*   28. the]
MS; ~: *corrector*   36. Berecynthivs:] *Croker* (*Berecinthius*.); *one line lower in MS*

mine beeinge the mother of 'em would haue [helpd
    mee] helpd mee
they are thinges wee make our selves. or grant there
    shoulde bee   40
a hell or an Elizium, singe I cannot
to orphevs harpe in the one, nor dance in the other.
but yf there bee a Cerberus yf I serue not
to make three sopps for his three heades that may
    serue,
for somethinge more then an ordinarie [a] breakefast
the cur is [vengeance] Divelishe hungrie. woulde I
    had   46
ran away with your fellowe marchants, I had then
provided for my fame. yet as I am
I haue one request to make, & that my freindes
concernes my bodie wch I pray you grant   50
& then I shall dye in peace.

officer: what is it?

Berecynthivs: marrye
that you woulde bee suitors to the proconsul for mee
that noe [needie] covetous Roman after I am dead
may begge to haue my skinne flayde of, or stuffe
    [m] it
with strawe like an aligator, & then showe it   55
in faires, and markets for a monster, thowgh
I knowe the sight will draw more fooles to gape on't
then a camell or an elephant, afore hande
I tell you, yf you doe my ghost shall haunt you.

officer: you shall haue buriall feare not.

Berecinthivs: & roome enough   60
to tumble in I pray you thowgh I take vp
more graue then Alexander. I haue ill lucke
yf I stincke not as much as hee, and yeelde the wormes
as large a supper.

1 marchant: are you not mad to talke thus?

Berecynthivs: I came crijnge into the worlde, and am resolude 65
to goe out merrilie, therefore despatch mee. exevnt.

   39. haue helpd] helpd *altered from* holpe *in MS*   44. that] *interlined above a*
caret in MS   44-5. serue, / for] *Croker; undivided MS*   45. somethinge . . .
ordinarie] *interlined above a caret before* a   54. or] *altered from* and *in MS*

[IV. iv]   Actus quarti, scæna quarta.
                         metellus. flaminivs.

metellus: There was never such a constancie.
flaminivs: you gieue it
22ᵛ   to faire a name, tis foolishe obstinacie
                for wᶜh Hee shall without my pittie suffer.
                what wee doe for the service of the republicꝗ
                & propagation of Romes glorious empire   5
                needes noe defence & wee shall wronge our iudge-
                   ments
                to feele compunction for it. haue you giuen order
                accordinge to the sentence, that the impostor
                ridinge vpon an asse, his face turnd to
                the hinder part, may in derision bee   10
                brought through Calipolis.
metellus: yes. and a paper
                vpon his head, in wᶜh with capitall letters
Enter Sempronivs   his fault's inscribde, and by three trompetters
                proclaimde before hym, and that donne to haue hym
                cõmitted to the gallies. Here comes Sempronivs   15
                to whom I gaue the charge
Sempronivs: I haue performd it
                in every circumstance.
flaminivs: how doe the people
                receiue it?
Sempronivs: as an acte of crueltie
                and not of iustice. it drewe teares from all
                the sad spectators. His demeanor was   20
                in the whole progresse, worth the observation
                but one thinge most remarkeable.
metellus: what was that?
Sempronivs: when the Cittie clarke with a lowde voice read the
                cawse
                for wᶜh hee was condemnde in takinge on hym
                the name of a kinge, with a setled countenance   25
                the miserable man repli'd I am soe.
                but when hee touchd his beeinge a cheatinge Iewe

---

IV. iv. Actus . . . flaminivs.] *one line in MS. Knight deletes Massinger's heading, and writes in l.h. and r.h. margin* Ent: Metellus: / & fflaminius: 13 SD. Enter Sempronivs] *MS*; *Knight writes* Enter: Sempronius *on top of Massinger's direction*

	His pacyence mou'd with a face full of anger
	Hee boldlye sayde 'tis false. I never saw
	such magnanimitie.
flaminivs:	frontlesse impudence rather. 30
Sempronivs:	or any thinge els you please.
flaminivs:	haue you forc'd on hym
	the habit of a slaue?
Sempronivs:	yes, and in that
	pardon my weakenesse, still there does appeare
	a kinde of maiestie in hym.
flaminivs:	you looke on it
	with the eies of foolishe pittie that deceiues you. 35
Sempronivs:	this way Hee comes, and I beleeue when you see hym
	you'll bee of my opinion.
officer:	make way there. Enter officers leadinge in
	Antiochus. (his head shaude in the habit of a slaue
Antiochus:	fate! 'tis thy will it shoulde bee thus, & I
	with pacyence obey it. was there ever
	in all precedent mappes of miserie 40
	Callamitie soe drawne out to the life
	as shee appeeres in mee? in all the changes
	of fortune such a metamorphosis
	antiquitie cannot showe vs. men may read there
	of kinges depos'd, and some in trivmph [read] lead
	by the prowde insultinge Roman. yet they were 46
	acknowledgde such, and died soe. my sad fate
	is of a worse condition, and Rome
	to mee more barbarous then ere yet to any
	brought in subiection. [it] is not sufficient 50
	that the lockes of this once royall head are shau'd of,
	my glorious robes changd to this slavishe habit
	this hande that graspd a scepter manaclde,
	or that I haue bene as a spectacle
	exposde to publicꝗ scorne, yf to make perfit 55
	the cruell reckoninge I am not compelde
	to liue beyonde this, & with stripes bee forcd

23ʳ

37. officer:] *MS*; *Knight writes* wᵗʰin: officer: *on top of Massinger's direction. In l.h.*
margin below he writes Ent: Antiochus: / & Gard: 50. is] *MS*; is it *Knight*
51. once] *Sisson*; oure *Croker*   52. glorious] *Croker*; glo⟨ ⟩ious *MS*   this]
Croker; t⟨ ⟩is *MS*

	to stretch my shruncke vp sinnewes at an ore	
	in the company of theeues, and murtherers,	
	my innocence, and their guilt noe way distinguishd	
	but equall in our suffringes.	
metellus:	you may yet	61
	redeeme all, and bee happie.	
flaminivs:	but persistinge	
	in this imposture thincke but what it is	
	to liue in hell on earth, and rest assur'd	
	it is your fatall portion.	
Antiochus:	doe what you please.	65
	I am in your power but still Antiochus	
	kinge of the lower Asia, noe impostor	
	that fower, and twenty yeares since lost a battaile	
	& challenge now mine owne wch tyrannous Rome	
	with violence keepes from mee.	
flaminivs:	stoppe his mouth.	70
Antiochus:	this is the very truth, and yf I liue	
	thrice nestors yeares in torture, I will speake	
	noe other language.	
metellus:	I begin to melt.	
flaminivs:	to the galley with hym.	
Antiochus:	Every place shall bee	74
	a temple in my pænitence to mee.	exevnt

Actus quinti, scæna prima.

[V. i]

Marcellus (proconsul of Sicilie) 2. & 3 marchant.

Marcellus:	vpon your recantation this Gallerien	
	was not Antiochus you had your pardons	
	signde by the senate?	
2 marchant:	yes my lorde.	
Marcellus:	troth tell mee	
	& freelie, (I am[o] noe informer) did you	
	beleeue, and knowe hym such, or raysd that rumor	
	for private endes of your owne.	
3 marchant:	may it please your excellence	6

75. *In l.h. margin, Knight writes* Act: 5:   V. i. Actus . . . marchant.] *one line in MS. In l.h. margin, Knight writes* Ent:. *He deletes* Actus . . . prima., *inserts* wth a letter *above a caret before* proconsul, *and alters* marchant. *to* marchant: w^m Pen: Curt: / & Attend^tę: Rowland: m^r Balls: Nick:

23ᵛ

	to vnderstand, the feare of death wrought on vs
	in a kinde to turne Apostatas: besides
	havinge prou'd our testimonies coulde not helpe hym
	wee studied our safeties.
2 marchant:	a desire to 10
	of the recoverie of our [our] owne kepd from vs
	with stronge hand by his violent persecutor
	Titus flaminivs, when Hee was at Carthage
	vrg'd vs to seeke redresse, nor was it fit
	wee shoulde oppose greate Rome.
Marcellus:	in worldlye wisdome 15
	you are excusable. but.
3 marchant:	wee beseech your honor
	presse vs noe further. a letter
Marcellus:	I doe not purpose it
	doe you knowe what this containes?
2 marchant:	noe my good lord
3 marchant:	perhaps ⟨w⟩ee b⟨e ⟩ warrant for our deaths
	as 'tis sayde of Bellerophon, yet wee durst not 20
	presume to open it.
Marcellus:	'twas manners in you.
	but Ile discharge you of that feare. there is
	noe hurt intended to you.
3 marchant:	wee thancke your lordship.
Marcellus:	how is the service of flaminivs spoke of
	in Rome?
2 Marchant:	with admiration, and many 25
	divine great honors to hym.
Marcellus:	the peoples voice
	is not oraculous ever. are you sure
	the galley in wᶜh your supposd kinge [rowes] is chainde,
	was bounde for Siracusa?
3 marchant:	she is now
	in the port my lord.

8. *In l.h. margin, Knight writes* All the / swords / ready   11. our owne] our *deleted probably by Knight*   17 SD. a letter] *Croker* (A letter.); ⟩e letter *Sisson*   19. ⟨w⟩ee . . . ⟩] *MS*; wee beare a *conj. Sisson*; wee bringe a *conj. McIlwraith*; We bring the *Cunningham*   warrant] *Cunningham*; ⟨ r⟩ant *MS*   deaths] *Cunningham*; ⟨ ⟩ths *MS*   25. Marchant:] *Croker* (*Marchant.*); Marchans: *MS, altered from* Marcellus: 29. Siracusa] sa *altered from* si *in MS*

Marcellus: Titus flaminivs in her?   30
3 marchant: vpon my certaine knowledge.
Marcell: keepe your selues
     conceald 'till you are calde for. when least hop'd for,
     you shall haue iustice.
2 marchant: your honors vassalls ever.   exevnt marchants.
Marcellus: Here. Here it is apparent y^t the Poet
     wrot truth though noe proofe els coulde bee alleagd
     to make it good that though the heavens lay open   36
     to humane wishes, and the fates were bounde
     to signe what wee desire, such clowdes of error
     involue our reason, wee still begge a curse
     and not a blessinge. how many borne vnto   40
     ample possessions, & like pettie kinges
     disposinge of their vassals, sated with
     the peace, and quiet of a cuntrie life,
     carried headlonge with ambition contend
     to weare the golden fetters of imployment.   45
     presuminge there's noe happinesse but in
     the service of the state. but when they haue tri'ed
     by a sad experience the burthen of 'em,
     when 'tis not in their power at any rate
     they woulde redeeme their calm securitie   50
     morgagd in wantonesse. alas what are wee
     that governe provinces but prayes expo'sd
     to everie subtle spie. & when wee haue
     like spunges suckde in welth, wee are squeezd out
     by the rough hande of the lawe, and faylinge in   55
     one sillable of our com̃ission, with
     the losse of what wee got with toyle, wee drawe
Enter Cornelia. & a moore waitingwoman   what was our owne
           in quæstion. you come timelye
     to turne my tir'd thowghts from a sad discourse
     that I had with my selfe.
Cornelia.   I rather feare s^r 60
     I bringe an argument alonge with mee
     that will increase, not lessen such conceptions.

52. provinces] *Croker*; provines *MS*   56. *In l.h. margin, Knight writes* Ent:
Cornelia: / & a Moore Woman: 58 SD. Enter . . . waitingwoman] *MS*; *deleted*
by Knight

24ʳ

	as I founde with you.	
Marcellus:	why sweete? what's the matter?
Cornelia:	when I but name Antiochus. though I spare
	to make a briefe relation how hee died,	65
	or what Hee is yf Hee nowe liue, a sigh
	& seconded with a teare I knowe must fall
	as a due tribute to hym.
Marcellus:	wᶜh I pay
	without compulsion. but why doe you
	lance this old sore?
Cornelia:	th' occasion cõmandes it	70
	and now I woulde forget it I am forcde
	in thanckefullnesse to call to memorie
	the favours for wᶜh wee must ever owe hym.
	you had the honor in his court at Sardis
	to bee stilde his freinde, an honor Rome, and
	Carthage	75
	were rivalls for, and did deserue the envie
	of his prime mignions, and favorites.
	His naturall subiectes planted in his favour,
	or rooted vp, as your dislike or prayse
	reported 'em; the good kinge holdinge what	80
	you spake to bee oraculous, & not
	to bee disputed. His magnificent guiftes
	confirmd his trewe affection, wᶜh you were
	more wearie to receaue then hee to gieue,
	yet still hee studied newe ones.
Marcellus:	pray you noe more.	85
[Marcellus:] Cor:	O 'tis a theme sʳ I coulde ever dwell on.
	but since it does offende you, I will speake
	of what concernes my selfe. Hee did not blushe
	in the height of his fælicitie, to confesse
	fabritivs, my lord, and father, for	90
	his much lou'd kinsman, and as such obserud hym.
	you may please to remember to, when at
	the publicꝗ sacrifice made to the gods
	after a longe infection, in wᶜh
	the Asian kinges, and Queenes were his assistants,
	with what respecte, and grace Hee did receaue mee;

66. or] *Croker* (Or); ⟨ ⟩r *MS*   75. Carthage] Car *altered from* Sar[dis] *in MS*

And at a sollemne tiltinge, when hee had   97
put on the richest armor of the worlde,
smilinge Hee sayde. His wordes are still, & shall bee
writ in the tablet of my Heart. faire cousin   100
soe Hee began, & then you thought mee faire to,
since I am turnd souldier, twere a solæcisme
in the language of the war to haue noe mistrisse,
and therefore as a prosperous omen to
my vndertakings, I desire to fight   105
(soe you with willingenesse gieue suffrage to it)
vnder your gratious colours; and then looseninge
a scarfe tied to mine arme, Hee did intreate mee
to fasten it on his. o with what ioy
I did obey hym, rapd beyonde my selfe   110
in my imagination to haue
soe greate a kinge my servant.

Marcellus: you had to
some private conference.

Cornelia   & you gaue way [to't] to it
without a signe of iealousie, & dispensde with
the Roman gravitie.

Marcellus: woulde I coulde againe   115
grant you like opportunitie ⟨   ⟩
is this remembred now?

Cornelia: it does prepare
a suite I haue wch you must not denie mee
to see the man, whoe as it is reported
in the exterior parts nature hath drawne   120
as his perfit coppie. there must bee somethinge in hym
remarkeable in his resembl[inge]ance only
of kinge Antiochus features.

Marcellus: 'twas my purpose
& soe much my Cornelia, flaminivs
shall not denie vs.

flaminivs: as my dutie bindes mee   Enter [Marcellus.]
flaminivs. & Demetrivs.

24^v

102. solæcisme] læ *altered from* lic *in MS*   103. haue] h *altered from* n *in*
MS   116. opportunitie] *conj. Croker* (opport[unitie . . . but . . .]); oppor⟨ ⟩*MS*;
opportunitie but why *conj. Sisson*   121. perfit] i *altered from* e *in MS*   123. *In*
l.h. margin, Knight writes Ent: fflaminius / &: R: Baxt: 125 SD. Enter . . .
Demetrivs.] *MS*; *deleted by Knight*

	my stay here beeinge but short, I come vnsent for
	to kisse your lordships hands.
Marcellus:	I answer you 127
	in your owne language sʳ—and yet your stay here
	may bee longer then you thincke.
flaminivs:	most Hono'rd Madam
	I cannot stoope to lowe in tendringe of 130
	my humblest service.
Cornelia:	you disgrace your courtship
	in overactinge it my lord. I looke not
	for such observance
flaminivs:	I am most vnhappie
	yf that your excellence make any scruple
	of doubt you may com̃ande mee.
Cornelia:	this assurance
	gieues mee encouragement to intreate a favour 135
	in wᶜʰ my lord beeinge a suitor with mee
	I hope shall finde a grant.
flaminivs:	though all that's mine
	bee comprehended in't.
Marcellus:	your promise sʳ
	shall not soe far ingage you. In respect 140
	of some familiar passages betwene [vs]
	[and] the kinge Antiochus when hee liu'd, and vs,
	and though it needes it not, for farther proofe
	that this is an impostor, wee desire
	some conference with hym.
flaminivs:	for your satisfaction 145
	I will dispense a little with the strictnes
	of my com̃ission. sirrha will the Captaine
	to bringe hym to the proconsull.
Cornelia:	his chaines tooke of
	that I intreate to. since I woulde not looke on
	the image of a kinge, I soe much honor'd 150
	bounde like a slaue.
flaminivs:	see this greate ladies will
	bee punctuallie obeyde. **exit Demetrivs.**
Marcellus:	your wisdome sʳ

126. but] b *altered from long* s *in MS*   137. with mee] *conj. Croker* (with me);
with *MS*   148. chaines] *Knight, who writes* es *over the final* e *of Massinger's* chaine

Hath donne the state a memorable service,
in stranglinge in the birth this dreadfull monster
and though with some your cruell vsage of hym
(for soe they call your fit severitie)   156
may finde a harshe interpretation, wise men
in iudgement must applaude it.

flaminivs: such as are
selected instruments for deepe designes
as things vnworthie of em, must not feele   160
or passions, or affections. & though I knowe
the Ocean of your apprehensions needes not
the rivolet of my poore cautions, yet
bolde from my longe experience I presume
(as a symbole of my zeale, and service to you)   165
to leaue this counsayle. when you are my lord
grac'd or distasted by the state, remember
your faculties are the states, and not your owne.
and therefore haue a care the emptie soundes
of freind, or enemie sway you not beyonde   170
the limits are assignde you. wee with ease
swimme downe the [torrent] streame, but to oppose
    the torrent
is dangerous, and to goe more or lesse
then wee are warranted fatall.

Marcellus: with my thanckes
for your soe graue advice, I'le put in practise   175
on all occasions what you deliver
& studie 'em as aphorismes. in the meane time
pray you accept such entertainment as
Syracusa can present you. when the impostor
arriues, let vs haue notice. pray you walke sᵣ. exevnt.

[V. ii]

        Actus quinti scæna vltima.
        Antiochus. Captaine. souldiers.

Captaine: waite at the Pallace gate, there is noe feare now
of his escape. Ile bee my selfe his guardian
till you heare further from mee.

161. or . . . &] *conj. Sisson*; or p⟨ ss ⟩s, o⟨ ff⟩ections. & *MS*; Or fa[vour]s, or affections. *Croker*   V. ii. Actus . . . souldiers.] *one line in MS. Knight deletes Massinger's SH., and writes in l.h.margin* Ent: Antiochus: / Capᵗ: (wᵐ patt:) & / Soldiers.

Antiochus:	what new engine
	hath crueltie founde out to rayse against
	this poore demolishd rampire? it is leveld 5
	with the earth alreadie. will they trivmph in
	the ruines they haue made? or is there yet
	one masterpeece of tyrannie in store
	beyonde that I haue suffer'd? yf there bee
	a viall of affliction not pourde out yet 10
	vpon this sinfull head I am prepar'd
	and will looke on the clowde before it breake
	without astonishement. scorne mee not captaine
	as a vaine bragart, I will make this good,
	and I haue strengths to doe it. I am armd 15
	with such varieties of defensiue weapons,
	lent to mee from my passiue fortitude,
	that there's noe torment of a shape soe horrid
	can shake my constancie. where lyes the scæne now?
	thowgh the hangeings of the stage were congeald gore
	the Chorus flintye executioners 21
	and the spectators, yf it coulde bee, more
	inhumane then flaminivs, the cue gieven
	the principall actor's readie.
Captaine:	yf I durst
	I coulde shewe my compassion.
Antiochus:	take heede Captaine. 25
	pittie in Roman officers is a crime
	to bee punnishde more then murther in colde blood.
	beare vp to tell mee where I am I take it
	is noe offence.
Captaine:	you are in Syracusa
	in the court of the proconsul.
Antiochus:	whoe? Marcellus? 30
Captaine:	that noble Roman. by hym we ⟨ ⟩ e⟨ ⟩
	but to what ende I am ignorant.
Antiochus:	Ha! Hee was
	my creature! and in my prosperitie prowde
	to holde dependance of mee, though I gracd hym

---

20. hangeings] *MS, Croker*; hangeinge *Sisson*   31. hym . . .⟩] *MS*; hym you are se[nt for] *Croker*   36. *In l.h. margin, Knight writes* ⟩nt: Marcellus: / fflaminius: / Cornelia: / Moore woman: / R: Baxt: Rowl: & / others

	with the title of a freinde, and his faire ladye 35
	in courtship stilde my mistrisse. can they bee
	infected with such barbarisme, as to make mee
	a spectacle for their sport?
Captaine:	they are heere, and soone
	they will resolue you. Enter Marcellus.
	flaminivs.Cornelia.Moore woman & servants.
Marcellus:	bee reserud. and let not 39
	the meere resemblance of his shape transport you
	beyonde your selfe. though I confesse the obiect
	does much amaze mee.
Cornelia:	you impose my lord
	what I want power to beare.
Marcellus:	let my example
	though your fierce passions make war against it.
	strengthen your reason.
Antiochus:	haue you taken yet 45
	a full viewe of mee? in what part doe I
	appeare a monster?
Cornelia:	His owne voice!
Marcellus:	forbeare.
Antiochus:	though I were an impostor as this fellowe
	labours you to beleeue, you breake the lawes
	of faire humanitie in addinge to 50
	affliction at the height, and I must tell you
	the reverence you shoulde pay vnto the shape
	of kinge Antiochus may challenge pittie
	as a due debt, not scorne. wisemen preserue
	dumbe pictures of their freindes, & looke vpon em
	with feelinge, and affection, yet not holde it 56
	a foolishe superstition. but there is
	in thanckefullnesse a greater tye on you
	to showe compassion.
Marcellus:	were it possible
	thow couldst bee [Dom Seb] kinge Antiochus.
Antiochus:	what then? 60
Marcellus:	I shoulde both say and doe

39 SD. Enter . . . servants.] *MS reads* Enter . . . flaminivs. / Cornelia . . . woman / &
servants. *Knight deletes Massinger's direction*   60. Dom Seb] *deleted by Massinger
and Knight*

Antiochus:	nothinge for mee,
	(as far as my persuasion coulde prevent it)
	not suitinge with the qualitie, and condition
	of one that owes his loyaltie, to Rome.
	and since it is by the inscrutable will 65
	of fate determinde that the royalties
	of Asia must bee conferd vpon her
	for what offence I knowe not, 'tis in vaine
	for men to oppose it. you expresse my lord
	a kinde of sorrow for mee, in w^{c}h madam 70
	you seeme to bee a sharer. that you may
	haue some proofe to defende it, for your mirth sake
	Ile play the iugler, or more subtle gipsey
	& to your admiration reveale
	strange misteries to you, w^{c}h as you are Romans 75
	you must receive for cunninge trickes, but gieue
	noe farther credit to 'em.
flaminivs:	at your perill
	you may gieue hym hearinge. but to haue faith in
	hym
	neighbours on treason. such an impudent slaue
	was never reade of.
Marcellus:	I dare stande his charmes 80
	with open eares. speake on.
Antiochus:	yf soe haue at you
	Can you call to your memorie when you were
	at Sardis with Antiochus, before
	His Græcian expedition, what Hee
	with his owne handes presented you, as a favour 85
	noe third man by to witnesse it?
Marcellus:	gieue mee leaue
	to recollecte my selfe. yes—sure 'twas soe.
	Hee gaue mee a faire sworde.
Antiochus:	'tis trewe, and you
	vowd never to part from it. is it still
	in your possession?
Marcellus:	the same sword I haue 90

61. mee,] *editor*; ∼., *MS*; ∼. *Croker*   77. 'em.] *altered from* 'em? *in MS*
78. may gieue] *Croker* (ma[y g]ieve); m⟨   ⟩ieue *MS*   79. neighbours on treason]
conj. McIlwraith; neighb⟨o   ⟩tre⟨ s   ⟩. *MS*; Neighbo[urs to] treason *Croker*

	and while I liue will keepe.
Antiochus:	will you not say
	it beeinge fower and twentye yeares since you
	were master of that guift, yf now I knowe it
	amonge a thousande others, that I haue
	the art of memorie?
Marcellus:	I shall receaue it 95
	as noe cõmon sleight. sirrha. fetch all the swordes
	for mine owne vse in my armorie. & doe you heare?
	doe as I gieue directions.
servant:	with all care s^r. exit servant.
Antiochus:	to entertaine the time vntill your servant
	returnes. there is noe sillable that pas'de 100
	betwene you, and Antiochus, wch I coulde not
	articulatelye deliver. you must still
	bee confident that I am an impostor
	or els the tricke is nothinge.
Cornelia:	Can this bee? Enter servant with many
	swordes⟨
Antiochus:	o welcome freind. most choice & curious swordes
	but mine is not amonge em.
Marcellus:	bringe the rest. Enter another servant with
	more swordes.
Antiochus:	I this is it. this is the sword I gaue you
	before I went to Greece. bee not amazde,
	nor let this trifle purchase a beleefe
	I am Antiochus. here is one will assure you 110
	theis are but iuglinge trickes of an affronter.
flaminivs:	they are noe more. a contract's seald betwene
	the divell, and this seducer, at the price
	of his damnde soule. & his familiar Dæmon
	acquaints hym with theis passages.
Marcellus:	I knowe not 115
	but I am thunderstrooke.
Cornelia:	I can containe
	my selfe noe longer.
Antiochus:	stay deare Madam. though

103. *In l.h. margin, Knight writes* Ent: R: Baxt: / wth Swords   106 SD. Enter
. . . swordes.] *MS reads* Enter . . . servant / with . . . swordes.   *In l.h. margin, Knight*
writes Ent: Rowland / wth swords: 116. Cornelia] C *written on top of* fl *in MS*

   credulitie bee excusable in your sex,
   to take away all colour of guilt in you
   you shall haue stronger proofes. the scarfe you
    gaue mee,   120
   as a testimonie you adopted mee
   into your service I ware on mine armor
   when I fought with marcus scaurus. and mine eie
   hath on the suddaine founde a pretious iewe⟨ll ⟩
   you dainde to receaue from mee. th⟨   ⟩ 125
   wch you weare on your ⟨   ⟩

26ᵛ Cornelia: I acknowledge
   it was the ⟨k⟩inge Antiochus guift.

Antiochus: I will
   make a discoverie of a secret in it
   of wch you yet are ignorant. pray you trust it
   for kinge Antiochus sake into my handes 130
   I thancke your readines. nay drie your eies,
   you hinder els the facultie of seeinge
   the cunninge of the lapidarie. I can
   pull out the stone, & vnder it you shall finde
   my name, and cipher I then vsde ingraven. 135

Cornelia: 'tis most apparent. though I loose my life for't
   theis knees shall pay their dutye.

Antiochus: by noe meanes.
   for your owne sake bee still incredulous
   since your faith cannot saue mee. I should knowe
   this moorishe woman. yes. tis shee. thou weret 140
   one of my laundrie. & thou wast calde Zanthia
   while thou were't mine I am glad thou hast lighted
    on
   soe gratious a mistrisse.

moore: mine owne kinge !
   o let mee kisse your feete. what cursed villaines
   haue thus transformd you.

flaminivs: tis not safe my lord   145
   to suffer this.

---

  125. dainde] *Croker*; d⟨ ⟩inde *MS* th⟨] *MS*; [The *Croker* 126. on] *altered from* in *in MS* your⟨] *MS*; your sl[eeve]. *Croker* 126–7. *The l.h. margin containing the speech headings has been torn away, together with part of the text.* 126. Cornelia:] *Croker* (*Cornelia.*); *missing in MS* I acknowledge] *Croker*; I ack⟨ *MS* 127. Antiochus:] *Croker* (*Antiochus.*); *missing in MS*

Marcellus: I am turnd statue. or
                 all this is but a vision.
Antiochus: your eare madam.
                 since what I now shall say is such a secret
                 as is knowne only to your selfe, and mee
                 and must exclude a third though your owne lord
                 from beeinge of the counsaile. Havinge gaynd   151
                 accesse, and privacie with you, my hot blood
                 (noe freinde to modest purposes) prompted mee
                 with pills of poysond language, candied ore
                 with hopes of future greatenesse to attempt   155
                 the ruine of your honor. I inforc'd then
                 my power to iustefie the ill & presde you
                 with mountainous promises of loue, and service.
                 But when the buildinge of your faith, and vertue
                 began to totter, and a kinde of grant   160
                 was offerd. my then sleepinge temperance
                 began to rowze it selfe, & breakinge through
                 the obstacles of lust, when most assurde
                 to inioy a pleasant hower I let my sute fall
                 & with a gentle reprehension taxde   165
                 your forwarde pronenesse, but with many vowes
                 nere to discover it wᶜʰ heavn can witnes,
                 I haue & will keepe faithfullie.
Cornelia: this is
                 the kinge Antiochus as sure as I am
                 the daughter of my mother.
Marcellus: bee advisde   170
flaminivs: this is little lesse then treason.
Cornelia: they are traytors
                 traytors to innocence and oppresd iustice
                 that dare affirme the contrarie.
Marcellus: pray you temper
                 the vio⟨len⟩ce of your passion,
                     ⟨   ⟩ b⟨   ⟩
Cornelia: ⟨   ⟩ but expresse   175

   150. lord] *MS*; ~, *corrector*   167–8. witnes, / I] *Cunningham*; *undivided MS*
174. the] *Croker* (The); ⟨ ⟩e *MS*   ⟨. . .⟩] *MS*; I beseech you *conj. Sisson*
175. Cornelia:] *Croker* (C[or]*neli*[*a*].); ⟨C ⟩rne⟨ *MS*   but expresse] *Croker*;
bu⟨t⟩ expr⟨e ⟩se *MS*

27ʳ

your thanckefulnesse for his soe m⟨a
& labour that the senate may restore hym
vnto his owne. Ile dye els.

Antiochus: liue longe madam
to nobler, & more profitable vses
I am a fallinge structure, and desire not   180
your honors shoulde bee buried in my ruines.
let it suffice my lord you must not see
the sun yf in the policie of state
it is forbidden. with compassion
of what a miserable kinge hath suffer'd   185
preserue mee in your memorie.

[Marcellus:] flam: you stande as
this sorcerer had bewitchde you. dragge hym to
his ore, and let his waightie chaines bee doublde

Marcellus: for my sake let the poore man haue what favour
you can affoord hym.

flaminivs: sʳ you must excuse mee.   190
you haue abusde the libertie I gaue you.
but villaine you pay deere for't. I will trust
the execution of his punnishement
to noe man but my selfe. His cries, and grones
shall bee my howerlye musicȝ. soe my lord   195
I take my leaue abruptlye

Cornelia: may all plauges
that ever follow'd tyrannie pursue thee.

Marcellus: pray you stay a little.
flaminivs: on noe termes
Marcellus: yeelde soe [muc] much
to my intreaties.

flaminivs: not a minute, for
your governement.

Marcellus: I will not purchase sʳ   200
your company at such a rate. & yet
must take the boldnesse vpon mee to tell you
you must, and shall stay.

176. soe m⟨a] *MS*; soe many⟨ *Croker*; soe many favours *conj. Cunningham*
177. hym] *Croker* (h[ym]); h⟨y ⟩ *MS*   192. *In l.h. margin,* Knight *writes* Be
ready: yᵉ .2. / Marchant℮: wᵐ Pen: / Curtis: & Garde: 198. noe] *altered from*
not *in MS*

flaminivs: how ?
Marcellus: nay what is more
               as a prisoner, not a ghest. looke not soe high
               Ile humble your prowde thoughts.
flaminivs: you dare not doe this   205
               without authoritie.
Marcellus: you shall finde I haue
               sufficient warrant with detayninge you
               to take this man in to my custodie
               thowgh 'tis not in my power what ere you are
               to doe you further favour. I thus free you   210
               out of this divells pawes.
Antiochus: I take it as
               a lesseninge of my torments.
flaminivs: you shall answer
               this in another place.
Marcellus: but you shall here
               yeelde an accompt without appeale for what
               you haue alreadie donne. you may peruse⟨   ⟩the
                 letter⟩⟨   215
               shake you alreadie? doe you finde I haue
27ᵛ   ⟨   ⟩nt call in the Asian marchants.
               ⟨   ⟩rt   Enter the 2 marchants &
                                                      a garde
               ⟨   ⟩now to bee hangde
               ⟨   ⟩n hym that pitties thee.
Marcellus: your accusers
               are readie & will proue that you tooke bribes   220
               of the Carthaginian marchants, to detaine
               their lawful prize, & for your sordid endes
               abusde the trust comitted by the state
               to right their vassalls. the wise senate, as
               they will rewarde your good, and faithfull service
               cannot in iustice without punnishement   226

---

214. what] *Croker* (wha[t]); wh⟨a *MS*   215. peruse] *Cunningham*; p⟨e se⟩
MS; perose *Croker*   letter)] *the parenthesis is uncertain*   216. doe . . . haue]
Croker (doe [y]ou finde [I] have); doe ⟨y⟩ou f⟨i ⟩de ⟨I⟩ ha⟨ *MS*   217–20. *The l.h.*
margin containing the speech headings has been torn away, together with part of the text
217. ⟨   ⟩nt] *MS*; sufficient warrant *conj. Sisson*   218 SD. Enter . . . garde] *MS*
reads Enter . . . marchants / & a garde   219. Marcellus . . . accusers] *conj.*
McIlwraith; ⟨   ⟩cusers *MS*   220. are readie] *conj. McIlwraith*; ⟨ e⟩adie *MS*

       passe ore your ill. guiltinesse makes you dumbe
       but 'till that I haue leasure, and you finde
       your tongue, to prison with hym.

flaminivs: I proue to late
       as heavn is mercifull, mans crueltie   230
       never escapes vnpunnishde. exevnt with flaminivs

Antiochus: how a smile
       labours to breake forth from mee. but what is
       Romes pleasure shall bee donne with mee?

Marcellus: pray you thincke s^r
       a Roman, not your constant freinde that tells you
       you are confinde vnto the Gyaræ   235
       with a stronge garde vpon you.

Antiochus: then 'tis easie
       to prophecie I haue not longe to liue
       though the manner how I shall dye is vncertaine.
       nay weepe not since 'tis not in you to helpe mee
       theis showers of teares are fruitlesse. may my storie
       teach potentates humilitie, and instructe 241
       prowde monarchs, though they governe humane
        thinges
       a greater power does rayse, or pull downe [th]
        kinges.

       The Ende.

235. *In l.h. margin, Knight writes* Ent: Garde / (agen)   243. *In l.h. margin,*
Knight writes fflorish *Beneath the text, Herbert writes his licence* This Play, called
Beleiue / as you liste, may bee acted. this / 6. of May. 1631. / Henry Herbert.

29^r   *Epilogue:*

The end of *Epilogues*, is to Inquire
the censure of the play. or to desire
pardon for whate amisse. In his intent
the maker vowes that hee is Innocent,
& for me & my fellowes I protest   5
& you may beleeve me, wee haue donne o^r best,
& reason to wee should, but whether you
conceave wee haue wth care dischargd whate due
reste yet in supposition, you may
yf you please resolue vs, yf o^r fate this day   10
prove prosperous, & you to vouchsafe to give
some signe yor pleasure is this worke shall live,
wee will finde out new wayes for yor delight,
& to o^r powre nere faile to doe you right.

29^v Act: 1: A writing out of the booke wth a small peece of siluer
                         for m^r Swansson:
                    .3. notes for m^r pollard:
Act: 2: A writing for m^r Taylor:
Act: 3: A letter. for m^r Robinson   5
     .2. letters for m^r Lowin:
Act: 5: A letter for m^r Benfeild

    1. Act . . . writing] *Croker* ([Act 1.]—A writing); ⟨ ⟩writing *MS*   small] s
altered from p *in MS*

THE EMPEROR OF THE EAST

INTRODUCTION

(a) *Date*

The Emperor of the East was completed by 11 March 1631, when, according to Malone, Sir Henry Herbert licensed it for performance: '*The Emperor of the East*, by Philip Massinger, licensed for the King's Company.'[1] The play cannot be earlier than 1626, the publication-date of its main source, *The Holy Court* (see below). There is no reason to suppose that it was written long before it was licensed, though it is worth noting that between 11 January and 6 May 1631 Massinger was revising the rejected *Believe As You List* (see above, pp. 293–4), and that *The Unfortunate Piety* (now lost) was licensed on 13 June 1631. To write two plays and rewrite a third in five months is not impossible, but during the comparatively quiet year 1630 Massinger may well have been at work on one or more of the plays which he submitted in the first half of 1631.[2]

(b) *Sources*

The story of *The Emperor of the East* is based on episodes from Byzantine history of the fifth century concerning the marriage of the emperor Theodosius the younger with the lowly-born Athenais (421) and the subsequent conflict for power with the emperor's sister Pulcheria. Gibbon said the story of the marriage 'might be deemed an incredible romance' if it had not been verified (chapter xxxii), though he naturally refused to accept the story of the apple of discord as authentic ('fit only for the Arabian Nights'). There had been dispute about which of the many versions of the events Massinger had used (up to and including Burton's brief redaction in *The Anatomy of Melancholy*), until in 1950, by a coincidence, two

---

[1] Adams, *Herbert*, p. 33.
[2] T. W. Baldwin, in *Organization and Personnel of the Shakespearean Company*, pp. 60–1, asserts that the play was written in 1630, 'probably for the winter', and was held up by the plague until 1631; there is nothing to support this (see Bentley, iv. 781).

scholars, P. G. Phialas and J. E. Gray, independently discovered
and reported the true source.[1] This is the first part of *The Holy
Court*, published in Paris in 1626, a translation by Thomas Hawkins
from the Jesuit Nicholas Caussin's *La Cour sainte* (1624), a long,
moralizing, romantic history. The fifth book of the translation, 'The
Fortunate Piety' is the only version of the Theodosius story to bring
together certain details found in Massinger's play (see Phialas, op.
cit., p. 481), and Massinger's indebtedness to Hawkins's translation
is clinched by close verbal similarities (which are noted in the
Commentary at the appropriate points). At the same time, both
Phialas and Gray overlooked the significance of one small piece of
evidence that Massinger, as was usual with him, consulted more
than one version of a story he was dramatizing and that he was
familiar with one or more of the old chronicles.[2] At I. ii. 325-7,
Athenais says that her father, dividing his estate between his two
sons and excluding her because he foresaw she would come into
great honour, yet left her ten thousand crowns to protect her from
present wants; and it is because her brothers withhold that legacy,
as well as turn her out of doors, that she repairs to the Emperor's
court. There is nothing of this legacy in *The Holy Court*. 'It
was sayd her Father well read in the knowledge of starres, foretold
the good fortune which should happen to her, & that making his
will, he left all his wealth to two Sonnes he had . . . making no
mētion of his daughter' (p. 496). This legacy, though more modestly
put at a hundred crowns ('*C. Numismata*'), is in the earliest of the
chronicles to give the story, by John Malalas of Antioch (*c.* 491-578;
editio princeps, Oxford, 1691, pt. 2, p. 52), and is repeated by such
later writers as Zonaras, whose work, translated into French in 1583,
Koeppel earlier supposed Massinger to have used.

Massinger has also made his own departures from the traditional
story. A minor one is that Theodosius is given the fatal apple when
he is out hunting instead of when returning from church at Epiphany;
this change is part of Massinger's desanctification of the 'holy court'
described below. The major change is in the ending. Whereas in
the source Paulinus was done to death by the jealous Theodosius,

[1] P. G. Phialas, 'The Sources of Massinger's *Emperour of the East*', *PMLA*, lxv
(1950), 473-82; J. E. Gray, 'The Source of *The Emperour of the East*', *RES*, new series, i
(1950), 126-35. The editor of *PMLA* acknowledged J. E. Gray's priority of publication.
[2] J. E. Gray, op. cit., p. 135, noting that 'several minor details have been altered',
mentioned 'the introduction of further information relating to the will of Athenais's
father', but went on, 'these require no special explanation'.

and Athenais/Eudoxia went into exile, Massinger contrives that all shall remain alive and become reconciled. Theodosius is convinced of the innocence of Athenais when he has listened to her as her pretended confessor: Phialas (op. cit., p. 474) gives a long list of analogues for the device of the confessional, chiefly from *novelle*, but including Marston's *Malcontent*, IV, ii. 30–82, and Davenport's *City Nightcap* (1624), III. 24. Paulinus escapes death through the contrivance of his keeper, Philanax, who learns that his prisoner must be innocent of adultery because he is a eunuch. Here, Phialas makes the interesting comment (p. 480) that the eponym of the play's ghost-character, Favorinus (see below), was a philosopher of the second century attached to the court of Hadrian who was charged with adultery and was acquitted on the grounds that he was a eunuch.

Two episodes in the play are additional to the Byzantine story. The first is the very English episode which introduces the villains of the contemporary scene, the Informer and the Projector. No source need be sought for this, and the significance of Massinger's introducing them is discussed below. The second is the scene in which the Empiric pretends to cure Paulinus's gout (IV. iii). Isaac D'Israeli, in his *Curiosities of Literature* (1834 edn., iii. 66–7; 1866 edn., pp. 227–8), remarking that the scene bore a 'striking resemblance' to one in Molière's *Le Malade imaginaire*,[1] suggested that both authors were indebted to the *Dottore* of the *commedia dell' arte*, one of whose characteristics was to make absurd mistakes in his pretentious diction.[2] In the commentary of his unpublished edition of 1948 (Yale), P. G. Phialas rightly attributed the extraordinary prescriptions of the Empiric to the *Dictionarium Theophrasti Paracelsi*. Mr. Phialas used the version in *Fasciculus Paracelsicae Medicinae Veteris*, Frankfurt, 1581. The *Dictionarium*, compiled by G. Dorn, went into many editions, and Massinger had plenty of choice.

The Emperor of the East, especially towards the end, shows signs of tired or hasty writing, and it is obvious that Massinger often reached out to Shakespeare rather than invent for himself. *Othello*

---

[1] See Commentary at IV. iii. 47–51.

[2] P. G. Phialas in 'Massinger and the *Commedia dell' arte*', *MLN*, lxv (1950), 113–14, seems to take D'Israeli too far in suggesting the influence on Massinger of the Venetian mountebanks as described by Coryate and Jonson, and in proposing the possible influence of the performances which Nicolini and Puncteus put on to sell their nostrums, licensed by Herbert in February and March, 1631; see Bentley, iv. 781.

is put to use for Theodosius's jealousy (see IV. iv. 100–49) and a strange amalgam of *Richard II* and *Antony and Cleopatra* ekes out his later distress (see V. ii. 80–105).

When we look at Massinger's play as a whole in relation to its main source, it is clear that Massinger was not interested in invoking the pious admiration which Caussin insistently demands for his unbelievably saintly family. Perhaps Pulcheria is not presented satirically, but the results of her holy and austere government are remarkable. Theodosius, with his interest in women (II. i. 246–95), is very different from the devout pupil in the source, and the younger sisters Arcadia and Flaccilla, who in the source happily and willingly vowed their virginity to God and their lives to devotion, spend their time in the play in mutinous muttering and protest against their puritanic education (see I. ii. 104–11, III. ii. 137–61). An even more striking change in the holy court is the gratuitous introduction of the Projector, the Suburbs Minion and the Master of the Habit in the second scene. These are dwellers in court, necessary to the weaknesses of the courtiers. The men 'owe their bravery' to the Projector's financial ingenuity, the 'sportful ladies' employ the Suburbs Minion, and all are educated by the Master of the Manners in the refinements which will mark their superiority to their fellow men. Although Pulcheria roundly abuses these men and banishes them the court, it is notable that they are brought before her by the Informer, who calls himself 'her ubiquitary spirit', and who was, historically, as corrupt and detestable as the projector. Hawkins dedicated his translation to the new queen, Henrietta Maria, and his quaint suggestion that the Byzantine court might prove a model for England may have moved Massinger to introduce rather more human reality into Caussin's picture of court life and saintly up-bringing. He called his next play (now lost), *The Unfortunate Piety*, an inversion of the title of Caussin's fifth book.

(c) *Text*

The Emperor of the East was entered in the Stationers' Register on 19 November 1631:

M^r. Iohn Waterson   Entred for his Copy vnder the hands of S^r. Henry Herbert & Mr Smethwicke warden a Play booke called the Emperor of the East   vj^d.

(Register D 231; Greg, *Bibliography*, i. 40; Arber, iv. 265)

The play appeared in an edition dated 1632, printed by Thomas Harper and published by John Waterson, as THE EMPEROVR OF THE EAST. A Tragæ-Comœdie. *The Scæne Constantinople.* This edition will be referred to as *32*; the title-page is reproduced on page 401. *32* is in quarto, A–M⁴ (48 leaves); see Greg, *Bibliography*, no. 459 (ii. 608). The contents are: A1ʳ, *title*; A1ᵛ, '*The* ACTORS *names.*'; A2ʳ, *dedication begins*, 'TO THE RIGHT HONORABLE, AND MY especiall good Lord, IOHN Lord MOHVNE, Baron of *Okehampton, &c.*'; A2ᵛ, *dedication ends, running-title 'The Epistle Dedicatorie.*', *signed* 'PHILIP MASSINGER.'; A3ʳ, *verse epistle*, 'To my worthy Friend, Mʳ. PHILIP MASSINGER . . .'; A3ᵛ, *verse epistle ends, signed* 'Aston Cokaine:', *second verse epistle, headed* 'A friend to the Author . . .' *and signed* 'Iohn Clauell.', *third verse epistle begins*, 'To my true friend, and Kinsman: . . .'; A4ʳ, *verse epistle ends, signed* 'William Singleton.', 'Prologue at the Blackfriers.' *begins*; A4ᵛ, *first prologue ends, followed by* 'Prologue at Court.'; B1ʳ, 'The Emperour of the East. *The Scæne Constantinople.*', *text begins*; M3ʳ, *text ends*, 'THE END.'; M3ᵛ, 'EPILOGVE.'; M4 *blank*. The text is in roman, 20 lines measuring approximately 80 mm. There are generally 37 lines to a page, but D1ʳ and H4ʳ have 36, E4ʳ has 35, and M1ʳ has 34.

Three skeletons were used in the printing; they were used in sequence as far as the inner forme of sheet G, after which the sequence becomes erratic; the third skeleton was unlocked and repositioned between its use for inner G and outer I. The full sequence is as follows (commencing with sheet B and placing the inner forme of each sheet before the outer): 1 2: 1 2: 3 1: 2 3: 1 2: 3 1: 1 2: 2 3b: 2 1: 3b 1: ? ?. The play as a whole is well printed. A simple variation in spelling-patterns shows that two compositors worked on the play. Compositor A preferred *-e* in *he, she* etc., and final *-y*; Compositor B preferred *-ee* and he mixed *-y* and *-ie*. In stage-directions, A generally put speakers' names in italics, B in roman. For the first six sheets, B–G, the two compositors alternated, and the shares show that the copy had not been cast-off by formes.[1] From sheet H to the end, it appears that compositor B set the whole work.

McIlwraith found press-corrections in eleven out of the 24 formes. Some of these introduce new readings (e.g. *feare* for *care* at I. ii. 291) and the most important of them provide strong evidence

---

[1] A set B1ʳ, B3ʳ, B3ᵛ, C3ʳ, C3ᵛ, D2ʳ, D4ᵛ, E3ᵛ, E4ʳ, E4ᵛ, F2ᵛ–4ᵛ, C2ʳ–3ᵛ. D1ʳ and D1ᵛ are indeterminate. B set the remainder, 27 pages to A's 19.

that Massinger visited the printing-house during the printing of the play; the ghost-character Favorinus (see below) disappears in the corrected sheets, being replaced by Paulinus, the metre at III. iii. 24 being preserved by reading 'good *Paulinus*' instead of '*Fauorinus*'.

The copy for *32* was probably in Massinger's own hand: a number of his spellings are scattered among more regular forms of the same words in pages set by both compositors, *e.g. thincke, ranck, sownde, prowde, gowte, hower, ghesse, ghest, waight*. His habit of grouping characters at the beginning of a scene without 'Enter' and separating the names by full-stops is found a number of times.

The stage-directions, which are full and interesting, are characteristic of Massinger's concern for detail. They contain indications for gesture and expression, e.g. '*Wringing her hands.*'; '*Pulcheria appeares troubled.*'; for business, e.g. '*Teares the deed.*'; '*All this time the informer kneeling to* Pulcheria, *and deliuering papers.*'; '*Walkes by.*'; '*Athen. kneeling, points to Theod. sword.*'; '. . . *the curtaines drawne aboue*, Theodosius, *and his* Eunuches *discouer'd.*'; for dress and appearance, *viz.*, '*Enter . . .* Athenais *newly habited.*'; '. . . Athenais *in sackecloth. Her haire loose.*' [see text note to V. iii. SD.]; '*Enter* Theodosius, *like a frier . . .*'. (Directions for properties are sometimes so phrased that it is just possible that the manuscript had been annotated by the stage-keeper. '*2. Pictures brought in.*'; '*Enter Seruant with the petition.*'; '*Enter* Countrieman *with the apple.*' (not previously mentioned); '*Paulinus brought in a chaire.*'; '*Enter* Cleon *with a parchement role.*')

The directions at I. i. 89 and III. ii for ceremonial entries are extremely full and elaborate. As a contrast, exits are often very vague; at III. ii. 38, we have '*Exeunt* Theodosius *and the traine.*' without any indication that Pulcheria, Athenais, Arcadia and Flaccilla (and presumably attendants) remain behind. There are other directions which are vague about the numbers and persons involved.

The strongest indications that the copy was Massinger's own working manuscript, or 'foul papers', are provided by the occasional irregularities in the naming of characters.

(i) At the opening of III. ii, Arcadia and Flaccilla appear in the elaborate ceremonial entry as Pulcheria's '*two young Sisters*'; when they speak, at III. ii. 135–61, they are '*1 Sister*' and '*2 Sister*'; their exit is '*Exeunt* Athenais *and the yong Ladyes.*' Both earlier and later in the play they are referred to by name. It seems likely that the sisters had originally been anonymous throughout the manuscript, that Massinger had then gone through inserting the two names he chose from the three names in his source (he rejected Marina), and that he overlooked one scene.

(ii) Pulcheria is attended by a confidential servant (it is he who draws up the petition which entraps Theodosius); in one brief appearance, II. i. 178–87, he enters as '*Seruant*', but two of his three speech-headings read '*Mar.*' and he exits as '*Mart.*'. The Servant is quite a busy character and at one time Massinger may have intended to give him a name (perhaps Martianus, which is found in *The Holy Court*); in the scene in question it looks as though Massinger is writing rather absent-mindedly and comes out half-way between designating by function and by name.

(iii) At III. ii. 171 (F4ᵛ), 'Favorinus' makes a brief appearance among Theodosius's eunuchs. In III. iii (G1ᵛ, G2ʳ), Favorinus appears again, as Theodosius's envoy to Pulcheria, but during the printing (of the inner forme of G) the name on its four appearances was changed to Paulinus (see above). At III. iv. 41 and 46 the name of the envoy appears only as Paulinus. Favorinus was evidently a real character, and not a misprint for Paulinus. Massinger presumably decided to economize on characters, or was asked to do so. The part could be distributed easily enough among the other characters, but perhaps in his manuscript Massinger failed to make the changes throughout, as he had failed to complete the naming of the sisters. In the printing house it must surely have been Massinger who noticed the relic of the discarded character and had the alterations made (preserving the scansion as we saw), though he failed to notice that he had left the name in the outer forme of F.

McIlwraith once suggested (*Review of English Studies*, v, (1929), 36–42) that the anomalies in naming were signs that Massinger undertook a revision after the initial poor reception of his play. In his unpublished textual introduction to the play, McIlwraith described his article as 'exploratory'. The preferable theory is that we are looking at changes during the play's composition. The signs of haste in the last speech in the play, noted in McIlwraith's article,[1]

---

[1] Massinger wrote 'My grace on all' twice (V. iii. 190 and 192) and in the Harbord copy he deleted the first of these. McIlwraith was surely right to suggest that after he had made Theodosius give pardon and blessing, he remembered that he had not liberated Cleon. He wrote in the necessary words, repeated the blessing, but forgot to delete the earlier one.

are not surprising in a manuscript which shows Massinger still thinking about the naming of his characters.[1]

The play is clearly and correctly divided into Acts and Scenes.

There are copies of *32* in the following libraries and institutions: Bodleian Library (2 copies); Boston Public Library; British Museum (5 copies); Cambridge University Library; Chapin Library, Williamstown; University of Chicago; Clark Library, University of California; University of Columbia, Butler Library; Library of Congress; Folger Shakespeare Library (2 copies); University of Glasgow; Harvard College Library (2 copies); Huntington Library; University of Illinois; King's College, Cambridge; University of Leeds, Brotherton Library; University of Liverpool; Merton College, Oxford; Pierpont Morgan Library; Newberry Library; University of Pennsylvania; Pforzheimer Collection; Princeton University; John Rylands Library, Manchester; Shakespeare Birthplace Trust, Stratford-upon-Avon; Sheffield University; University of Texas; Trinity College, Cambridge; Alexander Turnbull Library, Wellington, New Zealand; Victoria and Albert Museum (2 copies); Wadham College, Oxford; Worcester College, Oxford; Yale University.

The text of the present edition has been prepared from the British Museum copy, 644.e.77.

One copy of *32*, now in the Folger Shakespeare Library, has ink corrections in Massinger's own hand (see General Introduction, p. xxxii). There are 81 of them and they are cited in the textual footnotes as *Massinger MS*. The most famous correction is at I. ii. 178, where '*Constantinople* ?' is deleted and '*Courte* ?' inserted. Why *Constantinople* should have been printed, when both sense and metre prefer Court is an unsolved mystery. I have rejected one of Massinger's corrections, at IV. i. 14 (see text note and Commentary); and Massinger has sometimes obviously failed to make a necessary correction.

There have been no published editions of *The Emperor of the East* since 1632 except in the standard collected editions and Harness's expurgated selection.

(d) *Stage History*

The Emperor of the East, licensed for the King's company in March 1631, was 'diuers times acted, at the *Blackfriers*, and *Globe* Play-

---

[1] The mute 'Patriarch' disappears quite early in the play.

houses', according to the title-page. There is strong evidence that it was not a success. The Epilogue states with embarrassing candour that the maker, presumably Massinger, 'forc'd to it by necessitie' had conferred the part of the Emperor Theodosius on one too young for the burden, and the speaker doubts whether the young man had given satisfaction 'in his art / Of action and deliuerie'. T. W. Baldwin[1] thought that Massinger had prepared Theodosius for the leading boy actor John Thompson, but that the part had to be taken over by John Honyman on Thompson's death. But Bentley points out (iv. 781) that Thompson did not die until 1634. In any case he played women's parts. It is by no means certain that Massinger had to accept a younger actor because a more experienced one had died. The 'necessitie' may have been in the exigencies of repertory casting: there may have been no-one else available at the time except the tyro.

The poor reception of the play is spoken of or hinted at in the preliminary verses, and in the 'Prologue at Court'. John Clavell writes that the audience can have had no appetite for they rose without giving thanks. William Singleton says more flatly that he can applaud the play, however it was 'cried down' by those who, he claimed, were ill-disposed towards any play by Massinger.[2] The 'Prologue at the Blackfriers', which like the Epilogue surprises one by its lack of tact, also talks of malice or at least a tendency to undervalue whatever Massinger writes. In the 'Prologue at Court', the author appeals to the King for justice:

> . . . this poore worke suffer'd by the rage,
>   And enuie of some Catos of the stage:
> Yet still hee hopes, this Play which then was seene
>   With sore eyes, and condemn'd out of their spleen,
> May bee by you, The supreme iudge, set free,
>   And rais'd aboue the reach of calumnie.

This court-prologue raises questions of its own. Bentley points out (iv. 778–9) that the play is not in the list of those given at Court during the season of 1630–1. He also wonders why a court-performance is not advertised on the title-page. As the eleven plays given at court by the King's company in 1631–2 are not itemized, Bentley

---

[1] *Organization and Personnel of the Shakespearean Company*, pp. 60–1.
[2] The possibility of Massinger's share in a theatrical feud at this time is discussed in the introduction to Massinger's poem for Shirley's *The Grateful Servant*. See vol. v, pp. 414–15.

suggests that if the play was acted at Court it must have been during 1631–2, but he wonders whether the court-prologue could have been prepared for a performance which never took place.

In discussing this, it is necessary to note the similarity between the prologue and epilogue of *The Emperor of the East* and those of Jonson's *The New Inn*, published in 1631. *The New Inn* had also been a failure, when it was 'most negligently play'd' by the King's men in 1629. The Prologue uses the same images of sickly appetite in the audience found in Clavell's epistle to *The Emperor*. The Epilogue is unusually humble and deferential. There is a second epilogue, headed: 'Another Epilogue there was, made for the Play in the Poets defence, but the play liu'd not, in opinion, to haue it spoken' (Jonson, *Works*, vi. 491). This second epilogue was clearly intended for a court audience ('*To giue the* King, *and* Queene, *and* Court *delight*'), but the play was not performed at court. Jonson may have expected a court performance which did not take place, or he may have written a dummy-epilogue for the printed version which gave him a further opportunity of attacking the public audience and vindicating himself. At any rate, it seems very likely that Massinger imitated a pattern of verses from the published version of a play by a greater man which had also suffered an ignominious reception in the theatre. In writing his 'Prologue at Court', he need not even have expected a court-performance, but may have had his eye upon the understanding auditory of his readers. It is also a possibility that the Epilogue, which has a strange *ex post facto* air, is not the original but was specially written for publication.

Although *The Emperor of the East* was one of the plays of His Majesty's servants 'formerly acted at the Blackfriars and now allowed of to his Majesty's servants at the New Theatre', that is, assigned to Killigrew, in January 1689 (Nicoll, *History of Restoration Drama*, pp. 315–16), there is no record of its having been acted in the Restoration. No subsequent revival of the play is known. Lee's *Theodosius* (1680), though based on a different source, uses the incident of the blank charter devised by Pulcheria for Theodosius to sign, and Lee may have got this from Massinger (McManaway, *Studies*, p. 23).

THE
EMPEROVR
OF
THE EAST.

A Tragæ-Comœdie.

The Scæne Constantinople.

As it hath bene diuers times acted, at the *Black-*
friers, and *Globe* Play-houses, by the
Kings Maiesties Seruants.

Written by PHILIP MASSINGER.

LONDON,

Printed by THOMAS HARPER, for
John Waterson, ANNO 1632.

The ACTORS *names.*

THEODOSIVS the younger.

Paulinus, a Kinsman to the Emperour.
Philanax, Captaine of the Guard.
Timantus ⎫
Chrysapius ⎬ Eunuchs of the Emperours chamber.   5
Gratianus ⎭
Cleon, a trauailer, friend to *Paulinus*.
Informer.
Proiector.   10
Master of the manners.
Mignion of the suburbs.
Countryman.
Chirurgion.
Emperick.   15

Pulcheria, the protectresse.
Athenais, a strange virgin, after the Empresse.
Arcadia ⎫
Flaccilla ⎭ the younger sisters of the Emperour.

Seruants.   20
Mutes.

To The Right Honorable, and my especiall good Lord, IOHN Lord MOHVNE, Baron of *Okehampton, &c.*

My good Lord,

LET my presumption in stiling you so (hauing neuer deseru'd it in 5
my seruice) from the clemencie of your noble disposition finde
pardon. The reuerence due to the Name of *Mohune*, longe since
honored in three Earls of *Sommerset*, and eight Barons of *Munster*,
may challenge from all pennes a deserued celebration. And the
rather in respect those Titles were not purchas'd, but conferr'd, and 10
continued in your Ancestours, for many vertuous, noble, and still
liuing Actions; nor euer forfeited, or tainted, but when the iniquitie
of those times labour'd the depression of approued goodnesse, and
in wicked policie held it fit that Loyaltie, and Faith, in taking part
with the true Prince, should be degraded, and mulcted. But this 15
admitting no farther dilation in this place, may your Lordship please,
and with all possible breuitie to vnderstand, the reasons why I am
in humble thankfulnesse ambitious to shelter this Poem vnder the
wings of your Honorable protection. My worthy friend Mʳ *Aston
Cokaine* your Nephew, to my extraordinarie content, deliuer'd to 20
mee, that your Lordship at your vacant hours sometimes vouchsaf'd
to peruse such trifles of mine, as haue passed the Presse, & not alone
warranted them in your gentle suffrage, but disdain'd not to bestow
a remembrance of your loue, and intended fauour to mee. I professe
to the world, I was exalted with the bountie, and with good assurance, 25
it being so rare in this age to meete with one Noble Name, that in
feare to bee censur'd of leuitie, and weakenesse, dares expresse it selfe,
a friend, or Patron to contemn'd Poetrie. Hauing therefore no meanes
els left mee to witnesse the obligation, in which I stand most
willingly bound to your Lordship, I offer this Tragæ-Comœdie to 30
your gratious acceptance, no way despairing, but that with a cleere

aspect, you will daine to receiue it (it being an induction to my future endeauours) and that in the list of those, that to your merit truely admire you, you may descend to number,

Your Lordships   35
Faithfull Honorer;
Philip Massinger.

To my worthy Friend, Mʳ. PHILIP MASSINGER,
vpon his Tragæ-Comœdie, call'd
The Emperour of the East.

Suffer, my friend, these lines to haue the grace,
That they may bee a mole on Venus *face.*
There is no fault about thy Booke, but this,
And it will shew how faire thy Emperour is.
Thou more then Poet, our Mercurie (*that art*   5
Apollo's *Messenger, and do'st impart*
His best expressions to our eares) liue long
To purifie the slighted English tongue,
That both the Nymphes *of* Tagus, *and of* Poe,
May not henceforth despise our language so.   10
Nor could they doe it, if they ere had seene
The matchlesse features of the faerie Queene;
Read Iohnson, Shakespeare, Beaumont, Fletcher, *or*
Thy neat-limnd peeces, skilfull Massinger.
Thou knowne, all the Castillians *must confesse*   15
Vega de Carpio *thy foile, and blesse*
His language can translate thee, and the fine
Italian *witts, yeeld to this worke of thine.*
Were old Pythagoras *aliue againe,*
In thee hee might finde reason to maintaine   20
His Paradox; that soules by transmigration
In diuers bodies make their habitation,
And more; that all Poetik soules yet knowne
Are met in thee, vnited, and made one.
This is a truth, not an applause. I am   25
One that at farthest distance view thy flame,
Yet may pronounce, that were Apollo *dead,*
In thee his Poesie might all bee read.
Forbeare thy modestie. Thy Emperours veine

Shall liue admir'd, when Poets shall complaine 30
It is a patterne of too high a reach
And what great Phœbus *might the Muses teach.*
Let it liue therefore, and I dare bee bold
To say, it with the world shall not grow old.

Aston Cokaine.

A friend to the Author, and well-wisher to the Reader.

Who with a liberall hand, freely bestowes
His bounty, on all commers, and yet knowes
No ebbe, nor formall limits, but proceeds
Continuing his hospitable deeds,
With dayly welcome, shall aduance his name 5
Beyond the art of flatterie: with such fame
May yours (deare friend) compare. Your muse hath bene
Most bountifull, and I haue often seene
The willing seates receaue such as haue fedd,
And risen thankefull; yet were some mis-led 10
By Nicetie, *when this faire Banquet came*
(So I allude) their stomacks were to blame,
Because that excellent sharpe, and poinant sauce
Was wanting, they arose without due grace.
Loe thus a second time hee doth inuite you: 15
Bee your owne Caruers, and it may delight you.

Iohn Clauell.

To my true friend, and Kinsman: PHILIP MASSINGER.

I take not vp on trust; nor am I lead
By an implicit Faith: what I haue read
With an impartiall censure I dare crowne
With a deseru'd applause, how ere cri'd downe

30. *complaine]* Coxeter; ~. *32*

By such whose malice will not let 'em bee   5
Equall to any peece limnd forth by thee.
Contemne their poore detraction, and still write
Poems like this, that can indure the light,
And search of abler iudgments. This will raise
Thy Name, the others Scandall is thy praise.   10
This oft perus'd by graue witts, shall liue long,
Not dye as soone, as pass'd the Actors tongue,
(The fate of slighter toyes): And I must say
'Tis not enough to make a passing play,
In a true Poet. Workes that should indure   15
Must haue a Genius in 'em strong, as pure.
And such is thine friend; nor shall time deuoure
The well form'd features of thy Emperour.

William Singleton.

12. *pass'd*] 32²; *passe* 32¹· ²

Prologue at the Blackfriers.

But that imperious custome warrants it,
   Our Author with much willingnes would omit
This Preface to his new worke. Hee hath found
   (And suffer'd for't) many are apt to wound
His credit in this kind: and whether hee   5
   Expresse himselfe fearefull, or peremptorie,
Hee cannot scape their censures who delight
   To misapplie what euer hee shall write.
Tis his hard fate. And though hee will not sue,   10
   Or basely beg such suffrages, yet to you
Free, and ingenious spirits, hee doth now
   In mee present his seruice, with his vow
Hee hath done his best, and though hee cannot glorie
   In his inuention, (this worke being a storie,
Of reuerend Antiquitie) hee doth hope   15
   In the proportion of it, and the scope,
You may obserue some peeces drawne like one
   Of a stedfast hand, and with the whiter stone

To bee mark'd in your faire censures. More then this
   I am forbid to promise, and it is   20
With the most 'till you confirme it: since wee know
   What ere the shaft bee, Archer, or the bow,
From which 'tis sent, it cannot hit the white
   Vnlesse your approbation guide it right.

A4ᵛ

Prologue at Court.

As euer (Sir) you lent a gratious eare
   To oppress'd innocence, now vouchsafe to heare
A short petition. At your feete in mee
   The Poet kneeles, and to your Maiestie
Appeales for iustice. What wee now present,   5
   When first conceiu'd, in his vote and intent,
Was sacred to your pleasure; in each part
   With his best of fancie, iudgment, language, art,
Fashion'd, and form'd so, as might well, and may
   Deserue a wellcome, and no vulgar way.   10
Hee durst not (Sir) at such a solemne feast
   Lard his graue matter with one scurrilous ieast,
But labour'd that no passage might appeare,
   But what the Queene without a blush might heare:
And yet this poore worke suffer'd by the rage,   15
   And enuie of some Catos of the stage:
Yet still hee hopes, this Play which then was seene
   With sore eyes, and condemn'd out of their spleen,
May bee by you, The supreme iudge, set free,
   And rais'd aboue the reach of calumnie.   20

The Emperour of the East

The Scæne Constantinople

Act. 1. Scæne 1.

PAULINUS. CLEON.

Paulinus. In your six yeeres trauaile, friend, no doubt you haue
    met with
Many, and rare aduentures, and obseru'd
The wonders of each climate, varying in
The manners, and the men, and so returne,
For the future seruice of your prince and country,   5
In your vnderstanding betterd.
    Cleon.   Sir, I haue made of't
The best vse in my power, and hope my gleanings,
After the full crop others reapd before me,
Shall not when I am call'd on, altogether
Appeare vnprofitable: yet I left   10
The miracle of miracles in our age
At home behind me; euery where abroad
Fame with a true, though prodigall voyce, deliuer'd
Such wonders of *Pulcheria* the Princesse,
To the amazement, nay astonishment rather   15
Of such as heard it, that I found not one
In all the States and Kingdomes that I pass'd through,
Worthy to be her second.
    Paulinus.   She indeed is
A perfect Phœnix, and disdaynes a riuall.
Her infant yeeres, as you know, promis'd much,   20
But growne to ripenesse shee transcendes, and makes
Credulitie her debtor. I will tell you
In my blunt way, to entertaine the time,
Vntill you haue the happinesse to see her,

I. i. 1. six] *Coxeter*; fix *32*   6. of't] *editor*; oft *32*; of it *Mason*

How in your absence shee hath borne her selfe,   25
And with all possible breuitie, though the subiect
Is such a spatious field, as would require
An abstract of the purest eloquence
(Deriu'de from the most famous Orators
The nurse of learning, *Athens*, shew'd the world)   30
In that man, that should vndertake to bee
Her true Historian.
    Cleon.   In this you shall doe mee
A speciall fauour.
    Paulinus.   Since *Arcadius* death,
Our late great Master, the protection of
The Prince his Sonne, the second *Theodosius*,   35
By a generall vote and suffrage of the people,
Was to her charge assigned, with the disposure
Of his so many Kingdomes. For his person,
Shee hath so train'd him vp in all those arts
That are both great and good, and to be wished   40
In an Imperiall Monarch, that the Mother
Of the *Gracchi*, graue *Cornelia* (Rome still boasts of)
The wise *Pulcheria* but nam'd, must be
No more remembred. She by her example
Hath made the court a kinde of Academy,   45
In which true honour is both learnd, and practisd,
Her priuate lodgings a chaste Nunnery,
In which her sisters as probationers heare
From her their soueraigne Abbesse, all the precepts
Read in the schoole of vertue.
    Cleon.   You amaze me.   50
    Paulinus. I shall ere I conclude. For heere the wonder
Begins, not ends. Her soule is so immense,
And her strong faculties so apprehensiue,
To search into the depth of deepe designes,
And of all natures, that the burthen which   55
To many men were insupportable,
To her is but a gentle exercise,
Made by the frequent vse familiar to her.
    Cleon. With your good fauour let me interrupt you.
Being as she is in euery part so perfect,   60

B2ʳ (line 55)

47. lodgings] *Coxeter*; lodging's *32*

Me thinkes that all kings of our Easterne world
Should become riualls for her.
Paulinus.   So they haue,
But to no purpose. She that knowes her strength
To rule, and gouerne Monarchs, scornes to weare
On her free necke the seruile yoke of marriage.   65
And for one loose desire, enuie it selfe
Dares not presume to taint her. *Venus* sonne
Is blinde indeed, when he but gazes on her;
Her chastity being a rocke of Diamonds,
With which encountred his shafts flie in splinters,   70
His flaming torches in the liuing spring
Of her perfections, quench'd: and to crowne all,
Shee's so impartiall when she sits vpon
The high tribunall, neither swayd with pittye,
Nor awd by feare beyond her equall scale,   75
That 'tis not superstition to beleeue
Astrea once more liues vpon the earth,
Pulcheriaes brest her temple.
 Cleon.   You haue giuen her
An admirable character.
     Paulinus.   She deserues it,
And such is the commanding power of vertue,   80
That from her vitious enemies it compells
Pæans of prayse as a due tribute to her.   *Solemne lowd musick.*
 Cleon. What meanes this solemne musicke Sir?
     Paulinus.   It vshers
The Emperours morning meditation,
In which *Pulcheria* is more then assistant.   85
Tis worth your obseruation, and you may
Collect from her expence of time this day,
How her howres for many yeeres haue beene dispos'd of.
 Cleon. I am all eyes and eares.

Enter after a strayne of musicke, PHILANAX, TIMANTUS, *Patriarch,*
THEODOSIUS, PULCHERIA, FLACCILLA, ARCADIA, *followed by*
CHRYSAPIUS *and* GRATIANUS, INFORMER, *Seruants, Officers.*

 Pulcheria.   Your patience Sir.

B2ᵛ

68. her;] *Gifford*; ~. *32*   74. pittye] *Massinger MS*; piety *32*   83. musicke
Sir?] *Massinger MS* (musicke Sʳ?); musicke? *32*

Let those corrupted ministers of the court, 90
Which you complayne of, our deuotions ended,
Be cited to appeare. For the Embassadours
Who are importunate to haue audience,
From me you may assure them, that to morrow
They shall in publike kisse the Emperours robe, 95
And we in priuate with our soonest leasure
Will giue 'em hearing. Haue you especiall care too
That free accesse be granted vnto all
Petitioners. The morning weares. Pray you on Sir;
Time lost is ne're recouerd.

     Exeunt THEODOSIUS, PULCHERIA, *and the trayne.*

Paulinus.   Did you note 100
The maiesty she appeares in ?
 Cleon.   Yes my good Lord,
I was rauish'd with it.
 Paulinus. And then with what speede
Shee orders her dispatches, not one daring
To interpose; the Emperour himselfe
Without replie putting in act what euer 105
Shee pleas'd to impose vpon him.
 Cleon.   Yet there were some
That in their sullen lookes rather confessed
A forc'd constraint to serue her, then a will
To bee at her deuotion, what are they?
 Paulinus. Eunuchs of the Emperours chamber, that repine, 110
B3ʳ The globe and awfull scepter should giue place
Vnto the distaffe, for as such they whisper
A womans gouernment, but dare not yet
Expresse themselues.
 Cleon. From whence are the Embassadours
To whom she promisde audience?
 Paulinus.   They are 115
Imployd by diuers Princes, who desire
Alliance with our Emperour, whose yeeres now
As you see, write him man. One would aduance
A daughter to the honour of his bed,
A second, his fayre sister: to instruct you 120
In the particulars would aske longer time
Then my owne designes giue way to. I haue letters

From speciall friends of mine, that to my care
Commend a stranger virgin, whom this morning
I purpose to present before the Princesse,   125
If you please, you may accompany me.
    Cleon.   Ile wait on you.   *Exeunt.*

Act. *1. Scene 2.*

INFORMER, *Officers bringing in the* PROIECTOR, *the* SUBURBS
    MIGNION, *the* MASTER OF THE HABIT AND MANNERS.

    Informer. Why should you droope, or hang your working heads?
No danger is meant to you, pray beare vp,
For ought I know you are cited to receiue
Preferment due to your merits.
    Proiector.   Very likely,
In all the proiects I haue read and practisd   5
I neuer found one man compeld to come
Before the seat of iustice vnder guarde
To receiue honour.
    Informer.   No; it may be you are
B3ᵛ The first example. Men of qualities,
As I haue deliuer'd you to the protectresse,   10
Who knows how to aduance them, cannot conceiue
A fitter place to haue their vertues publish'de,
Then in open Court: could you hope that the Princesse
Knowing your pretious merits, will reward 'em
In a priuate corner? no, you know not yet   15
How you may be exalted.
    Suburbs Mignion.   To the gallowes.
    Informer.   Fy,
Nor yet depressde to the Gallies; in your names
You carry no such crimes: your specious titles
Cannot but take her: President of the Proiectors!
What a noyse it makes! The master of the habit,   20
How proud would some one country be that I know
To be your first pupill! Minion of the suburbs,
And now and then admitted to the Court,
And honor'd with the stile of Squire of Dames,
What hurt is in it? One thing I must tell you,   25

As I am the State scout, you may think me an informer.

    Master. They are *Synonima.*

    Informer.   Conceale nothing from her
Of your good parts, 'twill be the better for you,
Or if you should, it matters not, she can coniure,
And I am her vbiquitary spirit,   30
Bound to obey her, you haue my instructions,
Stand by, heeres better company.

        Enter PAULINUS, CLEON, ATHENAIS, *with a Petition.*

    Athenais.   Can I hope, Sir,
Oppressed innocence shall finde protection,
And iustice among strangers, when my brothers,
Brothers of one wombe, by one Sire begotten,   35
Trample on my afflictions?

    Paulinus.   Forget them,
Remembring those may helpe you.

B4ʳ   *Athenais.*   They haue robde mee
Of all meanes to prefer my iust complaint
With any promising hope to gaine a hearing,
Much lesse redresse: petitions not sweetened   40
With golde, are but vnsauorie, oft refused,
Or if receau'd, are pocketted, not read.
A suitors swelling teares by the glowing beames
Of Cholerick authority are dri'd vp,
Before they fall, or if seene neuer pittied.   45
What will become of a forsaken maide?
My flattering hopes are too weake to encounter
With my stronge enemy, despaire, and 'tis
In vaine to oppose her.

    Cleon.   Cheere her vp, shee faints, Sir.

    Paulinus. This argues weakenesse; thogh your brothers were   50
Cruell beyond expression, and the iudges
That sentenc'd you, corrupt, you shall finde heere
One of your owne faire sexe to doe you right,
Whose beames of iustice like the Sun extend
Their light, and heate to strangers, and are not   55
Municipall, or confinde.

    Athenais.   Pray you doe not feede mee
With aerie hopes; vnlesse you can assure mee

The greate *Pulcheria* will descende to heare
My miserable storie, it were better
I died without her trouble.
    Paulinus.   Shee is bound to it   60
By the surest chaine, her naturall inclination
To helpe th' afflicted, nor shall long delayes
(More terrible to miserable suitors
Then quicke deniralls) grieue you; Drie your faire eyes,
This roome will instantly bee sanctifi'd   65
With her bless'd presence; to her ready hand
Present your grieuances, and rest assur'd
You shall depart contented.
    Athenais.   You breath in mee
A second life.
B4ᵛ   *Informer.*   Will your Lordship please to heare
Your seruant a few words?
    Paulinus.   Away you rascall,   70
Did I euer keepe such seruants?
    Informer.   If your honestie
Would giue you leaue, it would bee for your profit.
    Paulinus. To make vse of an Informer? tell mee in what
Can you aduantage mee?
    Informer.   In the first tender
Of a fresh suite neuer begd yet.
    Paulinus.   Whats your suite Sir?   75
    Informer. 'Tis feasible, heere are three arrant knaues
Discouerd by my Art:
    Paulinus.   And thou the arch-knaue,
The greate deuoure the lesse.
    Informer.   And with good reason,
I must eate one a month, I cannot liue els.
    Paulinus. A notable canniball! but should I heare thee,   80
In what doe your knaues concerne mee?
    Informer.   In the begging
Of their estates.
    Paulinus.   Before they are condemned?
    Informer. Yes or arraigned, your Lordship may speake too late
    els.
They are your owne, and I will bee content
With the fift part of a share.

Paulinus.   Hence Rogue!

Informer.   Such Rogues   85

In this kinde will be heard, and cherish'd too.

Foole that I was to offer such a bargaine,

To a spic'd conscience chapman, but I care not,

What hee disdaines to taste others will swallow.   *Lowde Musick.*

Enter THEODOSIUS, PULCHERIA, *and the traine.*

Cleon. They are returned from the Temple.

Paulinus.   See, shee appeares,

C1ʳ What thinke you now?

Athenais.   A cunning Painter thus   91

Her vaile tane off, and awfull sword and ballance

Lay'd by, woulde picture iustice.

Pulcheria.   When you please,

You may intend those royall exercises

Suiting your birth, and greatenesse: I will beare   95

The burthen of your cares, and hauing purged

The body of your empire of ill humors,

Vpon my knees surrender it.

Chrysapius.   Will you euer

Bee awde thus like a Boy?

Gratianus.   And kisse the rod

Of a proude Mistrisse?

Timantus.   Bee what you were borne Sir.   100

Philanax. Obedience and Maiestie neuer lodg'd

In the same Inne.

Theodosius.   No more; hee neuer learned

The right way to command, that stopp'd his eares

To wise directions.

Pulcheria.   Reade ore the Papers

I left vpon my cabinet, two hours hence   105

I will examine you.

Flaccilla.   Wee spende our time well.

Nothing but praying, and poring on a booke,

It ill agrees with my constitution, sister.

Arcadia. Would I had beene borne some masquing Ladies woman,

Only to see strange sights, rather then liue thus.   110

I. ii. 85. Rogue!] *Coxeter*; ~, *32*   89 SD. *Musick.*] *Coxeter*; *Mus. 32*   92. off,]
Massinger MS; ~ʌ *32*   93. by,] *Massinger MS*; ~ʌ *32*

Flaccilla. We are gone forsooth, there is no remedy, sister.

         Exeunt ARCADIA *and* FLACCILLA.

Gratianus. What hath his eye found out?

Timantus.   'Tis fix'd vpon

That stranger Lady.

Chrysapius.   I am glad yet, that

Hee dares looke on a Woman.

CIv *All this time the* INFORMER *kneeling to* PULCHERIA, *and*

       deliuering papers.

 Theodosius.   *Philanax,*

What is that comely stranger?

 Philanax.   A Petitioner.   115

 Chrysapius. Will you heare her case, and dispatch her in your

  Chamber?

Ile vndertake to bring her.

 Theodosius.   Bring mee to

Some place where I may looke on her demeanour.

'Tis a louely creature!

 Chrysapius.   Ther's some hope in this yet.

    Exeunt THEODOSIUS, *Patriarch and the trayne.*

Pulcheria. No you haue done your parts.

Paulinus.   Now opportunity courts you,

Prefer your suite.

 Athenais.   As low as miserie   121

Can fall, for proofe of my humilitie,

A poore distressed Virgin bowes her head,

And layes hold on your goodnesse, the last altar

Calamitie can flie to for protection.   125

Great mindes erect their neuer falling trophees

On the firme base of mercie; but to triumphe

Ouer a suppliant by proud fortune captiued,

Argues a Bastard conquest: 'tis to you

I speake, to you the faire, and iust *Pulcheria,*   130

The wonder of the age, your sexes honor,

And as such daine to heare mee. As you haue

A soule moulded from heauen, and doe desire

To haue it made a star there, make the meanes

118. demeanour.] *Massinger MS*; demeaner.⌃ *32* 119. creature!] *Coxeter*; ~?
*32*¹﹐²; ~, *32*³   119 SD. *Exeunt . . . trayne.*] *Coxeter*; *follows* creature *32*
120–1. you, / Prefer] *32*; opportunity / Courts *McIlwraith*

Of your ascent to that celestiall height   135
Vertue wing'd with braue action: they draw neer
The nature, and the essence of the Gods,
C2ʳ Who imitate their goodnesse.
　　　Pulcheria.　　　　　　　　If you were
A subiect of the Empire, which your habit
In euery part denies—
　　　Athenais.　　　　　　O flie not to   140
Such a euasion; what ere I am,
Being a Woman, in humanitie
You are bound to right mee; though the difference
Of my religion may seeme to exclude mee
From your defence (which you would haue confinde)   145
The morall vertue, which is generall,
Must know no limits; by these blessed feete
That pace the paths of equity, and tread boldly
On the stiffe necke of tyrannous oppression,
By these teares by which I bath 'em, I coniure you   150
With pitty to looke on mee.
　　　Pulcheria.　　　　　　　Pray you rise,
And as you rise receiue this comfort from mee.
Beauty set off with such sweete language neuer
Can want an Aduocate, and you must bring
More then a guiltie cause if you preuaile not.   155
Some businesse long since thought vpon dispatched,
You shall haue hearing, and as far as iustice
Will warrant mee, my best aydes.
　　　Athenais.　　　　　　　　I doe desire
No stronger garde, my equitie needs no fauour.
　　　Pulcheria. Are these the men?
　　　Proiector.　　　　　　Wee were, an't like your highnesse,
The men, the men of eminence, and marke,   161
And may continue so, if it please your grace.
　　　Master. This speech was well proiected.
　　　Pulcheria.　　　　　　　　Does your conscience
(I will begin with you) whisper vnto you
What heere you stand accused of? are you named   165
The President of Proiectors?
　　　Informer.　　　　　　Iustifie it man,

140. denies—] *Coxeter;* ~. 32

And tell her in what thou art vsefull.

C2^v　　*Proiector.*　　　　　　　　　That is apparent,
And if you please, aske some about the court,
And they will tell you to my rare inuentions,
They owe their brauerie, perhaps meanes to purchase,　　170
And cannot liue without mee. I alas
Lende out my labouring braines to vse, and sometimes
For a drachma in the pound, the more the pitty.
I am all patience, and indure the curses
Of many, for the profit of one patron.　　175
　　Pulcheria. I do conceiue the rest. What is the second?
　　Informer. The mignion of the suburbs.
　　Pulcheria.　　　　　　　　　　　What hath he
To doe in Courte?
　　Mignion.　　　　I steale in now and then,
As I am thought vsefull, marry there I am calde
The Squire of Dames, or seruant of the sex,　　180
And by the allowance of some sportfull Ladies
Honor'd with that title.
　　Pulcheria.　　　　　　　Spare your Character,
You are heere desciphered; stand by with your compere.
What is the third? a creature I ne're heard of;
The master of the manners, and the habit,　　185
You haue a double office.
　　Master.　　　　　　　In my actions
I make both good, for by my theoremes
Which your polite, and terser gallants practise,
I rerefine the court, and ciuilize
Their barbarous natures: I haue in a table　　190
With curious punctualitie set downe
To a haires breadth, how low a new stamp'd courtier
May vaile to a country Gentleman, and by
Gradation, to his marchant, mercer, draper,
His linnen man, and taylor.
　　Pulcheria.　　　　　　　Pray you discouer　　195
This hidden mysterie.
　　Master.　　　　　　If the foresayde courtier
(As it may chance somtimes) find not his name

169. to] *Massinger MS*; too *32*　　178. Courte?] *Massinger MS*; *Constantinople?*
32　　192. stamp'd] *Massinger MS*; stamp'd (m *defective, inked in by Massinger*) *32*

C3ʳ Writ in the Citizens bookes, with a State hum
He may salute 'em after three dayes wayting:
But if he owe them money, that he may   200
Preserue his credit, let him, in policy, neuer
Appoint a day of payment, so they may hope still:
But if he be to take vp more, his page
May attend 'em at the gate, and vsher 'em
Into his Cellar, and when they are warm'd with wine,   205
Conduct 'em to his bedchamber, and though then
He be vnder his Barbers hands, assoone as seene,
He must start vp to embrace 'em, vayle thus low,
Nay though he call 'em cosins, 'tis the better,
His Dignity no way wrong'd in't.
    Paulinus.   Here's a fine knaue.   210
    Pulcheria. Does this rule hold without exception sirrha
For Courtiers in generall?
    Master.   No, deare madam,
For one of the last edition, and for him
I haue composde a Dictionary, in which
He is instructed, how, when, and to whom   215
To be proud or humble; at what times of the yeare
He may do a good deed for it selfe, and that is
Writ in Dominicall letters, all dayes else
Are his owne, and of those dayes the seuerall houres
Markt out, and to what vse.
    Pulcheria.   Shew vs your method,   220
I am strangely taken with it.
    Master.   Twill deserue
A pension, I hope. First a strong cullise
In his bed to heighten appetite: Shuttle-cock
To keepe him in breath when he rises; Tennis Courts
Are chargeable, and the riding of great horses   225
Too boystrous for my yong Courtier, let the old ones
I thinke not of, vse it; next his meditation
How to court his Mistresse, and that he may seeme witty,
Let him be furnish'd with confederate iests
Between him and his friend, that on occasion   230
C3ᵛ They may vent 'em mutually: what his pace, and garbe
Must be in the presence, then the length of his sword,

231. 'em] *Massinger MS*; em *32*

The fashion of the hilt, what the blade is
It matters not, 'twere barbarisme to vse it,
Vnlesse to shew his strength vpon an andiron,   235
So the sooner broke, the better.
    Pulcheria.   How I abuse
This pretious time! Proiector, I treat first
Of you and your disciples; you roare out,
All is the Kings, his will aboue his lawes:
And that fit tributes are too gentle yokes   240
For his poore subiects; whispering in his eare,
If he would haue their feare, no man should dare
To bring a sallad from his country garden,
Without the paying gabell; kill a hen,
Without excise: and that if he desire   245
To haue his children, or his seruants weare
Their heads vpon their shoulders, you affirme,
In policy, tis fit the owner should
Pay for 'em by the pole; or if the Prince want
A present summe, he may command a city   250
Impossibilities, and for non-performance
Compell it to submit to any fine
His Officers shall impose: is this the way
To make our Emperor happy? can the groanes
Of his subiects yeeld him musick? must his thresholds   255
Be wash'd with widdowes and wrong'd orphans teares,
Or his power grow contemptible?
    Proiector.   I begin
To feele my selfe a rogue againe.
    Pulcheria.   But you are
The Squire of Dames, deuoted to the seruice
Of gamesome Ladies, the hidden mystery   260
Discouer'd, their close bawde; thy slauish breath
Fanning the fires of lust, the Goe-between
This female, and that wanton Sir, your art
Can blinde a iealous husband, and disguisde
Like a Millainer or Shoomaker, conuey   265
A letter in a pantophle or gloue
Without suspition, nay at his table
In a case of picketoothes; you instruct 'em how

---

   242. their] *32²*, *Massinger MS*; them *32¹*   **244. gabell]** *Coxeter*; gubell *32*

To parley with their eyes, and make the temple
A mart of loosenesse: to discouer all   270
Thy subtile brokages, were to teach in publick,
Those priuate practises which are, in iustice,
Seuerely to bee punish'd.
    Mignion.   I am cast,
A iurie of my patronesses cannot quit mee.
    Pulcheria. You are master of the manners, and the habit,   275
Rather the scorne of such as would liue men,
And not like Apes with seruile imitation,
Studie prodigious fashions. You keepe
Intelligence abroad that may instruct
Our giddie youth at home what new found fashion   280
Is now in vse, swearing hees most compleate
That first turnes monster. Know villaines, I can thrust
This arme into your hearts, strip off the flesh
That couers your deformities, and shew you
In your owne nakednesse. Now though the law   285
Call not your follies death, you are for euer
Banish'd my brothers court. Away with 'em.
I will heare no reply.   *Exeunt* INFORMER, *Officers,* PRISONERS.
    The curtaines drawne aboue, THEODOSIUS, *and his*
       EUNUCHES [*and* PHILANAX] *discouer'd.*
    Paulinus.   What thincke you now?
    Cleon. That I am in a dreame, or that I see
A seconde *Pallas.*
    Pulcheria.   These remou'd, to you   290
I cleare my browe, speake without feare sweete mayde,
Since with a milde aspect and ready eare,
I sit prepar'd to heare you.
    Athenais.   Know greate Princesse,
My father, though a *Pagan*, was admir'd
For his deepe serch into those hidden studies,   295
Whose knowledge is deni'd to common men:
The motion, with the diuers operations
Of the superior bodies, by his long
And carefull obseruation were made
Familiar to him, all the secret virtues   300

271. Thy] *32²*; The *32¹*   288. SD. *and* PHILANAX] *after Gifford; not in 32*
291. feare] *32³, Massinger MS*; care *32¹,²*

Of plants, and simples, and in what degree
They were vsefull to mankinde, hee could discourse of.
In a word conceiue him as a Prophet honourd
In his owne countrie. But being borne a man,
It lay not in him to defer the hower   305
Of his approching death, though long foretold:
In this so fatall hower hee call'd before him
His two sonnes, and my selfe, the deerest pledges
Lent him by nature, and with his right hand
Blessing our seuerall heades, hee thus began;   310
    Chrysapius. Marke his attention.
    Philanax.   Giue mee leaue to marke too.
    Athenais. If I could leaue my vnderstanding to you,
It were superfluous to make diuision
Of whatsoeuer els I can bequeath you,
But to auoide contention, I allot   315
An equall portion of my possessions
To you my sonnes: but vnto thee my daughter,
My ioy, my darling (pardon mee though I
Repeate his words) if my prophetick soule
Ready to take her flight, can truely ghesse at   320
Thy future fate, I leaue the strong assurance
Of the greatenesse thou art borne to, vnto which
Thy brothers shall be proud to pay their seruice,
    Paulinus. And all men els that honour beauty.
    Theodosius.   Vmph.
    Athenais. Yet to prepare thee for that certaine fortune,   325
And that I may from present wants defend thee,
I leaue ten thousand crownes, which sayd, being call'd
To the fellowship of our Deities, he expird,
And with him all remembrance of the charge
Concerning me, left by him to my brothers.   330
    Pulcheria. Did they deteyne your legacy?
    Athenais.   And still do.
His ashes were scarce quiet in his vrne,
When in derision of my future greatnesse,
They thrust me out of doores, denying me
One short nights harbor.

   321. strong] *Massinger MS*; strange *32*   324. Vmph.] *Massinger MS* (vmph.);
Nimph. *32*; Umph! *Gifford*

Pulcheria. Weepe not.

Athenais. I desire 335
By your perswasion, or commanding power,
The restitution of mine owne, or that
To keepe my frailty from temptation,
In your compassion of me, you would please
I as a handmaid may be entertaind 340
To do the meanest offices to all such
As are honor'd in your seruice.

Pulcheria. Thou art welcome.
What is thy name?

Athenais. The forlorne *Athenais.*

Pulcheria. The sweetnes of thy innocence strangely takes me;
Takes her vp and kisses her.

Forget thy brothers wrongs, for I will be 345
In my care a mother, in my loue a sister to thee;
And were it possible thou could'st be woone
To be of our beleefe—

Paulinus. May it please your excellence,
That is an easie taske, I, though no schollar,
Dare vndertake it; cleere truth cannot want 350
Rhetoricall perswasions.

Pulcheria. Tis a work,
My Lord, will well become you; break vp the Court,
May your endeuors prosper.

Paulinus. Come my faire one,
I hope my conuert.

Athenais. Neuer, I will die
As I was borne.

Paulinus. Better you nere had beene. [*Exeunt.*]

Philanax. What does your maiesty think of? the maid's gone. 356

Theodosius. She's wondrous faire, and in her speech appear'd
Peeces of schollarship.

Chrysapius. Make vse of her learning
And beauty together, on my life she will be proud
To be so conuerted.

Theodosius. From foule lust heauen guard me. *Exeunt.*

342–3. welcome. / What] *Coxeter*; *undivided 32* 344 SD. *Takes . . . her.*] *Coxeter*;
after l. 343 in 32 347. woone] *Massinger MS*; wooned *32* 355. *Exeunt.*]
Coxeter; *not in 32*

Act. 2. Scæne 1.

PHILANAX, TIMANTUS, CHRYSAPIUS, GRATIANUS.

Philanax. WE only talk when we should do.
Timantus. Ile second you,
Begin, and when you please.
Gratianus. Be constant in it.
Chrysapius. That resolution which growes cold to day,
Will freeze to morrow.
Gratianus. 'Slight, I think sheele keepe him
Her ward for euer, to her selfe ingrossing   5
The disposition of all the fauors
And bounties of the Empire.
Chrysapius. Wee that by
The neerenesse of our seruice to his person,
Should raise this man, or pull downe that, without
Her licence hardly dare prefer a suit,   10
Or if wee doe, 'tis cross'd.
Philanax. You are troubled for
Your proper ends, my aimes are high and honest.
The wrong that's done to Maiesty I repine at:
I loue the Emperor, and 'tis my ambition
To haue him know himselfe, and to that purpose   15
Ile run the hazard of a check.
Gratianus. And I
The losse of my place.
Timantus. I will not come behinde,
Fall what can fall.
Chrysapius. Let vs put on sad aspects
To draw him on; charge home, weele fetch you off,
Or ly dead by you.

Enter THEODOSIUS.

Theodosius. How's this? clouds in the chamber,   20
And the ayre cleere abroad?
Philanax. When you our Sunne
Obscure your glorious beames, poore we that borrow
Our little light from you, cannot but suffer
A generall Eclipse.

Timantus.　　　　Great Sir, 'tis true,
For 'till you please to know, and be your selfe,　　　　25
And freely dare dispose of what's your owne
Without a warrant; we are falling meteors,
And not fix'd starres.
　　Chrysapius.　　　The pale fac'd Moon that should
Gouerne the night, vsurps the rule of day,
And still is at the full in spite of nature,　　　　30
And will not know a change.
　　Theodosius.　　　　　　Speak you in riddles?
I am no *Oedipus*, but your Emperor,
And as such would be instructed.
　　Philanax.　　　　　　　Your command
Shall be obeyd, till now I neuer heard you
Speak like your selfe; and may that power by which　　35
You are so, strike me dead, if what I shall
Deliuer, as a faithfull subiect to you,
Hath root, or growth from malice, or base enuy
Of your Sisters greatnesse; I could honor in her
A power subordinate to yours, but not　　　　40
As 'tis predominant.
　　Timantus.　　　Is it fit that she,
In her birth your vassall, should command the knees
Of such as should not bow but to your selfe?
　　Gratianus. Shee with security walkes vpon the heads
Of the nobility, the multitude　　　　45
As to a Deitie offring sacrifice,
For her grace, and fauour.
　　Chrysapius.　　　　　Her proude feete euen wearied
With the kisses of petitioners,
　　Gratianus.　　　　　While you,
To whom alone such reuerence is proper,
Passe vnregarded by her,
　　Timantus.　　　　　You haue not yet　　　　50
Bene Master of one houre of your whole life,
　　Chrysapius. Your will and faculties kept in more awe,
Then shee can doe her owne,
　　Philanax.　　　　And as a bondman,

D2ᵛ

II. i. 28. fix'd] *Massinger MS*; fixed *32*　　41. Is] *Massinger MS*; It *32*
48. petitioners,] *editor*; ~. *32*　　53. owne,] *editor*; ~ₐ *32*

O let my zeale finde grace, and pardon from you,
That I descende so low, you are designed   55
To this or that imployment, suiting well
A priuate man I grant, but not a Prince;
To bee a perfit horseman, or to know
The words of the chace, or a faire man of armes,
Or to bee able to pierce to the depth,   60
Or write a comment on th' obscurest Poets,
I grant are ornaments, but your maine scope
Should bee to gouerne men, to guarde your owne,
If not enlarge your empire.
    Chrysapius.   You are built vp
By the curious hand of nature to reuiue   65
The memorie of *Alexander*, or by
A prosperous successe in your braue actions
To riuall *Cæsar.*
    Timantus.   Rouze your selfe, and let not
Your pleasure bee a copye of her will,
    Philanax. Your pupill age is pass'd, and manly actions   70
Are now expected from you,
    Gratianus.   Doe not loose
D3ʳ Your subiects heartes,
    Timantus.   What is't to haue the meanes
To bee magnificent, and not exercise
The boundlesse vertue?
    Gratianus.   You confine your selfe
To that which strict Philosophie allowes of,   75
As if you were a priuate man.
    Timantus.   No pompe,
Or glorious showes of royaltie, rendring it
Both lou'd, and terrible.
    Gratianus.   'Slight you liue, as it
Begets some doubt, whether you haue or not
Th' abilities of a man.
    Chrysapius.   The Firmament   80
Hath not more starres then there are seuerall beauties
Ambitious at the height to impart their deare,
And sweetest fauours to you.
    Gratianus.   Yet you haue not

69. will,] *editor*; ~ ∧ *32*

Made choice of one, of all the sex, to serue you,
In a Physicall way of courtshippe.

  Theodosius.   But that I would not 85
Beginne the expression of my being a man,
In blood, or staine the first white robe I weare
Of absolute power, with a seruile imitation
Of any tyrannous habit, my iust anger
Prompts mee to make you in your suffrings feele, 90
And not in words to instruct you, that the licence
Of the loose, and saucie language you now practised,
Hath forfeited your heades.

  Gratianus.   How's this?

  Philanax.   I know not
What the play may proue, but I assure you that
I doe not like the prologue.

  Theodosius.   O the miserable 95
Condition of a Prince! who though hee varie
More shapes then *Proteus* in his minde, and manners,
Hee cannot winne an vniuersall suffrage,

D3ᵛ From the many-headed monster, Multitude.
Like *Æsops* foolish Frogges they trample on him, 100
As a senselesse blocke, if his gouernement bee easie.
And if hee proue a Storke, they croke, and rayle
Against him as a tyranne. Ile put off
That maiestie, of which you thinke I haue
Nor vse, nor feeling, and in arguing with you, 105
Conuince you with strong proofes of common reason,
And not with absolute power, against which, wretches,
You are not to dispute. Dare you that are
My creatures, by my prodigall fauours fashion'd,
Presuming on the neerenesse of your seruice, 110
Set off with my familiar acceptance,
Condemne my obsequiousnesse to the wise directions
Of an incomparable Sister, whom all parts
Of our world, that are made happy in the knowledge
Of her perfections, with wonder gaze on? 115
And yet you that were only borne to eate
The blessings of our mother earth, that are
Distant but one degree from beasts (since slaues

  100. foolish] *Massinger MS*; folish *32* 114. in the] *Massinger MS*; in *32*

Can claime no larger priuiledge) that know
No farther then your sensuall appetites,   120
Or wanton lust haue taught you, vndertake
To giue your soueraigne lawes to follow that
Your ignorance markes out to him?   *Walkes by.*
   Gratianus.   How were wee
Abus'd in our opinion of his temper?
   Philanax. Wee had forgot 'tis found in holy writ,   125
That Kings hearts are inscrutable.
   Timantus.   I ne're reade it,
My studie lies not that way.
   Philanax.   By his lookes
The tempest still increases.
   Theodosius.   Am I growne
So stupid in your iudgments, that you dare
With such security offer violence   130
To sacred maiestie? will you not know
The Lyon is a Lyon, though he show not
His rending pawes? or fill th' affrighted ayre
With the thunder of his rorings? you bless'd Saints,
How am I trenched on? is that temperance   135
So famous in your cited *Alexander*,
Or Roman *Scipio* a crime in mee?
Cannot I bee an Emperour, vnlesse
Your wiues, and daughters bow to my proud lusts?
And cause I rauish not their fairest buildings   140
And fruitfull vineyards, or what is dearest,
From such as are my vassalls, must you conclude
I doe not know the awfull power, and strength
Of my prerogatiue? am I close handed
Because I scatter not among you that   145
I must not call mine owne? Know you court leeches,
A Prince is neuer so magnificent,
As when hee's sparing to inrich a few
With th' iniuries of many; could your hopes
So grossely flatter you, as to beleeue   150
I was born and traind vp as an Emperour, only
In my indulgence to giue sanctuarie,
In their vniust proceedings, to the rapine
And auarice of my groomes?

D4ʳ

Philanax.   In the true mirror
Of your perfections, at length wee see   155
Our owne deformities.
    Timantus.   And not once daring
To look vpon that maiestie wee now sleighted.
    Chrysapius. With our faces thus glewd to the earth, wee beg
Your gratious pardon.
    Gratianus.   Offring our neckes   160
To bee trod on, as a punishment for our late
Presumption, and a willing testimony
Of our subiection.
    Theodosius.   Deserue our mercie
In your better life heereafter; you shall finde,
Though in my Fathers life I helde it madnesse

D4ᵛ To vsurp his power, and in my youth disdainde not   165
To learne from the instructions of my sister,
Ile make it good to all the world, I am
An Emperor; and euen this instant graspe
The Scepter, my rich stock of maiesty
Intire, no scruple wasted.
    Philanax.   If these teares   170
I drop, proceed not from my ioy to heare this,
May my eye-bals follow 'em.
    Timantus.   I will shew my selfe
By your suddain metamorphosis transform'd
From what I was.
    Gratianus.   And nere presume to aske
What fits not you to giue.
    Theodosius.   Moue in that sphere,   175
And my light with full beames shall shine vpon you.
Forbeare this slavish courtship, 'tis to me
In a kinde idolatrous.
    Philanax.   Your gratious sister.

        Enter PULCHERIA, SERVANT.

    Pulcheria. Has he conuerted her?
    Seruant.   And, as such, will
Present her when you please.
    Pulcheria.   I am glad of it.   180
Comand my Dresser to adorne her with

The robes that I gaue order for.
  Seruant.   I shall.
  Pulcheria. And let those pretious Iewels I tooke last
Out of my Cabinet, if't be possible,
Giue lustre to her beauties, and that done,   185
Command her to be neere vs.
  Seruant.   Tis a prouince
I willingly embrace.   *Exit* SERVANT.
  Pulcheria.   O my deare Sir,
You haue forgot your morning taske, and therefore
With a mothers loue I come to reprehende you,
But it shall bee gentlie.
  Theodosius.   'T will become you, though, 190
You said with reuerend duty. Know heereafter,
If my mother liu'd in you, how ere her sonne,
Like you shee were my subiect.
  Pulcheria.   How?
  Theodosius.   Put off
Amazement, you will finde it. Yet Ile heare you
At distance, as a sister, but no longer   195
As a gouernesse, I assure you.
  Gratianus.   This is put home,
  Timantus. Beyond our hopes.
  Philanax.   Shee stands as if his words
Had powerfull magick in 'em.
  Theodosius.   Will you haue mee
Your pupill euer? the downe on my chinne
Confirmes I am a man, a man of men,   200
The Emperour, that knowes his strength.
  Pulcheria.   Heauen grant
You know it not too soone.
  Theodosius.   Let it suffice
My wardships out. If your designe concernes vs
As a man, and not a boy, with our allowance
You may deliuer it.
  Pulcheria. A strange alteration!   205
But I will not contend. Bee, as you wish, Sir,
Your owne disposer, vncompeld I cancell

 182. *Seruant.*] *Coxeter; Mar. 32* 186. *Seruant.*] *Coxeter; Mar. 32* 187 SD.
Exit SERVANT.] *Coxeter; Exit Mart. 32*

All bondes of my authority.   *Kneeles.*

    Theodosius.   You in this
Pay your due homage, which perform'd, I thus
Embrace you as a Sister, no way doubting   210
Your vigilance for my safetie as my honor;
And what you now come to impart, I rest
Most confident, points at one of them.

    Pulcheria.   At both,
And not alone the present, but the future
E1ᵛ Tranquillity of your minde: since in the choice   215
Of her, you are to heate with holy fires,
And make the consort of your royall bed,
The certaine meanes of glorious succession,
With the true happinesse of our humane being,
Are wholy comprehended.

    Theodosius.   How? a wife?   220
Shall I become a votarie to *Hymen*,
Before my youth hath sacrific'd to *Venus*?
'Tis something with the soonest, yet to shew
In things indifferent, I am not auerse
To your wise counsailes, let mee first suruay   225
Those beauties, that in being a Prince I know
Are riualls for mee. You will not confine mee
To your election, I must see deere sister
With mine owne eyes.

    Pulcheria.   'Tis fit Sir, yet in this
You may please to consider, absolute Princes   230
Haue, or should haue, in Policie, lesse free will
Then such as are their vassals. For, you must,
As you are an Emperour, in this high businesse
Waigh with due prouidence, with whom alliance
May bee most vsefull for the preseruation,   235
Or your increase of Empire.

    Theodosius.   I approue not
Such compositions for our morall ends,
In what is in it selfe diuine, nay more,
Decreed in heauen. Yet if our neighbour Princes,
Ambitious of such neerenesse, shall present   240

---

235. preseruation,] *Massinger MS*; ~ ^ *32*   236. your increase of] *32*; increase
of your *Mason*

Their dearest pledges to mee (euer reseruing
The caution of mine owne content) Ile not
Contemne their courteous offers.
    Pulcheria.   Bring in the pictures.
                            2. *Pictures brought in.*
   Theodosius. Must I then iudge the substances by the shadowes?
The Painters are most enuious, if they want   245
Good colours for preferment: virtuous Ladies
Loue this way to bee flatterd, and accuse
The workeman of detraction, if he adde not
Some grace they cannot truely call their owne.
Is't not so *Gratianus*? you may challenge   250
Some interest in the science.
    Gratianus.   A pretender
To the art, I truely honor, and subscribe
To your maiesties opinion.
    Theodosius.   Let mee see,
Cleanthe, daughter to the King of *Epirus*,
Ætatis suæ, the fourteenth: ripe enough,   255
And forward too, I assure you. Let me examine
The Symmetries. If Statuaries could
By the foote of *Hercules* set downe punctually
His whole dimensions, and the countenance be
The index of the minde, this may instruct me,   260
With the aydes of that I haue read touching this subiect,
What shee is inward: the colour of her haire,
If it be, as this does promise, pale, and faint,
And not a glistering white; her brow, so so;
The circles of her sight, too much contracted;   265
Iuno's faire cowe eyes by old *Homer* are
Commended to their merit; heeres a sharpe frost,
In the tippe of her nose, which by the length assures mee
Of stormes at midnight, if I faile to pay her
The tribute she expects. I like her not: 270
What is the other?
    Chrysapius.   How hath hee commenc'd
Doctor in this so sweete and secret art,
Without our knowledge?
    Timantus.   Some of his forward pages
Haue rob'd vs of the honor.

E2ʳ

Philanax.   No such matter,
Hee has the theorie only, not the practick.   275
     Theodosius. Amasia, Sister to the Duke of *Athens*,
Her age eighteen, descended lineally
From *Theseus*, as by her pedegree
Will be made apparent. Of his lustie kinred?
E2ᵛ And loose so much time! 'tis strange! as I liue, shee hath   280
A Philosophicall aspect, there is
More wit then beauty in her face, and when
I court her, it must be in tropes, and figures,
Or shee will crie absurd. Shee will haue her elenchs
To cut off any fallacie I can hope   285
To put vpon her, and expect I should
Euer conclude in Syllogismes, and those true ones
In parte et toto, or sheele tire mee with
Her tedious Elocutions in the praise
Of the increase of generation, for which   290
Alone the sport in her moralitie
Is good and lawfull, and to bee often practis'd
For feare of missing. Fy on't, let the race
Of *Theseus* be match'd with *Aristotles*,
Ile none of her.
     Pulcheria.   You are curious in your choice, Sir,   295
And hard to please, yet if that your consent
May giue authority to it, Ile present you
With one, that if her birth, and fortunes answer'd
The rarities of her body, and her mind,
Detraction durst not tax her.
     Theodosius.   Let me see her,   300
Though wanting those additions, which we can
Supplie from our owne store: it is in vs
To make men rich, and noble, but to giue
Legitimate shapes and virtues, does belong
To the greate creator of 'em, to whose bounties   305
Alone 'tis proper, and in this disdaines
An Emperour for his riuall.
     Pulcheria.   I applaud
This fit acknowledgement, since Princes then

298. answer'd] *Mason*; answer 32, *Gifford*

Grow lesse then common men, when they contend
With him, by whom they are so.

      Enter PAULINUS, CLEON, ATHENAIS *newly habited.*

    Theodosius.   I confesse it.   310

E3ʳ   *Pulcheria.* Not to hold you in suspense, Behold the virgin
Rich in her naturall beauties, no way borrowing
Th' adulterate aydes of art. Peruse her better,
Shee is worth your serious view.
    Philanax.   I am amaz'd too.
I neuer saw her equall.
    Gratianus.   How his eye   315
Is fix'd vpon her!
    Timantus.   And as shee were a fort,
He would suddainly surprize, Hee measures her
From the bases to the battlements.
    Chrysapius.   Ha! now I view her better,
I know her; 'tis the mayd that not long since
Was a petitioner; her brauerie   320
So alters her, I had forgot her face.
    Philanax. So has the Emperour.
    Paulinus.   Shee holdes out yet,
And yeeldes not to th' assault.
    Cleon.   Shee is strongly guarded
In her virgin blushes.
    Paulinus.   When you know, faire creature,
It is the Emperour that honours you   325
With such a strict suruay of your sweete parts,
In thankefulnesse you cannot but returne
Due reuerence for the fauour.
    Athenais.   I was lost
In my astonishment at the glorious obiect,
And yet rest doubtfull whether he expects,   330
Being more then man, my adoration,
(Since sure there is diuinity about him,)
Or will rest satisfi'd if my humbled knees
In duty thus bowe to him.
    Theodosius.   Ha! it speakes.

    323. guarded] *Massinger MS*; garded *32*

  Pulcheria. Shee is no statue Sir.

  Theodosius.   Suppose her one,   335
And that shee had nor organs, voice, nor heat,
Most willingly I would resigne my Empire
E3ᵛ So it might be to after-times recorded
That I was her *Pigmalion*, though, like him,
I doted on my workmanship, without hope too   340
Of hauing *Cytherea* so propitious
To my vowes, or sacrifice, in her compassion
To giue it life or motion.

  Pulcheria.   Pray you be not rap'd so,
Nor borrow from imaginary fiction
Impossible aydes; she's flesh and blood, I assure you,   345
And if you please to honor her in the triall,
And be your owne security, as youle finde
I fable not, she comes in a noble way
To be at your deuotion.

  Chrysapius.   'Tis the maid
I offer'd to your highnesse, her chang'd shape   350
Conceal'd her from you.

  Theodosius.   At the first I knew her,
And a second firebrand Cupid brings to kindle
My flames almost put out: I am too cold,
And play with opportunity.

           May I taste then
The nectar of her lip? I do not giue it   355
The praise it merits: antiquity is too poore
To help me with a simile to expresse her.
Let me drink often from this liuing spring,
To nourish new inuention.

  Pulcheria.   Do not surfet
In ouer-greedily deuouring that   360
Which may without satiety feast you often.
From the moderation in receiuing them,
The choysest viands do continue pleasing
To the most curious palats; if you thinke her
Worth your embraces, and the soueraigne title   365
Of the Græcian Empresse,

  Theodosius.   If? how much you sinne,

340. I] *Massinger MS (J)*; I (*defective*) 32

Only to doubt it: the possession of her
Makes all that was before most pretious to me,
E4ʳ Common, and cheap: in this you haue shown your selfe
A prouident Protectresse. I already   370
Grow weary of the absolute command
Of my so numerous subiects, and desire
No soueraignty but here, and write downe gladly,
A period to my wishes.
 Pulcheria.   Yet before
It be too late, consider her condition,   375
Her father was a Pagan, she her selfe
A new conuerted Christian.
 Theodosius.   Let me know
The man to whose religious meanes I ow
So great a debt.
 Paulinus. You are aduanc'd too high Sir,
To acknowledge a beholdingnes; 'tis discharg'd,   380
And I, beyond my hopes, rewarded, if
My seruice please your Maiesty.
 Theodosius.   Take this pledge
Of our assured loue. Are there none here
Haue suits to prefer? on such a day as this
My bounty's without limit. O my dearest,   385
I will not heare thee speak; what euer in
Thy thoughts is apprehended, I grant freely:
Thou would'st plead thy vnworthinesse, by thy self
The magazine of felicity, in thy lownesse
Our Eastern Queens at their full height bow to thee,   390
And are in their best trim thy foyles, and shadowes.
Excuse the violence of my loue, which cannot
Admit the least delay. Command the Patriarch
With speed to do his holy office for vs,
That when we are made one—
 Pulcheria.   You must forbeare Sir,   395
She is not yet baptiz'd.
 Theodosius. In the same houre
In which she is confirmed in our faith,
E4ᵛ We mutually will giue away each other,
And both be gainers; weele heare no reply

391. foyles,] *Massinger MS*; ∼ ∧ *32* 395. one—] *Coxeter*; ∼. *32*

That may diuert vs. On.

  Pulcheria.   You may hereafter   400
Please to remember to whose furtherance
You ow this height of happinesse.

  Athenais.   As I was
Your creature when I first petition'd you,
I will continue so, and you shall finde me,
Though an Empresse, still your seruant.

    All go off but PHILANAX, GRATIANUS, *and* TIMANTUS.

  Gratianus.   Here's a marriage 405
Made vp on the suddain!

  Philanax.   I repine not at
The faire maids fortune, though I feare the Princesse
Had some peculiar end in't.

  Timantus.   Who's so simple
Only to doubt it?

  Gratianus. It is too apparent,
She hath preferr'd a creature of her owne,   410
By whose meanes she may still keepe to her selfe
The gouernment of the Empire.

  Timantus.   Where as if
The Emperor had espous'd some neighbour Queen,
Pulcheria with all her wisdome could not
Keepe her preheminence.

  Philanax.   Be it as it will, 415
'Tis not now to be alter'd, heauen I say
Turne all to the best.

  Gratianus. Are we come to praying againe?

  Philanax. Leaue thy prophanenesse.

  Gratianus.   Would it would leaue mee.
I am sure I thriue not by it.

  Timantus.   Come to the Temple. 419

  Gratianus. Eu'n where you will, I know not what to think on't.

              [Exeunt.]

    The end of the second Acte.

---

400. vs. On] *Massinger MS* (vs. on.); vs on *32* You] *Massinger MS*; You (*defective*) *32*
420. Eu'n] *32²*; Euen *32¹* on't] *32²*; on *32¹* Exeunt.] *Gifford*; *not in 32*

Act. 3. Scæna 1.

PAULINUS. PHILANAX.

Paulinus. NOR this, nor the age before vs euer look'd on
The like solemnitie.

Philanax.　　　　A suddain feuer
Kep'd mee at home. Pray you my Lord acquaint me
With the particulars.

Paulinus.　　　　You may presume
No pompe, nor ceremony could be wanting,　　　　　5
Where there was Priuiledge to command, and meanes
To cherish rare inuentions.

Philanax.　　　　　I beleeue it;
But the summe of all in briefe.

Paulinus.　　　　　Pray you so take it;
Faire *Athenais* not longe since a Suitor,
And almost in her hopes forsaken, first　　　　　10
Was Christned, and the Emperours mothers name
Eudoxia, as hee will'd, impos'd vpon her:
Pulcheria the euer matchlesse Princesse,
Assisted by her reuerend Aunt *Maria*,
Her God-mothers.

Philanax.　　　And who the masculine witnesse?　　15

Paulinus. At the new empresse suite I had the honor,
For which I must euer serue her.

Philanax.　　　　　'Twas a grace,
With iustice you may boaste of.

Paulinus.　　　　The marriage followed,
And as 'tis sayd, the Emperour made bold
To turne the day to night, for, to bed they went　　20
Assoone as they had din'd, and there are wagers
Lay'd by some merrye Lords, hee hath already
Fᵢᵛ Begot a boy vpon her.

Philanax.　　　That is yet
To be determin'd of; but I am certaine,
A Prince so soone in his disposition alter'd,　　　　25
Was neuer heard nor reade of.

Paulinus.　　　　But of late,
Frugall and sparing, now nor boundes, nor limits

To his magnificent bounties. Hee affirm'd,
Hauing receiu'd more blessings by his empresse
Then hee could hope, in thankefulnesse to heauen   30
He cannot be to prodigall to others.
What euer's offer'd to his royall hand
Hee signes without perusing it.
 Philanax.   I am heere
Inioyned to free all such as lye for debt,
The creditors to bee pay'd out of his coffers.   35
 Paulinus. And I all malefactors that are not
Conuicted or for treason or fowle murther,
Such only are excepted.
 Philanax.   'Tis a rare clemencie!
 Paulinus. Which wee must not dispute, but put in practise.
                Exeunt.

Actus 3. Scæn. 2.

*Lowd Musick. Showtes within: Heauen preserue the Emperour,
Heauen blesse the Empresse. Then in State,* CHRYSAPIUS, *Patriarch,*
PAULINUS, THEODOSIUS, ATHENAIS, PULCHERIA. *Her two young*
SISTERS *bearing vp* ATHENAIS *trayne. Followed by* PHILANAX,
GRATIANUS, TIMANTUS. *Suitors, presenting petitions. The
Emperour sealing them.* PULCHERIA *appeares troubled.*

 Pulcheria. Sir by your owne rules of Philosophie
You know things violent last not, royall bounties
Are great, and gratious while they are dispens'd
With moderation, but when their excesse
In giuing gyant-bulkes to others, take from   5
The Princes iust proportion, they loose
The names of vertues, and, their natures chang'd,
Grow the most dangerous vices.
 Theodosius.   In this, sister,
Your wisdome is not circular; they that sowe
In narrow boundes, cannot expect in reason   10
A croppe beyond their ventures; what I doe
Disperse, I lend, and will with vsury
Returne vnto my heape: I only then
Am rich, and happy, (though my coffers sound

With emptinesse) when my glad subiects feele,   15
Their plenty and felicitie is my gifte;
And they will finde, when they with cheerefulnesse
Supplie not my defectes, I being the stomacke
To the politick body of the State, the limbes
Grow suddainely faint, and feeble; I could vrge   20
Proofes of more finenesse in their shape and language,
But none of greater strength: dissuade mee not,
What wee will, we will doe; yet to assure you,
Your care does not offend vs, for an houre,
Bee happy in the conuerse of my best   25
And deerest comfort; may you please to licence
My priuacie some few minutes?
    Athenais.   Licence Sir,
I haue no will, but is deriu'd from yours,
And that still waites vpon you, nor can I
Bee left with such security with any,   30
As with the gratious Princesse, who receiues
Addition, though shee bee all excellence,
In being stilde your sister.
    Theodosius.   O sweete creature!
Let mee bee censur'd fond, and too indulgent,
Nay though they say vxorious, I care not,   35
Her loue, and sweete humility exact
A tribute far beyond my power, to pay
Her matchlesse goodnesse. Forward.
                   Exeunt THEODOSIUS *and the traine.*
    Pulcheria.   Now you finde
Your dying fathers prophecie that foretolde
Your present greatnesse, to the full accomplish'd.   40
For the poore aides, and furtherance I lent you,
I willingly forget.
    Athenais.   Eu'n that bindes me
To a more strict remembrance of the fauor,
Nor shall you from my foule ingratitude,
In any circumstance euer finde cause   45
T'upbraid me with your benefit.
    Pulcheria.   I beleeue so.
Pray you giue vs leaue: what now I must deliuer
Vnder the deepest seale of secrecy,

F2ᵛ

Though it be for your good, will giue assurance
Of what is look'd for, if you not alone   50
Heare, but obey my counsels.

    Athenais.   They must be
Of a strange nature, if with zealous speed
I put 'em not in practice.

    Pulcheria.   'Twere impertinence
To dwell on circumstances, since the wound
Requires a suddain cure, especially   55
Since you that are the happy instrument
Elected to it, though yong, in your iudgement
Write far aboue your yeeres, and may instruct
Such as are more experienc'd.

    Athenais.   Good madam,
In this I must oppose you, I am well   60
Acquainted with my weaknesse, and it will not
Become your wisdome (by which I am rais'd
To this titulary height) that should correct
The pride, and ouerweening of my fortune,

F3ʳ To play the parasite to it, in ascribing   65
That merit to me, vnto which I can
Pretend no interest; pray you excuse
My bold simplicity, and to my waight
Designe me where you please, and you shall finde
In my obedience, I am still your creature.   70

    Pulcheria. 'Tis nobly answer'd, and I glory in
The building I haue rais'd; go on, sweet Lady,
In this your vertuous progresse: but to the point,
You know, nor do I enuy it, you haue
Acquir'd that power, which, not long since, was mine,   75
In gouerning the Emperor, and must vse
The strength you hold in the heart of his affections,
For his priuate, as the publique preseruation,
To which there is no greater enemy,
Then his exorbitant prodigality,   80
How ere his sycophants, and flatterers call it
Royall magnificence, and though you may

III. ii. 49. your] *Coxeter*; you *32*   57. yong,] *Massinger MS*; ∼ ∧ *32*
62-3. wisdome (by . . . height)] *Massinger MS*; wisdome, by . . . height, *32*   81. it]
Massinger MS (*ink mark deleted*); it *32*

Vrge, what's done for your honor must not be
Curb'd, or be controul'd by you, you cannot in
Your wisdome but conceiue, if that the torrent   85
Of his violent bounties be not stopp'd, or lessen'd,
It will proue most pernitious. Therefore, Madam,
Since 'tis your duty, as you are his wife,
To giue him sauing counsells, and in being
Almost his idoll, may command him to   90
Take any shape you please, with a powerfull hand,
To stop him in his precipice to ruine.
    Athenais. Auert it heauen.
    Pulcheria.   Heauen is most gratious, madam,
In choosing you to be the instrument
Of such a pious work. You see he signes   95
What suit soeuer is preferr'd, not once
Inquiring what it is, yeelding himselfe
A prey to all; I would therefore haue you, Lady,
As I know you will, to aduise him, or command him,
As he would reap the plenty of your fauours,   100
F3ᵛ To vse more moderation in his bounties,
And that before he giues, he would consider,
The what, to whom, and wherefore.
    Athenais.   Do you think
Such arrogance, or vsurpation, rather,
Of what is proper, and peculiar   105
To euery priuate husband, and much more
To him an Emperor, can ranck with th'obedience
And duty of a wife? are we appointed
In our creation (let me reason with you)
To rule, or to obey? or 'cause he loues me   110
With a kinde of impotence, must I tyrannize
Ouer his weaknesse? or abuse the strength
With which he armes me to his wrong? or, like
A prostituted creature, merchandize
Our mutuall delight for hire? or to   115
Serue mine owne sordid ends? in vulgar nuptials
Priority is exploded, though there be
A difference in the parties, and shall I,

92. ruine.] *32*; ruin— *Gifford*   93. gratious] *Massinger MS*; gratious to you *32*
(to you *deleted by Massinger*)   111. of] *Massinger MS*; *not in 32*

His vassall from obscurity rais'd by him
To this so eminent light, presume to appoint him   120
To do, or not to do this, or that? when wiues
Are well accommodated by their husbands
With all things both for vse, and ornament,
Let them fix there, and neuer dare to question
Their wils or actions. For my selfe, I vow,   125
Though now my Lord would rashly giue away
His Scepter, and imperiall Diadem,
Or if there could be any thing more pretious,
I would not crosse it; but I know this is
But a triall of my temper, and as such   130
I do receiue it, or if't be otherwise,
You are so subtill in your arguments,
I dare not stay to heare them.
    Pulcheria.   Is't eu'n so?
I haue power ore these yet, and command their stay,
To hearken nearer to me.
    F4ʳ   *1 Sister.*   We are charg'd   135
By the Emperor, our brother, to attend
The Empresse seruice.
    2 Sister.   You are too mortifi'd sister,
(With reuerence I speak it) for yong Ladies
To keepe you company. I am so tir'd
With your tedious exhortations, doctrines, vses,   140
Of your religious morality,
That for my health sake, I must take the freedome
To enioy a little of those pretty pleasures
That I was borne to.
    1 Sister.   When I come to your yeeres,
Ile do as you do, but till then, with your pardon,   145
Ile lose no more time. I haue not learn't to dance yet,
Nor sing, but holy hymns, and those to vile tunes too;
Nor to discourse, but of Schoolemens opinions.
How shall I answer my sutors? since, I hope,
Ere long I shall haue many, without practice   150
To write, and speake somthing that's not deriu'd
From the fathers of Philosophy?

    135-61. *1 Sister . . . 2 Sister*] *32; Arcadia . . . Flaccilla Gifford*   139. I] *Mass-*
inger MS (J); I (*defective*) *32*

2 *Sister*.   We shall shame
Our breeding Sister, if we should go on thus.
  1 *Sister*. 'Tis for your credit, that we study
How to conuerse with men; women with women   155
Yeelds but a barren argument.
  2 *Sister*.   She frownes,
But you'll protect vs Madam?
  Athenais.   Yes, and loue
Your sweet simplicity.
  1 *Sister*.   All yong gyrles are so,
Till they know the way of't.
  2 *Sister*.   But when we are enter'd,
We shall on a good round pace.
  Athenais.   Ile leaue you Madam.   160
  1 *Sister*. And we our duties with you.

Exeunt ATHENAIS *and the yong Ladyes.*

F4ᵛ *Pulcheria*.   On all hands
Thus slighted? no way left? am I growne stupid
In my inuention? can I make no vse
Of the Emperors bounties? now 'tis thought: within there.

Enter a SERVANT.

Seruant. Madam.
  Pulcheria.   It shall be so; neerer; your eare. [*Whispers him.*]
Draw a petition to this end.
  Seruant.   Besides   166
The danger to prefer it, I beleeue
Twill nere be granted.
  Pulcheria.   How's this? are you growne,
From a seruant, my director? let me heare
No more of this. Dispatch. Ile master him   170
At his owne weapon.   *Exit* SERVANT.

Enter THEODOSIUS, PAULINUS, PHILANAX,
TIMANTUS, GRATIANUS.

Theodosius.   Let me vnderstand it,
If yet there be ought wanting that may perfect
A generall happinesse.
  Paulinus.   The peoples ioy

165. *Whispers him.*] *Gifford*; *not in* 32   171 SD. PAULINUS] *Gifford*; *Favorinus*
32   173. *Paulinus.*] *Gifford*; *Fauor. 32*

In seas of acclamations flow in
To wait on yours.
    Philanax.   Their loue with bounty leuied,   175
Is a sure guard. Obedience forc'd from feare,
Paper fortification, which in danger
Will yeeld to the impression of a reed,
Or of it selfe fall off.
    Theodosius.   True, *Philanax*:
And by that certain compasse we resolue   180
To steere our Barque of gouernment.

            Enter SERVANT *with the petition.*

    Pulcheria.   'Tis well.
    Theodosius. My deerest, and my all-deseruing Sister;
Gɪʳ As a petitioner kneele? it must not bee,
Pray you, rise, although your suite were halfe my Empire,
'Tis freely granted.
    Pulcheria.   Your alacritie   185
To giue hath made a begger; yet before
My suite is by your sacred hand and seale
Confirm'd, 'tis necessary you peruse
The summe of my request.
    Theodosius.   Wee will not wrong
Your iudgement, in conceiuing what 'tis fit   190
For you to aske, and vs to grant, so much,
As to proceede with caution; giue mee my signet,
With confidence I signe it, and heere vow
By my fathers soule, but with your free consent
It is irreuocable.
    Timantus.   What if shee now   195
Calling to memorie, how often wee
Haue cross'd her gouernment, in reuenge hath made
Petition for our heads?
    Gratianus.   They must euen off then,
No ransome can redeeme vs.
    Theodosius.   Let those iewells
So highly rated by the Persian merchants   200
Bee bought, and as a sacrifice from vs

       199. ransome] *Massinger MS*; ransone *32*

Presented to *Eudoxia*, shee being only
Worthy to weare 'em. I am angrie with
The vnresistable necessitie
Of my occasions, and important cares   205
That so long keepe mee from her.
                        Exeunt THEODOSIUS *and the trayne.*
  Pulcheria.   Goe to the Empresse,
And tell her, on the suddaine I am sicke,
And doe desire, the comfort of a visit,
If shee please to vouchsafe it. From me vse
Your humblest language: But when once I haue her   210
G1ᵛ In my possession, I will rise, and speake
In a higher straine, say it raise stormes, no matter.
Fooles iudge by the euent, my endes are honest.   *Exeunt.*

Act. 3. Scæne 3.

THEODOSIUS. TIMANTUS. PHILANAX.

  Theodosius. What is become of her? can shee that carries
Such glorious excellence of light about her,
Be any where conceal'd?
  Philanax.   Wee haue sought her lodgings,
And all we can learne from the seruants is,
Shee by your maiesties sisters wayted on,   5
(The attendance of her other officers
By her expresse command deni'd,)
  Theodosius.   Forbeare
Impertinent circumstances, whither went shee? speake.
  Philanax. As they ghesse, to the lawrell groue.
  Theodosius.   So slightly guarded!
What an earth-quake I feele in mee! and but that   10
Religion assures the contrarie,
The Poets dreames of lustfull Fawnes, and Satyres,
Would make me feare, I know not what.

---

    202. *Eudoxia,* shee] *Coxeter*; *Eudoxa.* Shee *32*   207. her, on the suddaine]
Gifford; her on the suddaine, *32*   III. iii. 9. guarded] *Massinger MS* (gaᵘrded);
garded *32*

Enter PAULINUS.

Paulinus.   I haue found her,
And it please your Maiestie.
  Theodosius.   Yes, it doth please mee.
But why return'd without her?
  Paulinus.   As shee made   15
Her speediest approches to your presence,
A seruant of the Princesses *Pulcheria*
Encounterd her; what 'twas, he whisperd to her
G2ʳ I am ignorant, but hearing it, she started,
And will'd me to excuse her absence from you,   20
The third part of an houre.
  Theodosius.   In this she takes
So much of my life from me; yet Ile beare it
With what patience I may; since 'tis her pleasure.
Go back, my good *Paulinus*, and intreat her   24
Not to exceed a minute.
  Timantus.   Here's strange fondnesse!   *Exeunt.*

[III. iv]   *Act. 3. Scæne 4.*

PULCHERIA, *Seruants.*

Pulcheria. You are certaine she will come?
  Seruant.   She is already
Enter'd your outward lodgings.
  Pulcheria.   No traine with her?
  Seruant. Your excellence sisters only.
  Pulcheria.   'Tis the better;
See the doores strongly guarded, and deny
Accesse to all, but with our speciall licence.   5
Why dost thou stay? shew your obedience,
Your wisdome now is vselesse.   *Exeunt Seruants.*

Enter ATHENAIS, ARCADIA, FLACCILLA.

Flaccilla.   She is sick sure,
Or, in fit reuerence to your Maiesty,
She had waited you at the doore.

  13 SD. PAULINUS] *32²* (Paulinus); Fauorinus *32¹*   13. *Paulinus.*] *32²* (*Paul.*);
Fauor. 32¹   15. *Paulinus.*] *32²* (*Paul.*); *Fauor. 32¹*   24. good *Paulinus*] *32²*;
Fauorinus 32¹

Arcadia.   'Twould hardly be
                              PULCHERIA *walking by.*
Excus'd, in ciuill manners, to her equall,   10
But with more difficulty to you, that are
So far aboue her.
    Athenais.   Not in her opinion;
G2ᵛ She hath beene too long accustom'd to command
T'acknowledge a superior.
    Arcadia.   There she walks.
    Flaccilla. If she be not sick of the sullens, I see not   15
The least infirmity in her.
    Athenais.   This is strange!
    Arcadia. Open your eyes; the Empresse.
    Pulcheria.   Reach that chaire:
Now sitting thus at distance, Ile vouchsafe
To looke vpon her.
    Arcadia.   How! sister! pray you awake,
Are you in your wits?
    Flaccilla.   Grant heauen, your too much learning   20
Does not conclude in madnesse.
    Athenais.   You intreated
A visit from me.
    Pulcheria.   True, my seruant vs'd
Such language, but now as a mistresse I
Command your seruice.
    Athenais.   Seruice!
    Arcadia.   She's stark mad, sure.
    Pulcheria. Youle finde I can dispose of what's mine owne   25
Without a guardian.
    Athenais.   Follow me. I will see you
When your frantique fit is ore. I do begin
To be of your beleefe.
    Pulcheria.   It will deceiue you.
Thou shalt not stirre from hence, thus as mine owne
I seize vpon thee.
    Flaccilla.   Help, help, violence   30
Offer'd to the Empresse person.
    Pulcheria.   'Tis in vaine:

III. iv. 19. sister!] *Massinger MS*; ~: 32   29. stirre] *Massinger MS* (Stirre);
str 32

Shee was an Empresse once, but, by my gift,
Which, being abus'd, I do recall my grant.
You are read in story; call to remembrance,
What the great *Hectors* mother, *Hecuba*   35
Was to *Vlysses*, *Ilium* sack'd.
G3ʳ   *Athenais.*   A slaue.
Pulcheria. To me thou art so.
Athenais.   Wonder and amazement
Quite ouerwhelme mee: how am I transform'd?
How haue I lost my liberty?

Knocking without: *Enter* SERVANT.

Pulcheria.   Thou shalt know
Too soone, no doubt. Who's that with such rudenesse   40
Beats at the doore?
Seruant.   The Prince *Paulinus*, madam,
Sent from the Emperor to attend vpon
The gratious Empresse.
Arcadia.   And who is your slaue now?
Flaccilla. Sister, repent in time, and beg a pardon
For your presumption.
Pulcheria.   It is resolu'd: 45
From me returne this answer to *Paulinus*;
She shall not come; she's mine; the Emperor hath
No interest in her.   *Exit* SERVANT.
Athenais.   Whatsoere I am,
You take not from your power ore me, to yeeld
A reason for this vsage.
Pulcheria.   Though my will is   50
Sufficient, to ad to thy affliction,
Know wretched thing, 'tis not thy fate, but folly
Hath made thee what thou art: 'tis some delight
To vrge my merits to one so vngratefull;
Therefore with horror heare it. When thou wert   55
Thrust as a stranger from thy fathers house,
Expos'd to all calamities that want
Could throw vpon thee, thine owne brothers scorne,
And in thy hopes, as by the world, forsaken,

35. mother,] *Massinger MS*; ~ ∧ *32*   39. shalt] *Coxeter*; shall *32*   44. beg
a] *Massinger MS*; beg *32*   51. Sufficient,] *Massinger MS*; ~ ∧ *32*

My pitty the last altar that was left thee,   60
I heard thy Syren charmes, with feeling heard them,
And my compassion made mine eyes vy teares
G3ᵛ With thine, dissembling Crocodile; and when Queenes
Were emulous for the imperiall bed,
The garments of thy sorrowes cast aside,   65
I put thee in a shape as would haue forc'd
Enuy from *Cleopatra*, had she seene thee;
Then, when I knew my brothers blood was warm'd
With youthfull fires, I brought thee to his presence,
And how my deepe designes, for thy good plotted,   70
Succeeded to my wishes, is apparent,
And needs no repetition.
  Athenais.   I am conscious
Of your so many, and vnequall'd fauors,
But finde not how I may accuse my selfe
For any facts committed, that with iustice   75
Can raise your anger to this height against me.
  Pulcheria. Pride and forgetfulnesse would not let thee see that,
Against which now thou canst not close thine eyes.
What iniury could be equall to thy late
Contempt of my good counsell? when I vrg'd   80
The Emperors prodigall bounties, and intreated
That you would vse your power to giue 'em limits,
Or, at the least, a due consideration
Of such as su'd, and for what, ere he sign'd it?
In opposition you brought against me   85
Th' obedience of a wife, that Ladyes were not,
Being well accommodated by their Lords,
To question, but much lesse to crosse their pleasures;
Nor would you, though the Emperor were resolu'd
To giue away his Scepter, hinder it,   90
Since 'twas done for your honor, couering with
False colors of humility your ambition.
  Athenais. And is this my offence?
  Pulcheria.   As wicked counsell
Is still most hurtfull vnto those that giue it;
Such as deny to follow what is good,   95

60. pitty] *Massinger MS*; pity *32* 64. the] *Massinger MS*; thy *32* 71. appa-
rent] *Massinger MS*; apparant *32* 80. counsell?] *Massinger MS*; ~, *32*

In reason, are the first that must repent it.
When I please you shall heare more, in the meane time
G4^r Thank your owne wilfull follie that hath chang'd you
From an Empresse to a bondewoman.
    Theodosius [*within*].   Force the doores,
Kill those that dare resist.

Enter THEODOSIUS, PAULINUS, PHILANAX,
CHRYSAPIUS, GRATIANUS.

    Athenais.   Deere Sir redeeme mee.   100
    Flaccilla. O suffer not, for your owne honors sake,
The Empresse you so late lou'd to bee made
A prisoner in the court.
    Arcadia.   Leape to his lippes,
You'll finde them the best sanctuarie.
    Flaccilla.   And trie then,
What interest my reuerend Sister hath   105
To force you from 'em.
    Theodosius.   What strange may-game's this?
Though done in sport, how ill this leuitie
Becomes your wisdome!
    Pulcheria.   I am serious Sir,
And haue done nothing but what you in honor,
And as you are your selfe an Emperour,   110
Stand bound to iustifie.
    Theodosius.   Take heed, put not these
Strange trialls on my patience.
    Pulcheria.   Doe not you Sir,
Denie your owne act; as you are a man,
And stand on your owne bottomes, 'twill appeare
A childish weakenes to make void a grant,   115
Sign'd by your sacred hand, and seale, and strengthend
With a religious oth, but with my licence,
Neuer to be recall'd. For some few minutes,
Let reason rule your passion, and in this,   *Deliuers the deed.*
Bee pleas'd to reade my interest; you will finde there   120
What you in me call violence, is iustice,
And that I may make vse of what's mine owne,

99. *within*] *Gifford: not in* 32

G4ᵛ According to my will. 'Tis your owne gift Sir,
And what an Emperour giues, should stand as firme
As the celestiall poles vpon the shoulders   125
Of *Atlas*, or his successor in that office
The greate *Alcides*.
    Theodosius.   Miseries of more waight,
Then 'tis faind they supported, fall vpon mee.
What hath my rashnesse done? in this transaction
Drawne, in expresse and formall termes I haue   130
Giuen and consign'd into your handes, to vse,
And handle, as you please, my deere *Eudoxia*.
It is my deed, I doe confesse it is,
And as I am my selfe, not to bee cancell'd:
But yet you may shew mercie, and you will,   135
When you consider that there is no beauty,
So perfit in a creature, but is soilde
With some vnbeseeming blemish; you haue labour'd
To build mee vp a compleate Prince, 'tis granted,
Yet as I am a man, like other Monarchs,   140
I haue defects and frayleties, my facilitie,
To send petitioners with pleas'd lookes from me,
Is all I can be charg'd with, and it will
Become your wisdome, (since 'tis in your power)
In charitie to prouide, I fall no further   145
Or in my oth, or honor.
    Pulcheria.   Royall Sir,
This was the marke I aim'd at, and I glorie
At the length, you so conceaue it. 'Twas a weakenes
To measure by your owne integritie
The purposes of others. I haue showne you   150
In a true mirror what fruite growes vpon
The tree of hudwinckt bounty, and what dangers
Precipitation in the managing
Your greate affaires produceth.
    Theodosius.   I embrace it
As a graue aduertisement, and vow heereafter   155
Neuer to signe petitions at this rate.

131. vse,] *Massinger MS*; ～ₐ *32*   132. handle] *Massinger MS*; obserue *32*
Eudoxia] *Massinger MS*; *Eudoxa 32*   145. I] *Massinger MS (J)*; I (*defective in*
some copies) *32*

Pulcheria. For mine, see Sir, 'tis cancel'd, on my knees
I redeliuer what I now beg'd from you.   *Teares the deed.*
Shee is my second gift.
    Theodosius.   Which if I part from
Till death diuorce vs—   *Kissing* ATHENAIS.
    Athenais.   So Sir,
    Theodosius.   Nay sweete chide not: 160
I am punish'd in thy lookes, defer the rest,
Till we are more priuate.
    Pulcheria.   I aske pardon too
If in my personated passion I
Appeard to harshe, and rough.
    Athenais.   'Twas gentle language,
What I was then considerd.
    Pulcheria.   O deere Madame,   165
It was *decorum* in the *Scæne*.
    Athenais.   This triall,
When I was *Athenais*, might haue pass'd,
But as I am the Empresse—
    Theodosius.   Nay no anger,
Since all good was intended.
        Exeunt THEODOSIUS, ATHENAIS, ARCADIA, FLACCILLA.
    Pulcheria.   Building on   169
That certaine base, I feare not what can follow.   *Exit* PULCHERIA.
    Paulinus. These are strange deuices *Philanax.*
    Philanax.   True my Lord,
May all turne to the best.
    Gratianus.   The Emperours lookes
Promis'd a calme.
    Chrysapius.   But the vex'd Empresse frownes
Presag'd a second storme.
    Paulinus.   I am sure I feele one,
In my legge already.
    Philanax.   Your old friend, the goute?   175
    Paulinus. My forc'd companion, *Philanax.*
    Chrysapius.   To your rest.
Hı^v   *Paulinus.* Rest and forbearing wine, with a temperate dyet,

160. vs—] *Coxeter*; ~. *32*   ATHENAIS.] *Massinger MS* (ais *added*); Athen. *32*
163. I] *Massinger MS* (*J*); I (*slightly defective*) *32*   164–5. language, / What]
Coxeter; *undivided 32*   168. Empresse—] *Coxeter*; ~. *32*

Though many Montebancks pretend the cure of't,
I haue found my best Physitians.
 Philanax.   Ease to your Lordship. *Exeunt.*

      The ende of the third Act.

      Actus 4. Scæn. 1.

    ATHENAIS. CHRYSAPIUS.

Athenais. MAKE mee her propertie?
 Chrysapius.   Your maiestie
Hath iust cause of distast, and your resentment
Of the affront in the point of honor cannot
But meete a faire construction.
 Athenais.   I haue only
The title of an Empresse, but the power   5
Is, by her, rauish'd from me. Shee suruayes
My actions as a gouernesse, and calls
My not obseruing all that shee directs
Folly, and disobedience.
 Chrysapius.   Vnder correction,
With griefe I haue long obseru'd it, and if you   10
Stand pleas'd to signe my warrant Ile deliuer
In my vnfainde zeale, and desire to serue you,
(Howere I run the hazard of my head for't
Should it arriue at the knowledge of the Princesse,)
Not alone, the reasons why things are thus carried, 15
But giue into your hands the power to clippe
The wings of her command.
 Athenais.   Your seruice this way
Cannot offend mee.
 Chrysapius. Bee you pleas'd to know then
But still with pardon, if I am too bold,
H2ʳ Your too much sufferance impes the broken feathers 20
Which carie her to this proude height, in which
Shee with securitie, soares, and still towres ore you,
But if you would imploy the strengths you hold

  IV. i. 13. I] *Massinger MS*; I (*defective*) *32*   14. Princesse] *32*; Empresse
Massinger MS; Emperour *conj. Greg*

In the Emperours affections, and remember
The orbe you moue in should admit no star els, 25
You neuer would confesse the managing
Of state affaires to her alone are proper,
And you sit by a looker on.
    Athenais.   I would not,
If it were possible I could attempt
Her diminution, without a taint 30
Of foule ingratitude in my selfe.
    Chrysapius.   In this
The sweetenesse of your temper does abuse you,
And you call that a benefit to your selfe
Which shee for her owne endes conferr'd vpon you.
'Tis yeelded shee gaue way to your aduancement: 35
But for what cause? that shee might still continue
Her absolute sway, and swinge ore the whole state,
And that shee might to her admirers vaunt,
The Empresse was her creature, and the giuer
To bee preferr'd before the gift.
    Athenais.   It may bee. 40
    Chrysapius. Nay 'tis most certaine: whereas would you please
In a true glasse to looke vpon your selfe,
And view without detraction your owne merits
Which all men wonder at; you would find that fate,
Without a second cause, appointed you 45
To the supremest honor. For the Princesse,
Shee hath raign'd long enough, and her remoue
Will make your entrance free to the possession
Of what you were borne to, and but once resolue
To build vpon her ruines, leaue the engines 50
That must bee vs'd to vndermine her greatenes
To my prouision.
    Athenais.   I thanke your care,
But a designe of such waight must not be
Rashly determin'd of, it will exact
A long and serious consultation from mee. 55
In the meane time *Chrysapius* rest assur'd
I liue your thankefull Mistrisse.   *Exit* ATHENAIS.

H2ᵛ

---

    37. swinge] *Massinger MS*; swing *32*   57 SD. ATHENAIS.] *Massinger MS* (enais
added); Ath: *32*

Chrysapius.   Is this all?
Will the Physick that I minister'd worke no further?
I haue playd the foole, and leauing a calme port
Embarqu'd my selfe on a rough sea of danger.   60
In her silence lies my safetie, which how can I
Hope from a woman? but the die is throwne,
And I must stand the hazard.

       Enter THEODOSIUS, PHILANAX, TIMANTUS,
            GRATIANUS, *Huntsmen.*

Theodosius.   Is *Paulinus*
So tortur'd with his gowte?
     Philanax.   Most miserablie,
And it ads much to his affliction, that   65
The payne denies him power to waite vpon
Your Maiestie.
     Theodosius.   I pittie him: hee is
A wondrous honest man, and what he suffers,
I know will grieue my Empresse.
     Timantus.   Hee indeed is
Much bound to her gratious fauour.
     Theodosius.   Hee deserues it,   70
Shee cannot finde a subiect vpon whom
Shee better may confer it: is the stagge
Safe lodg'd?
     Gratianus.   Yes Sir, and the houndes and huntsmen ready.
     Philanax. Hee will make you royall sport. Hee is a deere
Of ten at the least.

       Enter COUNTRYMAN *with the apple.*

     Gratianus.   Whither will this clowne?
H3ʳ   *Timantus.*   Stand backe.   75
     Countryman. I would zee the Emperour, why should you Courtiers
Scorne a poore Countryman? wee zweat at the Plough
To vill your mouths, you and you curs might starue els.
Wee prune the orchards, and you cranch the fruite;
Yet still you are snarling at vs.
     Theodosius.   What's the matter?   80
     Countryman. I would looke on thy sweete face.

         78. you curs] *32*; your curs *Mason*

Timantus.   Vnmannerly swaine.

Countryman. Zwaine, though I am a zwaine, I haue a heart yet,
As ready to doe seruice for my leege,
As any Princox Peacock of you all.
Zookers had I one of you zingle with this twigge,   85
I would so veeze you.

Timantus.   Will your Maiestie
Heare his rude language?

Theodosius.   Yes, and hold it as
An ornament, not a blemish. O *Timantus*!
Since that drad power by whom we are, disdaines not
With an open eare to heare petitions from vs,   90
Easie accesse in vs his deputies,
To the meanest of our subiects, is a debt,
Which we stand bound to pay.

Countryman.   By my granams ghost
'Tis a holsome zaying, our vicar could not mend it
In the pulpit on a Zunday.

Theodosius.   What's thy suite friend?   95

Countryman. Zute? I would laugh at that. Let the court begge
        from thee
What the poore countrie giues: I bring a present
To thy good grace, which I can call mine owne,
And looke not like these gay folke for a returne,
Of what they venture. Haue I giuent you? ha?   100

Chrysapius. A perillous knaue.

Countryman.   Zee heere a dainty Apple,
                          Presents the Apple.
Of mine owne graffing, zweete, and zownde I assure thee.

H3ᵛ   *Theodosius.* It is the fairest fruite I euer saw.
Those golden apples in the *Hesperian* orchardes
So strangely guarded by the watchfull Dragon,   105
As they requir'd greate *Hercules* to get 'em,
Nor those with which *Hippomenes* deceiu'd
Swift footed *Atalanta*, when I looke
On this, deserue no wonder. You behold
The pooreman, and his present with contempt: 110
I to their value prize both; he that could

88. blemish] *Coxeter*; blendish *32*   89. drad] *32*; dread *Coxeter*   95. thy]
Mason; they *32*   105. strangely] *32*; strongly *conj. Gifford*

So ayde weake nature, by his care, and labour,
As to compell a crabtree stocke to beare
A pretious fruite of this large size, and beauty,
Would by his industrie change a pettie village   115
Into a populous Citty, and from that
Erecte a flourishing Kingdome. Giue the fellow
For an encouragement to his future labours,
Ten Attick talents.
    Countryman.   I will wearie heauen
With my prayers for your Maiestie.   *Exit* COUNTRYMAN.
    Theodosius.   *Philanax*,   120
From mee present this raritie to the rarest
And best of women, when I think vpon
The boundlesse happinesse that from her flow to me
In my imagination I am rap'd
Beyond my selfe; but I forget our hunting,   125
To the forrest for the exercise of my body,
But for my mind, 'tis wholly taken vp,
In the contemplation of her matchlesse vertues.   *Exeunt.*

Act. 4. Scæna 2.

ATHENAIS. PULCHERIA. ARCADIA. FLACCILLA.

    Athenais. You shall know ther's a difference betweene vs.
    Pulcheria. There was I am certain not long since, when you
H4ʳ Kneel'd a petitioner to me, then you were happy
To bee neere my feete, and doe you hold it now
As a disparagement that I side you Lady?   5
    Athenais. Since you respect mee only as I was,
What I am shall be remembred.
    Pulcheria.   Does the meanes,
I practis'd to giue good, and sauing counsails
To the Emperour, and your new stamp'd maiestie
Still sticke in your stomach?
    Athenais.   'Tis not yet digested,   10
In troth it is not: why good gouernesse,
Though you are held for a grand Madam, and your selfe,
The first that ouerprize it, I nere tooke

Your words for *Delphian* oracles, nor your actions
For such wonders as you make 'em, there is one   15
When shee shall see her time, as fit and able
To be made partner of the Emperours cares,
As your wise selfe, and may with iustice challenge
A neerer interest. You haue done your visit,
So when you please, you may leaue me.
 Pulcheria.   Ile not bandye   20
Words with your mightinesse, prowd one, only this,
You carrie to much saile for your small barke,
And that when you least think vpon't may sincke you.
            Exit PULCHERIA.

 Flaccilla. I am glad shee is gone.
 Arcadia.   I feard shee would haue read
A tedious lecture to vs.

     Enter PHILANAX *with the apple.*

 Philanax.   From the Emperour,   25
This rare fruite to the rarest.
 Athenais.   How my Lord?
 Philanax. I vse his language Madame, and that trust,
Which hee impos'd on mee, discharg'd, his pleasure
Commands my present seruice.   *Exit* PHILANAX.
 Athenais.   Haue you seene
So faire an Apple?
 Flaccilla.   Neuer.
H4ᵛ *Arcadia.*   If the taste   30
Answer the beauty.
 Athenais.   Prettily beg'd, you should haue it,
But that you eate too much cold fruite, and that
Changes the fresh red in your cheekes to palenesse.
I haue other dainties for you;

      Enter SERVANT.

       you come from
Paulinus, how is't with that truely noble,   35
And honest Lord? my witnesse at the fount;
In a word the man to whose bless'd charity
I owe my greatenesse. How is't with him?
 Seruant.   Spiritely,

In his minde, but by the raging of his goute
In his body much distemper'd, that you pleas'd   40
To inquire his health, tooke off much from his paine,
His glad lookes did confirme it.
    Athenais.   Doe his Doctors
Giue him no hope?
    Seruant.   Little, they rather feare,
By his continuall burning, that hee stands
In danger of a feuer.
    Athenais.   To him againe,   45
And tell him that I heartely wish it lay
In mee to ease him, and from me deliuer
This choice fruite to him, you may say to that,
I hope it will proue Physicall.
    Seruant.   The good Lord
Will be oreioyde with the fauour.
    Athenais.   Hee deseru's more.   *Exeunt.*

I1^r
IV. iii]

Actus 4. Scæna 3.

PAULINUS *brought in a chaire.* CHIRURGION.

    Chirurgion. I haue done as much as art can doe, to stoppe
The violent course of your fit, and I hope you feele it,
How does your honor?
    Paulinus.   At some ease, I thanke you,
I would you could assure continuance of it,
For the moyetie of my fortune.
    Chirurgion.   If I could cure   5
The gout my Lord, without the Philosophers stone
I should soone purchase, it being a disease,
In poore men very rare, and in the rich
The cure impossible; your many bounties
Bid mee prepare you for a certaine truth,   10
And to flatter you were dishonest.
    Paulinus.   Your plaine dealing
Deserues a fee. Would there were many more such
Of your profession. Happy are pooremen,

If sicke, with the excesse of heate, or cold,
Caus'd by necessitous labour, not loose surfets,   15
They, when spare dyet, or kind nature faile
To perfit their recouery, soone arriue at
Their rest in death, but on the contrarie
The greate, and noble are expos'd as preyes
To the rapine of Physitians, and they   20
In lingring out what is remedilesse,
Aime at their profit, not the patients health;
A thousand trialls and experiments
Haue bene put vpon mee, and I forc'd to pay deere
For my vexation, but I am resolu'd   25
(I thanke your honest freedome) to be made
I1ᵛ A propertie no more for knaues to worke on.

Enter CLEON *with a parchement role.*

What haue you there?
   Cleon.   The triumphes of an artsman
O're all infirmities, made authenticall
With the names of Princes, Kings, and Emperours   30
That were his patients.
   Paulinus.   Some Empericke.
   Cleon. It may be so, but he sweares within three dayes
He will grub vp your goute by the rootes, and make you able
To march ten leagues a day in compleate armor.
   Paulinus. Impossible!
   Cleon.   Or if you like not him—   35
   Chirurgion. Heare him, my Lord, for your mirth; I will take order,
Hee shall not wrong you.
   Paulinus.   Vsher in your monster.
   Cleon. He is at hand, march vp:

Enter EMPERICK.

                          now speak for your self.   38
   Emperick. I come not (right honorable) to your presence, with
any base and sordid end of reward; the immortality of my fame is
the white I shoote at, the charge of my most curious, and costly

14. sicke,] *Massinger MS*; ~ₐ *32*   heate,] *Massinger MS*; ~ₐ *32*   15. surfets,] *Massinger MS*; ~ₐ *32*   27 SD. *Enter . . . role.*] *Gifford*; *follows* What . . .
there *in 32*   30. Kings,] *Massinger MS*; ~ₐ *32*   35. Impossible!] *Massinger
MS*; ~, *32*   37. Hee] *Massinger MS*; They *32*   38. self.] *Coxeter*; ~? *32*

ingredients defray'd, amounting to some seaventeene thousand
crownes, a trifle in respect of health, writing your noble name in my
Catalogue, I shall acknowledge my selfe amply satisfi'd.

Chirurgion. I beleeue so.   45

Emperick. For your owne sake I most heartily wish, that you had
now all the diseases, maladies, and infirmities vpon you, that were
euer remembred by old *Galen*, *Hippocrates*, or the later, and more
admired *Paracelsus*.

Paulinus. For your good wish, I thanke you.   50

I2ʳ   *Emperick.* Take mee with you, I beseech your good Lordship, I
vrg'd it that your ioy in being certainely, and suddainly freed from
them, may be the greater, and my not to bee paralleld skill the more
remarkable: the cure of the goute a toy, without boast bee it said, my
cradle practise, the cancer, the Fistula, the Dropsie, consumption
of Lunges, and Kidnyes, hurts in the braine, heart, or liuer, are
things worthy my opposition, but in the recouerie of my patients
I euer ouercome them, but to your goute,

Paulinus. I marry Sir, that cur'd I shall be apter
To giue credit to the rest.

Emperick.   Suppose it done Sir.   60

Chirurgion. And the meanes, you vse I beseech you?

Emperick. I will doe it in the plainest language, and discouer my
ingredients. First my *boteni Terebinthina*, of *Cypris*, my Manna, *ros
cœlo*, coagulated with *vetulos ouorum*, vulgarly yelkes of Egges, with
a little Cyath, or quantitie of my potable Elixir, with some few
scruples of sassa-fras and Guacum, so taken euery morning and
euening, in the space of three dayes, purgeth, clenseth, and dissi-
pateth the inward causes of the virulent tumor.

Paulinus. Why doe you smile?

Chirurgion. When hee hath done I will resolue you.   70

Emperick. For my exterior applications I haue these balsum-
unguentulums extracted from hearbes, plants, rootes, seeds,
gummes, and a million of other vegetables, the principall of which
are Vlissipona, or Serpentaria, Sophia, or Herba consolidarum,
Parthenium or commanilla Romana, Mumia transmarina, mixed
with my plumbum Philosophorum, and mater metallorum, *cum ossa
paraleli, est vniuersale medicamentum in podagra.*   77

Cleon. A coniuring balsamum!

Emperick. This applied warme vpon the pained place, with a
fether of Struthio cameli, or a bird of Paradise which is euery where
to bee had, shall expulse this tartarous, viscous, anatheos, and
malignant dolor.   82

Chirurgion. An excellent receipt, but does your Lordship
I2ᵛ Know what it is good for?

Paulinus.   I would be instructed.

Chirurgion. For the gonorrhea, or if you will heare it   85
In a plainer phrase, the pox.

Emperick.   If it cure his Lordship
Of that by the way, I hope Sir 'tis the better;
My medicine serues for all things, and the pox Sir,
Though falsely nam'd the Sciatica, or goute,
Is the more Catholick sickenesse.

Paulinus.   Hence with the rascall.   90
Yet hurt him not, he makes mee smile, and that
Frees him from punishment.   *They thrust off the* EMPERICK.

Chirurgion.   Such slaues as this
Render our art contemptible.

Enter SERVANT.

Seruant.   My good Lord,
Paulinus. So soone return'd?
Seruant.   And with this present from
Your greate, and gratious Mistrisse, with her wishes   95
It may proue Physicall to you.

Paulinus.   In my heart
I kneele, and thanke her bounty. Deere friend *Cleon*,
Giue him the cupboorde of Plate in the next roome,
For a reward.   *Exeunt* CLEON *and the* SERVANT.
                Most glorious fruite, but made
More pretious by her grace, and loue that sent it.   100
To touch it only comming from her hand
Makes mee forget all paine. A Diamond
Of this large size, though it would buy a Kingdome,
Hew'd from the rocke, and lay'd downe at my feete,
Nay though a Monarchs gift, will hold no value,   105
Compar'd with this, and yet ere I presume
To tast it, though sans question it is
I3ʳ Some heauenly restoratiue, I in duty

Stand bound to waigh my owne vnworthinesse:
Ambrosia is foode only for the Gods;   110
And not by humane lips to be prophan'd:
I may adore it as some holy Relick,
Deriu'de from thence, but impious to keepe it,
In my possession; the Emperour only,
Is worthy to inioy it.

Enter CLEON.

                         Goe good *Cleon*,   115
(And cease thie admiration at this obiect;)
From mee present this to my royall master,
I know it will amaze him, and excuse me
That I am not my selfe the bearer of it.
That I should bee lame now, when with wings of duty   120
I should flye to the seruice of this Empresse!
Nay no delayes good *Cleon*.
   Cleon.   I am gone Sir.   *Exeunt.*

Act. 4. Scæne 4.

THEODOSIUS. CHRYSAPIUS. TIMANTUS. GRATIANUS.

Chrysapius. Are you not tir'd Sir?
   Theodosius.   Tir'd? I must not say so
Howeuer, though I rode hard; to a huntsman,
His toyle is his delight, and to complaine
Of wearinesse, would shew as poorely in him,
As if a Generall should greiue for a wound,   5
Receau'd vpon his forhead, or his brest,
After a glorious victorie; lay by
These accoutrements for the chase.

Enter PULCHERIA.

   Pulcheria.   You are well return'd Sir,
From your Princely exercise.
   Theodosius.   Sister, to you
I owe the freedome, and the vse of all   10

116. thie] *Massinger MS*; this *32*   IV. iv. 8 SD. PULCHERIA.] *Massinger MS*
(eria *added*); Pulch. *32*

The pleasures I enioy; your care prouides
13ᵛ For my security, and the burthen which
I should alone sustaine, you vndergoe,
And by your painefull watchings, yeeld my sleepes
Both sound, and sure. How happie am I in   15
Your knowledge of the art of gouernement!
And credit mee, I glorie to behold you
Dispose of great designes, as if you were
A partner, and no subiect of my Empire.
    Pulcheria. My vigilance, since it hath well succeeded,   20
I am confident, you allow of, yet it is not
Approu'd by all.
    Theodosius.   Who dares repine at that,
Which hath our suffrage?
    Pulcheria.   One that too well knowes,
The strength of her abilities can better
My weake endeuours.
    Theodosius.   In this you reflect   25
Vpon my Empresse?
    Pulcheria.   True, for as shee is
The consort of your bed, 'tis fit shee share in
Your cares, and absolute power.
    Theodosius.   You touch a string
That sowndes but harshely to mee, and I must
In a brothers loue aduise you that heereafter   30
You would forbeare to moue it; since shee is
In her pure selfe a harmonie of such sweetenesse,
Compos'd of dutie, chaste desires, her beautie
(Though it might tempt a Hermit from his beades)
The least of her endowments. I am sorrie   35
Her holding the first place, since that the second
Is proper to your selfe, calls on your enuie.
Shee erre? it is impossible in a thought,
And much more speake, or doe what may offend mee.
In other things, I would beleeue you sister: 40
But though the tongues of Saints, and Angells tax'd her
Of any imperfection, I should be
Incredulous.
14ʳ   *Pulcheria.* Shee is yet a woman Sir.
    Theodosius. The abstract of what's excellent in the sex:

But to their mulcts, and frayleties a meere stranger;   45
Ile dye in this beleefe.

Enter CLEON with the apple.

Cleon.   Your humblest seruant,
The Lord *Paulinus,* as a witnesse of
His zeale, and dutie to your Maiestie,
Presents you with this iewell.
  Theodosius.   Ha!
  Cleon.   It is
Preferr'd by him.
  Theodosius.   Aboue his honor?
  Cleon.   No Sir,   50
I would haue said his patrimonie.
  Theodosius.   'Tis the same.
  Cleon. And he intreates, since lamenesse may excuse
His not presenting it himselfe, from mee
(Though far vnworthy to supplie his place)
You would vouchsafe to accept it.
  Theodosius.   Farther off,   55
You haue told your tale. Stay you for a reward?
Take that.   *Strikes him.*
  Pulcheria. How's this?
  Chrysapius.   I neuer saw him mou'd thus.
  Theodosius. Wee must not part so Sir, a guarde vpon him.

Enter Garde.

May I not vent my sorrowes in the aire,
Without discouerie? forbeare the roome,   60
Yet be within call.   *They all goe aside.*
         What an earth-quake I feele in mee!
And on the suddaine my whole fabrick totters.
My blood within mee turnes, and through my veines
Parting with naturall rednesse I discerne it,
Chang'd to a fatall yellow: what an army   65
Of hellish furies in the horrid shapes
Of doubts, and feares, charge on mee! rise to my rescue,
Thou stout maintainer of a chaste wifes honor,

50. him.] *32*; him— *Coxeter*   61. call.] *Massinger MS*; ∼, *32*   SD. *They* …
aside.] *editor*; *at l. 60 in 32*   63. veines] *Massinger MS*; vaines *32*

The confidence of her vertues; bee not shaken
With the wind of vaine surmises, much lesse suffer   70
14^v The diuell iealousie to whisper to mee
My curious obseruation of that
I must no more remember. Will it not bee?
Thou vninuited ghest, ill mannerd monster,
I charge thee leaue mee, wilt thou force mee to   75
Giue fuell to that fire I would put out?
The goodnesse of my memorie proues my mischiefe,
And I would sell my Empire, could it purchase
The dull art of forgetfulnesse. Who waites there?
    Timantus. Most sacred Sir.
    Theodosius.   Sacred, as 'tis accurs'd   80
Is proper to mee. Sirra, vpon your life,
Without a word concerning this, command
Eudoxia to come to mee; would I had   *Exit* TIMANTUS.
Nere knowne her by that name, my mothers name,
Or that for her owne sake shee had continued   85
Poore *Athenais* still.—No intermission?
Wilt thou so soone torment mee? must I reade
Writ in the table of my memorie,
To warrant my suspition, how *Paulinus*
(Though euer thought a man auerse to women)   90
First gaue her entertainement? made her way
For audience to my sister? then I did
My selfe obserue how hee was rauish'd with
The gratious deliuerie of her storie,
(Which was I grant the bait that first took me too)   95
Shee was his conuert, what the rethorick was
Hee vs'd I know not, and since shee was mine,
In priuate, as in publick, what a masse
Of grace and fauours hath shee heap'd vpon him!
And but to day this fatall fruite. Shee's come.   100

    Enter TIMANTUS, ATHENAIS, FLACCILLA, ARCADIA.

Can shee bee guiltie?
    Athenais.   You seeme troubl'd Sir,
My innocence makes mee bold to aske the cause
K1^r That I may ease you of it; no salute
After foure long houres absence?

Theodosius.   Prethee forgiue mee.   *Kisses her.*
Mee thinks I finde *Paulinus* on her lips,   105
And the fresh *Nectar* that I drew from thence
Is on the suddaine pal'd. How haue you spent
Your hours since I last saw you?
Athenais.   In the conuerse
Of your sweete sisters.
Theodosius.   Did not *Philanax*
From mee deliuer you an apple?
Athenais.   Yes Sir;   110
Heauen! how you frowne! pray you talke of something els,
Thinke not of such a trifle.
Theodosius.   How! a trifle?
Does any toy from mee presented to you,
Deserue to be so sleighted? doe you valewe
What's sent, and not the sender? from a peasant   115
It had deseru'd your thanks.
Athenais.   And meetes from you Sir
All possible respect.
Theodosius.   I priz'd it Lady
At a higher rate then you beleeue, and would not
Haue parted with it, but to one I did
Prefer before my selfe.
Athenais.   It was indeed   120
The fairest that I euer saw.
Theodosius.   It was?
And it had vertues in it, my *Eudoxia*
Not visible to the eye.
Athenais.   It may be so Sir.
Theodosius. What did you with it? tell mee punctually;
I looke for a strict accompt.
Athenais.   What shall I answer?   [*Aside.*]
Theodosius. Doe you stagger? ha?
Athenais.   No Sir, I haue eaten it.   126
It had the pleasantest tast. I wonder that
K1ᵛ You found it not in my breath.
Theodosius.   I'faith I did not,
And it was wondrous strange.

105. thinks] *Massinger MS*; thanks *32*   125 SD. Aside.] *Gifford²*; *not in 32*
128. I'faith] *Coxeter*; I faith *32*

Athenais.   Pray you try againe.

Theodosius. I find no scent of't heere. You play with me;   130
You haue it still?

Athenais.   By your sacred life, and fortune,
An oth I dare not breake, I haue eaten it.

Theodosius. Doe you know how this oth binds?

Athenais.   Too well, to breake it.

Theodosius. That euer man to please his brutish sense
Should slaue his vnderstanding to his passions,   135
And taken with soone fading white, and red,
Deliuer vp his credulous eares to heare
The magick of a Siren, and from these
Beleeue there euer was, is, or can bee
More then a seeming honestie in bad woman.   140

Athenais. This is strange language Sir.

Theodosius.   Who waites? come all.
Nay sister not so neere, being of the sex,
I feare you are infected to.

Pulcheria.   What meane you?

Theodosius. To show you a miracle, a prodigie
Which Affrick neuer equall'd. Can you think   145
This master peece of heauen, this pretious vellam,
Of such a puritie, and virgin whitenesse,
Could be design'd to haue periurie, and whoredome
In capitall letters writ vpon't?

Pulcheria.   Deere Sir,

Theodosius. Nay adde to this an impudence beyond   150
All prostituted boldnesse. Art not dead yet?
Will not the tempests in thy conscience rende thee
As small as *Atomes*? that there may no signe
Be left, thou euer wert so! wilt thou liue
Till thou art blasted with the dreadfull lightning   155
Of pregnant, and vnanswerable proofes,
Of thy adulterous twines? dye yet that I
K2ʳ With my honor may conceale it.

Athenais.   Would long since,
The Gorgon of your rage had turn'd mee marble,
Or if I haue offended—

---

136. white, and red,] *Massinger MS*; ∼ₐ∼∼ₐ *32*   145. neuer equall'd.]
Massinger MS; ∼: ∼ₐ *32*   160. offended—] *Coxeter*; ∼? *32*

Theodosius.   If! good Angels!   160
But I am tame: looke on this dombe accuser.
   Athenais. O I am lost!
   Theodosius.   Did euer cormorant
Swollow his prey and then digest it whole
As shee hath done this apple? *Philanax,*
As 'tis, from me presented it. The good Lady   165
Swore shee had eaten it; yet I know not how
It came intire vnto *Paulinus* hands,
And I from him receau'd it, sent in scorne
Vpon my life to giue me a close touch,
That he was wearie of thee. Was there nothing   170
Left thee to fee him, to giue satisfaction
To thy insatiate lust, but what was sent
As a deere fauour from mee? how haue I sind
In my dotage on this creature? but to her
I haue liu'd, as I was borne, a perfit virgin.   175
Nay more I thought it not enough to be
True to her bed, but that I must feede high,
To strengthen my abilities to cloye
Her rauenous appetite, little suspecting
Shee would desire a change.
   Athenais.   I neuer did Sir.   180
   Theodosius. Be dumbe, I will not waste my breath in taxing
Thy base ingratitude. How I haue rais'd thee,
Will by the world be to thy shame spoke often.
But for that ribawd, who held in my Empire
The next place to my selfe, so bound vnto me   185
By all the tyes of duty, and allegeance,
Hee shall pay deere for't, and feele what it is
In a wrong of such high consequence to pull downe
His Lords slow anger on him. *Philanax,*
Hee's troubl'd with the goute, let him be cur'd   190
With a violent death, and in the other world,
Thanke his Physitian.
   Philanax.   His cause vnheard Sir?
   Pulcheria. Take heede of rashnesse.

K2ᵛ

163. prey] *Massinger MS*; pray *32*   171. fee] *Massinger MS*; fee (f
defective) *32*

Theodosius.   Is what I command,
To bee disputed?
    Philanax.   Your will shall bee done Sir:
But that I am the instrument—
    Theodosius.   Doe you murmur?   195
                Exit PHILANAX *with the gard.*
What couldst thou say if that my licence should
Giue liberty to thy tongue?
        ATHENAIS, *kneeling, points to* THEODOSIUS' *sword.*
             Thou would'st dye? I am not
So to bee reconcil'd. See mee no more.
The sting of conscience euer gnawing on thee,
A long life bee thy punishment.   *Exit* THEODOSIUS.
    Flaccilla.   O sweete Lady   200
How I could weepe for her!
    Arcadia.   Speake deare Madam, speake.
Your tongue as you are a Woman, while you liue,
Should bee euer mouing, at the least the last part
That stirrs about you.
    Pulcheria.   Though I should sad Lady
In pollicie reioyce, you as a riuall   205
Of my greatenesse are remou'd, compassion,
Since I beleeue you innocent, commands mee
To mourne your fortune; credit mee I will vrge
All arguments I can alleage that may
Appease the Emperours furie.
    Arcadia.   I will grow too,   210
Vpon my knees, vnlesse hee bid mee rise,
And sweare hee will forgiue you.
    Flaccilla.   And repent too;
All this pother for an apple?
             Exeunt PULCHERIA, ARCADIA, FLACCILLA.
    Chrysapius.   Hope deare Madam,
K3ʳ And yeeld not to despaire, I am still your seruant,
And neuer will forsake you; though a while   215
You leaue the court, and city, and giue way
To the violent passions of the Emperour.
Repentance in his want of you will soone finde him.
In the meane time Ile dispose of you, and omit

No opportunity that may inuite him   220
To see his error.

  Athenais. Oh!   *Wringing her hands.*
  Chrysapius. Forbeare for heau'ns sake. [*Exeunt.*]

     The ende of the fourth act.

Act. 5. Scæne 1.

[V. i]

  PHILANAX. PAULINUS. *Guard. Executioners.*

 Paulinus. THIS is most barbarous! How haue you lost
All feeling of humanity, as honor,
In your consent alone to haue mee vs'd thus?
But to bee as you are a looker on,
Nay more a principall actor in't (the softnes   5
Of your former life consider'd) almost turnes mee
Into a senselesse statue.
  Philanax.   Would long since
Death by some other meanes had made you one,
That you might bee lesse sensible of what
You haue, or are to suffer.
  Paulinus.   Am to suffer?   10
Let such, whose happinesse, and heauen depend
Vpon their present being feare to part with
A fort they cannot long holde, mine to mee is
A charge that I am wearie of, all defences
By paine, and sickenesse batterd; Yet take heede,   15
Take heede Lord *Philanax*, that for priuate spleene
K3ᵛ Or any false conceiued grudge against mee,
(Since in one thought of wrong to you, I am
Sincerely innocent) you doe not that
My royall Master must in iustice punish,   20
If you passe to your owne heart, thorow mine,
The murther as it will come out discouer'd.
  Philanax. I murther you my Lord? heau'n witnesse for mee,
With the restoring of your health, I wish you
Long life, and happinesse: for my selfe I am   25

Compell'd to put in execution that
Which I would flie from, 'tis the Emperour,
The high incensed Emperours will commands
What I must see perform'd.
 Paulinus.   The Emperour!
Goodnesse, and innocence garde mee! wheeles, nor racks 30
Can force into my memorie, the remembrance
Of the least shadow of offence, with which
I euer did prouoke him. Though belou'd
(And yet the peoples loue is short, and fatall)
I neuer courted popular applause;   35
Feasted the men of action, or labour'd
By prodigall giftes to draw the needy souldier,
The tribunes, or centurions to a faction,
Of which I would rise vp the head against him.
I hold no place of strength, fortresse, or castle   40
In my command, that can giue sanctuarie
To malecontents, or countenance rebellion.
I haue built no palaces to face the court,
Nor doe my followers brauerie shame his traine,
And though I cannot blame my fate for want,   45
My competent meanes of life deserues no enuie.
In what then am I dangerous?
 Philanax.   His displeasure
Reflects on none of those particulars,
Which you haue mention'd, though some iealous Princes
In a subiect cannot brooke 'em.
 Paulinus.   None of these?   50
K4ʳ In what then am I worthy his suspition?
But it may, nay it must bee, some informer
To whom my innocence appear'd a crime,
Hath poyson'd his late good opinion of mee.
Tis not to dye, but in the censure of   55
So good a Master guilty, that afflictes mee.
 Philanax. There is no remedy.
 Paulinus.   No? I haue a friend yet,
Could the strictnesse of your warrant giue way to it,
To whom the state I stand in now deliuer'd,
That by faire intercession for mee would   60

So far preuaile, that my defence vnheard
I should not innocent, or guiltie suffer,
Without a fit distinction.
    Philanax.   These false hopes
My Lord abuse you. What man, when condemn'd,
Did euer find a friend? or who dares lend   65
An eye of pitty to that starcros'd subiect
On whom his soueraigne frownes?
    Paulinus.   Shee that dares plead
For innocence without a fee, the Empresse,
My greate, and gratious Mistrisse!
    Philanax.   There's your error.
Her many fauours which you hop'd should make you,   70
Proue your vndoing. Shee poore Lady is
Bannish'd for euer from the Emperours presence,
And his confirm'd suspition, to his wrong,
That you haue bene ouer familiar with her,
Doomes you to death. I know you vnderstand mee.   75
    Paulinus. Ouer familiar?
    Philanax.   In sharing with him,
Those sweete and secret pleasures of his bed,
Which can admit no partner.
    Paulinus.   And is that
The crime for which I am to dye? Of all
My numerous sinnes, was there not one of waight   80
Enough to sinke mee, if he borrow'd not
K4ᵛ The colour of a guilt I neuer saw,
To paint my innocence, in a deform'd
And monstrous shape? but that it were prophane
To argue heauen of ignorance, or iniustice,   85
I now should tax it. Had the stars that raign'd
At my natiuity such cursed influence,
As not alone to make mee miserable,
But in the neighbourhood of her goodnesse to mee
To force contagion vpon a Lady,   90
Whose purer flames were not inferior
To theirs, when they shine brightest? to dye for her
Compar'd with what shee suffers is a trifle.
By her example warn'd, let all greate women
Heereafter throw pride, and contempt on such   95

As truely serue 'em, since a retribution
In lawfull courtesies, is now stil'd lust,
And to be thankfull to a seruants merits
Is growne a vice, no vertue.
    Philanax.   These complaints
Are to no purpose: think on the long flight,   100
Your better part must make.
    Paulinus.   Shee is prepar'd,
Nor can the freeing of an innocent
From the Emperours furious iealousie hinder her.
It shall out, 'tis resolu'd, but to bee whisper'd
To you alone. What a solemne preparation   105
Is made heere to put forth an inch of taper
In it selfe almost extinguish'd! mortall poison?
The hangmans sword, the halter?
    Philanax.   Tis left to you,
To make choice of which you please.
    Paulinus.   Any will serue,
To take away my goute, and life together.   110
I would not haue the Emperour imitate
Romes Monster, *Nero*, in that cruell mercie
Hee shew'd to *Seneca*; when you haue discharg'd
What you are trusted with, and I haue giu'n you
Reasons beyond all doubt, or disputation,   115
Of the Empresses and my innocence, when I am dead,
Since 'tis my Masters pleasure, and high treason
In you not to obey it, I coniure you,
By the hopes you haue of happinesse heereafter,
Since mine in this world are now parting from mee,   120
That you would win the young man to repentance
Of the wrong done to his chaste wife *Eudoxia*,
And if perchance hee shed a teare for what
In his rashenesse hee impos'd on his true seruant,
So it cure him of future iealousie,   125
'Twill proue a pretious balsamum, and finde mee
When I am in my graue. Now when you please,
For I am readie.
    Philanax.   His words worke strangely on mee,
And I would doe, but I know not what to thinke on't.   *Exeunt.*

L1ʳ

Act. 5. Scæne 2.

PULCHERIA. FLACCILLA. ARCADIA. TIMANTUS.
GRATIANUS. CHRYSAPIUS.

Pulcheria. Still in his sullen mood? no intermission
Of his melancholy fit?
    Timantus.   It rather Madam
Increases, then grows lesse.
    Gratianus.   In the next roome
To his bed-chamber, wee watch'd, for hee by signes
Gaue vs to vnderstand, hee would admit   5
Nor company, nor conference.
    Pulcheria.   Did hee take
No rest as you could ghesse?
    Chrysapius.   Not any Madam;
Like a Numidian Lyon, by the cunning
Of the desperate huntsman taken in a toyle,
And forc'd into a spatious cage, hee walkes   10
About his chamber, wee might heare him gnash
His teeth in rage, which opend, hollow grones
And murmurs issu'd from his lippes, like windes
Imprison'd in the cauernes of the earth
Striuing for liberty; and sometimes throwing   15
His body on his bed, then on the ground,
And with such violence, that wee more then fear'd
And still doe, if the tempest of his passions
By your wisdome bee not lay'd, hee will commit
Some outrage on himselfe.
    Pulcheria.   His better Angell,   20
I hope will stay him from so foule a mischiefe,
Nor shall my care bee wanting.
    Timantus.   Twice I heard him
Say false *Eudoxia*, how much art thou
Vnworthy of these teares? then sigh'd, and straight
Rores out *Paulinus*, was his goutie age   25
To bee preferr'd before my strength and youth?
Then groand againe, so many wayes expressing
Th' afflictions of a tortur'd soule, that wee

L1ᵛ

Who wept in vaine, for what wee could not helpe,
Were sharers in his suffrings.
    Pulcheria.   Though your sorrow   30
Is not to bee condemn'd, it takes not from
The burthen of his miseries; wee must practise
With some fresh obiect to diuert his thoughts
From that they are wholly fix'd on.
    Chrysapius.   Could I gaine
The freedome of accesse, I would present him   35
With this petition. Will your highnes please   *A paper deliuer'd.*
To looke vpon it? You will soone finde there
What my intents, and hopes are.

Enter THEODOSIUS.

    Gratianus.   Ha! 'tis hee.
    Pulcheria.   Stand close,
And giue way to his passions, 'tis not safe
To stoppe them in their violent course, before   40
They haue spent themselues.
    Theodosius.   I play the foole, and am
Vnequall to my selfe, delinquents are
To suffer, not the innocent. I haue done
Nothing, which will not hold waight in the scale
Of my impartiall iustice: neither feele   45
The worme of conscience, vpbraiding mee
For one blacke deed of tyranny; wherefore then
Should I torment my selfe? great *Iulius* would not
Rest satisfi'd that his wife was free from fact,
But only for suspition of a crime   50
Su'd a diuorce, nor was this Roman rigour
Censur'd as cruell, and still the wise Italian,
That knowes the honor of his family
Depends vpon the purity of his bed,
For a kisse, nay wanton looke, will plough vp mischiefe,   55
And sowe the seedes of his reuenge in blood.
And shall I to whose power the law's a seruant,
That stand accomptable to none, for what
My will calls an offence, being compell'd,
And on such grounds, to raise an Altar to   60
My anger, though I grant 'tis cemented

L2^r

With a loose strumpets and adulterers gore,
Repent the iustice of my furie? no.
I should not: yet still my excesse of loue
Fed high in the remembrance of her choice　　　　　65
And sweete embraces, would perswade mee that
Conniuence, or remission of her fault,
Made warrantable by her true submission
For her offence, might bee excusable,
Did not the crueltie of my wounded honor　　　　70
With an open mouth denie it.
　　Pulcheria.　　　　　　　I approue of　　[*To* CHRYSAPIUS.]
Your good intention, and I hope 'twill prosper.
Hee now seemes calme. Let vs vpon our knees
Encompasse him.—Most royall Sir,
　　Flaccilla.　　　　　　　　Sweet brother.
　　Arcadia. As you are our Soueraigne, by the tyes of nature　75
You are bound to bee a Father in your care
To vs poore Orphans.
　　Timantus.　　　　Shew compassion Sir,
Vnto your selfe.
　　Gratianus.　　　The maiestie of your fortune
Should flie aboue the reach of griefe.
　　Chrysapius.　　　　　　And 'tis
Impair'd, if you yeeld to it.
　　Theodosius.　　　　　　　Wherefore pay you　　　80
This adoration to a sinfull creature?
I am flesh, and blood as you are, sensible
Of heat, and cold; asmuch a slaue vnto
The tyrannie of my passions, as the meanest
Of my poore subiects. The proud attributes　　　　85
(By oil'd tongu'd flatterie impos'd vpon vs)
As sacred, glorious, high, inuincible,
The deputie of heauen, and in that
Omnipotent, with all false titles els
Coind to abuse our frailetie, though compounded,　　90
And by the breath of Sycophants appli'd,
Cure not the least fit of an ague in vs.
Wee may giue poore men riches; confer honors
On vndeseruers; raise, or ruine such

L2ᵛ

　　V. ii. 71 SD. *To* CHRYSAPIUS.] *Coxeter*; *not in 32*

As are beneath vs, and with this puff'd vp,   95
Ambition would perswade vs to forget
That wee are men: but hee that sits aboue vs,
And to whom, at our vtmost rate, wee are
But pageant properties, derides our weakenesse.
In mee to whom you kneele, 'tis most apparent.   100
Can I call backe yesterday, with all their aides
That bow vnto my scepter? or restore
My minde to that tranquillitie, and peace
It then inioy'd? can it make *Eudoxia* chaste?
Or vile *Paulinus* honest?
    Pulcheria.   If I might   105
Without offence, deliuer my opinion,
    Theodosius. What would you say?
    Pulcheria.   That on my soule the Empresse
Is innocent.
    Chrysapius. The good *Paulinus* guiltlesse.
    Gratianus. And this should yeeld you comfort.
    Theodosius.   In being guiltie
Of an offence far, far transcending that   110
They stand condemn'd for. Call you this a comfort?
Suppose it could bee true? a corrasiue rather,
Not to eate out dead flesh, but putrifie
What yet is sownd. Was murther euer held
A cure for iealousie? or the crying blood   115
Of innocence, a balme to take away
Her festring anguish? as you doe desire
I should not doe a iustice on my selfe,
Adde to the proofes by which *Paulinus* fell,
And not take from 'em; in your charitie   120
Sooner beleeue that they were false, then I
Vnrighteous in my iudgement! subiects liues
Are not their Princes tennisballs to bee banded
In sport away, all that I can indure
For them, if they were guilty, is an atome   125
To the mountaine of affliction, I pull'd on mee,
Should they proue innocent.
    Chrysapius.   For your Maiesties peace
I more then hope they were not; the false oth

L3^r

104. it] *32*; I *Gifford*

Tooke by the Empresse, and for which shee can
Plead no excuse, conuicted her, and yeelds   130
A sure defence for your suspition of her.
And yet to be resolu'd, since strong doubts are
More grieuous for the most part, then to know
A certaine losse—
    Theodosius.   'Tis true *Chrysapius,*
Were there a possible meanes.
    Chrysapius.   'Tis offer'd to you,   135
If you please to embrace it. Some few minutes
Make truce with passion, and but read, and follow
What's there proiected, you shall finde a key,
Will make your entrance easie to discouer
Her secret thoughts, and then, as in your wisdome   140
L3ᵛ You shall thinke fit, you may determine of her,
And rest confirm'd, whether *Paulinus* died
A villaine or a Martyr.
    Theodosius.   It may doe,
Nay sure it must, yet howsoeuer it fall,
I am most wretched. Which way in my wishes,   145
I should fashion the euent, I am so distracted,
I cannot yet resolue of. Follow mee.
Though in my name, all names are comprehended,
I must haue witnesses, in what degree
I haue done wrong, or suffer'd.
    Pulcheria.   Hope the best Sir.   *Exeunt.*

[V. iii]
Act. 5. Scæna 3.

A sad song. ATHENAIS *in sackecloth. Her haire loose.*

Athenais.   *Why art thou slow, thou rest of trouble, Death,*
        To stoppe a wretches breath?
    That calls on thee, and offers her sad heart
        A prey vnto thy dart?
    I am nor young, nor faire, bee therefore bold,   5
        Sorrow hath made mee old,

---

134. losse—] *Coxeter;* ~. *32*   145. wretched.] *Massinger MS;* ~ₐ *32*
146. distracted,] *Massinger MS;* ~ₐ *32*   147. of.] *Massinger MS;* ~ₐ *32*   mee.]
Massinger MS; ~; *32*   V. iii. SD. *haire loose*] *Coxeter; loose haire 32*

> *Deform'd, and wrinkl'd, all that I can craue,*
>   *Is quiet in my graue.*
> *Such as liue happy, hold long life a Iewell,*
>   *But to mee thou art cruell:*   10
> *If thou end not my tedious miserie,*
>   *And I soone cease to bee.*
> *Strike, and strike home then, pitty vnto mee*
>   *In one short hours delay is tyrannie.*

Thus like a dying Swan, to a sad tune   15
I sing my owne dirge; would a requiem follow
Which in my penitence, I despaire not of,
L4ʳ This brittle glasse of life, already broken
With misery, the long and quiet sleepe
Of death would bee most welcome; yet before   20
Wee end our pilgrimage, 'tis fit that wee
Should leaue corruption, and foule sinnes behinde vs.
But with wash'd feete, and hands, the Heathens dare not
Enter their prophane temples; and for mee
To hope my passage to eternitie   25
Can bee made easie 'till I haue shooke of
The burthen of my sinnes in free confession,
Ayded with sorrow, and repentance for 'em,
Is against reason. 'Tis not laying by
My royall ornaments, or putting on   30
This garment of humility, and contrition,
The throwing dust, and ashes on my head,
Long fasts to tame my proud flesh, that can make
Attonement for my soule, that must be humbled,
All outward signes of penitence, els are vselesse.   35
Chrysapius did assure mee, hee would bring mee
A holy man, from whom (hauing discouer'd
My secret crying sinnes) I might receiue
Full absolution, and hee keepes his word.

     Enter THEODOSIUS, *like a frier, with* CHRYSAPIUS.

Welcome most reuerend Sir, vpon my knees   40
I entertaine you.
     Theodosius.   Noble Sir forbeare,

16. dirge;] *Coxeter*; dirg, *32*   34. soule,] *32*; ~; *Coxeter*   39 SD. *Enter* . .
CHRYSAPIUS.] *Coxeter*; *after* entertaine you *in 32*

The place, the sacred office that I come for,
Commandes all priuacie.   [*Exit* CHRYSAPIUS.]
                              My penitent daughter,
Bee carefull, as you wish remission from mee,
That in confession of your sinnes, you hide not   45
One crime, whose ponderous waight, when you would make
Your flight aboue the firmament, may sincke you.
A foolish modestie in concealing ought
Is now far worse then impudence to professe,
And iustifie your guilte, bee therefore free;   50
L4ᵛ So may the gates of mercie open to you.
     Athenais. First then, I aske a pardon, for my being
Ingratefull to heau'ns bountie.
     Theodosius.   A good entrance.
     Athenais. Greatenesse comes from aboue, and I rais'd to it
From a low condition, sinfully forgot   55
From whence it came, and looking on my selfe
In the false glasse of flatterie, I receiu'd it
As a debt due to my beautie, not a gift
Or fauour from the Emperour.
     Theodosius.   'Twas not well.
     Athenais. Pride wayted on vnthankfulnesse, and no more   60
Remembring the compassion of the Princesse,
And the meanes shee vs'd to make mee what I was,
Contested with her, and with sore eyes seeing
Her greater light, as it dimm'd mine, I practis'd
To haue it quite put out.
     Theodosius.   A greate offence,   65
But on repentance not vnpardonable.
Forward.
     Athenais. O Father, what I now must vtter,
I feare in the deliuerie will destroy mee,
Before you haue absolu'd mee.
     Theodosius.   Heau'n is gratious.
Out with it.
     Athenais. Heau'n commands vs to tell truth.   70
Yet I most sinfull wretch, forswore my selfe.
     Theodosius. On what occasion?

---

43. *Exit* CHRYSAPIUS.] *Coxeter*; *not in* 32   47. flight] *Massinger MS*; flights 32
may] *Coxeter*; that may 32

   Athenais.   Quite forgetting that
An innocent truth can neuer stand in need
Of a guiltie lye, being on the suddaine ask'd
By the Emperour my husband, for an Apple   75
Presented by him, I swore I had eaten it,
When my grieu'd conscience too well knowes, I sent it
To comfort sicke *Paulinus*, being a man,
I truely lou'd and fauour'd.
   Theodosius.   A cold sweate,
Mi^r Like the iuice of Hemlocke bathes mee.   *Aside.*
   Athenais.   And from this   80
A furious iealousie getting possession
Of the good Emperours heart, in his rage hee doom'd
The innocent Lord to dye, my periurie
The fatall cause of murther.
   Theodosius.   Take heed daughter,
You iuggle not with your conscience, and religion,   85
In stiling him an innocent from your feare,
And shame to accuse your selfe. The Emperour
Had many spies vpon you, saw such graces,
Which vertue could not warrant, showr'd vpon him;
Glances in publick, and more liberall fauours   90
In your priuate chamber meetings, making way
For foule adulterie; nor could hee bee
But sensible of the compact pass'd betweene you,
To the ruine of his honor.
   Athenais.   Heare mee Father,
I look'd for comfort, but in this you come   95
To adde to my afflictions.
   Theodosius.   Cause not you
Your owne damnation, in concealing that
Which may in your discouerie finde forgiuenesse.
Open your eyes, set heauen, or hell before you.
In the reuealing of the truth, you shall   100
Prepare a palace for your soule to dwell in,
Stor'd with celestiall blessings; whereas if
You palliate your crime, and dare beyond
Playing with lightning, in concealing it,
Expect a dreadfull dungeon, fill'd with horror,   105

        85. iuggle] *Massinger MS*; niggle *32*

And neuer-ending torments.
    Athenais.   May they fall
Eternally vpon mee, and increase,
When that which wee call time hath lost its name;
May lightning cleaue the centre of the earth,
And I sinke quicke, before you haue absolu'd mee,   110
Into the bottomlesse Abysse, yf euer
In one vnchaste desire, nay in a thought
I wrong'd the honor of the Emperours bed.
I doe deserue, I grant, more then I suffer
In that my feruor, and desire to please him,   115
In my holy meditations press'd vpon me,
And would not bee kept out; now to dissemble
(When I shall suddainely bee insensible,
Of what the world speaks of mee) were meere madnesse:
And though you are incredulous, I presume,   120
If as I kneele now, my eyes swolne with teares,
My hands heaud vp thus, my stretch'd heartstrings ready
To breake a sunder, my incensed Lord
(His storme of iealousie blowne ore) should heare mee,
Hee would beleeue I lied not.
    Theodosius.   Rise, and see him,   *Discouers himselfe.*
On his knees with ioy affirme it.
    Athenais.   Can this bee?   126
    Theodosius. My sisters, and the rest there, all beare witnesse.

Enter PULCHERIA, ARCADIA, FLACCILLA, CHRYSAPIUS,
GRATIANUS, TIMANTUS [,PHILANAX].

In freeing this incomparable Lady
From the suspition of guilt, I doe
Accuse my selfe, and willingly submit   130
To any penance, shee in iustice shall
Please to impose vpon mee.
    Athenais.   Royall Sir,
Your ill opinion of mee's soone forgiuen.
    Pulcheria. But how you can make satisfaction to
The poore *Paulinus,* hee being dead, in reason   135
You must conclude impossible.

---

111. yf euer] *Massinger MS*; If euer *32³*; I feuer *32²*; If feuer *32¹*   127 SD.
PHILANAX] *Coxeter*; *not in 32*   132-3. *rearranged by Coxeter*; *32 reads* Royall . . .
forgiuen.

Theodosius.   And in that
I am most miserable; the Ocean
M2ʳ Of ioy, which in your innocence flow'd high to mee,
Ebbs in the thought of my vniust command,
By which hee died. O *Philanax* (as thy name   140
Interpreted speakes thee) thou hast euer bene
A louer of the King, and thy whole life
Can witnesse thy obedience to my will,
In putting that in execution, which
Was trusted to thee; say but yet this once   145
Thou hast not done what rashly I commanded,
And that *Paulinus* liues, and thy reward
For not performing that which I inioin'd thee,
Shall centuple what euer yet thy dutie,
Or merit challeng'd from mee.
Philanax.   'Tis too late Sir.   150
Hee's dead, and when you know hee was vnable
To wrong you, in the way that you suspected,
You'll wish it had bene otherwise.
Theodosius.   Vnable?
Philanax. I am sure hee was an *Eunuch*, and might safely
Lye by a Virgins side, at foure yeares made one,   155
Though to hold grace with Ladies hee conceald it.
The circumstances, and the manner how
You may heare at better leasure.
Theodosius.   How! an *Eunuch*?
The more the proofes are, that are brought to cleare thee,
My best *Eudoxia*, the more my sorrowes.   160
Athenais. That I am innocent?
Theodosius.   That I am guiltie
Of murther, my *Eudoxia*. I will build
A glorious monument to his memorie,
And for my punishment liue, and dye vpon it,
And neuer more conuerse with men.

Enter PAULINUS.

Paulinus.   Liue long Sir,   165
M2ᵛ May I doe so to serue you. And if that
I liue does not displease you, you owe for it
To this good Lord.

Theodosius.   My selfe, and all that's mine.
Philanax. Your pardon is a payment.
Theodosius.   I am rap'd
With ioy beyond my selfe. Now my *Eudoxia*   170
My iealousie puff'd away thus, in this breath
I scent the naturall sweetenesse.   *Kisses her.*
    Arcadia.   Sacred Sir,
I am happy to behold this, and presume,
Now you are pleas'd, to moue a sute, in which
My sister is ioyn'd with mee.
    Theodosius.   Prethee speake it,   175
For I haue vow'd to heare before I grant,
I thanke your good instructions.
    Arcadia.   'Tis but this Sir,
Wee haue obseru'd the falling out, and in,
Betweene the husband and the wife showes rarely,
Their iarres, and reconcilements strangely take vs.   180
    Flaccilla. Anger and iealousie that conclude in kisses
Is a sweete war in sooth.
    Arcadia.   Wee therefore, brother,
Most humbly beg you would prouide vs husbands
That wee may tast the pleasure of't.
    Flaccilla.   And with speede Sir,
For so your fauour's doubl'd.
    Theodosius.   Take my word,   185
I will with all conuenience; and not blush
Heereafter to bee guided by your counsailes.
I will deserue your pardon. *Philanax*
Shall bee remembred, and magnificent bounties
Fall on *Chrysapius.*   190
M3ʳ Let *Cleon* bee deliuer'd and rewarded.
My grace on all, which as I lend to you,
Returne your vowes to heauen, that it may please
(As it is gratious) to quench in mee
All future sparkes of burning iealousie.   [*Exeunt.*]

THE END.

190. Fall on *Chrysapius.*] *Massinger MS*; Fall on *Chrysapius*. My grace on all. *32*
195 SD. *Exeunt.*] *Gifford*; *not in 32*

M3ᵛ

EPILOGVE.

Wee haue reason to be doubtfull, whether hee
  On whom (forc'd to it by necessitie)
The maker did conferre his Emperours part
  Hath giuen you satisfaction, in his art
Of action and deliuerie; 'tis sure truth   5
  The burden was too heauie for his youth
To vndergoe: but in his will wee know
  Hee was not wanting, and shall euer owe
With his, our seruice, if your fauours daine
  To giue him strength, heereafter to sustaine   10
A greater waight. It is your grace that can
  In your allowance of this write him man
Before his time, which if you please to doe
  You make the Player, and the Poet too.

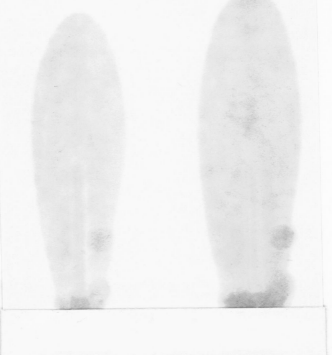